ALBANIA

BUSINESS INTELLIGENCE REPORT

VOLUME 1

PRACTICAL INFORMATION, OPPORTUNITIES, CONTACTS

International Business Publications, USA
Washington DC, USA - Albania

ALBANIA

BUSINESS INTELLIGENCE REPORT

VOLUME 1 PRACTICAL INFORMATION, OPPORTUNITIES, CONTACTS

UPDATED ANNUALLY

Cover Design: **International Business Publications, USA**

We express our sincere appreciation to all government agencies and international organizations which provided information and other materials for this report

2018 Updated Reprint International Business Publications, USA
ISBN 1-4330-0049-0

This report provides basic information for starting or/and conducting business in the country. The extraordinary volume of materials covering the topic, prevents us from placing all these materials in this report. For more detailed information on issues related to any specific investment and business activity in the country, please contact Global Investment Center, USA
Please acquire the list of our business intelligence and marketing reports and other business publications. We constantly update and expand our business intelligence and marketing materials. Please contact the center for the updated list of reports on over 200 countries.

For additional analytical, business and investment opportunities information,
please contact Global Investment & Business Center, USA
at (703) 370-8082. Fax: (703) 370-8083. E-mail: ibpusa3@gmail.com
Global Business and Investment Info Databank - www.ibpus.com

Printed in the USA

ALBANIA

BUSINESS INTELLIGENCE REPORT

VOLUME 1

PRACTICAL INFORMATION, OPPORTUNITIES, CONTACTS

TABLE OF CONTENTS

BUSINESS AND DEVELOPMENT PROFILES

BASIC & DEVELOPMENT PROFILES

Capital and largest city	Tirana 41°19′N 19°49′E
Official languages	Albanian
Demonym	Albanian
Government	Unitary parliamentary constitutional republic
• President	Ilir Meta
• Prime Minister	Edi Rama
Legislature	Kuvendi
Formation	
• Principality of Arbanon	1190
• Anjou Kingdom of Albania	February 1272
• Princedom of Albania	1368
• League of Lezhë	2 March 1444
• Proclamation of independence from the Ottoman Empire	28 November 1912
• Principality of Albania (Recognised)	29 July 1913
• Albanian Republic (1st republic)	31 January 1925
• Albanian Kingdom	1 September 1928
• People's Republic of Albania (2nd republic)	11 January 1946
• People's Socialist Republic of Albania (3rd republic)	28 December 1976
• Republic of Albania (4th republic)	29 April 1991
Current constitution	28 November 1998
Area	
• Total	28,748 km^2 (11,100 sq mi) (140th)
• Water (%)	4.7
Population	
• January 2017 estimate	2,876,591
• 2011 census	2,821,977
• Density	98/km^2 (253.8/sq mi) (63rd)
GDP (PPP)	2018 estimate
• Total	$37.923 billion
• Per capita	$13,193[3]
GDP (nominal)	2018 estimate
• Total	$14.120 billion
• Per capita	$4,912
Gini (2013)	34.5 medium
HDI (2015)	▲ 0.76 high · 75th

Currency	Lek (ALL)
Time zone	CET (UTC+1)
• Summer (DST)	CEST (UTC+2)
Date format	dd/mm/yyyy
Drives on the	right
Calling code	355
ISO 3166 code	AL
Internet TLD	.al

Albania officially the **Republic of Albania** is a country in Southeastern Europe. The country spans 28,748 square kilometres (11,100 square miles) and had a total population of 3 million people as of 2016. It is a unitary parliamentary constitutional republic with the capital in Tirana, the country's most populous city and main economic and commercial centre. The country's other major cities include Durrës, Vlorë, Sarandë, Shkodër, Berat, Korçë, Gjirokastër and Fier.

Albania lies in the southwestern portion of the Balkan Peninsula bordered by Montenegro to the northwest, Kosovo to the northeast, the Republic of Macedonia to the east, and Greece to the south and southeast. Most of the country is mountainous, including the Albanian Alps in the north, the Korab Mountains in the east, the Ceraunian Mountains in the south and the Skanderbeg Mountains in the center. The country's coast touches the Adriatic Sea to the west and the Ionian Sea to the southwest that forms the Albanian Riviera. It is less than 72 km (45 mi) from Italy across the Strait of Otranto, which connects the Adriatic to the Ionian.

Previously in classical antiquity, Albania has been populated by various Illyrian, Thracian and Greek tribes, as well as several Greek colonies established in the Illyrian coast. In the third century BC, the region was annexed by the Roman Empire and became an integral part of the Roman provinces of Dalmatia, Macedonia and Illyricum. The unified Principality of Arbër emerged in 1190, established by archon Progon in the Krujë, within the Byzantine Empire. In the late thirteenth century, Charles of Anjou conquered the Albanian territories from the Byzantines and established the medieval Kingdom of Albania, extending from Durrës along the coast to Butrint in the south. In the mid-fifteenth century, it was conquered by the Ottomans.

The modern nation state of Albania emerged in 1912 following the defeat of the Ottomans in the Balkan Wars.

The modern Kingdom of Albania was invaded by Italy in 1939, which formed Greater Albania, before becoming a Nazi German protectorate in 1943. After the defeat of Nazi Germany, a Communist state titled the People's Socialist Republic of Albania was founded under the leadership of Enver Hoxha and the Party of Labour. The country experienced widespread social and political transformations in the communist era, as well as isolation from much of the international community. In the aftermath of the Revolutions of 1991, the Socialist Republic was dissolved and the fourth Republic of Albania was established.

Albania is a democratic and developing country with an upper-middle income economy. The tertiary sector dominates the country's economy followed by the secondary and primary sector.

Following the end of communism in 1990, the country went through a process of transition from a centralized economy to a market-based economy. It also provides universal health care and free primary and secondary education to its citizens.

Albania has a high Human Development Index and is ranked 13th in the Happy Planet Index, 38th in the Global Gender Index, 52nd in the Social Progress Index and 37th for Life Expectancy. The country is a member of the United Nations, World Bank, UNESCO, NATO, WTO, COE,

OSCE and OIC. It is also an official candidate for membership in the European Union. In addition it is one of the founding members of the Energy Community, including the Organization of the Black Sea Economic Cooperation and Union for the Mediterranean.

GEOGRAPHY

Location: Southeastern Europe, bordering the Adriatic Sea and Ionian Sea, between Greece and Serbia and Montenegro

Geographic coordinates: 41 00 N, 20 00 E

Map references: Europe

Area:
total: 28,750 sq km
land: 27,400 sq km
water: 1,350 sq km

Area—comparative: slightly smaller than Maryland

Land boundaries:
total: 720 km
border countries: Greece 282 km, The Former Yugoslav Republic of Macedonia 151 km, Serbia and Montenegro 287 km (114 km with Serbia, 173 km with Montenegro)

Coastline: 362 km

Maritime claims:
continental shelf: 200-m depth or to the depth of exploitation
territorial sea: 12 nm

Climate: mild temperate; cool, cloudy, wet winters; hot, clear, dry summers; interior is cooler and wetter

Terrain: mostly mountains and hills; small plains along coast

Elevation extremes:
lowest point: Adriatic Sea 0 m
highest point: Maja e Korabit (Golem Korab) 2,753 m

Land use:
arable land: 21%
permanent crops: 5%
permanent pastures: 15%
forests and woodland: 38%
other: 21%

Irrigated land: 3,410 sq km

Natural hazards: destructive earthquakes; tsunamis occur along southwestern coast

Environment—current issues: deforestation; soil erosion; water pollution from industrial and domestic effluents

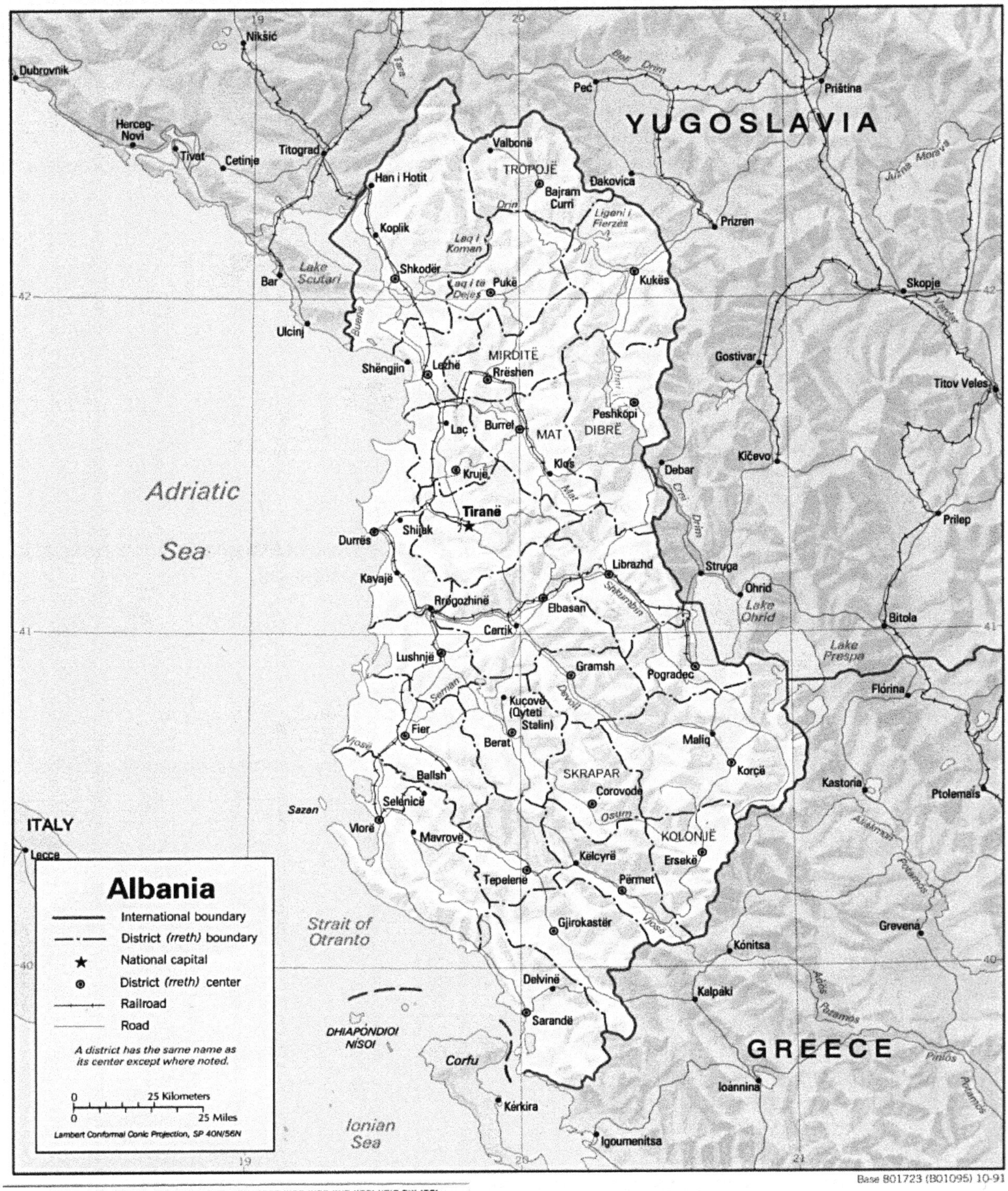

Environment—international agreements:
party to: Biodiversity, Climate Change, Wetlands
signed, but not ratified: none of the selected agreements

Geography—note: strategic location along Strait of Otranto (links Adriatic Sea to Ionian Sea and Mediterranean Sea)

Natural resources: petroleum, natural gas, coal, chromium, copper, timber, nickel

PEOPLE

Population: 3,364,571

Age structure:
0-14 years: 33% (male 568,642; female 530,088)
15-64 years: 61% (male 957,561; female 1,105,870)
65 years and over: 6% (male 84,280; female 118,130)

Population growth rate: 1.05%

Birth rate: 20.74 births/1,000 population

Death rate: 7.35 deaths/1,000 population

Net migration rate: -2.93 migrant(s)/1,000 population

Sex ratio:
at birth: 1.08 male(s)/female
under 15 years: 1.07 male(s)/female
15-64 years: 0.87 male(s)/female
65 years and over: 0.71 male(s)/female
total population: 0.92 male(s)/female

Infant mortality rate: 42.9 deaths/1,000 live births

Life expectancy at birth:
total population: 69 years
male: 65.92 years
female: 72.33 years

Total fertility rate: 2.5 children born/woman

Nationality:
noun: Albanian(s)
adjective: Albanian

Ethnic groups: Albanian 95%, Greeks 3%, other 2% (Vlachs, Gypsies, Serbs, and Bulgarians)
note: other estimates of the Greek population ranged from 1% (official Albanian statistics) to 12% (from a Greek organization)

Religions: Muslim 70%, Albanian Orthodox 20%, Roman Catholic 10%
note: all mosques and churches were closed in 1967 and religious observances prohibited; in November 1990, Albania began allowing private religious practice

Languages: Albanian (Tosk is the official dialect), Greek

Literacy:
definition: age 9 and over can read and write
total population: 93%

GOVERNMENT

Country name:

conventional long form: Republic of Albania
conventional short form: Albania
local long form: Republika e Shqiperise
local short form: Shqiperia
former: People's Socialist Republic of Albania
etymology: the English-language country name seems to be derived from the ancient Illyrian tribe of the Albani; the native name "Shqiperia" is derived from the Albanian word "Shqiponje" ("Eagle") and is popularly interpreted to mean "Land of the Eagles"

Government type:
parliamentary republic

Capital:
name: Tirana (Tirane)
geographic coordinates: 41 19 N, 19 49 E
time difference: UTC+1 (6 hours ahead of Washington, DC, during Standard Time)
daylight saving time: +1hr, begins last Sunday in March; ends last Sunday in October

Administrative divisions:
12 counties (qarqe, singular - qark); Berat, Diber, Durres, Elbasan, Fier, Gjirokaster, Korce, Kukes, Lezhe, Shkoder, Tirane, Vlore

Independence:
28 November 1912 (from the Ottoman Empire)

National holiday:
Independence Day, 28 November (1912) also known as Flag Day

Constitution:
history: several previous; latest approved by the Assembly 21 October 1998, adopted by referendum 22 November 1998, promulgated 28 November 1998
amendments: proposed by at least one-fifth of the Assembly membership; passage requires at least a two-thirds majority vote by the Assembly; referendum required only if approved by two-thirds of the Assembly; amendments approved by referendum effective upon declaration by the president of the republic; amended several times, last in 2016 (2017)

Legal system:
civil law system except in the northern rural areas where customary law known as the "Code of Leke" prevails
International law organization participation:
has not submitted an ICJ jurisdiction declaration; accepts ICCt jurisdiction

Citizenship:
citizenship by birth: no
citizenship by descent only: at least one parent must be a citizen of Albania
dual citizenship recognized: yes
residency requirement for naturalization: 5 years

Suffrage:
18 years of age; universal

Executive branch:
chief of state: President of the Republic Ilir META (since 24 July 2017)

head of government: Prime Minister Edi RAMA (since 10 September 2015); Deputy Prime Minister Niko PELESHI

cabinet: Council of Ministers proposed by the prime minister, nominated by the president, and approved by the Assembly

elections/appointments: president indirectly elected by the Assembly for a 5-year term (eligible for a second term); a candidate needs three-fifths majority vote of the Assembly in 1 of 3 rounds or a simple majority in 2 additional rounds to become president; election last held in 4 rounds on 19, 20, 27, and 28 April 2017 (next election to be held in 2022); prime minister appointed by the president on the proposal of the majority party or coalition of parties in the Assembly

election results: Ilir META elected president; Assembly vote - 87 - 2 in fourth round

Legislative branch:
description: unicameral Assembly or Kuvendi (140 seats; members directly elected in multi-seat constituencies by proportional representation vote to serve 4-year terms)
elections: last held on 25 June 2017 (next to be held in 2021)

election results: percent of vote by party - PS 48.3%, PD 28.9%, LSI 14.3%, PDIU 4.8%, PSD 1%, other 2.7%; seats by party - PS 74, PD 43, LSI 19, PDIU 3, PSD 1

Judicial branch:
highest court(s): Supreme Court (consists of 17 judges, including the chief justice); Constitutional Court (consists of 9 judges, including the chairman)

judge selection and term of office: Supreme Court judges, including the chairman, appointed by the president with the consent of the Assembly to serve single 9-year terms; Constitutional Court judges appointed by the president with the consent of the Assembly to serve single 9-year terms with one-third of the membership renewed every 3 years; chairman elected by the People's Assembly for a single 3-year term
subordinate courts: Courts of Appeal; Courts of First Instance

Political parties and leaders:
Democratic Party or PD [Lulzim BASHA]
Party for Justice, Integration and Unity or PDIU [Shpetim IDRIZI] (formerly part of APMI)
Social Democratic Party or PSD [Skender GJINUSHI]
Socialist Movement for Integration or LSI [Monika KRYEMADHI]
Socialist Party or PS [Edi RAMA]

Political pressure groups and leaders:
Confederation of Trade Unions of Albania or KSSH [Kol NIKOLLAJ]
Omonia [Leonidha PAPA]
Union of Independent Trade Unions of Albania or BSPSH [Gezim KALAJA]

International organization participation:
BSEC, CD, CE, CEI, EAPC, EBRD, EITI (compliant country), FAO, IAEA, IBRD, ICAO, ICC (national committees), ICCt, ICRM, IDA, IDB, IFAD, IFC, IFRCS, ILO, IMF, IMO, Interpol, IOC, IOM, IPU, ISO (correspondent), ITU, ITUC (NGOs), MIGA, NATO, OAS (observer), OIC, OIF, OPCW, OSCE, PCA, SELEC, UN, UNCTAD, UNESCO, UNIDO, UNWTO, UPU, WCO, WFTU (NGOs), WHO, WIPO, WMO, WTO

Diplomatic representation in the US:

chief of mission: Ambassador Floreta FABER (since 18 May 2015)
chancery: 2100 S Street NW, Washington, DC 20008
telephone: [1] (202) 223-4942
FAX: [1] (202) 628-7342
consulate(s) general: New York

Diplomatic representation from the US:
chief of mission: Ambassador Donald LU (since 13 January 2015)
embassy: Rruga e Elbasanit, 103, Tirana
mailing address: US Department of State, 9510 Tirana Place, Dulles, VA 20189-9510
telephone: [355] (4) 2247-285
FAX: [355] (4) 2232-222

Flag description:
red with a black two-headed eagle in the center; the design is claimed to be that of 15th-century hero George Kastrioti SKANDERBEG, who led a successful uprising against the Ottoman Turks that resulted in a short-lived independence for some Albanian regions (1443-78); an unsubstantiated explanation for the eagle symbol is the tradition that Albanians see themselves as descendants of the eagle; they refer to themselves as "Shqiptare," which translates as "sons of the eagle"

National symbol(s):
black double-headed eagle; national colors: red, black

National anthem:
name: "Hymni i Flamurit" (Hymn to the Flag)
lyrics/music: Aleksander Stavre DRENOVA/Ciprian PORUMBESCU
note: adopted 1912

ECONOMY

Albania, a formerly closed, centrally-planned state, is a developing country with a modern open-market economy. Albania managed to weather the first waves of the global financial crisis but, the negative effects of the crisis caused a significant economic slowdown. Since 2014, Albania's economy has steadily improved and economic growth reached 3.8% in 2017. However, close trade, remittance, and banking sector ties with Greece and Italy make Albania vulnerable to spillover effects of possible debt crises and weak growth in the euro zone.

Remittances, a significant catalyst for economic growth, declined from 12-15% of GDP before the 2008 financial crisis to 5.8% of GDP in 2015, mostly from Albanians residing in Greece and Italy. The agricultural sector, which accounts for more than 40% of employment but less than one quarter of GDP, is limited primarily to small family operations and subsistence farming, because of a lack of modern equipment, unclear property rights, and the prevalence of small, inefficient plots of land. Complex tax codes and licensing requirements, a weak judicial system, endemic corruption, poor enforcement of contracts and property issues, and antiquated infrastructure contribute to Albania's poor business environment making attracting foreign investment difficult. Since 2015, Albania has launched an ambitious program to increase tax compliance and bring more businesses into the formal economy. In July 2016, Albania passed constitutional amendments reforming the judicial system in order to strengthen the rule of law and to reduce deeply entrenched corruption.

Albania's electricity supply is uneven despite upgraded transmission capacities with neighboring countries. However, the government has recently taken steps to stem non-technical losses and has begun to upgrade the distribution grid. Better enforcement of electricity contracts has improved the financial viability of the sector, decreasing its reliance on budget support. Also, with help from international donors, the government is taking steps to improve the poor road and rail networks, a long standing barrier to sustained economic growth.

Inward FDI has increased significantly in recent years as the government has embarked on an ambitious program to improve the business climate through fiscal and legislative reforms. The government is focused on the simplification of licensing requirements and tax codes, and it entered into a new arrangement with the IMF for additional financial and technical support. Albania's three-year IMF program, an extended fund facility arrangement, was successfully concluded in February 2017. The Albanian Government has strengthened tax collection amid moderate public wage and pension increases in an effort to reduce its budget deficit. The country continues to face high public debt, exceeding its former statutory limit of 60% of GDP in 2015 and reaching 72% in 2016.

GDP (purchasing power parity):

$35.87 billion (2017 est.)
$34.59 billion (2016 est.)
$33.46 billion (2015 est.)
note: data are in 2017 dollars
unreported output may be as large as 50% of official GDP
country comparison to the world: 126

GDP (official exchange rate):
$13 billion (2017 est.)

GDP - real growth rate:
3.7% (2017 est.)
3.4% (2016 est.)
2.2% (2015 est.)
country comparison to the world: 85

GDP - per capita (PPP):
$12,500 (2017 est.)
$12,000 (2016 est.)
$11,600 (2015 est.)
note: data are in 2017 dollars
country comparison to the world: 122

Gross national saving:
15.6% of GDP (2017 est.)
15.9% of GDP (2016 est.)
16.3% of GDP (2015 est.)
country comparison to the world: 122

GDP - composition, by end use:
household consumption: 77.6%
government consumption: 10.9%
investment in fixed capital: 27%
investment in inventories: 0%
exports of goods and services: 29.7%
imports of goods and services: -45.2% (2017 est.)

GDP - composition, by sector of origin:
agriculture: 22.6%
industry: 23.8%
services: 53.7%
(2017 est.)

Agriculture - products:
wheat, corn, potatoes, vegetables, fruits, olives and olive oil, grapes; meat, dairy products; sheep and goats

Industries:
food; footwear, apparel and clothing; lumber, oil, cement, chemicals, mining, basic metals, hydropower

Industrial production growth rate:
3.5% (2017 est.)
country comparison to the world: 83

Labor force:
1.407 million (2017 est.)
country comparison to the world: 135

Labor force - by occupation:
agriculture: 41.8%
industry: 11.4%
services: 46.8% (2017 est.)

Unemployment rate:
14% (2017 est.)
15.2% (2016 est.)
note: these official rates may not include those working at near-subsistence farming
country comparison to the world: 170

Population below poverty line:
14.3% (2012 est.)

Household income or consumption by percentage share:
lowest 10%: 4.1%
highest 10%: 19.6% (2015 est.)

Distribution of family income - Gini index:
29 (2012 est.)
30 (2008 est.)
country comparison to the world: 136

Budget:
revenues: $3.486 billion
expenditures: $3.765 billion (2017 est.)

Taxes and other revenues:
26.8% of GDP (2017 est.)
country comparison to the world: 105

Budget surplus (+) or deficit (-):

-2.1% of GDP (2017 est.)
country comparison to the world: 88

Public debt:
71.3% of GDP (2017 est.)
72% of GDP (2016 est.)
country comparison to the world: 50

Fiscal year:
calendar year

Inflation rate (consumer prices):
2.1% (2017 est.)
1.3% (2016 est.)
country comparison to the world: 98

Central bank discount rate:
1.25% (31 December 2017 est.)
1.75% (31 December 2016 est.)
country comparison to the world: 125

Commercial bank prime lending rate:
7.2% (31 December 2017 est.)
9.65% (31 December 2016 est.)
country comparison to the world: 117

Stock of narrow money:
$3.979 billion (31 December 2017 est.)
$3.397 billion (31 December 2016 est.)
country comparison to the world: 112

Stock of broad money:
$6.665 billion (31 December 2017 est.)
$5.75 billion (31 December 2016 est.)
country comparison to the world: 122

Stock of domestic credit:
$8.147 billion (31 December 2017 est.)
$7.065 billion (31 December 2016 est.)
country comparison to the world: 114

Current account balance:
-$1.201 billion (2017 est.)
-$899 million (2016 est.)
country comparison to the world: 139

Exports:
$960.9 million (2017 est.)
$789.1 million (2016 est.)
country comparison to the world: 159

Exports - commodities:
apparel and clothing, footwear; asphalt, metals and metallic ores, crude oil; cement and construction materials, vegetables, fruits, tobacco

Exports - partners:
Italy 50.5%, Serbia 8.1%, Kosovo 7.5%, Greece 4.2%

Imports:
$4.084 billion (2017 est.)
$3.671 billion (2016 est.)
country comparison to the world: 132

Imports - commodities:
machinery and equipment, foodstuffs, textiles, chemicals

Imports - partners:
Italy 29%, Germany 9.4%, China 8.7%, Greece 7.8%, Turkey 7.8%, Serbia 4.1%

Reserves of foreign exchange and gold:
$3.274 billion (31 December 2017 est.)
$3.109 billion (31 December 2016 est.)
country comparison to the world: 102

Debt - external:
$8.579 billion (31 December 2017 est.)
$8.421 billion (31 December 2016 est.)
country comparison to the world: 120

Stock of direct foreign investment - at home:
$6.056 billion (31 December 2016 est.)
$5.459 billion (31 December 2015 est.)
country comparison to the world: 102

Exchange rates:
leke (ALL) per US dollar -
121.9 (2017 est.)
124.14 (2016 est.)
124.14 (2015 est.)
125.96 (2014 est.)
105.48 (2015 est.)

ENERGY

Electricity - production:
4.726 billion kWh (2014 est.)
country comparison to the world: 120

Electricity - consumption:
7.793 billion kWh (2014 est.)
country comparison to the world: 100
Electricity - exports:
288.5 million kWh (2014 est.)
country comparison to the world: 74

Electricity - imports:
3.355 billion kWh (2014 est.)
country comparison to the world: 48

Electricity - installed generating capacity:
1.878 million kW (2015 est.)
country comparison to the world: 109

Electricity - from fossil fuels:
5.2% of total installed capacity
country comparison to the world: 203

Electricity - from nuclear fuels:
0% of total installed capacity
country comparison to the world: 40

Electricity - from hydroelectric plants:
94.8% of total installed capacity
country comparison to the world: 9

Electricity - from other renewable sources:
0% of total installed capacity (2015 est.)
country comparison to the world: 151

Crude oil - production:
20,510 bbl/day (2014 est.)
country comparison to the world: 69

Crude oil - exports:
23,320 bbl/day
country comparison to the world: 57

Crude oil - imports:
3,440 bbl/day
country comparison to the world: 79

Crude oil - proved reserves:
168.3 million bbl (1 January 2015 est.)
country comparison to the world: 63

Refined petroleum products - production:
2,228 bbl/day (2012 est.)
country comparison to the world: 107

Refined petroleum products - consumption:
25,000 bbl/day (2015 est.)

country comparison to the world: 121
Refined petroleum products - exports:
354.2 bbl/day (2012 est.)
country comparison to the world: 117

Refined petroleum products - imports:
20,770 bbl/day (2012 est.)
country comparison to the world: 109

Natural gas - production:
19 million cu m (2015 est.)
country comparison to the world: 89

Natural gas - consumption:
19 million cu m
country comparison to the world: 112

Natural gas - exports:
0 cu m (2015 est.)
country comparison to the world: 55

Natural gas - imports:
0 cu m (2015 est.)
country comparison to the world: 155

Natural gas - proved reserves:
849.5 million cu m (1 January 2014 est.)
country comparison to the world: 105

Carbon dioxide emissions from consumption of energy:
3.962 million Mt (2012 est.)
country comparison to the world: 130

COMMUNICATIONS

Telephones - fixed lines:
total subscriptions: 250,000
subscriptions per 100 inhabitants: 8 (2014 est.)
country comparison to the world: 123

Telephones - mobile cellular:
total: 3.4 million
subscriptions per 100 inhabitants: 111 (2014 est.)
country comparison to the world: 133

Telephone system:

general assessment: despite new investment in fixed lines, teledensity remains low with roughly 10 fixed lines per 100 people; mobile-cellular telephone use is widespread and generally effective

domestic: offsetting the shortage of fixed-line capacity, mobile-cellular phone service has been available since 1996; by 2011, multiple companies were providing mobile services, and mobile teledensity had reached 100 per 100 persons; Internet broadband services initiated in 2005, but growth has been slow; Internet cafes are popular in Tirana and have started to spread outside the capital

international: country code - 355; submarine cable provides connectivity to Italy, Croatia, and Greece; the Trans-Balkan Line, a combination submarine cable and land fiber-optic system, provides additional connectivity to Bulgaria, Macedonia, and Turkey; international traffic carried by fiber-optic cable and, when necessary, by microwave radio relay from the Tirana exchange to Italy and Greece (2011)

Broadcast media:

3 public TV networks, one of which transmits by satellite to Albanian-language communities in neighboring countries; more than 60 private TV stations; many viewers can pick up Italian and Greek TV broadcasts via terrestrial reception; cable TV service is available; 2 public radio networks and roughly 25 private radio stations; several international broadcasters are available (2010)

Radio broadcast stations:

AM 13, FM 46, shortwave 1

Television broadcast stations:

65 (3 national, 62 local); 2 cable networks

Internet country code: .al

Internet hosts: 15,528
country comparison to the world: 124
Internet users:
total: 1.7 million
percent of population: 56.5% (
country comparison to the world: 104

TRANSPORTATION

Railways:
total: 447 km (none electrified)
standard gauge: 447 km 1.435-m gauge (1995)

Highways:
total: 18,000 km
paved: 5,400 km
unpaved: 12,600 km

Waterways: 43 km plus Albanian sections of Lake Scutari, Lake Ohrid, and Lake Prespa (1990)

Pipelines: crude oil 145 km; petroleum products 55 km; natural gas 64 km (1991)

Ports and harbors: Durres, Sarande, Shengjin, Vlore

Merchant marine:
total: 8 cargo ships (1,000 GRT or over) totaling 28,394 GRT/41,429 DWT

Airports: 9

Airports—with paved runways:
total: 3
2,438 to 3,047 m: 3

Airports—with unpaved runways:
total: 6

over 3,047 m: 1
1,524 to 2,437 m: 1
914 to 1,523 m: 2
under 914 m: 2

Heliports: 1

MILITARY

Military branches: Army, Navy, Air and Air Defense Forces, Interior Ministry Troops, Border Guards

Military manpower—military age: 19 years of age

Military manpower—availability:
males age 15-49: 763,949

Military manpower—fit for military service:
males age 15-49: 622,013

Military manpower—reaching military age annually:
males: 32,954

Military expenditures—dollar figure: $60 million

Military expenditures—percent of GDP: 2%

TRANSNATIONAL ISSUES

stateless persons: 7,443

Disputes—international: the Albanian Government supports protection of the rights of ethnic Albanians outside of its borders but has downplayed them to further its primary foreign policy goal of regional cooperation; Albanian majority in Kosovo seeks independence from Serbian Republic; Albanians in The Former Yugoslav Republic of Macedonia claim discrimination in education, access to public-sector jobs, and representation in government

Illicit drugs: increasingly active transshipment point for Southwest Asian opiates, hashish, and cannabis transiting the Balkan route and—to a far lesser extent—cocaine from South America destined for Western Europe; limited opium and cannabis production; ethnic Albanian narcotrafficking organizations active and rapidly expanding in Europe

IMPORTANT INFORMATION FOR UNDERSTANDING ALBANIA

OFFICIAL NAME: Republic of Albania

Geography
Area: 28,748 sq. km. (slightly larger than Maryland).
Major cities: *Capital*--Tirana (600,000, est.). *Others*--Durres (200,000, 2005 est.), Shkoder (81,000, 2005 est.), Vlore (72,000,est.).
Terrain: Situated in the southwestern region of the Balkan Peninsula, Albania is predominantly mountainous but flat along its coastline with the Adriatic Sea.
Climate: Mild, temperate; cool, wet winters; dry, hot summers.

People

Population (est.): 3,600,523.
Growth rate (est.): 0.529%.
Ethnic groups (2004 est., Government of Albania): Albanian 98.6%, Greeks 1.17%, others 0.23% (Vlachs, Roma, Serbs, Montenegrins, Macedonians, Balkan Egyptians, and Bulgarians).
Religions: Muslim (Sunni and Bektashi) 70%, Albanian Orthodox 20%, and Roman Catholic 10%.
Official language: Albanian.
Health (est.): *Life expectancy*--males 74.95 years; females 80.53 years. *Infant mortality rate*--20.02 deaths per 1,000 live births.

Government
Type: Parliamentary democracy.
Constitution: Adopted by popular referendum November 28, 1998.
Independence: November 28, 1912 (from the Ottoman Empire).
Branches: *Executive*--President (chief of state), Prime Minister (head of government), Council of Ministers (cabinet). *Legislative*--140-seat unicameral People's Assembly or Kuvendi Popullor (100 members elected by direct popular vote; 40 by proportional vote; all serve 4-year terms). *Judicial*--Constitutional Court, High Court, multiple district and appeals courts.
Suffrage: Universal at age 18.
Main political parties: Democratic Party of Albania (DP); Albanian Socialist Party (SP); Socialist Movement for Integration (LSI); Albanian Republican Party (PR); Demo-Christian Party (PDK); Union for Human Rights Party (PBDNJ); New Democracy Party (PDR); Social Democratic Party (PSD); Social Democracy Party (PDS).

Economy
Natural resources: Oil, gas, coal, iron, copper and chrome ores.

GEOGRAPHY

Albania shares a border with Greece to the south/southeast, Macedonia to the east, Kosovo to the northeast, and Montenegro to the northwest. Western Albania lies along the Adriatic and Ionian Sea coastlines. Albania's primary seaport is Durres, which handles 90% of its maritime cargo.

PEOPLE AND HISTORY

Over 90% of Albania's people are ethnic Albanian, and Albanian is the official language. Religions include Muslim (Sunni and Bektashi), Albanian Orthodox, and Roman Catholic.

Scholars believe the Albanian people are descended from a non-Slavic, non-Turkic group of tribes known as Illyrians, who arrived in the Balkans around 2000 BC. After falling under Roman authority in 165 BC, Albania was controlled nearly continuously by a succession of foreign powers until the mid-20th century, with only brief periods of self-rule.

Following the split of the Roman Empire in 395, the Byzantine Empire established control over present-day Albania. In the 11th century, Byzantine Emperor Alexius I Comnenus made the first recorded reference to a distinct area of land known as Albania and to its people.

The Ottoman Empire ruled Albania from 1385-1912. During this time, much of the population converted to the Islamic faith, and Albanians also emigrated to Italy, Greece, Egypt and Turkey. Although its control was briefly disrupted during the 1443-78 revolt, led by Albania's national hero, Gjergj Kastrioti Skenderbeu, the Ottomans eventually reasserted their dominance.

The League of Prizren (1878) promoted the idea of an Albanian nation-state and established the modern Albanian alphabet, updating a language that survived the hundreds of years of Ottoman rule despite being outlawed. By the early 20th century, the weakened Ottoman Empire was no longer able to suppress Albanian nationalism. Following the conclusion of the First Balkan War, Albanians issued the Vlore Proclamation of November 28, 1912, declaring independence and the Great Powers established Albania's borders in 1913. Albania's territorial integrity was confirmed at the Paris Peace Conference in 1919, after U.S. President Woodrow Wilson dismissed a plan by the European powers to divide Albania among its neighbors.

During the Second World War, Albania was occupied first by Italy (1939-43) and then by Germany (1943-44). After the war, Communist Party leader Enver Hoxha, through a combination of ruthlessness and strategic alliances, managed to preserve Albania's territorial integrity during the next 40 years, but exacted a terrible price from the population, which was subjected to purges, shortages, repression of civil and political rights, a total ban on religious observance, and increased isolation. Albania adhered to a strict Stalinist philosophy, eventually withdrawing from the Warsaw Pact in 1968 and alienating its final remaining ally, China, in 1978.

Following Hoxha's death in 1985 and the subsequent fall of communism in 1991, Albanian society struggled to overcome its historical isolation and underdevelopment. During the initial transition period, the Albanian Government sought closer ties with the West in order to improve economic conditions and introduced basic democratic reforms, including a multi-party system.

In 1992, after the sweeping electoral victory of the Democratic Party, Sali Berisha became the first democratically elected President of Albania. Berisha began a more deliberate program of economic and democratic reform but progress on these issues stalled in the mid-1990s, due to political gridlock. At the same time, unscrupulous investment companies defrauded investors all over Albania using pyramid schemes. In early 1997, several of these pyramid schemes collapsed, leaving thousands of people bankrupt, disillusioned, and angry. Armed revolts broke out across the country, leading to the near-total collapse of government authority. During this time, Albania's already inadequate and antiquated infrastructure suffered tremendous damage, as people looted public works for building materials. Weapons depots all over the country were raided. The anarchy of early 1997 alarmed the world and prompted intensive international mediation.

A UN Multinational Protection Force restored order, and an interim national reconciliation government oversaw the general elections of June 1997, which returned the Socialists and their allies to power at the national level. President Berisha resigned, and the Socialists elected Rexhep Meidani as President of the Republic.

During the transitional period of 1997-2002, a series of short-lived Socialist-led governments succeeded one another as Albania's fragile democratic structures were strengthened. Additional political parties formed, media outlets expanded, non-governmental organizations and business associations developed. In 1998, Albanians ratified a new constitution via popular referendum, guaranteeing the rule of law and the protection of fundamental human rights and religious freedom. Fatos Nano, Chairman of the Socialist Party, emerged as Prime Minister in July 2002.

On July 24, 2002, Alfred Moisiu was sworn in as President of the Republic. A nonpartisan figure, he was elected as a consensus candidate of the ruling and opposition parties. The peaceful transfer of power from President Meidani to President Moisiu was the result of an agreement between the parties to engage each other within established parliamentary structures. This "truce" ushered in a new period of political stability in Albania, making possible significant progress in democratic and economic reforms, rule of law initiatives, and the development of Albania's relations with its neighbors and the U.S.

The "truce" between party leaders began to fray in summer 2003 and progress on economic and political reforms suffered noticeably due to political infighting. The municipal elections of 2003 and national elections of 2005 were an improvement over past years, adding to the consolidation of democracy despite the continued presence of administrative errors and inaccuracies in voter lists.

In 2005, the Democratic Party and its allies returned to power, pledging to fight crime and corruption, decrease the size and scope of government, and promote economic growth. Their leader, Sali Berisha, was sworn in as Prime Minister on September 11, 2005.

Since the election, Prime Minister Berisha's government has made the fight against corruption and organized crime a priority, although the former has met with limited success. The opposition has criticized the government's approach to fighting corruption and crime as unconstitutional and an attempt to undermine independent institutions. While previously relations between the government and opposition SP party were characterized as antagonistic, both sides have at times shown willingness to work together to achieve major policy objectives, such as the constitutional reforms of early 2008.

Another politically contentious process was the pre-electoral period prior to the 2007 local elections. Although the February 18, 2007 local elections were generally peaceful and democratic, over-politicized debate during the preceding months resulted in procedural and administrative problems during the conduct of the elections. A major positive step forward was the performance of the police force.

The fragility of the Albanian electoral system was tested again during the parliamentary by-election in zone 26 (Shijak) on March 11, 2007. The left-wing opposition parties withdrew their commissioners from the polling stations and the counting center, in spite of prior concessions from the Central Elections Commission (CEC) to the opposition's demands. Opposition commissioners left and took with them one of the seals that mark the ballots. By midday, the opposition candidate also announced his withdrawal from the parliamentary race. However, the right of citizens to vote prevailed and the process continued thanks to the technical arrangements of the CEC. The only visible sign of violence was the wounding of a Democratic Party commissioner, who was fired upon by a militant.

Both elections were an indication of lack of political will to cooperate and of the need for a comprehensive electoral reform of the Albanian electoral system.

On July 20, 2007 President Bamir Topi was elected within Parliament after six members of the opposition coalition broke ranks to vote for his candidacy. Out of 90 deputies present at the session, 85 voted for Topi, while Neritan Ceka, head of the opposition Democratic Alliance party, won five votes. Topi, 50, a former agriculture minister, succeeded President Alfred Moisiu for a five-year mandate.

GOVERNMENT AND POLITICAL CONDITIONS

The unicameral People's Assembly (Kuvendi Popullor) consists of 140 seats, 100 of which are determined by direct popular vote. The remaining seats are distributed by proportional representation. All members serve 4-year terms. The Speaker of Parliament (Jozefina Topalli) has two deputies, who along with eight permanent parliamentary commissions assist in the process of legislating Albanian affairs. Parliamentary elections were held on June 28, 2009; as of end-June, results were not yet finalized.

The President is the head of state and elected by a three-fifths majority vote of all Assembly members. The President serves a term of 5 years with the right to one re-election. Although the position is largely ceremonial, the Constitution gives the President authority to appoint and dismiss some high-ranking civil servants in the executive and judicial branches, and this authority can have political implications. The President is also commander in chief of the armed forces, and chairs the National Security Commission. The current President's term expires on July 23, 2012.

The Prime Minister is appointed by the President and approved by a simple majority of all members of the Assembly. The Prime Minister serves as the Chairman of the Council of Ministers (cabinet), which consists of the Prime Minister, Deputy Prime Minister, and other ministers. Members of the Council of Ministers are nominated by the Prime Minister, decreed by the President, and approved by a parliamentary vote.

Albania's civil law system is similar to that of other European countries. The court structure consists of a Constitutional Court, a Supreme Court, and multiple appeal and district courts. The Constitutional Court is comprised of nine members appointed by the Assembly for one 9-year term. The Constitutional Court interprets the Constitution, determines the constitutionality of laws, and resolves disagreements between local and federal authorities. The Supreme Court is the highest court of appeal and consists of 11 members appointed by the President with the consent of the Assembly for 9-year terms. The President chairs the High Council of Justice, which is responsible for appointing and dismissing other judges. The High Council of Justice is comprised of 15 members--the President of the Republic, the Chairman of the High Court, the Minister of Justice, three members elected by the Assembly, and nine judges of all levels elected by the National Judicial Conference.

The remaining courts are divided into three jurisdictions: criminal, civil, and military. There are no jury trials under the Albanian system of justice. A college of three judges, sometimes referred to as a "jury" by the Albanian press, renders court verdicts.

Principal Government Officials
President--Bamir Topi
Prime Minister--Sali Berisha
Deputy Prime Minister--Genc Pollo
Minister of Defense--Gazmend Oketa
Minister of Foreign Affairs--Lulzim Basha

ECONOMY

Currency	Lek (ALL)
Fiscal year	Calendar year
Trade organisations	WTO, BSEC
Statistics	
GDP	$32.259 billion (PPP, 2015), $14.520 billion (Nominal, 2015)
GDP rank	96th (PPP, 2015 est.)
GDP growth	2.1% (Real, 2014 est.)

GDP per capita	$11.700 (PPP, 2015 est.) $5.260 (Nominal, 2015)
GDP by sector	agriculture: 18.4%, industry: 16.3%, services: 65.3% (2014 est.)
Inflation (CPI)	2.0% (CPI, 2012 est.)
Population below poverty line	10.3%
Gini coefficient	34.5
Labour force	1.280 million
Labour force by occupation	Agriculture: 18.4%, Industry: 16.3%, Services: 65.3% (December 2014 est.)
Unemployment	13.3%
Average gross salary	385 € / 430 $, monthly
Main industries	perfumes and cosmetic products, food and tobacco products; textiles and clothing; lumber, oil, cement, chemicals, mining, basic metals, hydropower
Ease-of-doing-business rank	68th
External	
Exports	$2.47 billion
Export goods	textiles and footwear; asphalt, metals and metallic ores, crude oil; vegetables, fruits, tobacco
Main export partners	Italy 43.3% China 9.7% Spain 8.4% Kosovo 7.4% India 6.1%
Imports	$5.067 billion (2014)
Import goods	machinery and equipment, foodstuffs, textiles, chemicals
Main import partners	Italy 36.1% Greece 9.6%

	China 7.2% Turkey 5.7% Germany 4%
Public finances	
Public debt	$7.825 billion (December 2014)
Revenues	$3.3 billion (Budget 2014)
Expenses	$4.50 billion (Budget 2014)
Economic aid	recipient: ODA: $366 million (top donors were Italy, EU, Germany) (2003 est.)
Credit rating	Standard & Poor's: B (Domestic) B+ (Foreign) BB+ (T&C Assessment) Outlook: Positive
Foreign reserves	$2.825 billion (December 2014)

The **economy of Albania** has undergone a transition from its Communist past into an open-market economy since the early 1990s. The country is rich in natural resources, and the economy is mainly bolstered by agriculture, food processing, lumber, oil, cement, chemicals, mining, basic metals, hydro power, tourism, textile industry, and petroleum extraction. As of 2014, exports seem to gain momentum and have increased 300% from 2008, although their contribution to the gross domestic product is still moderate (the export of products per capita as of 2014 is around $1,100).

Albania's transition from a socialist centrally planned economy to free-market capitalism has been largely successful. There are signs of increasing investments, and power cuts are reduced to the extent that Albania is now exporting energy. In 2012, its GDP per capita (expressed in Purchasing Power Standards) stood at 30% of the EU average, while AIC (Actual Individual Consumption) was 35%.Still, Albania has shown potential for economic growth, as more and more businesses relocate there and consumer goods are becoming available from emerging market traders as part of the current massive global cost-cutting exercise. Albania, Cyprus, and

Poland are the only countries in Europe that recorded economic growth in the first quarter of 2010. International Monetary Fund (IMF) predicted 2.6% growth for Albania in 2010 and 3.2% in 2011.

Albania and Croatia have discussed the possibility of jointly building a nuclear power plant at Lake Shkoder, close to the border with Montenegro, a plan that has gathered criticism from Montenegro due to seismicity in the area. In addition, there is some doubt whether Albania would be able to finance a project of such a scale with a total national budget of less than $5 billion. However, in February 2009 Italian company Enel announced plans to build an 800 MW coal-fired power plant in Albania, to diversify electricity sources. Nearly 100% of the electricity is generated by ageing hydroelectric power plants, which are becoming more ineffective due to increasing droughts. However, there have been many private investments in building new hydroelectric power plants such as Devoll Hydro Power Plant and the Ashta hydropower plant.

The country has large deposits of petroleum and natural gas, and produced 26,000 barrels of oil per day in the first quarter of 2014 (BNK-TC). Natural gas production, estimated at about 30 million m^3, is sufficient to meet consumer demands.

Other natural resources include coal, bauxite, copper and iron ore.Albania has the largest onshore oil reserves in Europe. Albania's crude output amounted to more than 1.2 million tonnes in 2015, including 1.06 million by Canada's Bankers Petroleum, 87,063 tonnes from Canada's Stream Oil and 37,406 tonnes by Albpetrol on its own. Three foreign firms produced the rest.

Agriculture is the most significant sector, employing a significant proportion of the labor force and generating about 21% of GDP. Agriculture in Albania employs 47.8% of the population and about 24.31% of the land is used for agricultural purposes. Domestic farm products accounted for 63% of household expenditures and 25% of exports in 1990. As part of the pre-accession process of Albania to the EU, farmers are being aided through IPA 2011 funds to improve Albanian agriculture standards. Albania produces significant amounts of tobacco, olives, wheat, maize, potatoes, vegetables, fruits, sugar beets, grapes; meat, honey, dairy products, and traditional medicine and aromatic plants, figs (13th largest producer in the world) and sour cherries. Albania's proximity to the Ionian Sea and the Adriatic Sea give the underdeveloped fishing industry great potential. World Bank and European Community economists report that Albania's fishing industry has good potential to generate export earnings because prices in the nearby Greek and Italian markets are many times higher than those in the Albanian market. The fish available off the coasts of Albania are carp, trout, sea bream, mussels, and crustaceans.

"Tourism is gaining a fair share of Albania's GDP with visitors growing every year. As of 2014 exports seem to gain momentum and have increased 300% from 2008, although their contribution to the GDP is still moderate (the exports per capita ratio currently stands at 1100 $) . Although Albania's growth has slowed in 2015 tourism is expanding rapidly and foreign investments are becoming more common as the government continues the modernization of Albania's institutions

Albania's economy has improved substantially over recent years and has outperformed many other countries in the region. However, it is still considered one of the poorest countries in Europe. According to the Bank of Albania, per capita income was $3,675 in 2008, expected to reach $4,000 in 2009. According to some preliminary data by the World Bank's Poverty Assessment Program, 12.4% of the population lived below the poverty line in 2008, marking a considerable improvement from 25.4% in 2002. The official unemployment rate is 12.7%. Almost 60% of all workers are employed in the agricultural sector, although the construction and service industries have been expanding recently. Tourism has been boosted significantly by ethnic Albanian tourists from throughout the Balkans. The GDP is comprised of services (50%), agriculture (19%), industry (12%), construction (14%), and transport and communication (6%). The Albanian economy has been partially sheltered from the global financial crisis and the economic downturn. In April 2009, the International Monetary Fund (IMF) predicted that Albania would be one of two countries in Europe to enjoy a positive growth rate for 2009, but lower remittances from Albanian workers abroad (approximately 9.6% of the GDP in 2008), mostly in Greece and Italy, and smaller exports will put a strain on economic activity.

The global financial crisis has reduced Albanian citizens' trust of commercial banks, even though the domestic banking sector has remained largely insulated from the crisis. Although bank deposits dropped by 10% since September 2008, withdrawals have diminished recently and deposits have stabilized during the second quarter of 2009. Lower liquidity has forced commercial banks to tighten lending procedures. In February 2009, the growth rate of loans dropped to 29% from 35% in 2008. In general, the banking sector remains viable and able to further finance the economy, as the ratio of loans to deposits, approximately 65%, is still low compared to western standards.

Albania was the last of the central and eastern European countries to embark upon democratic and free market reforms. Furthermore, Albania started from a comparatively disadvantaged position due to Hoxha's catastrophic economic policies. The transition from a centrally planned economy to a market-oriented system has been almost as difficult for Albania as the country's communist period.

The democratically elected government that assumed office in April 1992 launched an ambitious economic reform program meant to halt economic deterioration and put the country on the path toward a market economy. Key elements included price and exchange system liberalization, fiscal consolidation, monetary restraint, and a firm income policy. These were complemented by a comprehensive package of structural reforms, including privatization, enterprise and financial sector reform, and creation of the legal framework for a market economy and private sector activity.

Results of Albania's efforts were initially encouraging. Led by the agricultural sector, real GDP grew, and Albania's currency, the lek, stabilized. The speed and vigor of private entrepreneurial response to the opening of Albania's economy was better than expected. In 1995, however, progress stalled. The collapse of the infamous pyramid schemes of the late 1990s and the instability that followed were a tremendous setback, from which Albania's economy continues to recover.

The Albanian Government signed a free trade agreement (FTA) with the European Union (EU) as part of its Stabilization and Association Agreement negotiations. The interim agreement entered into force in December 2006, with a duty-free regime for almost 90% of agricultural and industrial products. On the fiscal side it will also significantly reduce revenue collection.

Albania has FTAs with Macedonia, Croatia, Bulgaria, Romania, Bosnia, Turkey, and Moldova. Albania also previously established an FTA with the UN Interim Administration Mission in Kosovo (UNMIK), which was transferred to the Republic of Kosovo in 2009. In April 2006, these bilateral agreements were replaced by a multiregional agreement that entered into force in May 2007 based on the Central European Free Trade Agreement (CEFTA) model.

The EU remains, by far, Albania's main trading partner, providing 60.7% of Albania's imports and receiving 79.7% of exports for 2008. Trade with Italy and Greece represent the largest share of EU trade, with a combined 67.7% of imports and 88.6% of exports. The impact of CEFTA in Albania's trade with member countries has been insignificant.

U.S. trade with Albania is very low. In 2008, U.S. exports to Albania totaled $67 million compared with $49 million in 2007, an increase of 36.7%. Part of this increase was due to the 8% depreciation of the dollar against the domestic currency. U.S. imports from Albania decreased 26% in 2008 ($5.1 million) from $6.9 million in 2007. However, there are some discrepancies between U.S. and Albanian trade figures. Major U.S. investment to date has been limited to large-scale infrastructure contracts with the government; Lockheed Martin and Bechtel are principal U.S. participants. In 2008, Refinery Associates of Texas became the first significant U.S. investor representing 20% of the consortium that privatized 85% of the shares of the state-owned oil refinery ARMO.

Albania is trying to attract foreign investment and promote domestic investment, but significant impediments exist. The Albanian Government faces the daunting task of standardizing and uniformly applying business laws, improving transparency in business procedures, resolving property ownership disputes, restructuring the tax systems (including tax collection), and reducing corruption.

Business growth has been hampered by Albania's inadequate energy and transportation infrastructure despite some significant investments in both sectors during the last few years. The capital, Tirana, and the main port of Durres generally receive electricity most of the day, but frequent power outages plague every other city, small town, and rural village. Although recent steps have been taken to improve the transportation infrastructure, Albania has a limited railway system and just one international airport. Because of the mountainous terrain and poor road conditions, overland goods transport is arduous and costly. However, the government has invested heavily in road construction over the last three years, and the country now sports a new, modern highway along its entire coastline, from Shkoder in the north to the southern resort city of Sarande. In addition, completion of the 170-kilometer Durres-Kukes highway in fall 2009 will provide a major transportation corridor connecting markets in the central Balkans through Kosovo to the port of Durres.

MILITARY AFFAIRS

Since the fall of communism in Albania in 1991, the country has played a constructive role in resolving several of the interethnic conflicts in south central Europe, promoting peaceful dispute resolution and discouraging ethnic Albanian extremists. Albania sheltered many thousands of Kosovar refugees during the 1999 conflict. Albania is part of the international force serving in Bosnia (EUFOR), and Albanian peacekeepers are part of the International Security Assistance Force (ISAF) in Afghanistan and previously contributed to the international stabilization force in Iraq prior to its mandate expiring in December 2008. While in Iraq, Albania was one of only four nations to contribute troops to the combat phase of Operation Enduring Freedom.

Albania worked with the international community to restructure its armed forces and strengthen democratic structures, including addressing military reforms, in its pursuit of NATO membership. Since 1999, Albania has spent approximately $108 million annually on military expenditures, roughly 1.35% of its GDP. According to Government of Albania projections, military expenditures were to reach 2% of GDP in 2008. With bilateral and multilateral assistance, the Ministry of Defense is transitioning to a smaller, voluntary, professional military, and reducing the vast amounts of excess weaponry and ammunition that litter the country and pose a significant public hazard and proliferation risk. The Albanian Government and the international community are working together on a project that will make Albania a mine-free country by 2010. Most high- and medium-priority mine clearance has been completed in the mined areas of northeast Albania, a legacy of the 1999 Kosovo crisis. However, a significant amount of unexploded ordnance remains to be demilitarized in the country.

Albania and the U.S. enjoy a military partnership and are signatories to treaties including the 2003 Prevention of Proliferation of Weapons of Mass Destruction and the Promotion of Defense and Military Relations and the 2004 Supplementary Agreement to the Partnership for Peace Status of Forces Agreement, which defined the status of American military troops in Albania, further enabling military cooperation. In May 2003, Albania, Croatia, Macedonia, and the U.S. created the Adriatic Charter, modeled on the Baltic Charter, as a mechanism for promoting regional cooperation to advance each country's NATO candidacy. In spite of strong EU objections, Albania also signed in May 2003 a bilateral agreement with the United States on non-surrender of persons, based on Article 98 of the statute of International Criminal Court.

In 2004 President George W. Bush authorized the use of the Nunn-Lugar Cooperative Threat Reduction program funds for projects in Albania, marking the first time such funds were used outside the former Soviet Union. With this funding the United States has assisted the Government of Albania with the destruction of a stockpile of chemical agents left over from the communist regime. Under this program, Albania became the first nation in the world to complete destruction of declared chemical weapons holdings under the Chemical Weapons Convention in July 2007. Albania received an invitation to become a NATO member at the April 2008 NATO Summit in Bucharest. The U.S. Senate unanimously ratified Albania's Protocols of Accession to NATO on September 25, 2008, and President Bush signed the Accession Protocols on October 24, 2008. Albania became a member of NATO on April 1, 2009.

FOREIGN RELATIONS

Albania is currently pursuing a path of greater Euro-Atlantic integration. Its primary long-term goals are to gain EU membership and to promote closer bilateral ties with its neighbors and with the U.S. Albania is a member of a number of international organizations, as well as multiple regional organizations and initiatives, including NATO, the Organization for Security and Cooperation in Europe (OSCE), the UN, the Stability Pact, the Adriatic Charter, and the World Trade Organization (WTO). In June 2006, Albania and the EU signed a Stabilization and Association Agreement, the first step to EU membership, which will focus on implementing essential rule of law reforms and curbing corruption and organized crime. Albania filed its application for EU candidacy on April 28, 2009.

Albania maintains good relations with its neighbors. It re-established diplomatic relations with the Federal Republic of Yugoslavia following the ousting of Slobodan Milosevic in 2000, and maintains excellent relations with the Republic of Montenegro, which gained its independence after the dissolution of the Serbia and Montenegro union in 2006. Albanian, Macedonian, and Italian law enforcement agencies are cooperating with increasing efficiency to crack down on the trafficking of arms, drugs, contraband, and human beings across their borders. Albania has also arrested and prosecuted several ethnic Albanian extremists on charges of inciting interethnic hatred in Macedonia and Kosovo. Tensions occasionally arise with Greece over the treatment of the Greek minority in Albania or the Albanian community in Greece, but overall relations are good.

U.S.-ALBANIAN RELATIONS

Albania enjoys friendly and cooperative bilateral relations with the U.S. Pro-U.S. sentiment is widespread among the population. Even while the U.S., which had closed its mission to Albania in 1946, was being vilified by communist propaganda during the Hoxha regime, ordinary Albanians remembered that Woodrow Wilson had supported Albanian independence in 1919. Albanians credit the NATO bombing of Serbia in 1999 with saving thousands of Kosovo Albanians, and they greatly appreciate the U.S. Government's continued support for a stable, free, and democratic Kosovo.

In 2003, Albania and the U.S. signed and ratified a number of agreements, including a treaty on the Prevention of Proliferation of Weapons of Mass Destruction and the Promotion of Defense and Military Relations; the Adriatic Charter; and an agreement regarding the non-surrender of persons to the International Criminal Court. The U.S. strongly supports Albania's EU membership goal, as it did Albania's pursuit of NATO membership. Working toward NATO membership, the

U.S. and Albania signed a Supplementary Agreement to the Partnership for Peace Status of Forces Agreement, an important step in strengthening bilateral cooperation and enhancing security, peace, and stability in the region. The U.S. Senate unanimously ratified Albania's Protocols of Accession to NATO on September 25, 2008, and President Bush signed the Accession Protocols on October 24, 2008.

Since FY 1991, the U.S. has provided Albania with more than $616 million in assistance, not counting U.S. Department of Agriculture (USDA) food aid. The aid has served to facilitate Albania's transition from the most isolated and repressive communist state in Europe to a modern democracy with a market-oriented economy, and to support long-term development. In 2007, the U.S. gave over $21.1 million to Albania under the Support for East European Democracy (SEED) Act program. Albania was among the first countries selected to participate in the Threshold Program under the Millennium Challenge Account, winning a grant of $13.8 million and a second Threshold grant of $16 million in 2008. The program targets two critical stumbling blocks to development--corruption and rule of law.

Despite daunting problems at home, Albania has wholeheartedly supported U.S. anti-terrorism efforts by freezing terrorist assets, shutting down non-governmental organizations (NGOs) with possible links to terrorist financing, expelling extremists, and providing hundreds of military troops for the U.S.-led actions in Afghanistan and Iraq. Albania has played a moderating role in the region and has fully supported UN mediation efforts in Kosovo.

Principal U.S. Embassy Officials

chief of mission: Ambassador Donald LU (since 13 January 2015)

Donald Lu was sworn in as U.S. Ambassador to the Republic of Albania on December 17, 2014. Prior to that assignment, he worked on the Ebola crisis in West Africa as Deputy Coordinator for Ebola Response in the State Department. His overseas postings include Deputy Chief of Mission in India, Azerbaijan and Kyrgyzstan. He also served for a year as Chargé d'Affaires at the U.S. Embassy in Azerbaijan.

Deputy Chief of Mission--Stephen Cristina
Political/Economic Section Chief--Paul Poletes
Political Officers--Tony Baird, Michael Gray
Economic/Commercial Officer--Victor Myev
Consular Officer--Abigail Aronson
USAID Director--Roberta Mahoney
Public Affairs Officer--Bix Aliu
Defense Attaché--Brian Moore
Regional Security Officer--Patrick Leonard
Management Officer--vacant

The U.S. Embassy is located at 103 Tirana Rruga Elbasanit, Tirana; telephone: [355] (4) 224-7285; facsimile: [355] (4) 223-2222.

TRAVEL AND BUSINESS INFORMATION

The U.S. Department of State's Consular Information Program advises Americans traveling and residing abroad through Country Specific Information, Travel Alerts, and Travel Warnings. **Country Specific Information** exists for all countries and includes information on entry and exit requirements, currency regulations, health conditions, safety and security, crime, political disturbances, and the addresses of the U.S. embassies and consulates abroad. **Travel Alerts** are issued to disseminate information quickly about terrorist threats and other relatively short-term conditions overseas that pose significant risks to the security of American travelers. **Travel**

Warnings are issued when the State Department recommends that Americans avoid travel to a certain country because the situation is dangerous or unstable.

For the latest security information, Americans living and traveling abroad should regularly monitor the Department's Bureau of Consular Affairs Internet web site at http://www.travel.state.gov, where the current Worldwide Caution, Travel Alerts, and Travel Warnings can be found. Consular Affairs Publications, which contain information on obtaining passports and planning a safe trip abroad, are also available at http://www.travel.state.gov. For additional information on international travel, see http://www.usa.gov/Citizen/Topics/Travel/International.shtml.

The Department of State encourages all U.S. citizens traveling or residing abroad to register via the State Department's travel registration website or at the nearest U.S. embassy or consulate abroad. Registration will make your presence and whereabouts known in case it is necessary to contact you in an emergency and will enable you to receive up-to-date information on security conditions.

Emergency information concerning Americans traveling abroad may be obtained by calling 1-888-407-4747 toll free in the U.S. and Canada or the regular toll line 1-202-501-4444 for callers outside the U.S. and Canada.

The National Passport Information Center (NPIC) is the U.S. Department of State's single, centralized public contact center for U.S. passport information. Telephone: 1-877-4-USA-PPT (1-877-487-2778); TDD/TTY: 1-888-874-7793. Passport information is available 24 hours, 7 days a week. You may speak with a representative Monday-Friday, 8 a.m. to 10 p.m., Eastern Time, excluding federal holidays.

Travelers can check the latest health information with the U.S. Centers for Disease Control and Prevention in Atlanta, Georgia. A hotline at 800-CDC-INFO (800-232-4636) and a web site at http://wwwn.cdc.gov/travel/default.aspx give the most recent health advisories, immunization recommendations or requirements, and advice on food and drinking water safety for regions and countries. The CDC publication "Health Information for International Travel" can be found at http://wwwn.cdc.gov/travel/contentYellowBook.aspx.

Further Electronic Information

Department of State Web Site. Available on the Internet at http://www.state.gov, the Department of State web site provides timely, global access to official U.S. foreign policy information, including Background Notes and daily press briefings along with the directory of key officers of Foreign Service posts and more. The Overseas Security Advisory Council (OSAC) provides security information and regional news that impact U.S. companies working abroad through its website http://www.osac.gov

Export.gov provides a portal to all export-related assistance and market information offered by the federal government and provides trade leads, free export counseling, help with the export process, and more.

STARTING AND CONDUCTING BUSINESS IN ALBANIA - PRACTICAL INFORMATION[1]

DOING BUSINESS IN ALBANIA

MARKET OVERVIEW

Following the collapse of communism in 1992, Albania continues to make strides in its transition from a closed, centrally planned economy to a modern, open-market economy. The country is pursuing aggressively its Euro-Atlantic integration agenda. In 2000, Albania became a World Trade Organization (WTO) member and in June 2006, the Government of Albania (GOA) signed a Stabilization and Association Agreement (SAA) with the European Union (EU), the first step towards the EU accession process. In April 2009, Albania became a North Atlantic Treaty Organization (NATO) member country and at the same time, submitted its application for EU candidacy status, both considered major milestones in the country's history.

A small country with a population of 2.83 million people (2011 census) and a landmass approximately the size of Maryland, Albania's economy posted strong growth in the 2000s, with an average annual growth rate of 6 percent from 2000 to 2008. Although Albania largely was spared from the initial severe fallout of the 2008 financial crisis, the prolonged European crises, coupled with a challenging fiscal and budgetary environment and structural problems in the local economy, has caused economic output to steadily decline since 2009. 2015 GDP growth likely will decline to 0.7 percent, the lowest in more than a decade, and far from the government's initial projection of 3.1 percent. Faced with mounting public debt (approximately 70 percent of GDP), large government arrears to the private sector, and a weak economy, the government signed a $457 million arrangement with the International Monetary Fund at the end of 2015 and took out two development policy loans worth a total of $220 million from the World Bank in May 2014. The three-year IMF arrangement aims to help Albania pay back government arrears, pursue fiscal consolidation, and to improve debt sustainability. The World Bank development policy loans are intended to modernize Albania's public financial management system to reduce and better manage Albania's public debt. The Albanian government hopes these loans, coupled with better customs and tax collections, will spur economic growth and help the government reduce its public debt. The IMF estimates that the economy will grow by 2 percent in 2014, boosted by an increase in exports and a modest recovery in domestic demand.

Inflation in 2015 averaged 1.9 percent. The official unemployment rate during 2015 rose to 16.9 percent from 14.4 percent in 2012 and domestic labor costs remain among the lowest in Europe. In 2015, the Albanian lek was stable versus both the dollar and the euro. The banking sector in Albania remains viable, profitable, and well capitalized; however, increasing rates of nonperforming loans (around 25 percent) and low domestic

lending are growing concerns for the sector. At the end of February 2014, deposits totaled $940 million and loans totaled $590 million.

Estimated GDP for 2015 was $12.8 billion and GDP per capita was $4,598. Although GDP per capita has increased over the last decade, it is still amongst the lowest in the region. The Albanian economy has four main sectors. The service sector is the largest and comprises 57.8 percent of GDP, followed by agriculture at 19.5 percent, construction at 10.7 percent, and industry at 12 percent of GDP. The economy remains characterized by a narrow base of exports,

[1] Country Commercial Guide for Albania, US Governmetn Information

a wide base of imports, and low competitiveness. The agriculture sector employs half of the country's workforce, mostly in small subsistence-level family farms.

Albania's Foreign Direct Investment (FDI) inflow increased significantly over the last six years, averaging $1 billion each year from 2008 to 2015. Canada is Albania's largest foreign direct investor, representing 20 percent of Albania's FDI stock, followed by Switzerland (14.5 percent), Austria (14.2 percent), Greece (12.9 percent), Italy (12.4 percent), Turkey (7.5 percent), and the Netherlands (6.9 percent). FDI primarily focuses on the processing, extraction, and financial sectors.

Albania's trade deficit reduced from $2.9 billion to $2.53 billion in 2015 reflecting an increase in heavy crude oil, textile, and footwear exports. The European Union remains Albania's main trading partner. In 2015, the EU provided 64 percent of the country's imports and received 76.7 percent of exports. Albania's primary importing partners are Italy, Greece, China, Turkey, and Germany. Major exporting partners are Italy, Spain, Malta, Kosovo, and China.

Albania's trade with the United States remains small but is increasing. U.S. exports to Albania in 2015 reached $122 million, up from only $66 million in 2009. Agricultural products, ferroalloys, footwear, and textiles serve as the main exports to the United States, while meat, oil, transportation equipment, and computer and electronic equipment comprise the majority of Albanian imports from the United States.

Albania has a free trade agreement (FTA) with Turkey and is a signatory to the Central European Free Trade Agreement (CEFTA), which includes the eight countries of Albania, Macedonia, Montenegro, Kosovo, Moldova, Croatia, Serbia, and Bosnia and Herzegovina. Albania also enjoys important trade benefits with EU members since it signed and ratified the Stabilization and Association Agreement (SAA). In June 2009, Albania also signed an FTA with the European Free Trade Association (EFTA). EFTA member states include Iceland, Liechtenstein, Norway, and Switzerland. The agreement with Liechtenstein and Switzerland entered into force in November 2010 and the agreement with Iceland and Norway entered into force in 2011.

Overall, the Albanian market is a developing market. The government's main task at present is to maintain positive economic growth rates, while combating a challenging fiscal and budgetary environment.

MARKET CHALLENGES

Every sector in Albania is open to foreign investors and there are no legal barriers to market entry. The government has made significant reforms to make foreign investment

more attractive. Improvements in administrative procedures, such as business registration, licensing, e-procurement, e-taxes, and simplification of taxes are examples. Nonetheless, major challenges remain:

Corruption: Corruption is pervasive in Albania. This subject is discussed in depth in Chapter 6.

Weak judicial system and poor enforcement of contracts: While significant reforms of the judicial system are underway, the courts are slow, inefficient, and subject to political pressure and corruption. Enforcement of court decisions and contracts also presents a challenge.

Property issues: The official register of real estate property titles is incomplete and poorly maintained. Multiple claims on the same property are common and significant legislative and legal gaps in the restitution and compensation process remain.

Lack of proper infrastructure: Despite major improvements in infrastructure in recent years, the country's physical infrastructure is still developing and needs further investment.

Reference or market prices: The application of so-called reference or market prices by the customs authorities for calculating custom taxes remains a concern for businesses and foreign investors. Market prices are supposed to be used to combat fiscal evasion, but businesses allege these rates are artificially high. In 2014, Customs pledged to eliminate reference prices for goods originating in the United States and European Union by 2015.

Frequent legislative changes: One of the major challenges reported by the business community is frequent legislative changes and a lack of proper consultations with the business community.

MARKET OPPORTUNITIES

Despite its small size and population, Albania offers opportunities for trade and investment in a variety of sectors. Although the government has completed many major privatizations, several opportunities remain in the oil, mining, insurance, and real estate sectors. Chapter 4 of this guide spells out in detail some of the sectors that may offer the best opportunities for trade and investment.

Albania is rich in natural resources such as oil, gas, copper, chrome, iron, nickel, and coal. Higher world prices and renewed interest from private companies are creating business opportunities in the oil and gas sector and the government plans to auction 13 new oil and gas exploration licenses in 2014. The country's geographic location also allows for considerable water/hydroelectric and wind potential. The Law on Concessions enables the government to offer concession contracts in the hydroelectric, wind generation, and mining sectors. The government also has entered into production sharing agreements with several partners in the oil sector. Aside from possibility of direct investments or concessions, these sectors also represent potential opportunities to provide equipment, machinery, and financing for other investors.

The telecommunications sector has experienced spectacular growth in the last five years. Four mobile companies operate in the market and have made significant investments in developing the country's telecom infrastructure. Three out of four operators were issued Third Generation (3G) licenses during 2010-2012 which further boosted the market. In addition, another license to develop a wireless broadband national network is underway. Broadband services also are developing. The scheduled transfer from analogue broadcasting to digital broadcasting also will bring business opportunities. Overall, the on-going liberalization and expansion of the sector continues to fuel the demand for physical facilities and equipment.

Public investment in infrastructure has slowed in the last two years. Nonetheless, investment opportunities may exist in roads, water supply, and waste treatment, as well as port infrastructure and terminal projects. The government's transportation sector policy has emphasized the privatization and commercialization of road, maritime, railway, and civil aviation services.

Most of the large-scale privatizations of state-owned companies were completed by 2009. The few remaining opportunities for privatization include: state-owned oil extraction company Albpetrol, insurer INSIG, the remaining state-owned shares of recently privatized oil refinery ARMO (less than 15 percent state-owned shares), and telecom operator Albtelekom (16.7 percent state-owned shares).

Both the public and private health sectors are expanding and there is growing demand for modern medical equipment. As Albanians increasingly demand modern medical services, the demand for medical devices and pharmaceuticals will increase in the coming years.

Agro-processing is another sector with potential opportunities as there is strong demand for packaging and distribution facilities, refrigeration and storage capacity, and quality control in this sector. The government is focusing on modernizing the agricultural sector; so there may be significant demand for modern agriculture machinery in the coming years.

Tourism has the potential to play a leading role in Albania's economic development. The tourism sector represents one of the most important sources of revenue for the economy. The country's geographic location, seasonal climate, and combination of archaeological, historical, and religious sites can be harnessed to develop a highly attractive tourism industry. The sector is underdeveloped in comparison with the region and future development of resorts, marinas, and other tourism infrastructure represents opportunities for goods and services.

MARKET ENTRY STRATEGY

Before entering the local market, companies should consider having an agent and/or local distributor. Agents can be found by contacting the U.S. Embassy's Economic and Commercial Section, the American Chamber of Commerce in Albania, local chambers of commerce and industry, the Albanian Investment Development Agency, law firms, consulting companies, and other business organizations.

It is recommended that companies interested in investing in Albania visit the country. This is especially important for companies in the high-tech, telecommunications, and

service sectors. Most companies that come to Albania give detailed presentations and provide demonstrations of their products and/or services. For consumer goods, however, companies may work solely through agents or local distributors.

http://www.aida.gov.al

http://www.amcham.com.al

SELLING U.S. PRODUCTS AND SERVICES

USING AN AGENT OR DISTRIBUTOR

In order to conduct business effectively in Albania, it is essential for U.S. firms to select local sales partners. Collecting meaningful information and gaining access to markets can be difficult without local representatives who have the contacts and know-how to conduct business in this small but complex market. Many foreign firms have found that it is more efficient and cost effective to hire a good local agent or distributor rather than conduct direct sales. U.S. companies seeking to market and distribute their goods will find a considerable number of merchants, agents, middlemen, wholesalers, and retailers available in Albania.

All the typical distribution channels are available in Albania, although they often lack the sophistication of distribution networks found in western markets. Directly contacting potential agents or distributors from a list sometimes works, but is not recommended, as it is difficult to evaluate a prospective business partner from long-distance without an introduction or a third-party evaluation.

Before choosing a local partner, we highly advise U.S. exporters to consider the reputation and financial references of the local potential partner and to find out if the local partner represents any competing products, and their experience in the market. Often funds for product marketing need to be provided by the U.S. company in order to ensure wide promotion and distribution of goods. Once contacts have been established and initial investigation performed, it is advisable for the U.S. companies to visit the country for a final evaluation.

Since liquidity is currently an issue of concern in the domestic economy, it is highly recommended that U.S. companies ask for a confirmed letter-of-credit when conducting business with a new local partner. To gauge the creditworthiness of potential partners, a U.S. company may consider asking the local partner to provide a creditworthiness report issued by the Credit Registry of the Central Bank of Albania or asking the local company to grant a power of attorney to the U.S. company to query the Credit Registry for a report.

The following consulting offices, law firms, and other professional organizations may also be helpful in determining the credibility of a potential business partner:

http://www.kalo-attorneys.com

http://www.bogalaw.com

http:// www.wolftheiss.com

http:// www.hmh-al.net

http://www.tonucci.it

http://www.zkt-lawfirm.com

http://www.pbm.al/

http://www.pwc.com/al

http://www.deloitte.com

http://www.kpmg.com

http://www.ey.com

The American Chamber of Commerce in Albania is an excellent resource for finding a potential partner. The chamber has approximately 270 members interested in conducting business with U.S. companies.

http://www.amcham.com.al/

The U.S. Embassy can provide a series of complimentary and fee-based services to facilitate the entrance of U.S. companies in the Albanian market. For more details, please contact:

Ms. Edi Jacellari
Commercial Assistant
United States Embassy Tirana
E-mail: USALbusiness@state.gov

ESTABLISHING AN OFFICE

Albanian law recognizes a variety of legal forms for businesses entities. Because these business entities vary from each other in terms of their legal responsibilities, the list of documents required for their initial registration also varies. Registration procedures for businesses have been streamlined thanks to the establishment of the National Registration Center for Businesses (NRC) or "One Stop Shop" which became operational in September 2007. For more information on how to register an office in Albania and where to get assistance, please visit the National Center for Business Registration at: http://www.qkr.gov.al

The Law on Entrepreneurs and Commercial Companies of April 2008 is the main legal statute that governs the activities of companies and establishes the type of legal structure under which companies may operate. This law conforms Albanian legislation with the EU's *acquis communitaire.* The legal types of business entities that can be registered with the NRC are as follows:

Sole Entrepreneur

Unlimited Partnership

Limited Partnership

Limited Liability Company (Shpk)

Joint Stock Company

Branches and Representative Offices

Joint Ventures

Sole Entrepreneur

The Sole Entrepreneur trades under his own name and such trade must be registered as a business name. Individuals interested in establishing this type of business should file an application and an identification document with the NRC in the district where the business will be conducted. The application form includes identification data, address, and type of business and an exemplar of the sole proprietor's signature.

Unlimited Partnership

All partners are unlimitedly and jointly liable for the debts of the entity. Creditors can claim against a partner for the debts of the partnership, only if they have failed in their claims against the partnership as a whole. In unlimited partnerships, the partners are all considered administrators of the partnership, unless the contrary is stipulated in the bylaws. Each partner represents the partnership with third parties. An unlimited partnership should issue annual financial reports. The rights, duties and obligations of partners are governed by written bylaws, which should be filed with the National Registration Center

Limited Partnership

A limited partnership, which is seldom used in practice, consists of one or more general partners (unlimited) with unlimited liability and one or more limited partners whose liability is limited to the amount of their agreed contributions of the initial capital. A limited partner may not take part in the management of the partnership, even if he is given a proxy, otherwise he incurs unlimited liability. The Articles of Incorporation of the limited partnership should contain:

The total amount or value of the contributions of all partners;

The amount or value of the contribution made by each general or unlimited partner;

The percentage of the participation of all general partners and of each limited partner in the partnership's profits and in the remaining value after its dissolution.

All decisions are made in conformity with the Articles of Incorporation.

Limited Liability Company (Shpk)

This is the most common form of conducting business in Albania. Its members enjoy limited liability and, unless the articles of the bylaws provide otherwise, members have the right to transfer their shares to other persons, upon decision of three fourths of the shareholders. It can be established by one or more partners, legal or natural persons, who are responsible for losses only to the extent of their contribution to the capital of the

company. The capital is divided into shares and there are no mandatory requirements for their nominal value. The contributions to capital can be in cash or in any asset, tangible or intangible. The law does not permit contributions in services. Administrators nominated through the General Assembly of the shareholders manage the limited liability company. Extraordinary decisions, increases or decreases in the share capital, mergers and acquisitions are to be approved by at least three quarters of the capital shareholders. The law requires annual financial statements to be prepared by the company. The transformation of this form of business into unlimited and limited partnership is subject to decision of general assembly of the shareholders that takes valid decisions upon majority vote of ¾ of shareholders and after approval of financial statements for the last two years.

Joint Stock Company

Its capital is divided into shares, with shareholders held responsible for losses only to the extent of their contribution to the capital. The minimum initial capital required is lek 2 million (approx. $20,000) for companies with no public offering, and lek 10 million (approx. $100,000) for public offerings. The Commercial Law provides for the adoption by joint stock companies of a flexible administration system. This type of companies may choose to adopt either the "monistic" system (with a board of directors/administrators conducting both management and supervising functions) or the "dualistic" system (with board of directors/administrators and supervisory board conducting supervising functions). The supervisory council exercises control over the board of director's performance. This council should have not less than three and not more than 21 members. The capital is fully subscribed when the partners have promised to bring assets to the company in cash or in kind for an amount equaling the capital. At the moment of the subscription, at least one quarter of the nominal value of the shares representing contributions in cash must be paid. Payment of the remaining value shall be made in installments upon the decision of the management bodies of the company. Shares of contributions in kind must be fully paid at the moment of subscribing. The law does not permit contributions in services. The shares of a joint stock company may be ordinary or privileged.

Branches and Representative Offices

Under the Commercial Law, a foreign investor can also operate in Albania through a branch or representative office. The branch or representative office should be registered in the National Registration Center and should have a legal representative empowered by the head office to administer the office. For tax purposes, the branch is treated in the same manner as an Albanian entity.

Joint Ventures

Albanian legislation recognizes joint ventures under the term of simple company, since it is based on an agreement only and no legal personality is granted to this partnership. Joint ventures are overseen by the provisions of the Civil Code (articles 1074 -1112) and may be concluded by two or more persons, whether individuals or legal entities, foreign or national, agreeing to engage in an economic activity in order to share profits deriving from it. There is no minimum capital requirement. Partners are liable to perform the contributions provided in the contract. Unless otherwise agreed, every partner may take part in the management of the partnership and has full power to carry out any acts which are within the scope of the partnership. Every partner is entitled to receive its share of the profits after the accounts have been approved, unless otherwise agreed. Partners are jointly responsible for fulfilling the obligations imposed upon them by law and by the partnership agreement; unless they prove they were not at fault.

Consultants recommend that parties interested in establishing an office in Albania consult/hire local attorneys to guide them through the business establishment process.

For detailed information, please visit http://www.qkr.gov.al

FRANCHISING

Franchising is a relatively new concept for the business community in Albania. Provisions on franchising have been introduced into the Civil Code. In general, no specific registration or government approval is required in order to establish a franchise enterprise. Current economic conditions could encourage the entry of international franchising. The combination of a weakly saturated Albanian market and a strong domestic demand for merchandise and services from developed countries would make Albania a promising destination for a range of franchised businesses. There is a strong franchising presence in a few sectors in Albania, such as Century 21 and Re-Max in the real estate sector, and Western Union and Money Gram in the money transfer sector. There is also strong market potential for franchises in the advertising, restaurant, catering, equipment, and apparel sectors.

DIRECT MARKETING

Direct marketing is not well developed in Albania. E-mail marketing is used but does not have great efficacy, because the low penetration of internet limits its appeal to a limited pool of people for a limited range of services and products. Facebook is widely used for direct marketing, especially by small businesses which have small marketing budgets.

Direct calls or text (sms) are rarely used and are not efficient. Direct marketing by mail is far more common and households receive such mail on a daily basis. Offers usually come from local supermarket chains, electronics and home appliance stores, restaurants, and personal service providers.

Catalog and Internet shopping is in its early stages. Many online merchants do not ship to Albania or charge prohibitively high shipping charges.

Albania is still a cash-based economy and has a low number of credit card holders. In order to promote the use of credit cards, local banks have just started to introduce special discounts of various consumer goods in partnership with other companies.

JOINT VENTURES/LICENSING

Existing legislation permits joint ventures, mixed ownership investment, and both foreign and domestic investment. In the most common joint venture scheme, a foreign company provides capital, equipment, and merchandise, while the local company provides buildings, warehouses, office space, personnel, and channels of distribution. U.S. firms considering such ventures should carefully review the viability of potential domestic

partners. Consultants recommend that parties interested in forming joint ventures hire local attorneys to guide them through the business establishment process.

SELLING TO THE GOVERNMENT

Interested companies can visit the Public Procurement Agency's webpage at www.app.gov.al to learn about government procurement opportunities. The implementation of e-procurement procedures in January 2009 has contributed to improved access to information, reduction of procedural costs for businesses, and a reduction in the overall level of corruption. However, businesses still complain that problems occur in the drafting of technical and financial criteria of contracts which result in biased and distorted competition. There are also problems with the proper implementation of public procurement procedures and the high number of appeals is a clear indication of these numerous infringements. In some cases, not all the tender documents are in English and the agency's website sometimes is slow. For large and complex projects, it is important to consider having a local representative/partner, who can assist in accessing tender information and managing participation in the tender.

Internationally financed public procurements are usually the most transparent. Tenders financed by the World Bank, European Bank for Reconstruction and Development (EBRD), and similar institutions must meet international standards for tenders.

The Albanian government has held observer status to the WTO Government Procurement Agreement since 2001.

DISTRIBUTION AND SALES CHANNELS

U.S. companies seeking to enter the market and distribute their goods can find a considerable number of merchants, agents, middlemen, wholesalers, and retailers in Albania. Most distribution channels are in place and a number of large retailers have entered the Albanian market in the last year. The majority of Albanian trade goes through the Port of Durres, which is the largest port in Albania and handles more than 90 percent of maritime trade. Albania also has two smaller ports; Vlore in the south and Shengjin in the north. Land-based trade can clear customs at border-crossings with Greece, Macedonia, Kosovo, or Montenegro.

Small private shops still dominate the retail industry and many shops carry Italian and Greek goods. However, modern retail practices are quickly becoming the standard in major urban areas and several large shopping malls have opened in recent years. Carrefour, Conad, Euronics, and Pre-Alpina all have a significant presence in the market. Inditex with several of its brands including Zara, Pull&Bear, Massimo Dutti, Bershka, and Stradivarius, entered the market on April 2014. There also are local retailers like Megatek (DIY), GoTech, Globe, and Neptun (Electronics and appliances). The first shopping mall (QTU) opened its doors in 2005 and was followed by the City Park shopping mall in 2009, and Tirana East Gate (which houses Carrefour) in December 2011.

Capital goods and specialized equipment are normally sold directly to manufacturers and businesses. When selling capital goods or equipment to businesses, a good agent is essential.

Consumer-oriented trade shows are also an important part of the retail scene in Albania.

SELLING FACTORS/TECHNIQUES

Per capita income has been steadily rising for a decade but remains low by European standards. In 2015, estimates put GDP per capita around $4,596 (Note: This number does not take into account the large informal economy). Companies developing their marketing strategies must take into account these figures and the fact that most consumers purchase goods and services based primarily on price. Nonetheless, American goods are recognized for their high quality and relatively competitive prices. Other factors to take into consideration when introducing new products/services are the need for aggressive promotional campaigns including, mass advertising especially for non-branded products. Also, support to the local partner with resources and training is necessary. For durable goods, it is essential to offer efficient after the sales services.

Accurate statistics for market-size are not generally available. Typically, one agent or distributor can effectively cover the entire country. Several foreign companies have used their partners in Albania to expand into Kosovo and other neighboring markets like Montenegro and Macedonia (which have significant Albanian speaking populations). Improvements in road infrastructure connecting Albania with neighboring countries, particularly with Kosovo, have facilitated the growth of regional trade.

ELECTRONIC COMMERCE

E-commerce is not widely used in Albania, but is expected to grow in the coming years. Credit cards in Albania are not widely used outside of major hotels, grocery stores, and department stores. Albania remains a predominately cash economy. Although the use of debit cards has increased significantly in recent years, many use the cards solely to withdraw their salary. Catalog shopping and Internet shopping is in its early stages, because of the low use of credit cards, low purchasing power, and the high cost of shipping.

Use of cell phones to pay for goods and services is in its very early stages and users are a limited category of businesses and individuals. The use of cell phones is currently limited for mobile banking and is used mostly by businesses while individuals use it only to pay utility bills.

TRADE PROMOTION AND ADVERTISING

The advertising industry is growing rapidly in Albania. Both consumers and companies are beginning to understand the effectiveness of advertising and the importance of marketing products.

All forms of media are widely used (television, newspapers, magazines, radio, and outdoor billboards), although television remains the predominant medium. To a lesser extent, trade shows, sales promotion literature, and event sponsorship are also used to advertise goods and services.

The U.S. Embassy is able to arrange Single Company Promotions, which help expose a company to major business and government decision makers in Albania.

For more information on this service, please consult Chapter 10 of this guide or contact the Embassy.

Please see the following links for more information:

Media Outlets and Advertising:

http://www.top-channel.tv
http://www.visionplus.tv
http://www.tvklan.com
http://www.monitor.com.al
http://www.panorama.com.al
http://www.shqiptarja.com
http://www.balkanweb.com/gazetav5/
http://www.gazeta-shqip.com
http://www.mapo.al
http://www.monitor.com.al
http://ogilvyalbania.com
http://www.ddb.com

http://www.ashley-holmes.al
http://marketingmedia.al/
http://www.klikekspogroup.com

For a list of advertising agencies, please contact Commercial Assistant Ms. Edi Jacellari at Jacellarie@state.gov .

Trade Events/Fairs are particularly good promotion channels for industrial products. Local and foreign firms rely on trade fairs to build business connections, gain market visibility, and learn about new technology. A list of local trade fairs can be found at the end of this document or at the following link: www.qendraepanaireve.com .

PRICING

Consumers in Albania are price sensitive and consistently seek bargains for their purchases. Imports into Albania are subject to 20 percent VAT, which is assessed on the Cost Insurance Freight (CIF) value of an imported shipment plus applicable duty. Import duties vary from 0 percent to 15 percent.

The 20 percent Value Added Tax (VAT) is applicable on all goods and services sold in Albania with a few specific exemptions.

Prices are set by the market with a few exceptions like the price of electricity, which is regulated by the government. The government also defines the margin of all the different entities involved in the chain of distribution of pharmaceuticals, including pharmacies.

SALES SERVICE/CUSTOMER SUPPORT

Retailers in Albania may require assistance in designing point-of-sale promotions. Foreign companies may have to advise their agents and distributors on shelving displays, product location, promotional campaigns and promotional literature.

Although sales support and customer service are relatively undeveloped as marketing tools, service provided by local distributors to customers has improved.

Firms selling capital equipment or technology should emphasize customer service and product quality. American companies seeking to operate in Albania may want to consider providing training to their distributors/agents in order to communicate the firm's distinctive corporate policies, behavior and standards, and offer after sale service.

PROTECTING YOUR INTELLECTUAL PROPERTY

Albania is not on the Special 301 Watch List or Priority Watch List. However, intellectual property rights (IPR) infringement and theft are common due to weak legal structures and poor enforcement. Albanian law protects copyrights, patents, trademarks, stamps, mark of origin, and industrial designs, but there remains a significant gap between the law's intent and its enforcement. Regulators are ineffective at collecting fines and prosecutors rarely press charges for intellectual property theft. U.S. companies should consult an attorney experienced in IPR issues and avoid potential risk by establishing solid commercial relationships and drafting tight contracts.

Protecting Your Intellectual Property in Albania:

Several general principles are important for effective management of intellectual property ("IP") rights in Albania. First, it is important to have an overall strategy to protect your IP. Second, IP is protected differently in Albania than in the U.S. Third, rights must be registered and enforced in Albania, under local laws. Your U.S. trademark and patent registrations will not protect you in Albania. There is no such thing as an "international copyright" that will automatically protect an author's writings throughout the entire world. Protection against unauthorized use in a particular country depends, basically, on the national laws of that country. However, most countries do offer copyright protection to foreign works under certain conditions, and these conditions have been greatly simplified by international copyright treaties and conventions.

Registration of patents and trademarks is on a first-in-time, first-in-right basis, so you should consider applying for trademark and patent protection even before selling your products or services in the Albanian market. It is vital that companies understand that intellectual property is primarily a private right and that the U.S. government generally cannot enforce rights for private individuals in Albania. It is the responsibility of the rights' holders to register, protect, and enforce their rights where relevant, retaining their own counsel and advisors. Companies may wish to seek advice from local attorneys or IP consultants who are experts in Albanian law. The U.S. Embassy can provide a list of local lawyers upon request

While the U.S. Government stands ready to assist, there is little we can do if the rights holders have not taken these fundamental steps necessary to securing and enforcing their IP in a timely fashion. Moreover, in many countries, rights holders who delay

enforcing their rights on a mistaken belief that the USG can provide a political resolution to a legal problem may find that their rights have been eroded or abrogated due to legal doctrines such as statutes of limitations, laches, estoppel, or unreasonable delay in prosecuting a law suit. In no instance should U.S. Government advice be seen as a substitute for the obligation of a rights holder to pursue its case.

It is always advisable to conduct due diligence on potential partners. Negotiate from the position of your partner and give your partner clear incentives to honor the contract. A good partner is an important ally in protecting IP rights. Consider carefully, however, whether to permit your partner to register your IP rights on your behalf. Doing so may create a risk that your partner will list itself as the IP owner and fail to transfer the rights should the partnership end. Keep an eye on your cost structure and reduce the margins (and the incentive) of would-be bad actors. Projects and sales in Albania require constant attention. Work with legal counsel familiar with Albanian laws to create a solid contract that includes non-compete clauses, and confidentiality/non-disclosure provisions.

It is also recommended that small and medium-size companies understand the importance of working together with trade associations and organizations to support efforts to protect IP and stop counterfeiting. There are a number of these organizations, both Albania or U.S.-based. These include:

* The U.S. Chamber and local American Chambers of Commerce

* National Association of Manufacturers (NAM)

* International Intellectual Property Alliance (IIPA)

* International Trademark Association (INTA)

* The Coalition Against Counterfeiting and Piracy

* International Anti-Counterfeiting Coalition (IACC)

* Pharmaceutical Research and Manufacturers of America (PhRMA)

* Biotechnology Industry Organization (BIO)

IP Resources

A wealth of information on protecting IP is freely available to U.S. rights holders. Some excellent resources for companies regarding intellectual property include the following:

* For information about patent, trademark, or copyright issues -- including enforcement issues in the US and other countries -- call the STOP! Hotline: 1-866-999-HALT or register at www.StopFakes.gov .

* For more information about registering trademarks and patents (both in the U.S. as well as in foreign countries), contact the US Patent and Trademark Office (USPTO) at: 1-800-786-9199.

* For more information about registering for copyright protection in the US, contact the US Copyright Office at: 1-202-707-5959.

* For more information about how to evaluate, protect, and enforce intellectual property rights and how these rights may be important for businesses, a free online training program is available at www.stopfakes.gov .

* For US small and medium-size companies, the Department of Commerce offers a "SME IP Advisory Program" available through the American Bar Association that provides one hour of free IP legal advice for companies with concerns in Brazil, China, Egypt, India, Russia, and . For details and to register, visit: http://www.abanet.org/intlaw/intlproj/iprprogram_consultation.html

* For information on obtaining and enforcing intellectual property rights and market-specific IP Toolkits visit: www.StopFakes.gov This site is linked to the USPTO website for registering trademarks and patents (both in the U.S. as well as in foreign countries), the U.S. Customs & Border Protection website to record registered trademarks and copyrighted works (to assist customs in blocking imports of IP-infringing products) and allows you to register for Webinars on protecting IP.

* The U.S. Commerce Department has positioned IP attachés in key markets around the world. You can get contact information for the IP attaché who covers Albania at: http://www.uspto.gov/ip/global/index.jsp

DUE DILIGENCE

Due diligence is often necessary for U.S. companies. Specialized legal and accounting firms can provide due diligence services in Albania. For a list of major legal and accounting firms please see below.

When considering a potential agent or distributor, a background check of a potential business partner, plus frequent visits by the export sales manager, are recommended. One of the standard programs of the Embassy's Economic and Commercial Section is the International Company Profile (ICP), designed to assist U.S. companies to enter international business relationships with greater confidence by providing background information on a prospective business partner. For more information contact the Embassy or visit http://tirana.usembassy.gov/doing-business-local.html

LOCAL PROFESSIONAL SERVICES

Local professional business services exist. The American Chamber of Commerce in Albania http://www.amcham.com.al is a good place to start when looking for legal and other business services in Albania. The U.S. Embassy's Economic and Commercial Office can also provide lists of local professional services upon request.

WEB RESOURCES

Department of Commerce and Department of State Websites:

http://tirana.usembassy.gov/business.html
http://www.buyusa.gov
http://www.export.gov

Legal Firms:

http://www.kalo-attorneys.com
http://www.bogalaw.com.al
http:// www.wolftheiss.com
http://www.zkt-lawfirm.com
http://www.tonucci.it
www.ffconsulting.al

Auditing, Tax and Advisory Services:

http://www.pbm.al
http://www.deloitte.com
http://www.kpmg.com
http://www.ey.com
http://www.pwc.com/al/en/

Business Associations:
http://www.amcham.com.al
http://www.aida.gov.al
http://www.cci.al
http://www.fiaalbania.com

Government Institutions:
http://www.qkr.gov.al
http://www.qkl.gov.al
http://www.minfin.gov.al
http://www.ekonomia.gov.al
http://www.energjia.gov.al
http://www.tatime.gov.al
http://www.bankofalbania.com
http://www.instat.gov.al
http:// www.app.gov.al
http://www.dogana.gov.al

Advertising:
http://www.ogilvyal.com
http://www.ddb.com
http://rtadvertising-al.com

Media Outlets:
http://www.tvklan.com

http://www.top-channel.tv
http://www.visionplus.tv
http://www.monitor.com.al

LEADING SECTORS FOR EXPORT AND INVESTMENT

ERG - ENERGY

Albania has lacked a secure electricity supply for several years and its energy insecurity remains an impediment to economic growth. The country suffered frequent and recurring electricity shortages from 1992 to 2008 due to a lack of proper maintenance of inherited generation sources, a lack of new investments in new generation sources, gradual deterioration of transmission infrastructure, overdependence on hydro-generation, limited importing capacities, and general mismanagement of the sector.

At present, domestic generation is fully reliant on hydroelectric power plants (HPP) and is thus vulnerable to weather conditions. The average annual demand for electricity in 2015 reached 7,961 GWh, while the average annual generation output in 2015, considered a very good year, reached 6,956 GWh. The gap between supply and demand is met by either importing energy or load shedding (rolling blackouts). The government has embarked on a reform process in the energy sector to address this energy unreliability. The strategy aims at securing additional electricity through:

* The construction of new alternative generation sources through private investment;

* The promotion of energy diversification;

* The construction of new interconnection lines to increase Albania's integration into the European network;

* The improvement of electricity distribution and consumption.

* Liberalization of the energy market

In the last decade, the government also has undertaken a series of public investments and initiatives, including policy and regulatory reforms aimed at promoting private investments in the energy sector and addressing energy insecurity. These initiatives include:

Higher Transmission Capacities: The government has financed projects to build interconnection lines to raise importing capacities and integrate Albania into the European energy network. It completed a 100MW interconnection line between Albania and Montenegro in 2011. The investment was financed by German development bank Kreditanstalt für Wiederaufbau (KfW). In February 2010, the government also received KfW financing for the construction of an interconnection line between Albania and Kosovo which started in 2014 as well as a ring line in southern Albania. The government also has authorized the construction of two 400 kV undersea interconnection cable lines that would connect Albania and Italy but the project has yet to start.

Higher Distribution Efficiency: In 2009, the government unbundled the Albanian Power Corporation (KESH) into three separate generation, transmission and distribution entities. In an attempt to improve the efficiency of the system and reduce large technical and non-technical loses (theft) as well as bill collection, the government privatized the distribution grid with Czech company CEZ. However, due to the prolonged dispute between CEZ and the government, the government took over the administration of distribution arm in late 2012. Negotiations between CEZ and the government over the failed privatization are ongoing as of 2014. As a result, inefficiency in the system remains a concern for the electrical system in Albania.

Diversification of Generation Sources: In 2008-2009, the government funded the construction of the Vlora Thermo dual fired (oil/gas) power plant. The plant has an installed capacity of 97MW and would generate 700 GWh per year, representing approximately 10 percent of the country's overall consumption. The plant's capacity remains underused because its natural gas capacity has yet to come online and high oil prices make power general from fossil fuels cost prohibitive. The plant may now serve as a backup when hydro-electric production falls short.

Private Investment in Energy Generation: Albania's total installed capacity at the end of 2015 totaled 1,878 MW, out of which 98 MW are in thermo and the rest is hydro. Fully 81.5 percent of the generation capacity is state owned, with 88 percent coming from the cascade of three HPPs with a total installed capacity of 1,350 MW. However, private generation share is increasing because of privatization of small and medium sized HPPs as well as the construction of new ones under concession contracts. Several small HPPs including the medium sized Ashta I and II (53MW) have currently entered the system increasing the share of private generation capacity. Privately owned generation capacity at the end of 2015 stood at 347 MW, mostly fueled by the privatization of five small HPPs with an installed capacity of 83 MW during 2015.

Hydropower: The government has approved 110 concession contracts for the construction of 310 HPPs with capacities ranging from 1 MW to 320 MW. Most of the concessions would be for HPPs with an installed capacity of less than 10 MW. The construction of these HPPs would double the country's existing hydro capacity. The Kalivaci HPP (93MW) is the mid-sized HPP currently under construction and the larger Devoll Power 275 MW HPP cascade started construction in 2015. The project will develop in stages with an estimated time of completion in 2019. Additional capacity is available with the Vjose and Osum rivers.

Wind power & Other: The government has issued licenses for the construction of several wind farms with a total installed capacity of 1,367MW, with the largest being 500MW. All of these licenses were issued in 2007-2008, but none of these projects has started to date.

Opportunities

The energy sector represents good investment and trade opportunities in a variety of areas. The construction of new generation sources, construction of new transmission lines, improvements in distribution, and the promotion of energy efficiency using renewable energy sources, all represent opportunities to provide equipment, services, and financing.

In addition, the Trans-Adriatic Pipeline that will pump Azeri gas through Greece and Albania into Southern Italy might also drive the demand of investing in thermo plant generation capacities in Albania, which needs to diversify its energy sources. The pipeline is scheduled to start in 2015 and complete before 2020.

The state-owned companies for both electric power transmission and generation will continue to make investments to increase transmission efficiency and to maintain generation capacities. The distribution arm also needs to make significant investments in its distribution system as it needs to reduce losses that presently account for 55 percent of the system's electricity. Additional projects relating to dam safety also are potential opportunities for the export of U.S. goods and services.

The Albanian government has approved a legal framework that regulates concession contracts for investment in the energy sector. The Law on Concessions allows companies to submit unsolicited proposals. The government has approved more than 100 concession contracts in the electricity generation sector, although only a few have progressed past the approval stage.

WEB RESOURCES

http://www.ekonomia.gov.al
http://www.energjia.gov.al
http://www.ere.gov.al
http://www.kesh.com.al
http://www.akbn.gov.al
http://www.ost.al
http://www.aida.gov.al

MIN – MINING AND MINERALS

Albania is a country with considerable mineral resources. The estimated geological reserves are shown in the table below.

No	Mineral	Geological reserves	No	Mineral	Geological reserves
		Million tons			Million tons
1	Chrome	36.9			
2	Iron - Nickel	220 102	21	Rock Salt	68,246
	Nickel - Silicate				
3	Copper	53	22	Decorative Stones, marbles Decorative Stones ophiolites	299 70.4
4	Tar sands	406	23	Clays	262.7
5	Bitumen	0.864	24	Kaolin	1.9
6	Pirobitumens	6.4	25	Volcanic Glass	18.65
7	Titanomagnetites	137	26	Magnezites	1.135
8	Bauxite	12	27	Feldspar + albitophyres	71.64
9	Dolomite	> 158.5	28	River-bed gravels	242.4 mil. m3
10	Coal	770.4	29	Fluorite	0.758
11	Peat-Turfs	156	30	Sulphur	0.2
12	Tufe	5	31	Pyrophylite	6
13	Barite	0.72	32	Talc	0.616
14	Limestone	Huge quantities	33	Chalk	2

15	Mergele	> 2.6	34	Phosphorite	57.1
16	Trepele	6.4	35	Sand+Carbonatic Aggregates	25.4
17	Olivine	108.6	36	Polymetals	1.031
18	Gypsum	84.4	37	Platinum	848 kg
19	Silica sands, quartzites	> 200.5	38	Gold	13742.4 kg
20	Basalt	Uunlimited			

The mining and minerals industry was state-owned until the late 1990s, when a gradual restructuring of the industry started. Privatization of Albanian mineral resources is accomplished through the granting of prospecting, exploration and exploitation permits to Albanian and foreign companies.

Under the new Law on Mining of 2010, Albanian and foreign companies may acquire rights to research, explore, and exploit. Minerals are divided into four groups: 1-metallic

minerals, non-metallic minerals, coal and bitumen; 2- construction materials; 3-precious stones and semi-precious stones; and 4- radioactive minerals and substances. The Ministry of Energy and Industry approves its Annual Mineral Plan defining mineral zones as "bid areas" and "open areas," while "concession areas" are approved by the Council of Ministers. For the "bid areas," companies will compete; while for "open areas," group mining rights are granted on the first-come first-serve basis. Taxes applicable on the mining extraction are royalties that vary depending on the type of mineral from 3 percent - 10 percent, VAT 20 percent, and corporate income tax 15 percent (oil and gas has a different level of profit tax – see section on Oil and Gas.)

Albania became compliant with the Extractive Industries Transparency Initiative (EITI) on May 3, 2015. The new Albanian mining law approved in 2010 obligates the companies to implement EITI. In the framework of EITI, Albania has published only one report, for 2010, and the impact of EITI in increasing transparency in the sector remains to be seen.

Companies operating in the mining sector are mainly small to medium domestic and foreign companies, with foreign companies focusing mainly on cement, chromite, copper, and bitumen. Despite progress and increase of production, the mining sector has not yet maximized its potential. Current investment levels are not commensurate with the underlying resource potential; especially in the chromite mining. Cement production is the one subsector that has attracted most of the investments, fueled mostly by the construction boom that Albania experienced from 2000 - 2009.

Production of major minerals in Albania

Minerals	Unit	2008	2009	2010	2011	2012	2015
Chromite	ton	229,899	268,718	322,597	349,873	365,749	529,592
Copper	ton	105,000	114,286	139,926	305,284	479,720	507,105
Iron Nickel & Nickel Silicate	ton	353,320	68,840	269,300	363,723	75,017	215,086
Coal	ton	1,500	2,000	2,500	1,200	0	0

Limestone	m3	3,837,529	3,271,617	2,363,445	2,445,680	2,727,451	3,257,513
Slab Limestone	m3	18,341	39,749	34,132	29,885	36,357	36,739
Massif Limestone	m3	3,964	5,403	7,331	7,116	10,864	1,003
Bedded Sandstone	m3	25,237	45,415	22,902	23,989	29,249	22,316
Clay	ton	695,469	819,341	803,326	973,256	961,052	1,181,242
Gypsum	ton	87,261	71,276	77,400	93,248	91,021	126,349

Major companies operating in extraction are:

Locally-owned AlbChrome operates the Bulqiza chrome mine, an enrichment plant in Bulqiza, a selection plant in Klosi, a ferrochrome smelter in Burrel-Mat, a chrome mine in Pjoska-Pogradec, and a Ferrochrome smelter in Elbasan.

Turkish company Ber-Oner operates under a 30-year concession signed in 2001. It has three large copper mines at Munelle, Lak Rroshi, Karme 2. The consortium also has the enrichment plant at Fush Arrez, which was recently expanded to have a total ore processing capacity of 600,000 tons per year. In May 2014, the Chinese company Jiangxi Copper entered the Albanian market through the acquisition of 50 percent of the shares of Ber-Oner's mother company in Turkey.

The Chinese-Turkish Consortium Illyria Minerals Industry (Kurum Energy, Resources and Metallurgy Sh.a.-KERM, a subsidiary of Kurum Holding A.S. of Turkey, and Sichuan Jiannanchun International Group Ltd, a major Chinese group of companies) signed a concession contract in 2010 for Kalimash and Vlahne chromite mines and Kalimashi dressing plant.

Kurum also operates the only iron-steel plant in Albania, with an annual production capacity of 550,000 tons.

Alfa Nikel signed a concession agreement in 2011 to use the mineral resources in Bilisht, Korca District in the South East of Albania. The Bilisht site has a production capacity of 200,000 tons annually.

The French company Bitumi Selenica sh.a. has a concession contract to operate the Selenica bitumen mine and the bitumen smelting furnace.

In addition to these concessions, many other foreign companies, including Greek, Italian, Canadian, Australian, Swiss and American, have entered the market with research and exploration permits. These include Tirex-Canada, Balkan Resources-Canada, Adriatik Nickel-UK, Empire Mining Corporation, Mineral Invest, JAB resources, etc.

Small and large size investments have also taken place in construction materials, with a focus on asphalt and cement production that constitute a considerable part of total production in all mineral production. In January 2010, an investment of approximately $325 million for the construction of a cement factory by TITAN Group was finalized.

The government has signed a number of concessions with local and foreign companies for the construction of cement factories. Some of these investments are yet to materialize

OPPORTUNITIES

Considering the large number of companies involved in mining and exploration, the mining sector represents good opportunities in trade of technology and services.

Web Resources

http://www.energjia.gov.al
http://www.akbn.gov.al
http://www.albeiti.org
http://www.gsa.gov.al

OGM – OIL AND GAS

Albanian oil fields have good potential for production development. Geological reserves are estimated to reach 437 million tons (3.27 billion barrels -- 78 percent reserves of sandstone fields and 22 percent reserves of limestone fields). The government recently announced that it plans to auction 13 new oil and gas exploration licenses in 2014.

In 1990, following almost 45 years of isolation, many foreign companies started exploration onshore and offshore and some others signed production sharing agreements (PSA) with the government. Albania's territory is divided into onshore and offshore blocks. The state-owned oil company Albpetrol currently manages all free blocks available for exploration and exploitation, but the government announced in 2014 that it would develop a public auction process to license these blocks to interested investors.

To date, the government has issued licenses for the exploration, development, and exploitation of several blocks with the following companies: Emanuelle Energy Limited – Blocks Adriatik 2, 3 and 4 (offshore); San Leon Energy –Durres Block (offshore); Cairn (Capricorn Albania Limited) and Dyas Albania B.V. – Block Jon 5 (offshore); Petromanas Energy - Blocks D-E (onshore); Petromanas 25 percent and Shell 75 percent - Blocks 2-3 (onshore); Bankers Petroleum - Block F (onshore). The following blocks are free: Rodoni North Block (offshore); Blocks 4, 5, Dumre, A, B, C, 1, 6, 7, 8, C, Velca, and Panaja (onshore.)

In addition, Albpetrol has signed nine PSAs for the development and exploitation of the following oil fields, each with 25 years term:

Patos Marinza - Bankers Petroleum (2004); Ballsh Hekal - Stream Oil and Gas (2007); Cakran Mollaj - Stream Oil and Gas (2007); Gorisht Koculit - Stream Oil and Gas (2007); Delvina - Stream Oil and Gas (2007); Kucova – Sherwood International Petroleum (2007); and Visoka - Transoil Group (2009); Amonica, Drashovica, Finiq-Karne and Pekisht-Murriz – Phoenix Petroleum (2015); and, Divjake, Ballaj-Kryevidh, Povelce, panaja and Frakull – Phoenix Petroleum (2015)

Since 1992, dozens of companies have operated in the oil and gas sector in Albania including: Occidental; Shell; Chevron; OMV; BP Petroleum; AGIP; Edison Gas; Hamilton Brothers; Shell; Deminex; INA Naftaplin; Coparex; Lundin Petroleum; Beach Petroleum; Hellenic Petroleum; DMW Petroleum AG; IPC; Anschutz; MOL; Clyde Expro PLC; Premier Consolidated Oilfields; etc. As a result, a dozen onshore and offshore wells were drilled and thousands of new 2D and some 3D seismic profiles have been completed.

In the last few years, the rise in the price of oil in international markets has brought renewed interest to Albania's oil sector. Bankers Petroleum started the development and exploitation of Patos Marinza in 2006. Average oil production for the first quarter of 2014 for Bankers Petroleum reached 19,911 barrels of oil per day (bopd), more than doubling 2010 production.

Stream Oil and Gas also has started investing in the development and exploitation of oil and gas fields. In addition, Transoil Group is exploring a Production Sharing Agreement (PSA) of its own. However, oil production and investments of both companies are small.

Heavy crude oil production in Albania has tripled over the last decade, from as low as 420 thousand tons in 2004 to more than 1.2 million tons in 2015, with Bankers Petroleum driving almost the entire increase. Bankers capital investments have intensified in the last few years and in 2015 CAPEX reached USD 234 million while in 2014 Bankers plans to invest around USD 300 million. This, together with ambitious exploratory efforts especially by Pertomanas and Shell, which to date have invested close to USD 200 million in exploratory wells, has created opportunities for exports of goods and services in the oil sector.

Company	Oil and Gas Field	2011	2012	2015
Bankers Petroleum	Patos-Marinza (ton crude)	761,000	879,200	1,061,000
Stream Oil & Gas	Ballsh-Hekal (ton crude)	5,900	7,640	5,900
Stream Oil & Gas	CakranMollaj (ton crude)	28,300	41,600	35,250
Stream Oil & Gas	Gorisht-Kocul (ton crude)	39,200	41,100	45,920
Stream Oil & Gas	Delvine (Nm3 gas)	76,000	-	-
Sherwood International	Kuçove (ton crude)		300	100
Transoilgroup	Visoke (ton crude)	350	14,950	22,300
Phœnix Petroleum	Amonicë; (ton crude)			1,510
Albpetrol Sh.a.	Other (ton Crude)	59,000	45,000	37,320

Although Albania has refining capacities, the technology is outdated and most of the oil gets exported for further refining. As such, Albania imports large quantities of refined oil byproducts for its domestic needs. In 2015, Albania imported under HS code 2710 around 600,000 tons or $660 million and under HS code 2711 close to 74,000 tons or $70 million.

Gas market: Albania has no natural gas production and the country is not connected with any of the regional gas networks. The Trans-Adriatic Pipeline (TAP), scheduled to start construction in early 2015, will transport natural gas from the Shah Deniz II field in Azerbaijan through Greece and Albania to southern Italy. TAP will start with a capacity of 10 billion cubic meters (bcm), but a second phase can increase capacity to 20 bcm. Current TAP shareholders are BP (20 percent), SOCAR (20 percent), Statoil (20 percent), Fluxys (16 percent), Total (10 percent), E.ON (9 percent) and Axpo (5 percent). TAP has already started announcing tenders and its construction will create significant opportunities for companies operating in the sector. For opportunities on TAP please visit http://www.trans-adriatic-pipeline.com

The Albanian government also has issued two licenses for LNG terminals, but to date none of the projects has advanced beyond the approval stage.

OPPORTUNITIES

New oil and gas licenses, both onshore and offshore, may represent excellent opportunities for U.S. oil and gas companies as well as affiliated oil and gas service providers. The arrival of the Trans-Adriatic Pipeline may also bring opportunities for salt-

dome gas storage, thermal energy generation, pipeline and compressor station construction and maintenance, and infrastructure improvements.

Web Resources

http://www.trans-adriatic-pipeline.com/
http:// www.akbn.gov.al
http:// www.energjia.gov.al
http://www.alb-petrol.com/
http://www.streamoilandgas.com
http://www.ildce.com
http://www.sanleonenergy.com
http://www.petromanas.com
http://www.bankerspetroleum.com
http://www.transoilgroup.com
http://www.cairnenergy.com

TES - TELECOMMUNICATION

Albania's key telecom parameters

Sector	2009	2010	2011*	2012	H1 2015
Broadband					
Broadband subscribers (thousand)	80	120	174	215	210
Broadband penetration rate	2.5 percent	3.75 percent	6 percent	7.6 percent	7.4 percent
Subscribers to Telecoms Services					
Fixed-line telephone subscribers (thousand)	363	330	339	311	280
Penetration rate	11.3 percent	10.3 percent	12 percent	11 percent	10 percent
Mobile phone subscribers (million)	4.16	4.5	5.2	5.6	4.86
Penetration rate	130 percent	140 percent	185 percent	198 percent	172 percent
Active mobile phone users (million)**			3.07	3.5	3.37
Penetration rate			109 percent	125 percent	119 percent

**In 2011, the penetration rate is calculated with the new figure on the population as result of 2011 census.*

*** In 2011, Electronic Communication Regulator (AKEP) for the first time published data about the number of active mobile sim cards.*

Electronic communication market revenue

Sector	2009	2010	2011	2012
Overall Market Revenue(million US$)	615	570	520	554
Mobile sector (AMC, Vodafone, Eagle, and Plus)	472	416	390	420
Fixed line (Albtelekom)	112	108	93	104
Other operators	31	46	37	30

No revenue data reported for cable TV services. Financial Data for 2015 are not available yet.

The electronic communication sector in Albania is generally liberalized. The Law on Electronic Communications, enacted in June 2008, introduced the general authorization

regime where electronic communications networks and services that do not require the use of limited resources (numbers and frequencies) can receive individual licenses. General authorizations are issued by telecom regulator, the Agency of Postal and Electronic Communications (AKEP).

The market has experienced remarkable growth in the last decade and its growth potential has attracted international investment in all segments of the sector, with the primary focus being in mobile and broadband segments. The electronic communication sector has experienced steady revenue growth until 2011, when for the first time the revenue declined from $570 million in 2010 to $520 million, mostly due to the decline in prices for services offered by the operators in all segments of communication. There are nearly 200 operators in the e-communication market (including ISP) but the three mobile operators Vodafone, AMC, and Eagle along with the fixed-line operator Albtelekom represent 91 percent of total revenue of the e-communication sector with mobile telephony accounting for 75 percent of market revenue.

Mobile service first entered the market in 1996 and began to grow significantly around 2000. The rapid growth in mobile telephony was fueled by the low penetration rate of fixed telephony. Today the sector has close to 5.6 million subscribers compared to 15,000 in 2000. Mobile telephony has a penetration rate of 172 percent, far higher than the EU average. Future sector growth is expected to come from increasing average revenue per user by providing new data services.

Albania's broadband market offers significant growth potential due to low penetration levels. In the first half of 2015, broadband penetration was only 7.4 percent. In addition to Albtelekom, several regional competitors have emerged to offer broadband services over their own fiber, cable, and wireless networks. Internet access is available through a variety of means and all operators are aggressively pursuing strategies to increase the number of customers receiving broadband access.

Triple-play platforms offering cable TV, broadband, and fixed telephony also are increasingly popular.

OPPORTUNITIES

Overall, the electronic communication market represents good opportunities for trade and investment. Investment could create opportunities for U.S. companies to provide equipment and solutions, especially in the broadband sector. The 3G entrance also has boosted the demand for equipment, including smart phones.

WEB RESOURCES

http://www.akep.al
http://www.mpptt.gov.al
http://www.amc.al
http://www.vodafone.al
http://www.eaglemobile.al
http://www.albtelecom.al
http://www.tring.al
http://www.asc.al
http:// www.abcom-al.com
http://www.primo.al
http://www.abissnet.al

MED – MEDICAL EQUIPMENT

Albania has a predominantly public healthcare system, but private services are increasingly popular. The State remains the major provider of healthcare services. The public health service is organized in three levels: primary healthcare; secondary hospital service; and tertiary hospital service. The Ministry of Health takes the leading role in the public sector; it develops health policies, proposes the health care budget and the investment program for the sector, and monitors the work of state-owned health institutions. The Public Institute of Health Insurance in Albania is based on compulsory payroll contribution from both employees and employers and it is subsidized by the government for other segments of the population. It administers the primary healthcare system and some approved services in the secondary and tertiary healthcare service.

The government has been investing in the secondary and tertiary public healthcare to improve physical infrastructure and technology. Albania has in total 41 public hospitals: 22 district hospitals, 11 regional hospitals, four university hospitals, one trauma university center, two psychiatric hospitals, and the National Centre on Child Development and Rehabilitation. The system is financed by the state budget and equipment and other major investments are purchased directly by publicly owned institutions. The Law on Public Procurement requires open electronic tenders for all purchases of goods and services.

Reform in the health sector is ongoing and the government currently plans to develop hospital care through the incorporation of the hospital services under the health insurance scheme.

The private sector also is developing at a fast pace. It covers most of the pharmaceutical and dental services offered in the country. The number of clinics for specialized diagnosis has increased significantly in major urban areas and private hospital development is making progress. Four private, western standard hospitals have opened in Tirana in the last few years. American Hospital, Hygeia, German Hospital, and Salus Hospital all offer a wide range of specialized services.

The development of private clinics, opening of private hospitals, and investments by the government in the public health sector have all raised the demand for medical equipment, and represent good opportunities for U.S. manufacturers of healthcare equipment.

Albania imports 100 percent of the medical equipment that is used in the market. The primary suppliers of such equipment are manufacturers from the EU and to a lesser degree the United States. Public expenditure for healthcare is low. In 2014, the government has earmarked only $19 million for capital investments in the health care sector. $13 million of this allocation is for improvements in hospital infrastructure and technology.

OPPORTUNITIES

There are good opportunities in the Albanian market for U.S. manufacturers of medical equipment for both the public and private sectors. U.S.-manufactured medical devices and equipment enjoy an excellent reputation in Albania for their state-of-the-art technology, quality, and reliability. Price and after the sale technical assistance are two factors to be considered in Albanian market.

Products that might represent some export opportunities for U.S. manufacturers include: diagnostic imaging (CT, MRI) and radiation therapy equipment; computer tomography imaging equipment; electrocardiographs; cardiovascular diagnostic equipment; pace makers (the American Hospital and the Universal Hospital have strong cardiology departments); digitalized x-ray equipment; clinical laboratory equipment (there are many independent labs); non-invasive surgical devices; anesthesia and intensive care equipment; ultrasound equipment; urology equipment; laboratory and testing equipment; tissue and blood bank related equipment (there is a national blood bank although reputable hospitals do some of this type of testing before transfusion); needles; catheters; medical lasers; endoscopes; laser instruments, and a whole range of dentistry equipment and products.

Interested companies should visit the Agency of Public Procurement Portal www.app.gov.al to monitor for tenders in the public sector. The private market also presents opportunities and the most efficient way to enter the market is to engage local contacts such as dealers, agents, representatives, or partners. In addition to the Albanian Procurement platform, companies should also monitor the World Bank announcements since the later has been involved in financing the modernization of the health sector in Albania.

WEB RESOURCES

http:// www.shendetesia.gov.al
http:// www.app.gov.al
http://www.spitaliamerikan.com
http://www.hygeia.al/
http://www.german-hospital-tirana.com
http://www.salus.al

DGR - PHARMACEUTICALS

The pharmaceutical service in Albania is predominantly private with three, small, local private manufacturers, 216 pharmaceutical warehouses, 1,020 pharmacies, 210 pharmaceutical private agencies, and 42 hospital pharmacies (which are the only public pharmacies).

The Ministry of Health monitors the pharmaceutical industry and all drugs must be registered with the National Center of Drug Control. To date, there are more than 3,855 drug form-doses registered in Albania. For the registration process for drugs, please visit www.qkkb.gov.al

In the public healthcare system, the government sets profit margins for actors involved in the distribution chain and subsidizes prescription medicines. The Health Care Insurance Institute (ISKSH) develops an annual reimbursement list outlines which drugs will be subsidized by the government. For 2014, ISKSH has earmarked close to $84 million for the reimbursement of 477 prescription medicines.

Two commissions annually approve the drugs that are reimbursable by the Health Insurance Institution. They commissions also define the profit margin for importers and secondary distributors as well as pharmacies. The two entities are the Drug Commission on Drafting and Reviewing the Reimbursement List and the Drug Pricing Commission and they are appointed by the Minister of Health and approved by the Council of Ministers. For more information, please visit http://www.isksh.com.al .

The drug market in Albania has an estimated value of $220 million. Imported products dominate the market. Locally manufactured products account for a small share of the total market. In 2015, Albanian imports under chapter 30 "pharmaceutical products" reached close to $162 million. Although U.S. exports account for a small share of the market, it should be noted that the share might be larger because U.S. products are often imported from their European offices. Generic drugs are popular in the market due to lower prices.

Opportunities

Pharmaceuticals that treat cardiovascular disease, cancer, and diabetes will be in demand in the Albanian market as these are the leading causes of death in the country. U.S. suppliers might also consider the pharmaceutical market for vitamins and minerals. The market for food supplements is also under-developed and represents another good opportunity for U.S. companies.

Web Resources

http://www.qkkb.gov.al
http://www.isksh.com.al
http://www.imoh.gov.al

TRA – TRAVEL AND TOURISM

The Albanian government considers tourism as a key strategic economic sector, touting its potential to act as a catalyst for the development of the rest of the country. Located in the heart of the Mediterranean, Albania could well be Europe's last tourism "secret."

The country is rich in tourist resources, including mountains, valleys, forests, rivers, lakes, and especially beaches. Apart from its natural assets, Albania offers many opportunities to explore the country's cultural heritage with well-known archaeological sites dating back to pre-Roman, Roman, Greek, and medieval times. Amphitheaters, castles, Roman cities, monasteries, and old churches are among the archeological points of interest that Albania has to offer, some of which are UNESCO protected sites.

Traditional villages, ancient castles, and a beautiful coastline are part of its heritage. Albania surprises visitors with the diversity of its landscapes, which can change quickly and dramatically. Landscapes range from typical Mediterranean terrain in the west and southwest, to mixed landscapes in the central areas, to steep mountains in the inner part of country. Albania's coastline is one of the country's greatest assets. It stretches for about 450 km from north to south with two distinct coastal zones: the Adriatic and the Ionian. Besides its beautiful coastline which is mostly underdeveloped, Albania also has great potential for mountain tourism.

Opportunities

Tourism is the only sector of the Albanian economy with a positive trade balance. The country traditionally has been the summer vacation destination for the Albanian diaspora as well as ethnic-Albanians from Macedonia and Kosovo. The number of foreign visitors has increased substantially in recent years. In 2015, approximately 3.5 million foreigners came to Albania, mostly for tourism. The pristine and diversified nature and culture has attracted the attention of western media. Lonely Planet's Best in Travel 2011 proclaimed Albania the number one travel destination of the top 10 countries for 2011. A growing number of U.S. citizens have visited southern Albania during day excursions from cruise ships.

The government has worked to improve infrastructure and since 2006 it has spent more than $2 billion expanding road infrastructure and building new passenger terminals in ports and airports. While the road infrastructure is improving, tourist accommodations have developed chaotically and are far from international standards. Official statistics on the number of hotels and beds are contradictory and not very reliable as the sector remains highly informal. One of the major issues that needs to be addressed to boost the tourism industry is the size and quality of accommodations. Only a few hotels are large enough to accommodate large groups of tourists. There is untapped demand for a chain of small to mid-size hotels that could accommodate the growing number of package tours, which traditionally stay in Tirana where the only sizable hotels currently exist.

Albania also does not have any high-end resorts. Given growing tourism demand from EU tourists seeking cheaper beach destinations and the influx of Balkan tourists to the region, a high-end beach resort may be a lucrative investment. Such investments may also create opportunities for U.S. companies to offer services in the design and implementation stage as well as management and auxiliary services.

The removal of the moratorium on recreational boats in 2015 might also create opportunities for trade on motor boats, speed boats, sail boats, and other personal water craft.

WEB RESOURCES

http://www.turizmi.gov.al

http://www.albaniantourism.com

AGRICULTURAL SECTORS

Albania is a relatively small country, with a resident population of about 2.8 million. It has a total area of 28,750 square kilometers, of which 24 percent (696,000 hectares) is agricultural land, 36 percent (1,014,000 hectares) forest, and 15 percent (423,000 hectares) pastures and other types of land. Nearly 50 percent of the labor force works, directly or indirectly, in agriculture.

Although agriculture is no longer the dominant sector of the Albanian economy, it still contributes approximately 20 percent to the GDP. The government considers the agriculture sector to be of crucial importance for Albania's economic development and hopes to boost agriculture production by providing financial support to farmers and facilitating private investment in the agro processing sector. For example, over the last three years the government has distributed almost $30 million to develop fruit and olive orchards, vineyards, and greenhouses.

Albania is a net agricultural importer. In 2015, imports of agricultural products totaled $870 million, representing approximately 26 percent of Albania's agricultural consumption. The United States was by far the largest exporter of edible meat to Albania in 2015, exporting about $25.5 million. Corn, wheat, animal feed, flour, and edible oils also represent U.S. export opportunities to Albania. In 2015, Albania imported $95 million in grains, mainly wheat, $25 million in animal feed, $43 million in edible oil, $20 million in flour, and $20 million in corn.

Despite a mild climate, fertile land, and abundant water resources including rainfall, surface, and ground water, the agriculture sector remains largely untapped due to the small size of farms and low mechanization. Furthermore, the low use of fertilizers and pesticides in agriculture creates the opportunity for the development of organic agriculture. Opportunities are available for foreign investors in the production and processing of high-value crops and well as in some niche markets.

As Albania's economy develops, demand for high-end and niche agricultural products will increase. The recent expansion of large retail and food service outlets has led to better marketing and a growing demand for product variety. As a result, there will be numerous opportunities to both invest in Albanian agriculture and export U.S. agriculture products to the Albanian market.

OPPORTUNITIES

Good prospects exist for U.S. exporters in the following sub sectors:

Grain: The Albanian market consumes about 500 metric tons of grain per year, most of which is imported. In 2015, Albania imported 292,000 tons of wheat. In the past, there have been some sporadic efforts to import wheat from the United States, but the main barrier to trade remains the poor infrastructure in Albanian ports. Albania's main port, Durres, is shallow and does not allow for large vessels. The government is planning to deepen the port and improve warehouse capacities in order to maximize the economic benefits of the Durres-Kukes road. Albania produces large amounts of maize, mostly for

animal feed, but in 2015 imported a combined 150,000 tons of maize and animal feed worth about $45 million. The main competitors for U.S. wheat and maize are eastern countries, primarily Russia and Ukraine, as well as Argentina.

Livestock: There are interesting prospects for U.S. exporters of red and poultry meat, and edible offal. Despite the fact that Albania produces large amounts of red meat and other products, the country imports considerable amounts of live animals and meat products, mainly for the meat processing industry. In 2015, total imports for livestock were about $92 million with about 70 percent of it consisting of edible meat. Total imports of poultry amounted to $35 million of which $15 million were imported from the United States.

Animal feed: Albania is a net importer of protein meals for animal feed. There is no local production of soybeans, so traditionally soybean meal and other soy products are imported. Imports have come primarily from neighboring countries and, as in the case of wheat and other bulk products, attempts to import directly from the U.S. have not succeeded due to the poor import infrastructure. In 2015, Albania imported 88,000 tons of animal feed worth about $25 million. Imports have increased by almost 35 percent as demand is high due to growing local and foreign investment in the poultry and pork sectors.

WEB RESOURCES

http://www.bujqesia.gov.al

TRADE REGULATIONS, CUSTOMS AND STANDARDS

IMPORT TARIFFS

Albania enjoys a liberal trade regime. Foreign trade was liberalized in 1990 and follows guidelines set by the European Union (EU) and World Trade Organization (WTO). Albania has been a member of WTO since 2000. The Customs Tariff Nomenclature is based on the Harmonized Commodity Description and Coding System (HS).

The Directorate General of Customs is the institution responsible for the management of customs in the Republic of Albania. Major pieces of legislation regulating customs activity include:

* Law no.8449 of 27.01.1999 "Customs Code of the Republic of Albania" which is in line with Regulation 2913/92/EEC "The Community Customs Code."

* Law no.8474 of 14.04.1999 "On the Combined Nomenclature of Goods" based on Regulation 2263/2000/EC which amended Annex I of Regulation EEC 2658/87. The nomenclature of goods in Albania changes every year as a result of the fulfillment of WTO requirements and Free Trade Agreements. For 2014 nomenclature please visit the link: http://www.dogana.gov.al/sites/default/files/NK percent202014.pdf

* Decision of Council of Ministers No 205 dated April 13, 1999, "On the Implementation of Provisions of the Customs Code", based on Regulation 2454/1993/EC.

* Free Trade Agreements (SAA, CEFTA, FTA with Turkey and EFTA countries).

The Stabilization and Association Agreement (SAA) with the EU entered into force on April 1, 2009, following ratification by EU member countries. The SAA foresees the establishment of a free trade area according to the commitments of Albania under the agreements signed with the WTO. The agreement foresees the implementation of a transitional period, which establishes a free trade area between the two parties, over a

period of ten years, divided in two five year periods. The first period foresees: (i) tariff reduction for sensitive industrial products, agricultural products, processed agricultural products and fish products; (ii) different transitional periods for further liberalization of trade in services, public procurement, technical barriers to trade, etc. The agreement also foresees the elimination of all quantitative trade restrictions, or other measures with a similar effect and the gradual elimination of custom tariffs, to ensure the complete liberalization of imports of industrial products; convergence and harmonization of trade legislation with EU legislation; and, elimination of fiscal discrimination resulting from tariffs and taxes which are applicable in both parties' territories.

As such, Albania implements preferential tariffs on products originating from member countries of the European Community, CEFTA, EFTA, and Turkey. The following link contains the complete 2014 list:

http://www.dogana.gov.al/sites/default/files/origjina/Tarifa_Preferenciale_2014.pdf

Albania also is a signatory to the International Technology Agreement under the WTO umbrella, which provides free import of information technology equipment.

Customs duties/tariffs vary from zero to 15 percent based on the type of goods. Other taxes imposed on imported products include 20 percent VAT (with a few exemptions) and the excise tax, which applies to limited categories of products. VAT and excise tax are calculated on the basis of the CIF price plus duty. For customs tariffs and excise tax levels please see the Customs Administration website at http://www.dogana.gov.al and, the Tax Administration's website at http://www.tatime.gov.al/gdt/Tax_legislation_in_Force.aspx . For certain items, taxes and tariffs are levied based on a government-determined fair market price (the so called reference price) or the global market price regardless of the actual price paid.

Import regulations are generally not available in English. In order to learn about customs duties, taxes, and quality requirements for a specific product, U.S. exporters must contact freight forwarders or business consultants in Albania.

TRADE BARRIERS

There are no significant non-tariff trade barriers. However, administrative bureaucracy, including the use of sanitary or phytosanitary measures (SPS), can delay the movement of goods and increase costs. In addition, the application of market prices, often referred to as "reference prices" in calculating customs dues and other taxes at customs, have become a concern and are a potential barrier for many businesses involved in trade activity.

IMPORT REQUIREMENTS AND DOCUMENTATION

The importer is responsible for providing the necessary import documents to customs. The following are the main documents required for imports and exports however, the exporter should consult with the importer for a complete list of documents needed:

1. Certificate of the quality of goods
2. Certificate of the analysis of goods
3. Certificate of the origin of goods
4. Original purchase invoice (sales contract for the goods is optional)
5. Transportation documents (CMR, BL, AWB)
6. VAT number of Importer
7. Import authorization for certain goods

It is obligatory to describe the sanitary characteristics of food or medical products.

U.S. EXPORT CONTROLS

Most technology can be freely exported from the United States to Albania, but some equipment requires validated export licenses from the Bureau of Industry and Security (BIS), formerly the Bureau of Export Administration (U.S. Department of Commerce). The BIS is responsible for implementing and enforcing the Export Administration Regulations (EAR), which regulate the export and re-export of most U.S. commercial items. The items that BIS regulates are often referred to as "dual-use" items (i.e., items that have both commercial and military or proliferation applications) but purely commercial items without an obvious military use are also subject to the EAR. Export licenses can be obtained from the Bureau of Industry and Security. The need for an export license depends on the product's Export Commodity Control Number (ECCN), available from the manufacturer, or from BIS by calling (202) 482-3332 or - 4811. The EAR does not control all goods, services, and technologies. Other U.S. government agencies regulate more specialized exports. A list of other agencies involved in export controls can be found on the BIS website at: http://www.bis.doc.gov/ or in Supplement No. 3 to Part 730 of the EAR.

In 2007, Albania approved the Law on the State Control over Import-Export of Dual Use Military Goods and Commodities/Technologies. Starting in June 2009, any company operating in Albania, public or private, dealing with import-export, transit, transshipping, transfer, exhibition of dual use military goods and commodities/ technologies, or that serves as broker for these goods, included in the EU list of control and approved by the Council of Ministers, are legally bound to get licensed or authorized prior to the start of procedures by the State Export Control Agency in compliance with the Albanian legislation in force.

For more information please visit the State Export Control Authority (AKSHE) web page: http://www.akshe.gov.al .

TEMPORARY ENTRY

Effective February 25, 2015 Albania became a party to the Customs Convention on Carnet (ATA) for temporary import of goods. ATA Carnets are accepted for transit, are not accepted for postal traffic, and are not accepted for unaccompanied goods. For information on obtaining an ATA export document, please visit the following website:

http://www.atacarnet.com/ .

The Albanian customs regime is structured as follows:

Free Circulation Regime – Import or release of goods into free circulation, as a category of customs regime, means the permanent placing of goods in the territory of Albania. Products set under such a regime are subject to all trade policy measures, such as custom duties and other related payments.

Export – Export regime is applied on all Albanian products destined for export outside the Albanian customs territory.

Active Processing (Fason Regime) - The active processing regime implies that foreign goods undergo operations of transformation or processing on Albania's customs territory without the application of measures of economic policy, except for the customs processing fees, provided resulting products are exported.

Processing Under Customs Control – This regime allows goods to be imported from outside Albania for processing operations, which change their nature or state, without being subject to import duties or other trade policy measures. Duty becomes payable when the finished product is put on free circulation. The duty is then payable on the finished product as if it had been imported directly.

Temporary Permit Regime – Under such a regime, non-Albanian goods destined for re-export can be used in the Albanian customs territory being completely or partially exempted from import duties and any trade policy measures if they are not experiencing any change except depreciation. The maximum period for goods to be under such regime is one year. After this period, they should be re-exported.

Passive Processing - Albanian products are allowed to be exported temporarily outside the Albanian customs territory, so that they can be processed and products gained from these operations may be placed in free circulation (re-imported) with complete or partial exception from import duties.

Transit Regime - Transit of goods and vehicles means movement of goods and/or vehicles between foreign countries through the territory of Albania without application of economic policy measures thereof. Goods transported through the territory of Albania are exempt from customs duty, VAT, and excise taxes.

Temporary Warehouse regime – Products are considered to have the status of temporary storage from the moment they are present in the customs office until the time their destination is determined. Such goods are held in specific areas approved by customs authorities.

LABELING AND MARKING REQUIREMENTS

According to the Law on Food, all food products destined for end consumers must have labels in Albanian and should include: name of the product; ingredients; quantity of special ingredients or categories of ingredients; net quantity/weight/volume; expiration date; manner of storage;

pertinent consumer warnings; and importer's full address. The label in Albanian is not a requirement for the exporter but the importing company.

Directions on the labeling for non-food products in Albanian are less specific than food products. The law for the protection of the consumers approved in 2008 requires that

non-food products destined for end consumers have labels in the Albanian language which include name of the products, address of the producer and/or importer, brand or any other distinguishing sign of the manufacturer importer or supplier, weight, quantity, size and dimensions and any other identification feature necessary for the identification and use of the product.

PROHIBITED AND RESTRICTED IMPORTS

There are no specific prohibited imports. There are categories of products that need licenses and registration before being imported to Albania like insecticides, pesticide, pharmaceuticals, etc. Special import provisions are enforced for strategic sectors such as import of weapons, munitions, and dual-use items.

CUSTOMS REGULATIONS AND CONTACT INFORMATION

The General Directorate of Customs is responsible for the management, organization, and control of customs activity in Albania. The customs value of goods includes the price of the goods as well as transport and insurance expenses. For certain items, taxes are levied based on a government-determined fair market price or prices on the stock exchange regardless of the actual price paid.

For more information about customs regulations in Albania, you can contact:

General Directorate of Customs

Tirana, Albania

Tel: ++ 355 4 223 4499

Fax: ++ 355 4 224 3914

http://www.dogana.gov.al

TRADE STANDARDS

Albania has specific institutions for standardization, conformity assessment, accreditation and product certification. In certain areas, such as processed foods, beverages, and pharmaceutical products, individual ministries or agencies issue sector-specific standards and certificates.

Albania, has adopted standards regimes developed in other Western countries. ISO and EN are the primary standards-making bodies. Albania is a correspondent member without the right to vote in the International Organization for Standards (ISO) and an affiliate member to the European Organization of Standards (CEN & CENELEC). Since April 2009, it is also an associate member to the IEC with a limited vote right. The Stabilization and Association Agreement with the EU stipulates that Albania must adopt European Community technical regulations, European standards, and conformity assessment procedures.

Application of Albanian standards is voluntary unless specifically provided otherwise in law. Aside from standards concerning products for human ingestion, most standards are not enforced by legislation. Standards are developed or adopted by Technical Committees composed of interested parties from different sectors and industries. The work of the committees is then passed on to the national standards organization -- the General Directorate of Standardization (DPS). DPS is the official local inquiry point for issues relating to Technical Barriers to Trade (TBT), while the obligations under WTO/SPS Agreement are passed to Ministry of Agriculture, Rural Development and Waters and the National Food Authority

STANDARDS ORGANIZATIONS

General Directorate of Standardization (DPS) (www.dps.gov.al) is a legal entity acting as the National Standards Body of the Republic of Albania in charge of organizing all standardization activities at the national level. DPS represents the Republic of Albania at European and International Organizations dealing with standards like CEN, CENELEC, ISO, IEC and serves as a liaison to WTO officials.

The law on standardization establishes the rules and procedures for the development of all national standardization activities and the establishment and functioning of the General Directorate of Standardization. DPS is responsible for the development, adoption, approval, implementation, and the publication of the Albanian Standards in all fields except that of telecommunication. It also is responsible for publishing European and international standards. All standards published by DPS have voluntary status. A full list of the most recent standards can be found in the following link: http://www.dps.gov.al/standard/advance_search.php .

Ministry of Agriculture and Food and Consumer Protection: Albania follows WTO agreements on Sanitary and Phyto-Sanitary Procedures. To import food and agricultural products, companies must receive a license from the National Food Authority (AKU). When applicable, products also must pass sanitary, psychopathologic or veterinary control. Additional information on sanitary requirements can be obtained from the Ministry of Agriculture, Rural Developments, and Waters (www.bujqesia.gov.al) and the National Food Authority (www.aku.gov.al)

National Center for Drug Control–NCDC (www.qkkb.gov.al) represents an institution specialized in the analysis, control, and registration of drugs. It operates under the Ministry of Health and works in accordance with WHO principles. NCDC is the licensing authority for drug imports and maintains the drug registry in Albania.

NIST Notify U.S. Service

Member countries of the World Trade Organization (WTO) are required under the Agreement on Technical Barriers to Trade (TBT Agreement) to report to the WTO all proposed technical regulations that could affect trade with other Member countries. Notify U.S. is a free, web-based e-mail subscription service that offers an opportunity to review and comment on proposed foreign technical regulations that can affect your access to international markets. Register online at Internet URL: http://www.nist.gov/notifyus/

CONFORMITY ASSESSMENT

The conformity assessment body is the General Directorate of Metrology (GDM) www.dpm.gov.al which operates in accordance with the Law "On metrology." GDM implements the metrology policy in Albania in the three categories: scientific, industrial and legal metrology.

The GDM policy is to develop the national metrology system, in line with European standards; fulfilling the country needs and requirements and to harmonize technical procedures for the conformity of measurements, in order to avoid technical barriers to trade and enhance the quality of life of Albanian citizens. The national Metrology System includes national standards laboratories, calibration laboratories, testing laboratories and legal persons authorized to conduct the business of legal metrology

GDM is a member with full rights of OIML (International Organization of Legal Metrology), EURAMET (European Association of the National Metrology Institutions), IMEKO (International Measurement Confederation) and an associated member of WELMEC (European Cooperation for Legal Metrology) and BIPM-CGPM (General Conference on Weights and Measures). For tariffs and rates charged by the GDM, check the following link: http://dpm.gov.al/images/stories/DPM/sherbimet/tarifat-dhe-sherbimet-e-dpm-2015.pdf

PRODUCT CERTIFICATION

Product certification is done on a voluntary basis, unless specifically provided otherwise under law. Most legal product certifications concern sanitary characteristics of foodstuffs and medicine.

The accreditation of product certification is done from the Albanian Accreditation Directorate and/or from foreign Institutions.

In 2014, the DPA hopes to reach an agreement with the European Accreditation Body (EA) to become a signatory of the mutual recognition agreements in the field of testing laboratories. This would allow the recognition at the European level of testing by accredited laboratories from the DPA.

ACCREDITATION

The Albanian Accreditation Directorate (DPA) is recognized by the Albanian Government as the single national accreditation body to assess, in concordance with internationally agreed standards, organizations that provide certification, testing, and inspection and calibration services. The DPA operates a management system in line with the requirements of S SH ISO/IEC 17011. It is a full member of the International Laboratory Accreditation Cooperation (ILAC) and of the International Accreditation Forum (IAF) and since November 2011, an associate member of the European Accreditation Organization EA. Laboratory accreditation is not compulsory for every sector. It is, however, mandatory for laboratories dealing with safety and health issues.

Accreditations conducted by foreign accreditation bodies are recognized for the purposes of authorization or registration, only in specific cases.

PUBLICATION OF TECHNICAL REGULATIONS

Approved technical regulations are published in the Official Gazette which can be found at the following address: www.legjislacioni.gov.al Furthermore, each agency publishes its own publications. The DPS publishes a quarterly standards bulletin (in Albanian) and the annual Catalogue of Albanian Standards. The DPS is, according to the law, the National Authority for Notifications and a reference for draft standards, technical rules and procedures for conformity assessment.

Proposed technical regulations are not easily accessible to the public. With proposed regulations, however, the DPS will notify WTO officials in order to solicit comments.

LABELING AND MARKING

According to the Law on Food, all food products destined for end consumers must have labels in Albanian and should include: name of the product; ingredients; quantity of special ingredients or categories of ingredients; net quantity/weight/volume; expiration date; manner of storage; pertinent consumer warnings; and importer's full address. The label in Albanian is not a requirement for the exporter but is the responsibility of the importing company.

Directions on the labeling of non-food products in Albanian are less specific than food products. The law for the protection of the consumers approved in 2008 requires that non-food products destined for end consumers have labels in the Albanian language which include name of the products, address of the producer and/or importer, brand or any other distinguishing sign of the manufacturer, importer, or supplier, weight, quantity, size and dimensions and any other identification feature necessary for the identification and use of the product.

CONTACTS

General Directorate of Standardization
Mr. Riza Hasanaj
Director
Rruga "Mine Peza", Nr. 143/3,
Tirana, Albania
Phone: + 355 (4) 224 7175
Fax: + 355 (4) 224 7177
Email: hasanaj.r@dps.gov.al
http://www.dps.gov.al

National Food Authority
Mr. Afrim Bakaj
Director
Rruga Muhamet Gjollesha, 56,
Tirana, Albania Phone: +355 (4) 225 2658 Fax: +355 (4) 225 2658
http:www.aku.gov.al

Accreditation Directorate
Mr. Armond Halebi
Director
Rr " Sami Frashri", Nr.33, Tiranë.Tirana, Albania
Phone: +355 (4) 226 9097 /226 9325
http://www.dpa.gov.al

General Directorate of Metrology
Mr. Petrit Rama
Director
Adresa: Autostrada Tiranë-Durrës, km 10
Tirana, Albania Phone: +355 (4) 223 3462 Fax: +355 (4) 222 8244
E-mail: metrology@dpm.gov.al
http://www.dpm.gov.al

Points of Contact at the U.S. Embassy are:
Mr. Donald Brown
Economic/Commercial Officer
United States Embassy
Rruga Elbasanit 103
Tirana, Albania
tel: +(355) (4 2247 285
fax: + (355) (4 2232 222
e-mail: BrownDA8@state.gov

Ms. Edi Jacellari
Commercial Assistant
United States Embassy
Rruga Elbasanit, 103

Tirana, Albania
Tel. +355 (4) 224 7285 x 3116
Fax: +355 (4) 223 2222
E-mail: JacellariE@state.gov

Mr. Frank Nikolla
Economic Assistant
United States Embassy
Rruga Elbasanit, 103
Tirana, Albania
Tel. +355 (4) 224 7285 x 3065
Fax: +355 (4) 223 2222
E-mail: NikollaF@state.gov

TRADE AGREEMENTS

Albania joined the WTO in 2000 and applies WTO rules on import licensing. From October 1999 to December 2006, Albanian exports to European Union (EU) countries benefited from an asymmetric regime in the form of autonomous measures. Therefore, Albanian exports were subject to various reductions and discounts on duties when entering the EU market. The regime was applicable both to agricultural and industrial goods.

On June 12, 2006, Albania signed the Stabilization and Association Agreement (SAA) with the EU after prolonged negotiations. A vital step for eventual EU membership, the SAA established a free trade area between Albania and the EU over a course of 10 years. The Interim Foreign Trade Agreement (part of the SAA) entered into force on December 1, 2006. This liberalized trade relations between the EU and Albania in terms of tariff barriers for both agricultural and industrial goods. The SAA was ratified on April 2009 and supersedes the Interim Agreement, which is now an integral part of the SAA.

Trade with neighboring countries has improved since 2003, when the first bilateral Free Trade Agreement (FTA) entered into force. On December 19, 2006, all of Albania's bilateral trade agreements with countries in the region were consolidated into the multilateral Central European Free Trade Agreement (CEFTA), which includes eight countries (Albania, Macedonia, Montenegro, Kosovo, Moldova, Croatia, Serbia and Bosnia and Herzegovina). CEFTA officially came into effect on July 26, 2007. Albania's trade with its neighbors has experienced modest growth from a low base and is inhibited in part by poor infrastructure such as ports and roads.

Albania also has an FTA with Turkey (signed in 2006 and entered into force on May 2008). In June 2009, Albania signed an FTA with the European Free Trade Association (EFTA). EFTA member states are Iceland, Liechtenstein, Norway and Switzerland. The agreements with Liechtenstein and Switzerland entered into force in November 2010 and the agreements with Iceland and Norway entered into force during 2011.

WEB RESOURCES

http://www.ekonomia.gov.al
http://www.dogana.gov.al
http://www.dps.gov.al
http:/www.dpmk.gov.al
http:/www.albanianaccreditation.gov.al
http:www.aku.gov.al
http://www.bujqesia.gov.al
http://www.shendetesia.gov.al
http://www.qkkb.gov.al

TRADE AND PROJECT FINANCING

METHODS OF PAYMENT

Trade financing options for imports to Albania have improved in recent years as a result of the development of financial sector which has increased its range of services, quality, and presence across the country. It has streamlined several procedures and introduced ways to accommodate trade financing requirements. The most commonly used international payment mechanisms are now available by the banking sector to facilitate transactions including letters of guarantee and letters of credit.

Bank-to-bank trade finance alternatives can be structured with or without a letter of credit. A considerable number of larger importers regularly receive goods under a short-term supplier credit agreement. Importers are free to arrange payments through long-term supplier loans when they make larger purchases. For transactions abroad, the most preferred forms of payment are letters of credit or payments in advance. U.S. Export-Import Bank (Ex-Im) provides insurance policies to U.S. exporters to allow more flexible payment terms.

HOW DOES THE BANKING SYSTEM OPERATE

The banking sector is regulated by the Law 9662 "On banks in the Republic of Albania" of December 2006. The banking law stipulates the core principles in conducting banking activity in Albania as well as the guidelines to ensure sound management and administrative procedures for domestic and foreign banks. The banking sector is dominated by commercial banks fully owned by private shareholders. Currently, there are 16 banks operating in Albania, only two of which are Albanian owned. The Austrian bank Raiffeisen remains the predominant bank with approximately 23 percent of the banking sector's total assets followed by the National Commercial Bank with 21 percent. The Italian Intesa San Paolo, the Greek Alpha Bank, the French Societe General and Credit Agricole are some other notable international banks present in the Albanian market.

The banking sector in Albania remains sound, profitable, and well capitalized. It has in general been spared from the global financial turmoil, primarily due to the low amount of loans relative to total deposits and the lack of a domestic housing/real estate bubble. The sector remained profitable even during the peak of the financial crisis when it suffered a reduction of deposits by approximately 15 percent which it quickly recovered

in the following year. In 2015, profits reached $88 million with a 0.5 percent return on assets and 6.4 percent return on equities. The banking sector has reached a stable stage after many years of expansion. In April 2014, there were 549 banking outlets nationwide, slightly less than in 2012, (there were just 127 in 2005). The number of debit/credit cards, ATMs, and Point-of-Sales terminals continues to grow rapidly. However, the annual volume of transactions with debit/credit cards remains very limited to approximately 1.3 percent of total deposits. As of April 2014, total assets of the banking sector amounted to approximately $12.5 billion consisting mostly of bank deposits.

Commercial banks have improved significantly the variety and quality of services for both retail and corporate banking. Banks have expanded their presence countrywide and introduced new instruments and services such as e-banking. The private sector has widely benefited from the expansion of these instruments, but businesses still report that high interest rates, distrust of the banking system, and high operating costs of banks remain concerns for investors looking for access to credit.

More recently, the banking sector is experiencing new challenges as deposits are stalling and the stock of outstanding loans is slightly contracting due to the slowdown of the domestic economy.

Banks continue to keep tight lending standards due to the rise of nonperforming loans. As of April 2014, nonperforming loans stood at 23.8 percent of all private loans compared to 4.3 percent before the 2008 financial crisis. However, capital adequacy at 18 percent – far above Basel requirements – indicates the sector has sufficient assets to withstand the negative trend. Moreover, the payment of a significant amount of government arrears to the private sector is expected to reduce the extent of bad loans and improve bank's confidence in the business sector in 2014 and 2015.

The regulatory framework is well-developed and continues to align itself with international practice. Central Bank of Albania (BOA) has tightened supervision rules over second tier banks as a result of the global financial crisis and the contagion risks posed by regional banks. In the fall of 2011, the BOA adopted new regulations on credit risk management and introduced several amendments to the Law on the Banks that would bolster the independence of local branches from their international parent company. In July 2012, local branches of two Greek banks were transformed into subsidiaries, in line with other foreign banks in Albania.

In November 2015, Moody's confirmed its rating for Albania's government debt obligations at B1 with a stable outlook. In December 2015, Standard & Poor lowered its sovereign credit ratings on Albania to B from B+ with a negative outlook due to the significant unanticipated increase in the general government debt burden. However, in April 2014 S&P improved its outlook for Albania to Stable from Negative seemingly due to GOA's recent loan agreements with IMF and World Bank which are expected to mitigate the pressure on public finances.

Albania also has 20 non-banking financial institutions and 121 savings and loans associations. These institutions target medium sized businesses that are not primarily served by the commercial banking sector. They offer loans from $1,000 to $500,000. A detailed list is in the following address:

http://www.bankofalbania.org/web/Unionet_e_Shoqerive_te_Kursim_Kreditit_5322_1.php

FOREIGN-EXCHANGE CONTROLS

There are no foreign exchange controls in Albania. The Bank of Albania is entitled to impose exchange restrictions for the making of payments and transfers for capital account transactions. However, such restrictions can only be introduced for a period not exceeding twelve months, and can only be extended for another similar period. In September 2009, the BOA amended the Regulation of Foreign Exchange Controls which does not include any restriction over international financial remittances. Exporting of hard currency by commercial entities, including juridical persons and sole traders must be done through bank transfer.

When the amount of funds to be transferred abroad is large enough to negatively impact Albania's balance of payments abroad the Central Bank reserves the right to break it down into smaller amounts. In 2009, following the global financial meltdown the BOA restricted the distribution of the domestic banking sector profits in order to maintain sufficient liquidity in the sector. The restriction was lifted in July 2010.

Repatriation of income (dividends, royalties and consultancy services) is allowed if no tax liabilities are outstanding in Albania. Transfers for current international payments (imports of goods and services, transportation, interest and principal payments and other purposes defined in the regulation) must be supported by documentation such as invoices, certificates, or transport documents, to the transferring bank. There is a limit of $10,000 of hard currency and other assets to carry with while crossing border check points. The violation of the rule is subject to penal charges.

U.S. BANKS AND LOCAL CORRESPONDENT BANKS

There are no American banks present in Albania. However, many banks in Albania may have different U.S. correspondent banks and some U.S. banks may have correspondent relations with more than one bank in Albania. As banking relationships can change quickly, the best source of current information on correspondent banking arrangements is the banks themselves. Contact information for all banks in Albania can be found on the Bank of Albania website: http://www.bankofalbania.org/web/Rregjistri_i_Bankave_tregetare_50_1.php

PROJECT FINANCING

In the absence of a stock market, the banking sector remains the main channel for project financing. The entrance of large European banks during the last few years has strengthened competition and has improved the intermediation role of the banking system as a primary developer of the economy. After a spectacular expansion before the 2008 crisis with average annual growth rates of about 50 percent – mostly due to the very low starting base – credit growth has slowed down considerably after the global financial meltdown. Since 2009, banks have restricted their lending policies and become more cautious in crediting especially for the private sector. In April 2014, total stock of

outstanding loans contracted by 2 percent mostly due to lower lending to the private sector. In April 2014, loans constituted 45 percent of total banking assets compare to 50 percent at the end of 2011. Corporate loans represent almost 73percent of banks' credit portfolios.

The cost of borrowing locally remains relatively high, characterized by mid-term loans and high interest rates. However, competition in the sector is driving interest rates down even in the domestic currency. BOA has adopted a relaxed monetary policy and reduced several times the key interest rate for the domestic currency to historical minimums. On May 30, the Bank of Albania lowered the key interest rate by 0.25 percent to the new record low of 2.5 percent marking the eleventh consecutive reduction since September 2011. While companies from Albania are free to borrow from foreign banks without restrictions, the inflow of foreign capital for this purpose has been minimal. Domestic banks have limited financial ability to issue credit, which has led some of them to use corporate loans for certain large-scale commercial projects.

US based Financing

U.S. Export-Import Bank

Ex-Im Bank is an independent U.S. Government agency that helps finance the overseas sales of U.S. goods and services. Ex-Im Bank will finance the export of all types of goods or services with the exception of military-related items (although there are exceptions to this rule). In 2005, Ex-Im Bank provided a $47.6 million long-term loan guarantee to support Lockheed Martin's sale of an air traffic control navigation system to upgrade Albania's air navigation system. That remains so far the only Ex-Im Bank's exposure to Albania.

Ex-Im Bank's major programs include:

* Working capital guarantees that cover 90 percent of the principal and interest on commercial loans to creditworthy small and medium-sized companies that need funds to buy or produce U.S. goods or services for export

* Export credit insurance policies to protect against the political and commercial risks of a foreign buyer defaulting on payment

* Guarantees of commercial loans to foreign buyers of U.S. goods or services that cover 100 percent of principal and interest against both political and commercial risks of non-

payment

* Direct loans that provide foreign buyers with competitive, fixed-rate financing for their purchases from the U.S.

For more information please visit: http://www.exim.gov/

U.S. Trade and Development Agency

The U.S. Trade and Development Agency (USTDA) is an independent U.S. government agency, which promotes American private sector participation in developing and middle-income countries, with special emphasis on economic sectors that represent significant U.S. export potential. Through funding of feasibility studies, orientation visits, specialized training grants, and various forms of technical assistance, USTDA helps U.S. businesses compete for infrastructure projects in emerging markets. USTDA assists in

building mutually beneficial partnerships between American companies and local project sponsors, which result in increased U.S. exports, and the completion of high quality, successful projects in host countries. USTDA in Albania has financed projects to study airports, roads, ports, railroads, and the energy sector, as well as increased activities in supporting private sector projects.

Contact:

1621 N. Kent Street #200 Arlington, VA 22209-2131 USA Tel: (703) 875-4357 Fax: (703) 875-4009

Website: www.ustda.gov

Overseas Private Investment Corporation:

Overseas Private Investment Corporation (OPIC) is a self-sustaining U.S. Government agency that sells investment services to small, medium, and large American businesses expanding into emerging markets around the world. OPIC's three main activities include risk insurance, project finance, and investment funds. OPIC financing through its investment guaranty program and the direct loan program is limited to $200 million.

OPIC established the Southeast Europe Equity Investment Fund (SEEF) I and II that are managed by Bedminster Capital Management. This fund is capitalized at $320 million and seeks equity investment opportunities in the communications, healthcare, consumer, and financial service industries across South East Europe and Turkey.

Contact:

Overseas Private Investment Corporation Information Officer, Office of External Affairs 1100 New York Avenue, NW Washington, D.C. 20527

E-mail: info@opic.gov

Web: http://www.opic.gov

WEB RESOURCES

Export-Import Bank of the United States: http://www.exim.gov

Country Limitation Schedule: http://www.exim.gov/tools/country/country_limits.html

OPIC: http://www.opic.gov

Trade and Development Agency: http://www.tda.gov/

SBA's Office of International Trade: http://www.sba.gov/oit/

USDA Commodity Credit Corporation: http://www.fsa.usda.gov/ccc/default.htm

U.S. Agency for International Development: http://www.usaid.gov

BUSINESS TRAVEL

BUSINESS CUSTOMS

Albania is a relationship-oriented society that places a premium on friendship, hospitality and trust. Business discussions are usually preceded by a series of questions concerning health, family, and the general well-being of the all parties. Business meetings generally take place over coffee and the time spent over a coffee is considered an integral part of the meeting and should not be dismissed as a waste of time.

Appointments should be made in advance of a business visit and exchange of business cards is common. Most Albanian businesspeople speak at least one foreign language and the most common are English and Italian. Computer usage is extensive and most of them utilize e-mail and Internet, with many companies now creating their own websites. Summer holidays stretch throughout mid-July till the end of August and it is frequently difficult to reach company management during this period.

Credit cards are accepted in major hotels, shopping malls, chain grocery stores, and high-end restaurants. Most retail transactions are still conducted in cash.

Business dress is recommended when meeting with government officials. Meetings with business people and visits to local businesses can be done in smart business casual.

Albanians are a very hospitable people and commonly exchange gifts.

TRAVEL ADVISORY

Business travelers to Albania should remember that the country's transportation network is limited. Despite recent infrastructure improvements in major traffic corridors, the roads in rural areas are often in poor condition. Drivers are aggressive and frequently disregard traffic laws.

Traveling at night outside urban areas is not recommended due to poor road conditions, a lack of adequate street lighting, and general safety concerns. Train service inside the

country is not recommended as railroads and trains are in very poor conditions. Tirana's international airport services the entire country.

As in all cases, travelers should take precautions to ensure their personal safety while travelling. Please refer to the State Department's Consular Information Sheet for Albania at: http://travel.state.gov/content/passports/english/country/albania.html

VISA REQUIREMENTS

On March 28, 2015, Albanian parliament approved a new law on foreigners, granting to U.S. citizens a favorable regime. An American citizen does not have to obtain a visa prior to entering Albania. An entry stamp will be issued at the point of entry and American citizens can stay in Albania for one year without a residency permit. If you depart Albania during the one-year period or after a one-year stay and return after three months or more, you may re-enter and stay in Albania for a new one-year period without having to apply for a residence permit.

If you plan to stay for more than one year in Albania, you need to apply for a residence permit. Please visit the U.S. Embassy web page for instructions on how to apply for a residence permit.

http://tirana.usembassy.gov/residency.html

U.S. Companies that require travel of foreign businesspersons to the United States should be advised that security evaluations are handled via an interagency process. Visa applicants should go to the following links.

State Department Visa Website: http://travel.state.gov/visa/

http://tirana.usembassy.gov/visas.html

TELECOMMUNICATIONS

Internet use is not widespread in most remote areas, but is common in Tirana and major urban areas. Internet cafes are everywhere and charge around $1 per hour while most hotels, bars and restaurant have wi-fi.

Cellular phones are widely used in Albania. There are currently four GSM companies offering mobile services: Albanian Mobile Communications (AMC), Vodafone, Eagle Mobile and plus. Vodafone, AMC and Eagle all offer 3G. Triple band (like Treo, Handspring, Blackberries, etc.) cell phones can be used in Albania, but since roaming charges are expensive, it is recommended to use prepaid cards offered by local carriers.

Albania's voltage is 220V and plugs and sockets in wide use are those of European type, C and F.

Albania's country code is +355, followed by the local land line or cellular phone number.

TRANSPORTATION

Public transportation is limited in Albania and most business travelers will want to travel by taxi or hire a car and driver for the duration of their visit. Avis Rent a Car, Hertz and some local rent-a-car companies offer services in Albania. A taxi from Mother Teresa International Airport to the center of Tirana costs approximately $20-25.

For longer periods of travel or standby use, a car and driver can be rented for approximately $10 per hour.

LANGUAGE

The national language of Albania is Albanian. Albania has a large pool of well-trained and talented linguists who can serve as translators/interpreters.

Translators generally charge approximately $100-200 per day. Most business people in Albania speak a foreign language. The most popular second languages are English, Italian, and Greek.

HEALTH

The quality of medical care at private hospitals and clinics in Tirana has improved in recent years but does not yet meet western practice standards. Medical care outside the capital is limited because of a lack of medical specialists, diagnostic aids, medical supplies, and prescription drugs. Tirana has four main private hospitals that offer modern facilities and a full range of services. These hospitals include the American Hospital, Hygeia Hospital, German Hospital, and Albanian-Italian Hospital Salus.

Travelers with previously diagnosed medical conditions should consult their physician before traveling to Albania. As prescription drugs may be unavailable locally, travelers may also wish to bring extra supplies of required medications.

U.S. medical insurance plans seldom cover health costs incurred outside the United States unless supplemental coverage is purchased.

For more information, you can visit the following web sites:

http://travel.state.gov/content/passports/english/country/albania.htmlhttp://tirana.usembassy.gov/medical-information.html

Resources:

http://spitaliamerikan.com

www.hygeia-tirana.com

http://www.spitaligjerman.com/

http://www.salus.al/

LOCAL TIME, BUSINESS HOURS, AND HOLIDAYS

EST +6

GMT +1

Most Albanian businesses are open Monday through Friday from 8 a.m. to 5 p.m. and occasionally are open on Saturday. There is no legislation regulating shop hours and many shops are open seven days a week up to late evening.

Government offices generally operate Monday through Thursday from 8 a.m. to 4:30 p.m. and on Friday from 8 a.m. to 2 p.m.

The Embassy will observe the following Albanian and U.S. holidays during the calendar year 2014:

January 1 New Year's Day (Albania/(U.S. Holiday)

January 2 New Year's Day

January 20 Martin Luther King's Birthday (U.S. Holiday)

February 17 President's Day (U.S. Holiday)

March 22 Nevruz

April 20 Catholic & Orthodox Easter

May 1 May Day

May 26 Memorial Day (U.S. Holiday)

July 4 Independence Day (U.S. Holiday)

August 29* Big Bajram

September 1 Labor Day (U.S. Holiday)

October 14 Columbus Day (U.S. Holiday)

October 5* Small Bajram

October 19 Mother Teresa's Day

November 11 Veterans Day (U.S. Holiday)

November 27 Thanksgiving (U.S. Holiday)

November 28 Independence Day

November 29 National Liberation Day

December 25 Christmas (Albania/(U.S. Holiday)

When an authorized American holiday falls on a Sunday, the office will be closed the following Monday. When such a holiday falls on a Saturday, the office will be closed the preceding Friday.

When an authorized Albanian holiday falls on a Saturday or Sunday, the office will be closed the following workday in accordance with local custom.

* The Muslim Holidays of Big and Small Bajram are subject to the sighting of the moon. These dates may change.

TEMPORARY ENTRY OF MATERIALS AND PERSONAL BELONGINGS

According to Albania customs regulations, temporary entry of materials and personal belongings is allowed only when the person submits the following documents and the

person has a contract of more than 6 months of duration. Only one shipment is allowed under this category:

> * Request signed from client directed to Tirana Directory of Customs asking for duty free import of PE (in Albanian)
>
> * Photocopy of passport (notarized)
>
> * Letter in original from from the individual's organization in Tirana stating the employment (period for at minimum 6 months should be specified.)

* Photocopy of job contract with the company (the person might delete all confidential information on the contract)

* Photocopy of NIPT of the organization (V.A.T tax number certificate)

* Photocopy of the lease contract of the house in Albania (notarized)

* Photocopy of residence permit in Albania (notarized), and

* Packing list

WEB RESOURCES

http://travel.state.gov/content/passports/english/country/albania.html

http://travel.state.gov/content/visas/english.html

http://tirana.usembassy.gov/service.html

http://tirana.usembassy.gov/residency.html

http://tirana.usembassy.gov/medical-information.html

IMPORTANT BUSINESS CONTACTS

ALBANIAN GOVERNMENT

Embassy of the Republic of Albania
2100 S St NW, Washington, DC 20008
Phone: (202) 223-4942
www.embassyofalbania.org
info@albanianembassy.org

Edi Rama – Prime Minister
http://www.kryeministria.al

Niko Peleshi – Deputy Prime Minister
http://www.kryeministria.al

Ditmir Bushati- Minister of Foreign Affairs
http://www.punetejashtme.gov.al

Mimi Kodheli - Minister of Defense
http://www.mod.gov.al

Shkelqim Cani - Minister of Finance
http://www.financa.gov.al

Damjan Gjiknuri – Minister of Energy and Industry
http://www.energjia.gov.al

Arben Ahmetaj- Ministry of Economy, Trade and Entrepreneurship
http://www.ekonomia.gov.al

Edmond Haxhinasto - Minister of Transportation and Infrastructure http://www.mpptt.gov.al

Edmond Panariti - Minister of Agriculture, Rural Development and Administration of Waters
http://www.bujqesia.gov.al

Klajda Gjosha -Minister of European Integration
http://www.mie.gov.al

Saimir Tahiri - Minister of Interior Affairs
http://www.punetebrendshme.gov.al

Nasip Naco - Minister of Justice
http://www.drejtesia.gov.al

Ilir Beqaj - Minister of Health
http://www.shendetsia.gov.al

Eglantina Gjermeni – Minister of Urban Development and Tourism
http://www.turizmi.gov.al

Mirela Kumbaro - Minister of Culture
http://www.kultura.gov.al

Erion Veliaj – Minister of Social Welfare and Youth
http://www.sociale.gov.al

Lindita Nikolla –Minister of Education and Sports
http://www.arsimi.gov.al

Lefter Koka - Minister of Environment
http://www.mjedisi.gov.al

Milena Harito - Minister of Innovation and Public Administration
http://www.inovacioni.gov.al

Ilirian Celibashi - Minister of State for Parliamentary Relations
http://www.kryeministria.al

Bledi Cuci - Minister of State for Local Government
http://www.kryeministria.al

OTHER GOVERNMENT INSTITUTIONS AND AGENCIES

Central Bank
http://www.bankofalbania.com

Institute of Statistics
http://www.instat.gov.al

Public Procurement Agency
http://www.app.gov.al

Business Licensing Center
http://www.qkl.gov.al

Business Registration Center
http://www.qkr.gov.al

Albanian Investment and Development Agency
http://www.aida.gov.al

General Directorate of Taxation
http://www.tatime.gov.al

General Directorate of Customs
http://www.dogana.gov.al
Energy Regulator
http://www.ere.gov.al
Electronic Communication and Postal Authority
http://www.ert.gov.al

National Agency of Information Society
http://www.akshi.gov.al/

Agency of Natural Resources
http://www.akbn.gov.al

Financial Supervising Authority
http://www.amf.gov.al

Competition Authority
http://www.caa.gov.al

Albania Patent and Trademark Office
http://www.alpto.gov.al

General Directorate of Metrology
http://www.dpmk.gov.al

General Directorate of Standardization
http://www.dps.gov.al

BUSINESS ASSOCIATIONS

American Chamber of Commerce in Albania
http://www.amcham.com.al

Chamber of Commerce and Industry Tirana
http://www.cci.al

Foreign Investors Association of Albania
http://www.fiaalbania.com

LAW FIRMS

http://www.bogalaw.com.al
http://www.kalo-attorneys.com
http://www.wolftheiss.com
http://ffconsulting.al
http://www.tonucci.it

http://www.zkt-lawfirm.com
http://www.hmh-al.net

AUDIT, TAX AND ADVISORY SERVICES FIRMS

http://www.pbm.al correspondent of http://www.russellbedford.com
http://www.deloitte.com/al
http://www.kpmg.com.al
http://www.pwc.com/al
http://www.ey.com

MAJOR MEDIA OUTLETS:

http://www.top-channel.tv
http://www.tvklan.tv
http://www.vizionplus.tv
http://www.oranews.com
http://www.news24.com

ECONOMY:

http://www.monitor.com.al

For commercial issues, requests and information please contact:
Mr. Donald Brown
Economic/Commercial Officer
United States Embassy
Rruga Elbasanit 103
Tirana, Albania
tel: +(355) (42) 247 285
fax: + (355) (42) 232 222
e-mail: BrownDA8@state.gov

Edi Jacellari
Commercial Assistant
United States Embassy
Rruga Elbasanit 103
Tirana, Albania
Tel.: + (355) (42) 247 285, ext. 3116
Fax: + (355) (42) 232 222
E-mail: JacellariE@state.gov

STRATEGIC ECONOMIC AND BUSINESS INFORMATION

INVESTMENT, LEGAL AND BUSINESS CLIMATE - STRATEGIC INFORMATION AND CONTACTS FOR STARTING BUSINESS

Albania is a relatively small country located in the Western Balkans with a population of approximately 3 million people and a landmass the size of Maryland. Although the country was largely spared from the severe fallout of the 2008 financial crisis, economic output has slowed since 2009, reflecting the prolonged European crisis in neighboring Italy and Greece where close to 1.2 million Albanians live and work and 66 percent of Albanian trade occurs. Faced with public debt ballooning to 70 percent of GDP and large arrears to the private sector, the government began an ambitious fiscal consolidation program and signed a EUR 330 million euro, three-year program with the IMF in February 2014. Albania's GDP grew by an estimated 2 percent in 2014, up from 1.4 percent in 2013 and the government estimates approximately 3 percent growth in 2015. Low petroleum and mineral prices and the ongoing economic crises in Italy and Greece are the two biggest obstacles that may keep Albania from meeting its 2015 growth targets.

With low domestic demand, low bank lending rates, and limited government spending, the Albanian government has been focused on promoting foreign direct investment (FDI) as the driver of growth in the economy by implementing a liberal foreign investment regime. In recent years, the government has enacted reforms to improve the overall business climate in the country by streamlining business procedures through e-government reforms and improved legislation in a variety of sectors. The government currently is drafting a new Law on Investment that will provide investment incentives and fast-track registration and licensing procedures for strategic foreign investors.

According to the 2015 World Bank Doing Business Report, Albania made progress in regulatory reforms, moving up 40 slots from 108 in 2014 to 68 out of 189 economies in 2015. Albania became an EU candidate country in June 2014 and currently is working to fulfill the criteria that would pave the way for the start of accession negotiations. The EU integration process may serve as a strong incentive for the country to push forward on structural reforms and improve the business climate as the country aligns its legislation with the EU.

The Albanian legal system does not discriminate against foreign investors. The Law on Foreign Investment allows 100 percent foreign ownership of companies and outlines specific protections for foreign investors. Albanian tax policy also does not distinguish between domestic and foreign investments. The U.S. - Albania bilateral investment treaty entered into force in 1998 and ensures that U.S. investors receive most-favored-nation treatment.

Foreign Direct Investment annual inflows in Albania have increased significantly since 2008, averaging close to USD 1 billion per year for the period 2008-2014. Greece and Canada are the largest source of Albanian FDI, representing 45 percent of Albania's USD 5.5 billion foreign investment stock in 2013, mostly in the telecommunications, financial intermediation, manufacturing, hydrocarbon, and mining sectors.

Investment opportunities for U.S. investors likely will increase in the coming years, focusing mostly in oil, gas, energy, infrastructure, financial intermediation, and manufacturing. The government plans to issue 13 oil and gas exploration licenses in the near future and construction on the Trans-Adriatic Pipeline is slated to begin in mid-2015. Upgrades to the electricity distribution and transmission grids also may create significant investment opportunities. The government also has announced plans to grant many public services to the private sector as public-private partnerships (PPPs) across a wide range of sectors.

Despite progress in these reforms, major challenges remain, with investors citing endemic corruption, weak law enforcement, insufficiently defined property rights, government red tape, lack of developed infrastructure, and frequent changes in the legal framework as major challenges to conducting business in Albania. Changes in political leadership also have raised questions about the legal certainty of licensing and concession agreements signed by previous governments.

1. OPENNESS TO, AND RESTRICTIONS UPON, FOREIGN INVESTMENT

Attitude toward Foreign Direct Investment

Albania has implemented a liberal foreign investment regime with the goal of increasing foreign direct investment. The Law on Foreign Investment allows 100 percent foreign ownership of companies and outlines specific protections for foreign investors. In addition, Albanian tax policy does not distinguish between domestic and foreign investments. The U.S. - Albania bilateral investment treaty entered into force in 1998 and ensures that U.S. investors receive most-favored-nation treatment. The government has taken measures to improve the overall business climate in the country by streamlining business procedures through e-government reforms and improved legislation in a variety of sectors.

Other Investment Policy Reviews

In 2010, the World Trade Organization conducted an Investment Policy Review of Albania, more information about this review can be found at:

https://www.wto.org/english/tratop_e/tpr_e/tp329_e.htm

Laws/Regulations of Foreign Direct Investment

The Law on Foreign Investment attempts to create a hospitable climate for foreign investors and stipulates the following:

No prior government authorization is needed for an initial investment and no sector is closed to foreign investment;

100 percent foreign ownership of companies is permissible;

Foreign investment may not be expropriated or nationalized directly or indirectly, except for designated special cases, in the interest of public use and as defined by law;

Foreign investors enjoy the right to expatriate all funds and contributions in kind from their investments; and

Foreign investors receive 'most favored nation' treatment according to international agreements and Albanian law.

The government of Albania (GOA) is in the process of drafting a new law on investments in strategic sectors, aiming to introduce guarantees to foreign investors. In an attempt to attract the much needed foreign direct investment, especially in manufacturing, the GOA recently approved a 500 hectare free economic zone in Spitalle near the major port of Durres and soon will announce a tender to select the developer of the zone. The fiscal incentives for the zone are not defined yet.

There are limited exceptions to this liberal investment regime, most of which apply to the purchase of real estate: agricultural land cannot be purchased by foreigners and foreign entities, but may be rented for up to 99 years; and commercial property may be purchased, but only if the proposed investment is worth three times the price of the land. There are no restrictions on the purchase of private residential property.

Investors in Albania are entitled to judicial protection of legal rights related to their investments. Foreign investors have the right to submit disputes to an Albanian court. In addition, parties to a dispute may agree to arbitration. Albania is signatory of the New York Convention and foreign arbitration awards are recognized by Albania. The Albanian Civil Procedure Code outlines provisions regarding domestic and international commercial arbitration. However, many companies complain that endemic corruption and inefficient court procedures undermine judicial protection in Albania and therefore choose to seek international arbitration as a means for dispute resolution.

Albania's tax system does not distinguish between foreign and domestic investors. Reforms are aimed at increasing the efficiency of tax administration and reducing corruption, informality in the economy (as high as 50 percent) makes tax administration a challenge. In an effort to address the sharp decline in government revenues during 2012-2013 and growing public debt, the government, in consultation with the International Monetary Fund, passed a new fiscal package in December 2013. The new fiscal package increased corporate income tax from 10 to 15 percent for medium and large companies and reduced the tax rate to 7.5 percent for companies with less than USD 80,000 in annual turnover. The package also implemented a progressive personal income tax and removed the cap for health insurance contributions and eliminated many tax breaks and incentives in the oil and gas sector. The government introduced improvements to the Value-Added Tax (VAT) law in January 2015, easing the VAT reimbursement process.

U.S. exporters often complain about the unequal application of base pricing, used by local customs to assess taxes and duties on goods imported into Albania.

Visa requirements to obtain residence or work permits are straightforward and do not pose an undue burden on potential investors. The only potential complication to obtaining a work permit is the requirement that a foreign employer maintain a mandated number of local employees. The Law on Foreigners states that a foreign employer will be granted a work permit if the number of foreign employees in the company does not exceed 10 percent of the total number of employees on the payroll for the 12 proceeding months.

The Law on Entrepreneurs and Commercial Companies sets guidelines on the activities of companies and the legal structure under which they may operate. The government adopted the law in 2008 to conform Albanian legislation to the European Union's Acquis Communitaire. The most common type of organization for foreign investors is a limited liability company.

The National Business Registration Center serves as a one-stop-shop for business registration. Starting a business is now easier with online publishing of forms and procedures, reduction of registration costs, and the consolidation of tax, health insurance, and labor registration into a single application. The Business Licensing Center streamlines the licensing process by abolishing many licensing requirements and simplifying other licensing procedures. The business registration page can be found at: www.qkr.gov.al and the business, licensing center is www.qkl.gov.al

Albania improved public procurement procedures by introducing an e-procurement law in 2006, which has been amended over the years to improve the public procurement processes. The legal framework on public procurement is governed by the following general principles: non-discrimination and equality of treatment of actual and potential bidders, transparency of procurement procedures, and, proportionality of requirements and obligations imposed on bidders. The legislation covers public entities' procurement of public goods, public services, and, public works with a few exceptions including, defense procurement, secret contracts, and contracts requiring special security measures, international obligations, service contracts awarded on the basis of an exclusive right, and other specific exclusions specified in the law.

The law stipulates the following procurement procedures: open procedures, restricted procedures, negotiated procedures, request for proposals and design contests.

The Public Procurement Advocate performs functions similar to an ombudsman by safeguarding the rights and interests of bidders against acts or omissions by contracting authorities. Despite improvements to the laws and regulations, companies continue to complain of nontransparent processes when competing for public tenders, whether it is 'fixed' technical specifications designed to lock out a potential bidder or a lack of clear communication with the relevant ministries. Public procurement opportunities are published on the website of the Public Procurement Agency www.app.gov.al.

In 2013, Albania approved a new law on concessions and public-private partnerships. All contracts signed or negotiated prior to the new law remain subject to the provisions of the previous law. The new law aims to better align Albanian policy with EU legislation and clarify the distinction between concession contracts and public-private partnerships. The law establishes the framework for promoting and facilitating the implementation of privately financed concessionary projects and aims to enhance transparency, fairness, efficiency, and long-term sustainability in the development of infrastructure and public service projects. Concessions may be identified by central or local governments or through third party unsolicited proposals. The law applies to the following sectors:

Electricity and heating: generation and distribution;
Health;
Natural gas distribution;
IT and database infrastructure: service and maintenance;
Urban and suburban rehabilitation and development
Prison and judicial infrastructure;
Recycling projects, rehabilitation of land and forests;
Industrial parks and mining;
Housing, governmental buildings;
Solid waste: collection, transfer, processing, depositing, and administration;
Telecommunication;
Tourism, leisure and hotels;
Culture and sports;
Science and education;
Transport (railway system, rail transport, ports, airports, roads, tunnels, bridges, parking facilities, public transport);
Social Services
Public lighting in the local government units

Water: production and distribution, treatment, collection distribution and administration of waste water, irrigation, drainage, cleaning of canals, dams;

Public services: management contracts, including those related to sectors specified above.

In order to promote investment in priority sectors, the government has announced that it may offer concessions to local or international investors for the symbolic price of one euro, but has not yet detailed specific concessions that will receive this treatment. The Government may, with the proposal of other central government agencies or local government, authorize concessions in other sectors other than those listed above. The law does not apply to concessions that require a separate operating license, unless that is included in the framework of the concession agreement.

Industrial Promotion

The GOA is eager to attract foreign investment across all sectors, particularly in job creating industries that will help the government address high unemployment rates.

Please see a detailed list of incentives under subchapter five. Interested investors should contact the Albanian Investment Development Agency (AIDA) (www.aida.gov.al), to learn more about specific sectors. The GOA is currently drafting a law on investments in strategic sectors that will outline incentives for investors in various sectors.

Limits on Foreign Control

There are no restrictions on foreign ownership or control in domestic corporations. According to the Albanian legislation 100 percent foreign ownership of companies is allowed. There also are no sector-specific restrictions that discriminate against market access applicable to foreign investment.

Privatization Program

The privatization process in Albania is nearing a conclusion, with only a few major privatizations remaining. These few opportunities include electricity distribution company, the state owned insurance company INSIG, 16 percent of the fixed line telephone company Albtelekom, the state owned oil company Albpetrol, and, 25 percent of oil refiner ARMO. SOEs operate in the energy generation, electricity transmission and distribution, water supply, ports, railway, insurance, postal services, and hydrocarbon sectors.

In recent years, the government has granted as PPPs a large number of services, previously performed by public administration and is in the process of granting a wider range of services under the same model. The Ministry of Economy announced at the end of 2014 a very aggressive program of granting more than 65 services as PPPs across all sectors. The tendering procedures are published online and bidding also can be done on line at the Public Procurement Agency website: www.app.gov.al

Screening of FDI

The government does not screen foreign direct investment.

Competition Law

The Law on Protection of Competition governs incoming foreign investment whether it is through mergers, acquisitions, takeovers, or green field investments, irrespective of the industry or sector. In the case of particular share transfers in insurance and banking industries, additional regulatory approvals are needed. Also, transactions between parties outside Albania – foreign to foreign transactions – are covered by the competition law, which explicitly states that it applies to all undertakings, whether domestic or foreign, whose activities have a direct or indirect effect on the Albanian market.

Investment Trends

The legal framework to promote investment has been improving and the country offers significant emerging opportunities across all sectors, especially in natural resources. Corruption and transparency remain a significant concern, however, especially in the natural resources sector, with many foreign companies reporting pressure to hire specific employees or sub-contractors affiliated with public officials. In June 2014, Albania became a European Union (EU) candidate country and now is working to fulfill the necessary criteria that would pave the way for the start of accession negotiations. The EU integration process likely will provide an incentive for Albania to continue on its reform path and to improve the business climate.

According to the 2015 World Bank's Doing Business Report, Albania made progress in regulatory reforms, moving up 40 slots from 108 in 2014 to 68 out of 189 in 2015.

Foreign Direct Investment annual inflows in Albania have increased significantly since 2008, averaging close to USD 1 billion per year for the period 2008-2014. The largest recipients of FDI inflows are extractive industries (primarily oil and gas), telecommunication, financial intermediation, and wholesale and retail sales. The government recently announced plans to license 13 oil and gas exploration blocks in 2015, which also may drive an increase in FDI in the coming years.

Foreign investors cite Albania's strategic location in the Balkans, vicinity with major European markets, free trade agreements with key markets (European Union, Turkey, CEFTA and EFTA countries), opportunities for investments in a wide range of sectors, and inexpensive and skilled labor force as major reasons for investing in Albania.

Table 1

Measure	Year	Index or Rank	Website Address
TI Corruption Perceptions index	2014	110 of 174	transparency.org/cpi2014/results
World Bank's Doing Business Report "Ease of Doing Business"	2015	68 of 189	doingbusiness.org/rankings
Global Innovation Index	2014	94 of 143	globalinnovationindex.org/content.aspx?page=data-analysis
World Bank GNI per capita	2013	USD 4,710	data.worldbank.org/indicator/NY.GNP.PCAP.CD

2. CONVERSION AND TRANSFER POLICIES

Foreign Exchange

The Central Bank of Albania (BOA) formulates, adopts, and implements foreign exchange policies and maintains a supervisory role in foreign exchange activities in accordance with the Law on the Bank of Albania No. 8269 and the Banking Law No. 9662. Foreign exchange is regulated by the 2009 Regulation on Foreign Exchange Activities no. 70 (FX Regulation).

The BOA maintains a floating free exchange rate regime for its domestic currency, the Lek (ALL). Foreign exchange is readily available at banks and exchange bureaus. However, when exchanging large amounts, preliminary notification may be necessary as the exchange market in Albania remains small. The ALL has remained stable compared to the Euro, but depreciated by approximately 25 percent compared to the dollar over the past year (largely due to Euro depreciation). Albanian authorities do not engage in currency arbitrage and do not view it as an efficient instrument to achieve competitive advantage.

Remittance Policies

The Banking Law does not impose any restrictions on the purchase, sale, holding, or transfer of monetary foreign exchanges. However, the Law on the Bank of Albania authorizes the bank to temporarily restrict the purchase, sale, holding, or transfer of foreign exchanges in order to preserve the foreign exchange rate or its official reserves. In practice, the Bank of Albania rarely uses such measures. The last time was in 2009 when the Bank temporarily tightened supervision rules over liquidity transfers by domestic banks to their foreign mother banks due to the widespread lack of liquidity in international financial markets. It also asked banks to not distribute dividends and to use them to increase shareholders' capital instead. The Bank lifted these restrictions in 2010.

The Law on Foreign Investment guarantees the right to transfer and repatriate any funds associated with an investment from Albania into a freely usable currency at a market-clearing rate. Only licensed entities (banks) may conduct foreign exchange transfers and waiting periods depend on office procedures adopted by the banks. Both Albanian and foreign citizens entering or leaving the country must declare assets in excess of ALL 1,000,000 (USD 8,000) in hard currency and/or precious items. Failure to declare such assets is considered a criminal act and punishable by confiscation of the assets and imprisonment. Legal parallel markets are not in place in Albania as the financial sector does not make use of convertible or negotiable instruments.

Although the Foreign Exchange Regulation provides that residents and non-residents may transfer capital within and into Albania without any restrictions, capital transfers out of Albania are subject to certain documentation requirements. Physical persons must submit a request indicating the reasons for the capital transfer, the amount of capital transferred outside the territory of Albania, and the address to which the capital will be transferred. Such persons also must submit a declaration on the source of the funds to be transferred. In January 2015, The FX Regulation was amended and the requirement to present the documentation showing the preliminary payment of taxes related to the transaction was removed.

Albania is a member of the Council of Europe Committee of Experts on the Evaluation of Anti-Money Laundering Measures and the Financing of Terrorism (MONEYVAL), a Financial Action Task Force-style regional body.

3. EXPROPRIATION AND COMPENSATION

The Albanian Constitution guarantees the right of private property. According to Article 41, the expropriation or limitation in the exercise of a property right only can occur in the public interest and with fair compensation. In the post-communist period, expropriation has been limited to land needed for the public interest, mainly infrastructure projects such as roads, energy infrastructure, water works, airports, etc. Compensation has generally been below market value and owners have complained that the compensation process is slow and unfair. Civil courts are responsible for resolving such complains.

Political change also can be of concern to foreign investors. Following 2013 elections and a peaceful transition of power, the new government revoked or attempted to renegotiate numerous concession agreements, licenses, and contracts signed by the previous government with both domestic and international investors. This has occurred in years past, as well.

There are many ongoing disputes regarding properties confiscated during the communist regime. Identifying land titles and ownership in Albania is a perpetual problem that makes restitution for expropriated properties extremely difficult. The restitution and compensation process started in 1993, but has been slow and marred by corruption. Many U.S. citizens of Albanian origin have long-running restitution disputes. Court cases tend to drag on for years without a final decision, forcing many to take their case to the European Court of Human Rights in Strasburg, France. The Court has so far issued 18 decisions in favor of Albanian citizens in civil cases involving protection of property with an assessed financial cost of approximately USD 12 million. Reportedly there are in total 379 applications pending for consideration. Even once a case is settled in Strasburg, enforcement of the decision is often slow or nonexistent.

The GOA has presented three methods of compensation for confiscation claims: restitution; compensation of property with similarly valued land in a different location; and cash settlement/financial compensation. In practice however, a lack of funding and the large amount of claimants has significantly slowed the restitution process.

Albanian governments have not engaged in expropriation actions against U.S. investments, companies or representatives. There have been limited cases when the government has revoked licenses, especially in the mining and energy sectors, based on contract violation claims.

4. DISPUTE SETTLEMENT

Legal System, Specialized Courts, Judicial Independence, Judgments of Foreign Courts

Albania has a civil law system similar to that of most other European countries. The Albanian Constitution provides for the separation of legislative, executive, and judicial branches; thus supporting the independence of the judiciary. The Civil Procedure Code enacted in 1996 governs civil procedure in Albania. The civil court system consists of district courts, appellate courts, and the Supreme Court. The district courts are organized in specialized sections according to the subject of the claim: civil disputes; family disputes; and commercial disputes.

In 2012, Albania approved the law on administrative courts, and these courts began operation in late 2013. The administrative courts of first instance, the Administrative Court of Appeal, and the Administrative College of the High Court now adjudicate administrative disputes. Administrative courts aim to enable fast adjudication of administrative cases. The Constitutional Court reviews whether laws or subsidiary legislation comply with the Constitution and in limited cases protects and enforces the constitutional rights of citizens and legal entities.

Parties may appeal the judgment of the first instance courts within 15 days, while Appellate Court judgments must be appealed to the Supreme Court within 30 days. A lawsuit against an administrative action is submitted to the administrative court within 45 days from notification and the law stipulates short procedural timeframes enabling faster adjudication of administrative disputes.

Albania does not have a specific commercial code, but defines commercial legislation through a series of commercial laws. Relevant laws include: Foreign Investment Law; Commercial Companies Law; Bankruptcy Law; Environmental Law; Corporate and Municipal Bonds; Transport Law; Maritime Code; Secured Transactions Law; Employment Law; Taxation Procedures Law; Banking Law; Insurance and Reinsurance Law; Concessions Law; Mining Law; Energy Law; Water Resources Law; Waste Management Law; Excise Law; Oil and Gas Law; Gambling Law; Telecommunications Law; Value Added Law; Sports Law; etc.

Albania is signatory of the New York Convention and foreign arbitration awards may be enforced in local courts. Investors often cite corruption and inefficiency in the judiciary as a serious impediment to conducting business in Albania and often seek out international arbitration as an alternative means for dispute resolution.

Bankruptcy

The Bankruptcy Law governs the reorganization or liquidation of insolvent businesses. It sets out non-discriminatory and mandatory rules for the repayment of the obligations by a debtor in a bankruptcy procedure. The law establishes statutory time limits for insolvency procedures, professional qualifications for insolvency administrators, and an Agency of Insolvency Supervision to regulate the profession of insolvency administrators. A simplified insolvency procedure for small businesses is also in place.

A bankruptcy procedure can be initiated by debtors, creditors, as well as by tax authorities. Tax authorities can request a bankruptcy procedure when the subject reports financial losses three years in a row. The bankruptcy proceedings can initiate when the debtor is unable to pay the obligations at the maturity date. In addition, the inability to pay the obligations in the near future shall also be a reason for the debtor to file for bankruptcy.

According to the provisions of the Bankruptcy Law the initiation of the bankruptcy proceeding would suspend the enforcement of the claims of all the creditors against the debtor subject to bankruptcy. Creditors of all categories should submit their claims to the bankruptcy administrator in order to be treated under the bankruptcy proceeding. The Bankruptcy Law provides specific treatment for different categories, dividing them into: secured creditors; unsecured creditors; and unsecured creditors of lower ranking (i.e. those whose claims would be paid after all the secured and unsecured creditors are satisfied). The claims of the secured creditors will be satisfied by the assets of the debtor, which secure such claims under security agreements. The claims of the unsecured creditors will be paid out of bankruptcy estate excluding the assets used for payment of the secured creditors, following the priority ranking described under the Albanian Civil Code.

Pursuant to the provisions of the Bankruptcy Law, the creditors have the right to establish a creditors committee and the creditors' assembly. The creditors' committee is appointed by the Commercial Section Courts, before the first meeting of the creditors' assembly. The creditors' committee represents the secured creditors, the unsecured creditors with the larger claims, and creditors with the small claims. The committee has the right: (i) to support and supervise the activities of the insolvency administrator; (b) to request and receive information about the insolvency proceedings; c) to inspect the books and records; and d) to order an examination of the revenues and cash balances.

In the event that the creditors and administrator agree that reorganizing the company is the best option, the administrator of the bankruptcy shall prepare a reorganization plan and submit it to the court for authorizing implementation.

According to the law on bankruptcy, foreign creditors have the same rights as domestic creditors with respect to the commencement of, and participation in, a bankruptcy proceeding. The claim is valued as of the date the insolvency proceeding is opened. Claims expressed in foreign currency are converted into Albanian currency according to the official exchange value applicable to the place of payment at the time of the opening of the proceeding.

The Albanian Criminal Code provides for several criminal offences in bankruptcy such as: (i) the bankruptcy provoked intentionally; (ii) concealment of bankruptcy status; (iii) concealment of assets after bankruptcy; and (iv) failure to comply with the obligations arising under bankruptcy proceeding.

According to 2015 Doing Business Report of the World Bank, Albania ranks 44 out of 189 countries in the insolvency index. A reference analysis of the 'resolving insolvency' can be found here: http://www.doingbusiness.org/data/exploreeconomies/albania/resolving-insolvency/

The number of bankruptcy cases in Albania is limited, with only a handful of bankruptcy proceedings filed during 2014.

Investment Disputes

In the past ten years, there have been two major investment disputes between the Albanian government and U.S. companies. Both disputes were settled in International Arbitration, one in favor of the U.S. company and the other in favor of the Albanian government. In both instances, both parties respected and enforced the findings of the arbitration.

The recent dispute between the GOA and the Czech power group, CEZ, following its failed privatization of the Albanian Electricity Distribution company was settled outside of court.

International Arbitration

Under the Albanian Constitution, ratified international agreements prevail over domestic legislation. Albania is a member state to the International Centre for the Settlement of Investment Disputes (ICSID Convention). It is also a signatory to the convention on the Recognition and Enforcement of Foreign Arbitral Awards (1958 New York Convention). They have ratified the 1927 Convention and the European Convention on Arbitration (Geneva Convention).

In order for an arbitration award locally recognized the claimant must enforce the award before the Court of Appeals.

The procedure for the recognition of a foreign arbitral award typically last around one month and either party may appeal the Court's decision to the Supreme Court. The appeal must be filed within 30 days from the date of decision or notification of the other party (if absent).

The possibility of bringing an action before the local court in order to avoid arbitration proceedings is remote. According to explicit provisions in the Albanian Code of Civil Procedure, if a party brings actions before local courts despite the parties' agreement to arbitrate, the court would, upon motion of the other party, dismiss the case without entertaining the merits of the case. The decision of the court to dismiss the case can be appealed to the Supreme Court, which has 30 days to consider the appeal.

An alternative to dispute settlement via the courts is private arbitration or mediation. Parties can engage in arbitration when they have agreed to such a provision in the original agreement, when there is a separate arbitration agreement, or by mutual agreement at any time when the dispute arises. Legislation distinguishes arbitration of international disputes from arbitration of domestic disputes in that the parties involved in an international dispute may agree to settle through either a domestic or foreign arbitration tribunal. Mediation also is applicable in resolving all civil, commercial, and, family disputes and is regulated by the law "On Dispute Resolution through Mediation." Arbitral awards are final and enforceable and can be appealed only in cases foreseen in the Code of Civil Procedure. Mediation is final and enforceable in the same way.

There are no consolidated institutions for dispute resolution through arbitration and arbiters are appointed ad hoc in compliance with the provisions of the Code of Civil Procedure. While for the mediation process, the law provides for the establishment of the National Chamber of Mediators and Chambers of Mediators as institutions to perform mediation. Mediators are licensed and registered at the Mediators Register at the Ministry of Justice, which maintains a list of mediators from which the parties can choose.

The provisions with respect to arbitration procedures and the recognition and enforcement of the foreign awards are stipulated in the Albanian Code of Civil Procedure. Albania does not have a separate law on arbitration. Although the arbitration chapter of the Code of Civil procedure stipulates only the rules for domestic arbitration, the country is signatory of the 1958 New York Convention and as such, recognizes the validity of the written arbitration agreements and arbitral awards in a contracting state.

ICSID Convention and New York Convention

.Albania is a member state to the International Centre for the Settlement of Investment Disputes (ICSID Convention). It is also a signatory to the convention on the Recognition and Enforcement of Foreign Arbitral Awards (1958 New York Convention).

Duration of Dispute Resolution

The Albanian Code of Civil Procedure requires the courts to reach a judgment within a reasonable amount of time, but it does not provide for a specific deadline when referring to commercial disputes. Reaching a final judgment in a commercial litigation may take up to several years if all the stages of the process are exhausted.

The procedure for the recognition of a foreign arbitral award should take on average approximately one month, however in certain cases this decision may be appealable. An appeal against a court decision that recognizes a foreign arbitral award does not automatically suspend the effects of the enforcement.

5. PERFORMANCE REQUIREMENTS AND INVESTMENT INCENTIVES

WTO/TRIMS

Albania does not have any performance requirements that are inconsistent with the World Trade Organization (WTO) Trade-Related Investment Measures (TRIMs) obligations. Albanian law does not impose performance requirements on foreign or domestic investors. Furthermore, the bilateral investment treaty between the two countries prohibits either party from mandating or enforcing performance requirements as a condition for the establishment, acquisition, expansion, management, conduct, or operation of a covered investment.

Investment Incentives

The Albanian Investment Development Agency (www.aida.gov.al) is the best source to find incentives offered across a variety of sectors. Distinct from the incentives listed below, individual parties may negotiate additional incentives directly through AIDA or with the Ministry of Economy, Trade, Tourism and Entrepreneurship.

The hydrocarbons sector, exploration and exploitation: Companies operating in the oil and gas extraction industry pay profit tax at the rate of 50 percent (different from the flat 15 percent corporate income tax applicable for all other taxpayers) after deduction of all capital expenditure and operating and administrative expenses, in accordance with the respective petroleum sharing agreement signed with the government (PSA are negotiated on a case by case basis).

The import of goods or services relating to the performance of exploration/research phase of petroleum operations, carried out by contractors who work for these operations, is VAT exempt.

Energy sector: Cement and iron imported for the construction of HPPs is VAT exempt.

Foreign tax credit: Albania applies foreign tax credits rights even in case there is no double tax treaty in place with the country where the tax is paid. If a double taxation treaty is in force, double taxation is avoided either through an exemption or by granting tax credit up to the amount of the applicable Albanian corporate income tax rate (currently 15 percent).

Corporate income tax exemption: Film studios and cinematographic productions, licensed and funded by the National Cinematographic Centre are exempted from paying corporate income tax.

Loss carry forward for corporate income tax purposes: Fiscal losses can be carried forward for three consecutive years (the first losses are used the first). However, they can't be carried forward if more than 50 percent of direct or indirect ownership of the share capital or voting rights of the taxpayer is transferred (changed) during the tax year.

Tax exemption of dividends designated for investments: Dividends and profit share paid by a resident or non-resident company to a resident taxpayer will not be subject to corporate income tax for the resident taxpayer. This applies, despite the participation quote, in amounts or number of shares, in shareholder capital of the voting rights or participation in initial capital of the beneficiary.

Incentives for manufacturing sector

Lease of public property: Government of Albania can lease public property of more than 500 m2, or grant a concession for the symbolic price of 1 euro if the properties will be used for manufacturing activities with an investment exceeding 10 million euro, or for inward processing activities. The GOA can also lease public property or grant a concession for the symbolic price of 1 euro for investments of more than 2 million euro on activities that address social and economic issues in a certain area, as well as activities related to sport, culture, tourism and cultural heritage. Criteria and terms are decided on a by case basis by the Council of Ministers.

Manufacturing activities are exempt from VAT on machinery and equipment.

The employer is exempt from the social security tax payment for 1 year for all new employees.

The state pays the salaries for 4 months for the new employees and offers various financing incentives for job training.

VAT credit for fuel: Taxpayers whose main business activity is the production of bricks and tiles and the transport of goods with technological means are allowed to credit VAT on the purchase of fuel used wholly and exclusively for their business activities, up to the limit of a certain percentage of the taxpayer's total annual turnover.

Manufacturing sector obtains VAT refunds immediately in the case of zero risk exporters, within 30 days if the taxpayer is an exporter, and within 60 days in the case of other taxpayers.

Apparel and footwear producers are exempt from 20 percent VAT on raw materials as long as the finished product is exported. In 2011, the GOA also removed customs tariffs for imported apparel and raw materials in the textile and shoe industries (e.g. leather used for clothes, cotton, viscose, velvet, sewing accessories, etc.)

Research and Development

The Agency for Research, Technology and Innovation (ARTI), is a public, legal institution whose mission is to evaluate, finance, monitor and manage programs and projects in the fields of science, technology and innovation in Albania. ARTI (http://www.akti.gov.al/) aims to fund projects in the field of Small and Medium Business as well as transfer, modernization and renewal of their technologies. The Agency is funded by the state budget, donations by both domestic and foreign individuals and private sector, EU programs and projects, from specific countries and partner organizations. There are no restrictions to apply for research and development projects for foreign firms operating in Albania.

Performance Requirements

Although visa, residence, and work permit requirements are straightforward and do not pose an undue burden on potential investors, the Law on Foreigners requires foreign investors to prove that foreign employees are less than 10 percent of total workforce before granting a work permit.

Data Storage

According to the current legislation in force, companies that have sensitive data (mostly in telecommunications, banking, energy sector, etc.) are not authorized to transfer data abroad. In order to do so, they need to get approvals and fulfill certain security criteria. As such, many companies operating in Albania are returning their data inside Albania. The two large private datacenters in Albania belong to the telecom operator Albtelecom and Albanian Telecommunication Union.

6. RIGHT TO PRIVATE OWNERSHIP AND ESTABLISHMENT

Albanian law permits private ownership and establishment of enterprises and property. Foreign investors do not need additional permission or authorization beyond that required of domestic investors. The government applies restrictions only on the purchase of real estate: agricultural land cannot be purchased by foreign individuals or foreign companies, but may be rented for up to 99 years. Commercial property may be purchased, but only if the proposed investment is worth three times the price of the land. There are no restrictions on the purchase of private residential property.

Both foreign and domestic investors continue to experience significant issues in resolving property disputes arising from unclear or incomplete documentation.

Foreigners can acquire concession rights on natural resources and on resources of the common interest, as defined by the Law on Concessions and Public Private Partnerships The National Licensing Center (NLC) serves as a one-stop-shop for business licenses. More information on the types of licenses and application procedures is outlined at www.qkl.gov.al

The 2007 'Law Establishing the National Registration Center' (NRC) allows business entities to register in a single place, in one day, for one euro. More information on the NRC can be found at www.qkr.gov.al.

Foreign and domestic investors have numerous options available for organizing business operations in Albania. The 2008 'Law on Entrepreneurs and Commercial Companies,' and 'Law Establishing the National Registration Center' (NRC) allows for the following legal types of business entities to be established through the NRC: Sole Entrepreneur; Unlimited Partnership; Limited Partnership; Limited Liability Company; Joint Stock Company; Branches and Representative Offices; and Joint Ventures.

7. PROTECTION OF PROPERTY RIGHTS

Real Property

Real Estate is registered at the Immovable Property Registration Office (IPRO). The procedures are cumbersome and registrants have complained of corruption within the process. Recent changes in legislation allow a notary public to have access to real estate registers and confirm the legal ownership of property. For large transactions, it is still advisable to hire an attorney to check documents and procedures for property registration.

Property legislation has developed in a piecemeal and uncoordinated way. Immovable property rights enforcement is not efficient and is a common source of corruption allegations and lengthy legal procedures. Through the use of international donor assistance the recording system has improved. The initial property registration process has also seen progress because the GOA is committed to identifying property owners and properly registering land titles.

The process of registering property remains cumbersome and difficult to navigate. Approximately 13 percent of properties nationwide are not yet registered, mostly in urban and high value coastal areas. Illegal construction is a major impediment to securing property titles. The legalization process to address large-scale illegal construction started in 2006 and is still ongoing. There are an estimated 350,000 illegal buildings in Albania. In an attempt to legalize property and punish illegal construction, the government's National Urban Construction Inspectorate (INUK) began a campaign of building demolition in late 2013. There were credible reports that the government demolished some homes without due legal process as part of a wider campaign to demolish illegally constructed buildings. Citizens also submitted complaints that INUK ignored citizens' requests to demolish some illegal buildings while choosing to demolish other buildings about which citizens had not complained. Unresolved property issues continue to undermine efforts to develop a functional land market.

The civil court system manages property rights disputes. Decisions from civil courts often take many years and authorities often do not enforce court decisions. In 2010 there were amendments to the law on foreign investments, which granted special protection to foreign investors on property disputes. However, the new law on strategic investments aims to fill in the gap and provide to foreign investors assistance on a large variety of issues including property title.

According to the 2015 World Bank's Doing Business Report, Albania performed poorly in the registering property category, ranking 118 out of 189 economies. It takes 22 days and 6 procedures to register a property and the associated cost can reach 10 percent of the total property value.

Intellectual Property Rights

Copyright

Albania is not and never has been on the Special 301 Watch List or Priority Watch List. However, IPR infringement and theft are common due to weak legal structures and poor enforcement. Counterfeit goods are present in the local market ranging from software to garments and machines. Albanian law protects copyrights, patents, trademarks, stamps, marks of origin, and industrial designs, but there remains a significant gap between the law's intent and its enforcement. Regulators are ineffective at collecting fines and prosecutors rarely press charges for IP theft. U.S. companies should consult an attorney experienced in IPR issues and avoid potential risk by establishing solid commercial relationships and drafting strong contracts.

The Albanian government persists in failing to enact key legislation that would strengthen IPR enforcement and address shortcomings in existing legislation.

The main institutions responsible for IPR enforcement include the Albanian Copyright Office (ACO), Audiovisual Media Authority (AMA), the General Directorate of Patents and Trademarks (GDPT), the General Directorate for Customs, Tax Inspectorate, Prosecutor's Office, police, and the courts. Most IP-related fines are never collected and the few cases that the regulatory agencies refer to prosecutors are rarely enforced.

The AMA, which regulates broadcast and cable television, has been ineffective in fighting content theft in the broadcast sector due to political disputes over the composition of the Board of Directors. In November 2014, all vacancies were filled but challenges persist. The Albanian Copyright Office (ACO), established in 2006, is the main institution responsible for monitoring and implementing Albanian copyright law, but the ACO lacks administrative and institutional capacity. Law enforcement on copyrights remains virtually nonexistent and copyright violations are rampant.

The number of copyright violation cases brought to court remains low. ACO sanctions are not effective and the low fines it levies are rarely collected and do not serve as an adequate deterrent. In 2010, a 'Law on Administrative Contraventions' was adopted to improve collection of fines for infringement of copyrights, but enforcement of this law remains weak to non-existent. The ACO, along with the customs, tax and police authorities, are responsible to report on the seizure of counterfeit goods. While official figures are not available, Customs does report the quantity of counterfeit goods destroyed annually. In case of seizure, the rights holder has the burden of proof and must first inspect the goods before any further action takes place. The rights holder is also responsible for the storage and destruction of the counterfeit goods.

Patents and Trademarks

The General Directorate for Patents and Trademarks (GDPT) is responsible for the registration and administration of patents, commercial trademarks and service marks, industrial designs, and geographical indications. The 2008 law on Industrial Property was amended in 2014 to reflect EU legislation on this matter. Despite adequate legislation, the GDPT still needs further capacity building and additional human resources to be effective. Specifically, examination procedures are lengthy due to the very limited number of examiners for patents and trademarks.

Albania became a contracting party to the WIPO Patent Law Treaty and a full member of the European Patent Organization in 2010. The government became party to the London Agreement on the implementation of article 65 of the European Convention for the Patents in 2013.

For additional information about treaty obligations and points of contact at local IP offices, please see WIPO's country profiles at http://www.wipo.int/directory/en/.

Resources for Rights Holders

Contact at mission on IP issues:
Donald A. Brown
Economic and Commercial Officer
Phone: + 355 (0) 4229 3115
E-mail: BrownDA8@state.gov
Country resources:
American Chamber of Commerce: www.amcham.com.al
Address: Rr. Deshmoret e 4 shkurtit, Sky Tower, kati 11 Ap 3 Tirana, Albania
Email: info@amcham.com.al
Phone: +355 (0) 4225 9779
Fax: +355 (0) 4223 5350

8. TRANSPARENCY OF THE REGULATORY SYSTEM

Albania's regulatory system has improved in recent years but still faces challenges. Uneven enforcement of legislation, cumbersome bureaucracy, and lack of transparency are all hindrances to the business community.

Albania has adopted legislation and established agencies that superficially provide transparent rules and regulations to foster competition and attract investment. The government has amended the 2003 'Law on Protection of Competition' several times and created the Agency for the Protection of Competition in 2004. The law seeks to promote clear rules of the game. However, the legislation's uneven enforcement is one of the major reasons for distorting competition in the market. The operational independence and administrative capacity of the Competition Authority also needs to be strengthened so it can serve as an able watchdog.

Other independent agencies and bodies, including the Energy Regulator, Telecom Regulator, and other major institutions operate to ensure transparency in specific sectors. New legislation on public procurement introduced e-procurement and resulted in improved transparency in public procurements. However, as in many other areas, the proper enforcement of the law remains a challenge and problems with tender procedures are frequent. Business registration and licensing are streamlined through the one-stop-shop centers for registration and licensing. Although business registration is an easy step, licensing still remains cumbersome in some sectors. Albanian legislation includes rules on disclosure requirements, formation, maintenance and alteration of capital, mergers and divisions, takeover bids, shareholders' rights, as well as corporate governance principles. The 'Law on Accounting and Financial Statements' includes reporting provisions that stipulate large companies will apply International Financial Reporting Standards, while small and medium businesses will apply National Financial Reporting Standards.

In an effort to improve the dialogue between the public and private sector and to increase transparency in the process of drafting and approving new laws and regulations, the government established the National Economic Council (NEC) in 2014. According to the law, the NEC serves as an institution to guarantee institutional cooperation between the private and public sector. The law regulating the Council's activity clearly stipulates the principles and timeline of the consultation process. Although the participation of the business community in the consultation process has increased, issues of concern remain. Oftentimes, laws are rushed into the approval process without providing ample time for business community to comment, while at other times stakeholder input is not incorporated into the final version. Many representatives of the business community complain that the NEC has not become a forum for effective private sector consultation as it was intended to be.

9. EFFICIENT CAPITAL MARKETS AND PORTFOLIO INVESTMENT

In the absence of a stock market, the country's banking sector remains the main channel for business financing. It is sound, profitable, and well-capitalized, although the high rate of non-performing loans remains a concern. At the end of 2014, non-performing loans reached 22.8 percent of all private loans, marking the first reduction compared to their peak level of 25 percent throughout most of the 2014. However, capital adequacy at 16.8 percent -- far above Basel requirements -- indicates the sector currently has sufficient assets, which totaled USD 12 billion in 2014. The banking sector is fully private and consists of 16 banks, most of which are subsidiaries of foreign banks. The Turkish National Commercial Bank is the largest bank, with 23.5 percent of the market, followed by Austrian Raiffeisen Bank with 20.5 percent market share. The market share of Greek banks has decreased significantly in recent years, with French and Italian banks filling the void. The two main Albanian banks possess approximately 12.5 percent of sector assets.

Money and Banking System, Hostile Takeovers

Albania's banking sector weathered the financial crisis better than many of its neighbors, largely due to a lack of exposure to international capital markets and domestic housing bubbles. There is sufficient liquidity in the market to enter and exit sizeable positions. The sector remained profitable even during the peak of the financial crisis when it suffered a reduction of deposits of about 15 percent. In 2014, profits reached approximately USD 100 million with a 0.9 percent return on assets and 10.5 percent return on equities. Market concentration remains high, as the five largest banks dominate the market with about 73 percent of total assets. The Bank of Albania has the flexibility to intervene in the currency market to protect exchange rates and official reserves, but only for a period not exceeding 12 months. In 2009, following the global financial crisis, the central bank restricted the distribution of domestic banking sector profits in order to maintain sufficient liquidity in the sector but lifted the restriction in July 2010. The Bank of Albania further loosened monetary policy in 2014 and again in March 2015, with official central bank interest rates reaching a historical low of 2 percent.

Foreigners are not required to prove a residency status to establish a bank account other than the normal know your client procedures. However, in the case of U.S. citizens, they are required to fill a form accepting the disclosure of their banking data to IRS authorities in the framework of U.S. Foreign Account Tax Compliance Act requirements.

Commercial Credit

The GOA has adopted policies promoting the free flow of financial resources as a mechanism to promote any type of foreign investment in Albania. The government and Central Bank refrain from restrictions on payments and transfers for international transactions. While being a shallow FX market, banks enjoy enough liquidity to support sizeable positions. Furthermore, portfolio investments remain limited mostly to company shares, government bonds, and real estate.

The credit market is quite competitive but interest rates can be high, currently between 7 and 11.5 percent. Most mortgage and commercial loans are denominated in euros as rate differentials between local and foreign currency average 2-4 percent. Commercial banks have improved the quality and quantity of services they offer and the private sector has benefited from the expansion of these instruments. However, the high rate of non-performing loans and the economic slowdown has forced commercial banks to tighten their lending standards, making access to local capital more difficult.

10. COMPETITION FROM STATE-OWNED ENTERPRISES

The privatization process of State Owned Enterprises (SOEs) in Albania is nearly complete and the few remaining SOEs primarily are in the utilities sector. SOEs operate mostly in the electrical sector (generation, transmission, and distribution), water supply, ports, railway, insurance, postal services, and hydrocarbon sectors.

SOEs are defined as legal entities, which are entirely state-owned or state-controlled and operate as commercial companies in compliance with the Law on Entrepreneurs and Commercial Companies. There is no discrimination between public and private companies operating in the same sector. The government requires SOEs to submit annual reports and undergo independent audits. SOEs are subject to the same tax levels and procedures and same domestic accounting and international financial reporting standards as all other commercial companies. The High State Audit is the institution that audits the activity of the SOEs. They also are subject to public procurement law. The SOEs purchase and supply goods and services from and to the domestic and foreign companies.

OECD Guidelines on Corporate Governance of SOEs

There are no legal binding requirements for the SOEs to adhere to OECD guidelines. The corporate governance structure of the SOE includes the Supervisory Board and the Directorate. The Supervisory Board is comprised of 3-9 members, who are not employed by the SOE and are appointed one-third by the Ministry of Economy, one-third by the Ministry of Finance and one-third by the line ministry or institution to which the company reports. The Supervisory Board and the Shareholder's Assembly, which is the highest decision making authority, appoint the Administrator for the SOE.

Sovereign Wealth Funds

Albania doesn't have a sovereign wealth fund.

11. CORPORATE SOCIAL RESPONSIBILITY

Public awareness of corporate social responsibility (CSR) in Albania is low and CSR remains a relatively new concept for the majority of the business community. The small amount of CSR engagement in Albania primarily comes from the energy, telecommunication, heavy industry, and banking sector and tends to focus on philanthropy and environmental issues. Efforts from international organizations to promote CSR awareness, however, are beginning to bear fruit. Thanks to the efforts of the international community and large international companies, the first Albanian CSR Network was founded in March 2013 as a business-led non-profit organization. The American Chamber of Commerce also formed a CSR subcommittee to promote CSR amongst its members in 2015. The government maintains relatively robust CSR, labor and employment rights, consumer protection, and environmental protection legislation, but enforcement and implementation is inconsistent.

OECD Guidelines for Multinational Enterprises

The Corporate Governance Code for unlisted joint stock companies incorporates the OECD definitions and principles on corporate governance, but is not legally binding. The code provides guidance for Albanian companies, aiming to provide a best-practice framework above the minimum legal requirements, and assists Albanian companies in developing a sound governance framework.

12. POLITICAL VIOLENCE

Political violence is rare. Albania's June 2013 elections and subsequent September 2013 transition to a new government were peaceful. However, four protesters were shot and killed by security forces during a violent political demonstration on January 21, 2011.

Albania is a source of stability in the region and maintains friendly relations with all neighboring countries.

13. CORRUPTION

Corruption remains a persistent and pervasive problem at all levels of Albanian society. Under the Albanian Criminal Code, both active and passive corruption, abuse of office, and undue influence are considered criminal offenses. In addition to basic corruption offenses, there are specific criminal provisions addressing active and passive corruption by persons exercising public functions, high state officials and locally elected persons, judges, prosecutors, and employees of the judicial bodies and the private sector. Provisions addressing cases of bribery by foreign public officials exist while penalties for corruption in the private sector have increased. There also are provisions addressing trading in influence. The legislation on conflict of interest and declarations of assets by public officials, their spouses and adult children also is in place and was amended several times to address the loopholes and improve the efficiency. In 2012, Parliament restricted the immunity of high-level public officials and judges while 2014 amendments of the Criminal Procedure Code enabled the proper enforcement of these constitutional changes. Despite these amendments, no high-level officials have been successfully prosecuted for corruption.

Police authorities and the Prosecutor General's Office are in charge of criminal investigations and law enforcement, while the High State Audit and internal auditing units within various state institutions, inspect, assess, and report alleged cases of corruption. The High Inspectorate for the Declaration and Audit of Assets and Conflict of Interest (HIDAACI) collects and audits the annual declaration of assets and properties of around 5,000 mid- and high-level public officials in central and local executive agencies and supervises the prevention of conflicts of interest. A Joint Investigative Unit against corruption and economic crime was established in 2007 in the Tirana District Prosecution Office. The unit is a multi-agency taskforce composed of police staff from the prosecutor's offices, the state, customs and tax police, and other relevant institutions, working together on specific investigations. Based on the first unit model, seven more units were established in regions throughout Albania to prosecute corruption and economic crimes outside Tirana. In the Judiciary, the High Council of Justice is in charge of the appointment and removal of judges and prosecutors in district and appeals courts. Specialized inspectors investigate allegations of misconduct of judges and the High Council of Justice then takes the relevant disciplinary measures.

Despite legislation and governmental structures designed to fight corruption, a culture of impunity is widespread and deeply rooted in Albania. Ordinary citizens and foreign investors alike can point to the judiciary, uneven enforcement of laws and property rights, the opaque regulatory environment, and government procurement as indicators of endemic corruption. Although the number of corruption cases investigated is rising, conviction rates remain low. Furthermore, high-level corruption cases of politicians or well-connected business leaders very rarely end in conviction. Perception of corruption continues to be high and Albania ranked 110th (last in Europe) out of 174 countries in the 2014 Transparency International Corruption Perception Index.

Transparency International Albania is the main international non-governmental watchdog organization in Albania. Other NGOs perform watchdog functions regarding corruption, but the role of civil society in denouncing corruption is weak.

UN Anticorruption Convention, OECD Convention on Combatting Bribery

The government has ratified several corruption-related international treaties and conventions and is a member of major international organizations and programs dealing with corruption and/or organized crime. Albania has ratified the Civil Law Convention on Corruption (Council of Europe), the Criminal Law Convention on Corruption (Council of Europe), the Additional Protocol to Criminal Law Convention on Corruption (Council of Europe), and the United Nations Convention against Corruption (UNCAC). Albania also has ratified a number of key conventions in the broader field of economic crime, including the Convention on Laundering, Search, Seizure and Confiscation of the Proceeds from Crime (2001) and Convention on Cybercrime (2002). Albania has been a member of the Group of States against Corruption (GRECO) since the ratification of the Criminal Law Convention on Corruption in 2001 and also is a member of the Stability Pact Anti-Corruption Network (SPAI). Albania is not a member of the OECD convention on Combating Bribery of Foreign Public Officials in international Business Transactions.

Resources to Report Corruption

Resources to report corruption
Government online portal to denounce corruption
www.stopkorrupsionit.al
Transparency International
Address:
Bulevardi "Gjergj Fishta",
Projekt 2000, Kulla 5, Ap. 6,
Tirana, Albania
Email: leginet@albaniaonline.net; info@alac.al
Tel: + 355 (0) 4 226 7457

14. BILATERAL INVESTMENT AGREEMENTS

The United States and Albania signed a bilateral investment treaty in 1995, which entered into force in January 1998. This treaty ensures that U.S. investors receive national or most-favored-nation treatment and provides for dispute settlement. There is no free trade agreement or bilateral taxation treaty between the two countries.

As of December 2014, Albania has concluded bilateral investment treaties with the following countries: Austria, Azerbaijan, Belgium, Bosnia and Herzegovina, Bulgaria, China, Croatia, Cyprus, Czech Republic, Denmark, Egypt, Finland, France, Germany, Greece, Hungary, Islamic Republic of Iran, Israel, Italy, Kosovo, Kuwait, Lithuania, Macedonia, Malta, Malaysia, Moldova,

Netherlands, Poland, Portugal, Republic of Korea, Qatar, Romania, Russia, San Marino, Serbia, Slovenia, Spain, Sweden, Switzerland, Tunisia, Turkey, Ukraine, United Kingdom, and the USA.

As of December 2014, Albania has signed treaties for the avoidance of double taxation with the following countries: Austria, Belgium, Bosnia and Herzegovina, Bulgaria, China, Croatia, Czech Republic, Egypt, Estonia, France, Germany, Great Britain, Greece, Hungary, India, Ireland, Italy, Korea, Kosovo, Kuwait, Lithuania, Luxembourg, Macedonia, Malaysia, Malta, Moldova, Montenegro, Netherlands, Norway, Poland, Qatar, Romania, Russia, Serbia, Singapore, Slovenia, Sweden, Switzerland, Turkey, and United Arab Emirates.

Albania has signed also free trade agreements with the EU, CEFTA countries (Macedonia, Montenegro, Croatia, Serbia, Bosnia and Herzegovina, Kosovo, and Moldova), EFTA countries (Switzerland, Liechtenstein, Norway, and Iceland), and Turkey.

Bilateral Taxation Treaties

Albania does not have a bilateral taxation treaty with the United States.

15. OPIC AND OTHER INVESTMENT INSURANCE PROGRAMS

The Overseas Private Investment Corporation (OPIC) signed an agreement with Albania in 1991. Albania also has ratified the World Bank's Multilateral Investment Guarantees Agency (MIGA) Convention. Both instruments provide investment guarantees against certain non-commercial risks (i.e., political risk insurance) to eligible foreign investors for qualified investments in developing member countries. MIGA's coverage is against the following risks: currency transfer restriction; expropriation; breach of contract; war; terrorism; civil disturbance; and non-honoring of sovereign financial obligations. MIGA and OPIC often cooperate on projects.

In 1998, OPIC supported the Southeast Europe Equity Investment Fund (SEEF I), which invested heavily in southeastern Europe. OPIC supported its successor, SEEF II, managed by Bedminster Capital. SEEF II has invested in the Albanian health and IT sectors.

For more information on OPIC please see www.opic.gov.

For more information on MIGA please see www.miga.org.

16. LABOR

Pursuant to the Labor Code and the recently amended "Law on the Status of the Civil Employee," both individual and collective employment contracts regulate labor relations between employees and management. Albania is a member of the International Labor Organization (ILO) since 1991 and has ratified 53 ILO international labor conventions, the entire set of fundamental and governance conventions as well as two protocols. The Albanian government has established the National Council of Labor, composed of government officials, trade unions, management, and employers' associations, to improve social dialogue between stakeholders. The institutions governing the labor market include: Ministry of Welfare and Youth, Ministry of Innovation and Public Administration, National Employment Service, State Labor Inspectorate, and private actors such as employment agencies, and vocational training centers.

Albania has adopted a large variety of regulations to monitor labor abuses, but their enforcement remains weak due to persistent informality in the work force. Law 108/2013 dated March 28, 2013 On Foreigners and various decisions of the Council of Ministers regulate the employment regime in Albania. While there are no special treatments of labor in specific economic zones, the Law on Foreigners limits to 10 percent of the total the number of foreigners hired by employers in Albania.

Both employees and managers have the right to form trade unions. Trade unions are organized both at the national level (according to industrial sector) and at the company level. The Labor Code guarantees the right to strike as part of the right to negotiate wages and working conditions. However, economically driven strikes are very rare in Albania. Employment contracts are applicable both to union and non-union workers. The two main national-level trade unions, both affiliated with the International Trade Union Confederation (ITUC) are the Confederation of Trade Unions (KSSH) and the Union of the Independent Trade Unions of Albania (BSPSH). Despite claiming independence from politics, the latter is associated with opposition while the former with the current government. Employment contracts can be limited or for an unlimited period, but typically cover an unlimited period of duration if not specified in the contract. Labor code does differentiate between layoffs and firing but in general, employers are able to reduce staffing without facing extensive severance payments.

Albania has a labor force of about 1.3 million people. The official estimated unemployment rate in the last quarter of 2014 was 18 percent, but unemployment for people aged 15-29 was estimated at 34 percent. Approximately 42 percent of the population is self-employed in the agricultural sector. Almost 1.2 million Albanians have emigrated to Italy and Greece since 1991 and a majority of young Albanians speak English, Italian, or Greek as a second language. Other foreign language skills are common, as well. However, since the financial crisis in 2008 and the negative economic situation in neighboring Italy and Greece, it is estimated that about 200,000 Albanian expats have returned to Albania, further increasing pressure on social services, especially in smaller towns.

While some members of the labor force are highly skilled, many work in low-skill industries or have outdated skill sets. Albania has a tradition of a strong secondary educational system, while vocational schools are less prevalent. In 2013 only 17 percent of high school pupils were enrolled in vocational schools. The new government has shifted its attention to the promotion of vocational education and in 2014 enrollment has increased by 40 percent. University education remains uneven and studying abroad remains the best option for qualified students. In 2014, the average salary in public administration was ALL 53,800 (USD 445) per month. Since July 2013, the minimum monthly wage applicable to both public administration and the private sectors is ALL 22,000 (USD 183), which still is among the lowest in the region.

17. FOREIGN TRADE ZONES/FREE PORTS/TRADE FACILITATION

Albania does not have any free trade zones or free ports, although the legislation exists to create them. The Law on the Establishment and Functioning of Economic Zones regulates the establishment of free trade zones and industrial parks near ports, airports, or at the crossroads of international transport. The Ministry of Economy proposes free trade zones, which are ratified by the Council of Ministers on a case-by-case basis. The Council of Ministers has the power to define the status of the zone (free zone or industrial park), area and boundaries, the economic activities to be performed within the zones, time constraints, the type of permission (lease, concession, etc.), and selection procedures for the developer. Industrial parks may be used for production, manufacturing, agro-processing, export-import, and supporting activities.

Following the approval of the Law on the Establishment and Functioning of Economic Zones in 2007, the government approved the construction of the following economic zones:

Economic zone with the status of Industrial Park in Koplik, Shkoder.
Economic zone with the status of Industrial Park in Shengjin, Lezhe.
Economic zone with the status of Industrial Park in Spitalle.
Economic zone with the status of Industrial Park in Vlora.
Economic zone with the status of Industrial Park in Shkoder.
Economic zone with the status of Industrial Park in Lezhe.
Economic zone with the status of Industrial Park in Laknas, Tirana.

Economic zone with the status of Free Zone in a territory in Vlora.
Economic zone with the status of Industrial Park in Rrashbull, Durres.
However, none of these projects has moved beyond the licensing phase.

Recently, the GOA approved another free economic zone located in Spitalle, in the vicinity of the Durres port, the major port in Albania. The zone will be granted to a developer for 35 years with the symbolic price of 1 euro and will host manufacturing, agro processing, warehousing, services, and trading activities. The GOA is expected to open a tender shortly for the selection of the developer. Fiscal incentives are defined on a per case basis for the free economic zones and the government currently is in the process of approving legislation defining the fiscal incentives for the free economic zones.

18. FOREIGN DIRECT INVESTMENT AND FOREIGN PORTFOLIO INVESTMENT STATISTICS

Table 2: Key Macroeconomic Data, U.S. FDI in Host Country/Economy

	Host Country Statistical source*		USG or international statistical source		USG or International Source of Data: BEA; IMF; Eurostat; UNCTAD, Other
Economic Data	Year	Amount	Year	Amount	
Host Country Gross Domestic Product (GDP) ($M USD)	2013	12,900	2013	12,900	www.worldbank.org/en/country
Foreign Direct Investment	Host Country Statistical source*		USG or international statistical source		USG or international Source of data: BEA; IMF; Eurostat; UNCTAD, Other
U.S. FDI in partner country ($M USD, stock positions)	2013	69	2013	(2)	BEA data available 3/19/14 at http://bea.gov/international/direct_investment_multinational_companies_comprehensive_data.htm
Host country's FDI in the United States ($M USD, stock positions)	2013	Not available	2013	0	BEA data available 3/19/14 at http://bea.gov/international/direct_investment_multinational_companies_comprehensive_data.htm
Total inbound stock of FDI as %	2013	0	2013	0	

host GDP					

* Domestic Sources: Bank of Albania http://www.bankofalbania.org/

Albanian Institute of Statistics http://www.instat.gov.al/

Table 3: Sources and Destination of FDI

The data on Albania on the IMF website http://cdis.imf.org are available only for inward investments for 2013. Data from IMF are compatible with data provided by Bank of Albania on FDI.

Direct Investment from/in Counterpart Economy Data					
From Top Five Sources/To Top Five Destinations (US Dollars, Millions)					
Inward Direct Investment			Outward Direct Investment		
Total Inward	3,929	100%	Total Outward	Not available	100%
Greece	1,473	38%			
Canada	1087	28%			
Austria	520	13%			
Netherlands	482	12%			
Turkey	384	10%			
"0" reflects amounts rounded to +/- USD 500,000.					

Source: IMF Coordinated Direct Investment Survey

Table 4: Sources of Portfolio Investment

Portfolio investment data for Albania are unavailable.

IMPORTANT BUSINESS AND LEGAL CONTACTS

CONTACT FOR MORE INFORMATION

Donald Brown
Economic and Commercial Officer
U.S.A. Embassy Tirana, Albania
Rruga Elbasanit, Nr. 103
Tirana, Albania
+355 4 224 7285
BrownDA8@state.gov

MACROECONOMIC ENVIRONMENT

Since 1991, the Albanian economy has undergone a substantial transformation from a command economy towards a free market economy.

Since 1993, the pace of economic reform has been quick and well co-ordinated. It aims at stabilisation of macro-economic indicators, price liberalisation, controlled inflation, wage restraints, efficiency-oriented structural reforms (infrastructure, energy etc.). The structure of the economy, has changed in response to the new economic environment. The service sector, which in the past was much underdeveloped, has boomed and continues to show high growth rates. In 2004 the country experienced economic contraction as a result of a general crisis after the collapse of the country's "pyramid schemes". Successful attempts made by the Albanian authorities to stabilise the economy were reflected in the achievements made during the second half of 2004, particularly after the signing of the IMF Assistance Agreement. An ESAF-2 was signed during the first half of 2005 as a support for the further consolidation of structural reforms during te next three years. The Government program for 2005 expects a 10 % increase in GDP growth rate and an inflation rate of the same level.

INDICATORS ON COST FACTORS

PERSONAL COST

SALARY

In Albania employer and employee are free to agree about salaries. However, in urban areas the following monthly salaries by categories are observed:

qualification	average grosssalary in Lek
unqualified work	8.000 - 15.000*
semiskilled work	6.000 - 9.000
skilled workman	15.000 - 20.000
handicraft master	18.000 - 30.000
engineer	20.000 - 80.000
administrative	20.000 - 50.000
manager	20.000 - 35.000

1 USD = 150 Lek (May 1999) Personal careers and long term experiences are taken under consideration. Generally, salaries paid in rural areas are lower than in urban areas

SOCIAL COST

The package of social costs arrives on 45,9 % of employee's gross salary. The repartition of the 45,9 % is as follows:

Object of insurance	*% to pay employer*	*in chargeof employee*	*Tota*
General insurance	34.2 %	11.7 %	45.9 %

TAX ON WAGES

Tax debtors are physical person resident in Albania for a period of 183 days during a taxable year. Individual being subject of retail sale are excluded from income tax. Artistic and scientific work are generally taxed by 5 % of the income. Object of tax are all salaries, rewarding fees for artistic, scientific and literary works, and revenues from house or ground renting of more than 10 000 leks. For wages 10 000 - 20 000 lek the tax is 5%, for 20 000 - 30 000 lek the tax is 500 lek + 10 %, for 30 000 - 50 000 lek the tax is 1500 lek + 15 %, and for wages 50 000 - 80 000 lek the tax is 4500 lek + 20 % Exempted from taxes are revenues of insurance and donations.

INSURANCE

INSIG is the first insurance entity in Albania. It offers various types of insurance such as insurance against fire and other risks, C A R, E A R machinery insurance, KASKO, Green Card, agriculture insurance, insurance of livestock, marine hull, travel insurance, insurance from burglary, travel health insurance, credit insurance, reinsurance and coinsurance activity. Under its Private Sector Recovery Project. The International Development Association the World Bank has approved a credit of US$ 10 million to the Albanian Government. The supporting of Political Risks Guaranty Facility. This Political risks guarantee facility is administrated by the Albanian Guarantee Agency and covers a range of political risks, including risks of civil disturbance. Thereby generating confidence among potential exporters to and investors in Albania.

CAPITAL MARKET

CREDIT RATES

Traditionally, commercial banks have been state-owned, but not the first private commercial banks are being established. Commercial banks offer mainly short term credits but provide also medium term credit lines geared to small and medium enterprises which are sponsored by bilateral and / or multilateral donors. The following interest rates are applied:

Short term credit, in lek	25 - 28%
Medium term credit, in lek	28-30 %
Long term credit, in lek	28-30 %

Generally, the national capital market is restricted to nationals. Only those foreign who have created joint ventures with local investors are eligible.

WATER

Prices for water are fixed by law at 60 Lek/m3 on community level. In Tirana, the following tariffs are applied:

Group 1	Hood and beverage, slaughters	20 lek/m3
Group 2	All other manufactured sectors	30 lek/m3
Group 3	Service sector	52 lek/m3

STRATEGY OF PRIVATIZATION

BASIC LEGAL FRAME

The basic law on which the process of privatisation is based is that of August 10, 1991, No.7512" On Sanction and Protection of Private Property, Free Initiative and Privatisation." This law is considered liberal, because it allows enough space for the regulation of privatisation process through the Government's decisions. At the same time is very broad, because it included many aspects of market economy.

Privatisation was only one part of this law. It defined the National Agency of Privatisation (NAP) as the central institution responsible to transfer state property into private property. NAP sets the rules and procedures for the privatisation up to the total transfer of ownership. A critical point in this law was the existence of many difficulties for the foreigners to participate in Albanian privatisation process. This was corrected only partially, by the Law No. 7653, "For some changes in Law No. 7512", dated 23.12.1992. Only five years later, the Decree No.1632, dated 1.11. 1996 " For some amendments of Law No.7512 and the Law No. 8159, "For approving with changes of decree No. 1632..", allowed definitely foreigners to buy sites and state properties through different privatisation methods, including Mass Privatisation. Law No.8159, dated 7.11.1996, defined the Ministry of Privatisation as the leading institution for the privatisation process and the NAP was independent by the Ministry of Privatisation. Law No. 7638, dated 19.11.1992, "On Commercial Companies" This law defines the forms of the organisation of commercial companies in the Republic of Albania. It clearly defines the forms of the organisation of commercial companies in the Republic of Albania. It clearly defines the right and duties of the partners in various types of companies, the main conditions including the contracts and statues of the companies, limitation as well as the rights of solving disagreements. It defines the rules, regulations and deadlines for the registration of existing companies and those to be founded in the future. This law is the base for registering and functioning of joint-stock companies (corporatisation).

Law No.7926, dated 20.4.1995 " On transformation of State-Owned Enterprises in Commercial Companies". The aim of this law was to make the corporatization of SOEs the first step of privatisation (mass privatisation in particularly). The law declared the every enterprise should be transformed in one or several anonymous or limited companies. In every one of them would be created a supervisory board. The whole transformation procedures had to be finished in less than four months.

The law no. 7926, is as well a law on ownership, because it defines the state institution responsible for the ownership of the state equity. The state as unique owner, was represented by the Ministry of Finance during 1995 - 199, by the Ministry of Privatisation from June 1996 to June 2004 and since 2004 by the Ministry of Public Economy and Privatisation. Implementation of the Law no.7926, faced many difficulties. In particular the time for transformation of SOEs (less than four months) was an utopia. Also many enterprises could no be transformed, because their debts were very much higher than their equity. There were changes in the articles of this law several times. The most important was the President Decree No. 1631, "For some changes in the Law No.7926..." (see annex 1, d.13). This Decree charged the Ministry of Privatisation to finish the transformation of SOEs.

President's Decree No. 1030, "On Issuing and Distribution of Privatisation Vouchers " (see annex 1, D2), approved with some changes by the Law No. 7918. (see annex 1, L22). This decree created the legal base for the privatisation of the state property by MPP. All the citizens over 18-years-old profited vouchers. Only those , who had obtained properties free of charge from the privatisation process, would not get any voucher. Vouchers have a nominal value, they are anonymous and tradable in the free market. Foreigners were not allowed to own vouchers until November 1996)Law 8162, dated 1.11.1996). Bank of Albania is charged to emit vouchers according to the criteria defined by the Ministry of Finance. The Savings Bank is charged with the registration and distribution of privatisation vouchers.

The privatisation of non- strategic SOEs is regulated by Council of Ministers Decisions (CMDs), until now. While the privatisation of strategic sectors is mostly regulated by laws. Some of them are:

- Law No. 7963, dated 13.7.1995 "On the privatisation of the Electrical Power Sector" (see Annex 1, L28).
- Law No. 7973, dated 26.6.1995 "On concessions and participation of private sector in public service and infrastructure" (see Annex 1, L30)
- Law No. 8026, dated 9.11.1995 "On the privatisation of the commercial companies of mining sector" (see Annex 1, L35)
- Law No. 8103, dated 28.3.1996 "On privatisation of Water Supply, and Waste Water Collection Enterprises" (see Annex 1, L46).

The privatization process is still considered to be the crucial point of the economic reform in transition countries it addresses.The interests of different groups and also dynamically helps the re-dimensioning of the role of the state in various aspects. In Albania, privatization started with the privatization of the trade and services networks in all the districts in the country, and continued with the privatization of small and medium sized enterprises, and eventually the massive privatization program for large enterprises. The privatization program that is being prepared by the Government includes the completion of privatization of medium enterprises , as well as privatization of the most strategic sectors of the country economy.

The program covers 80% of the overall assets of the economy in oil, electric power, telecommunication, transport infrastructure, water resources and tourism . The main factor is ensuring sustained economic growth is the attraction of private foreign capital to recover, and use efficiently, the electric power and mineral resources in the country. Within this framework, the Government considers as necessary steps to guarantee, the success of its economic program (i) further liberalization of the economy in these strategic sectors, that are still state monopoly and implementation of the privatization program. Considering the importance of the privatization program the Government has prepared the Strategic Sectors Privatization Strategy. According to this strategy, all enterprises or companies with state owned capital in the strategic sectors of the economy are considered as potential candidates for privatization.

The main sectors privatizating are:

- Small and medium-sized industrial enterprises, most of which are concentrated in the capital, Tirana, and are generally perceived to offer low-risk opportunities for investment;
- Large enterprises in the mining and utilities sectors;
- Electric Power Corporation, the electricity monopoly, which will probably contract out its management before privatization;
- The three state-owned commercial banks, which are to undergo significant restructuring

before they are sold. Under the guidance of the International Monetary Fund (IMF) and the World Bank, the Government is preparing to liquidate at least partially the National Commercial Bank and the Rural Commercial Bank.

Albania's oil reserves are estimated at some 550 million tons and both onshore and offshore exploration has aroused the interest of international oil companies. Early in 2005, the Government signed 5 oil exploration agreements with two international consortia covering six onshore blocks.

PRIVATIZATION HISTORY

The Albanian economic crisis of 1990 was not only a characteristic of Albania, but of all the Eastern and Central European countries, which had already taken the political decision of changing the system. Statistics like 44% decrease in the industrial production, 30.3% unemployment rate, 237% inflation rate in 1992 were recorded only in Albania which would experience the most difficult transition period. Such a situation arose the necessity of an accelerated reform, the most important part of which should be the property transformation through the privatisation process.

These enterprises called "industrial gigantic enterprises" like the metallurgical enterprise, petroleum and mining enterprises, chemicals enterprise and almost all the economy sectors were going through difficult moments, lacking proper production structures, being overpopulated and having production for production, while the market was in a miserable state lacking even the basic goods for living. The economic change in Albania, as in all the other ex-communist countries, started with the "simple to implement" reforms like liberalisation of prices, liberalisation of foreign trade and exchange rate, privatisation of small service and production units etc.

The legal basis that supported the process of privatisation in 1991 and which is still valid is Law 7512 of August 1991 "On the sanctioning and protection of private property, free initiative, private independent activities and privatisation". The approval of this law, which had the consensus of the first Albanian pluralist parliament, opened the path to a very fast privatisation of the small units, shops, fishing facilities, vehicles and machinery, which were mainly privatised by employees who used them before. Privatisation of small units in 1991-1992

Name	Number
Shops	12,000
Small units	5,000
Vehicles	2,000

Privatisation of the majority of small units opened the way to the implementation of privatisation programme of small, medium and big enterprises.

This programme would be massively implemented during 1993-1995 through the auction method in accordance with the decisions of the privatisation boards set up in all the districts of the country, in the cases of the first right of purchase for the ex-owners of the land on which the object was built or in the cases of selling the machinery to the employees using it. During 1993-

1995, 8967 objects were privatised. They were small enterprises, production lines or parts of big enterprises. 18.5% of these objects were privatised through the auction method, while 37.5% were privatised by employees, 21% by ex-owners of the land and the rest by Albanian citizens and a very few foreigners.

The conclusion was that most of the small and medium objects were privatised, but the auction method could not be successfully used for the privatisation of big and very big enterprises in the conditions of very low savings level of the population in the country, of pyramid schemes blooming and of the lack of foreign investors participation in the privatisation process. Under the influence of the quickness criteria as the main criteria of the privatisation process, at the beginning of 1995 efforts started to compile a new privatisation programme, i.e. the mass privatisation programme.

The basic principle of this method was privatisation in favour of those who had contributed in the foundation of state property, by not claiming allocation of the property to the best owner. About 1 million and one hundred thousand citizens over 18 years old would profit 74 million lek of privatisation bono. They would use these bono to privatise different enterprises transformed into joint-stock companies. The ex-political prisoners who had not used their privatisation money had a chance to use this money to buy shares in the enterprises to be purchased.

There were 97 enterprises, mainly big ones, that became object of privatisation through this programme, 17 of which were partly privatised. The creation of a shares market brought about the necessity to set up the stock exchange in Tirana, which was inaugurated at the end of 1995. Lack of the proper preparation of enterprises for privatisation, insufficient sensitisation of the population for this type of privatisation, lack of concordance between the demand and offer for shares in the market, weak economical-financial indicators of enterprises involved in this programme were some of the weak points of the mass privatisation programme, which was not have the necessary economical impact. Moreover, lack of investment funds participation in this privatisation process like intermediary financial institutions that would improve the structure of property by concentrating it in a few specialised hands had a negative impact in the results of this programme.

By analysing the process of privatisation of more than 12000 objects and small and medium enterprises, of 97 joint-stock companies, of some joint-venture companies, as well as by evaluating the stage the process had reached, the Nano Government elected in July 2004 set forth the necessity of compiling a mid-term strategy for privatisation which would re-orient and accelerate this process. Privatisation of strategic sectors like telecommunication, energy, ports, petroleum industry etc. is defined as one of the priorities of the Government economic programme.

The path was opened to privatisation by the strategy approved in the parliament in march 2005 which constitutes the basic legal and instructing document of privatisation. Following the strategy of privatisation the MoPEP and other institutions related to this process are working to prepare the sectorial policies based on a legal framework. This finally opens the way to the privatisation of the most important part of economy.

STRATEGY OF PRIVATIZATION L A W

No. 8306, dated 14.3.2005

ON THE STRATEGY FOR THE PRIVATIZATION OF STRATEGIC SECTORS Based on article 16 of law no. 7491, dated 29.4.1991 "On main constitutional provisions", on the proposal of the Council of Ministers

THE PEOPLE'S ASSEMBLY
OF THE REPUBLIC OF ALBANIA
D E C I D E D:

Article 1 Definitions

In understanding of this law: **"Right to ownership"** is the right to enjoy and make free of an object within limits defined by law. **"Right to use and develop"** are rights stemming from enjoyment of an object in order to make use of it, exploit and develop it. **"Golden share"** is a share of special characteristics which the state holds for a definite period of time in order to exercise exclusive rights on decision-making for special decisive society issues, but not for its daily work. **"Privatization vouchers"** are privatization money, privatization bonds and vouchers issued by the Bank of Albania. **"Strategic Investor"** is any juridical person who holds a financial guarantee and is a licentiate of an economic activity, at a special sector.

Article 2

The strategy for the privatization of strategic sectors prepared by the Council of Ministers is approved.

Article 3

State enterprises and trade companies with state capital operating in strategic sectors of the economy are open to privatization. By privatization is meant the total or partial transfer of the right to ownership, use and development to the juridical or physical person. Transfer of right to ownership will be realized through the sale of companies' shares or sale of special objects issued by companies or state enterprises.

Article 4 By strategic sectors of economy are meant: the industry of energy and mining, oil and gas, post, telecommunications, forests and water reserves, roadways and railroads, sea ports, airports, air and rail transport, as well as the sector of second level banks and insurance companies with total state capital.

Article 5 The definition of the form and structure of the privatization formula for companies with state capital in strategic sectors is made by law

Article 6 The Council of Ministers should, for each decision to be taken on the privatization of enterprises and companies operating in strategic sectors, foresee the necessary steps to confront social problems according to definitions made to laws for the privatization of relevant sectors.

Article 7 The privatization of these sectors will be carried out with the participation of strategic investors to whom not less than 30 percent of shares are offered. Definition criteria and procedures for the selection of strategic investors are decided by the Council of Ministers.

Article 8 Participation with privatization vouchers in order to privatize companies and enterprises of strategic sectors is defined in the privatization formula, but it should, in no case, be higher than 20 percent of the capital. The way to represent shareholders and the rights deriving from them are defined by the Council of Ministers.

Article 9 In the cases of total or partial transfer of property, the privatization formula is implemented. The privatization formula denotes the company's capital to be withheld by the state, the strategic investor or other investors, and the possible limit of participation with privatization vouchers. It will be considered case-by-case by the Council of Ministers. Each time the packet to be privatized with the participation of the strategic investor will be paid in cash.

Article 10 When the state has the right to decide on issues concerning public and strategic interests or when a certain level of control is required to be preserved, the state holds "the golden share" or a defined packet of shares under ownership. Such cases are defined on the sale contract laws for each sector. Rights stemming from "the golden shares" are defined on the sale contract. **Article 11** In order that the privatization procedures be implemented, from the moment the decision on the privatization of a company is issued, a minimum term of 6 months will be regarded during which the necessary legal transparency on data, procedures and decisions taken will be ensured.

Article 12 The Council of Ministers is in charge of formulating the necessary draft laws according to definitions and terms decided in the privatization strategy, as well as approve sub-legal acts which are necessary for the implementation of this strategy.

Article 13 The Ministry of Public Economy and Privatization with the attribute of the representative of the state property owner is in charge of carrying out the implementation of the privatization strategy on sectors as defined in article 4 (except for banking and insurance sectors conform to all relevant procedures in line with the approved legal framework.

Article 14 The Ministry of Finance is in charge of carrying out the implementation of the privatization strategy in the sector of the second level banks with total state capital and of insurance companies with total state capital, following all respective procedures in line with the approved legal framework.

Article 15 Second paragraph of article 3 of law no. 7512, dated 10.8.1991 "On sanctioning and protection of private property, free initiative, independent private activities and privatization" becomes invalid.

Article 16 This article becomes effective 15 days after being issued at the Official Gazette.
CHAIRMAN
Skënder Gjinushi

FOREIGN INVESTMENTS

INTERNATIONAL PROGRAMS IN ALBANIA

Albania is a member of the following international and European organisations:

- United Nations
- Council of Europe
- World Intellectual Property Organisation
- International Monetary Fund
- International Bank for Reconstruction and Development (World Bank)
- European Bank for Reconstruction and Development
- Islamic Development Bank

Some of the most important international aid programs in Albania are: World Bank /IDA, EC/PHARE, USA/ USAID, United Nations/ UNDP, Italy/ Project Co-financing, EC/Cross Border, Germany/GTZ, EBRD, Switzerland/ Swiss Trust Fund, Japan/OECF. Other countries that have aid throughout in Albania are: Austria, Greece, Netherland, Norway, Sweden end others.

The Albanian Economic Development Agency AEDA -operation of AEDA with international organisations and institutions-operation of AEDA with international organisations and institutions-operation of AEDA with international organisations and institutions-operation of AEDA with international organisations and institutions in its work to create a favourable investment environment in Albania, co-operates with its counterpart organisations in other countries and is an active partner in the organisations and institutions like UNIDO, UNDP, EBRD, MIGA, WAIPA, SIMEST, FINEST, etc. Growth of co-operation with counterpart bodies in other countries and exchange of experience with these bodies are indispensable for the better use of human and natural resources in Albania, and of the financial instruments and mechanisms offered to Albania by the United States and EU Throughout.

FOREIGN INVESTMENT PROTECTION AND AGREEMENTS CONCERNING AVOIDANCE OF DOUBLE TAXATION

The foreigners, either juridical or physical persons, enjoy the right of exercising different economic activities in the Republic of Albania and to invest their capital in different sectors of the Albanian economy. They are allowed to participate in economic activity and carry out investments in Albania, generally enjoying no less favorable conditions than those given to local subjects, aside from the right of landownership.

The most important law, which in reality provide a number of basic guarantees and protections for foreign investors is Law No. 7764, dated November 2,1994 " On Foreign Investments". According to this Law, all foreigners, either physical or legal persons, who intend to invest in Albania have no need to ask for permission or authorization, they shall not be expropriated or nationalized or be subject to any other equivalent measure.

The foreign investor enjoys the right to transfer all funds in currency and in kind related to his investment out of the Republic of Albania. The investor enjoys legal protection of his rights related to an investment made in Albania. Such protection is guaranteed for a dispute that arise between a foreign investor and an Albanian party. It is up to the disputing parties to define the procedures for the resolution of the dispute through arbitration.

In the event of the failure of such provision, the foreign investor has the right to submit the matter to an Albanian court or to an Arbitration Court in Tirana. In the event of a dispute involving discrimination, transfer of assets, or indirect expropriation of a foreign investment by the Albanian Government, the investor may submit the dispute to the International Center for the Settlement of Investment Disputes ("ICSID"). Special protection is guaranteed to foreign investments in Albania and to foreign investors from the states with which the Republic of Albania has signed agreements the concerning avoidance of double taxation and mutual guarantee of investments.

To provide security and protection against lost arising from political risks (thereby providing confidence to potential exporters and investors in Albania), the International development Association (the World Bank) has approved a credit of USD 10 million to the Albanian Government under its Private Sector Recovery Project to support a Political Risks Guarantee Facility, to be administered by the Albanian Guarantee Agency(AGA), a statutory corporation owned by the Government of Albania.

This is a Program to provide guarantees to private sector entities that have financial exposure in Albania for a productive purpose. The guarantee covers a range of political risks, including the risk of civil disturbance of the kind experienced in March of 2004.

BILATERAL AGREEMENTS ON PROMOTION AND PROTECTION OF RECIPROCAL INVESTMENTS AND THOSE ON AVOIDANCE OF DOUBLE TAXATION

Albania has signed a number of Bilateral Agreements on the Promotion and protection of Reciprocal Investments as an instrument for promotion foreign investment and co-operation. The following is a list of countries with which Albania has signed the Agreement (as per end 2004)

Austria	Israel	Malaysia
Bulgaria	Italy	Turkey
China	Netherlands	United Kingdom
Croatia	Poland	USA (OPIC)
Egypt	Rumania	Slovenia
France	Sweden	Switzerland
Germany	Greece	Tunisia

On the avoidance of double taxation Albania has signed Agreements with the following states (as per September 1996 - as ratified by the Albanian Parliament):

Croatia (1995)	Czech Republic (2004)
Greece (1995)	Russian Federation (1995)
Hungary (1992)	Italy (1995)
Malaysia (1995)	Poland (1995)
Turkey (1995)	Rumania (1995)

TAXATION SYSTEM

There are two level of taxation in Albania:

- at national level
- at regional level (municipality level)

Taxes at national level are by far the most important one, while those at municipality level are mostly related with hotels, restaurants, advertising, cleaning and ambulatory trade. National tax system in Albania can be classified as follows:

DIRECT TAXES:

a) On income:

- corporate income tax (tax on profit)
- personal income tax

b) On assets:

- tax on buildings
- tax on agriculture land

Both these taxes are marginal and normally doesn't play any important role

INDIRECT TAXES:

- value added tax
- excise tax
- custom duties on imports

Legal acts The main legal acts that determine the Albanian tax system are the followings

- Law nr. 7681, dated 4.3.1993 "On the administration of taxes and fees in the Republic of Albania"
- Law nr. 7677, dated 3.3.1993 " On the tax on profit"
- Law nr. 7678, dated 3.3.1993 " On excise tax"
- Law nr. 7679, dated 3.3.1993 " On small business tax"
- Law nr. 7928, dated 27.4.1995 " On value added tax"
- Law nr.7805, dated " On Property tax"

and their amendments. There are a number of circulators issued by the Ministry of Finance on the implementation of the legal acts concerning the tax system.

CORPORATE INCOME TAX (TAX ON PROFIT)

This tax applies to all legal persons, Albanian or foreigner, that exercise economic activity in territory of Albania and for that reason are considered as resident in Albania for tax purposes. This applies equally to companies with their seat in Albania and to branches of foreign companies. A tax on profit of 30% is level on profits made by resident companies in Albania, irrespective of their legal form. Normally the tax on profit is prepaid each quarter and by the end of the year the balance is set off. For companies that exercise economic activity in tourism, this tax is 40%. Companies that exercise economic activity in oil and gas exploitation pay an average of about 50% tax on profits depending on the quantity produced. Taxable income is determined according to the Law No.7671, dated 19.1.1993 "On the Accounting" and is in line with standard western business practices.

PERSONAL INCOME TAX

This tax is a progressive one. Foreigners are considered as residents in Albania and liable for personal income tax if they have an income in Albania and spend a period of more than 183 days in the country. The minimum wage and remuneration taxable is 10000 lek/month. The maximum level of personal tax is 20%. Other kind of income are taxed at 10%. Exempt the creative work is taxed at the level of 5%.

PROPERTY TAX

The tax on buildings and Agriculture land by Law 7805 on Property Tax, Revenues Tax on agriculture land which varies depending on the quality and dimensions of the agriculture activity. The tax on the building is paid by the owners of the buildings . It varies from 3 to 6 lek/m2 year for living houses depending on whether the house is ingle building, buildings in co-ownership or in the country side. For buildings for manufacturing activities or service activities including trade activity, the tax rate varies from 50 to 100 lek/m2 year. Tax on agriculture land varies depending on the quality of agriculture land from 1500 to 6000 lek/ha year.

VALUE ADDED TAX

The value added tax entered in force in July 1, 1996 and substituted the turnover tax that was applied up to that moment. The basic purpose of VAT law was to adapt the Albanian legislation to EU VAT directives and regulations. The value added tax is levied on all legal and natural persons that performs goods or services supply and is calculated based on the total sum paid for the goods or services. The tax rate is 20%.(Law 8240 dates 16.9.2004) For exports and international services the tax rates in 0%. Following the EU model certain transaction are VAT exempt e.g. services and supplies of goods related to financial activities, transaction related to shares, stocks, bonds and other securities, transactions related to bank accounts, transfers, cheques, transaction related to life insurance policy, management of pension funds, rental of residential property etc.

Business are required to register for this tax if their annual turnover exceeds 5 milion LEK (1 January 2005) Also goods supplied under the temporary importation regime for job processing activities, are VAT-exempt. VAT must be paid within the first 14 days of the next month. First, the taxpayer must have carried forward a VAT tax credit for six consecutive month, and second, the total refund claimed must exceed 400,00 lek

EXCISE TAX

Excise tax is applied on limited number of goods such as tobacco, cigars, cigarettes, alcoholic drinks, soft and fresh drinks, electrical energy, derivatives of petroleum and coffee. This tax is applied only for goods produced in Albania or imported. For goods produced in Albania the excise tax is calculated on the bases of the value of each lot of goods sold and for imported goods it is calculated on the bases of the custom value. Excise tax is not applied on above mentioned goods when they are exported. Excise tax for tobacco and tobacco products is 50% to 70% when produced in Albania and 100% to 105% when imported. Alcoholic drinks have an excise tax of 40% to 105% when produced in Albania and an additional of 25% when imported.

For derivatives of petroleum the excise tax is in the range of 25% to 85% and for some specials derivatives up to 300 %.Normally the excise tax stimulates the domestic production of goods rather than import of goods

The Government has prepared e new law on excise. In this law there will be applied the same excise system for both the products that are produced on the country and those imported.

TAX ON SMALL BUSINESS

This tax is applied on individuals exercising private economic activities. It includes learned professions as well as small scale individual ambulatory trade activity. It is calculated on the bases of the total revenues and varies from 2% to about 10% depending on the type of activity.

DIRECT TAXES ON BUSINESS

GENERAL REVIEW

There are three main direct taxes paid by registered taxpayers in the Republic of Albania .

Tax on profit, which is paid by taxpayers who exceed the VAT registration threshold.

Simplified tax on profit , which is paid by registered taxpayers having an annual circulation that does not exceed the VAT registration threshold.

Local tax on small business , which is paid by registered taxpayers having an annual circulation that does not exceed the VAT registration threshold.

The VAT registration threshold is 8 million lek per calendar year.

2.1. Principle of residence

The definition of tax residence criteria for individuals, legal entities and physical persons is closely related with the place where they pay their taxes.

Under the law, taxable Albanian residents are taxed in Albania on all incomes realized on a world level (incomes deriving inside or outside Albania). Non-residents are taxed in Albania only on incomes deriving from within the Republic of Albania .

In particular, for persons who are residents in countries with which Albania has signed Agreements (Treaties) to eliminate double taxes and when these agreements have entered in force, the provisions of these agreements will be adopted.

- The individual is regarded as an Albanian resident for tax purposes, when he has a permanent place of residence, when he has his own family, i.e. when he has vital and economic interests vested in Albania (place of vital interests), although he may work outside the country for indefinite periods of time, or have foreign citizenship.

- For tax purposes, an Albanian resident is also considered an individual who stays in Albania for a tax year, whether for the entire period or a part of it totaling above 183 days, regardless of citizenship or place of vital interests. The calculation of duration of stay in Albania includes the days of his physical presence, i.e. not only workdays, but also days of arrival, departure and holidays.

To conclude, a taxable Albanian resident is considered every individual (regardless of nationality or citizenship), who meets one or both of the above-mentioned requirements.

A legal entity is considered a taxable Albanian resident if:

- Its headquarters (head office) are in the Republic of Albania ; and/or

- Its place of business management is in the Republic of Albania .

A person is considered an Albanian taxable resident when he runs his own business and is registered as a physical trader in the Albanian Court and the Albanian Tax organs.

2.2. Subjects that pay direct taxes on business

- ***Tax on Profit***

As we pointed out, all taxpayers registered in tax organs, whose annual circulation exceeds the VAT registration threshold are subject to the tax on profit. This category of taxpayers includes:

- Legal entities created according to the Law " On trade companies" and that are registered to the VAT ;

• Legal entities established on the basis of Civil Code which have profit activities in the territory of the Republic of Albania ;

• All other legal entities established or recognized as such by special laws;

• Partnerships as defined by law;

• Legal entities, partnerships or all other groupings of persons established or organized on the basis of a foreign law and exercising their activity in the territory of the Republic of Albania through a permanent headquarter.

• Every other person regardless of their legal registration form, including traders, who are not subject to simplified tax on profits, but who are otherwise registered as Value Added Tax subjects.

• ***Simplified tax on profits***

The simplified tax on profits applies to all taxpayers who are not registered, or bound by law to register as taxpayers for Value Added Tax.

• ***Local tax on small business***

Subject to local tax on small business is every person who runs a business in the territory under the jurisdiction of a local government entity in the Republic of Albania at any given time of a calendar year and who is not subject to Value Added Tax.

2.3 Registration

• All taxpayers are registered once, in the moment they begin their economic activity, before starting their business. Taxpayers of local tax on small business and/or of simplified tariff on earnings are excluded from this rule in the year 2005. These taxpayers must re-register within the 20-th of March. If the taxpayers are not registered or re-registered in the right time the tax authorities do their registration. This registration has the same effects as if the taxpayers would have done the registration their self.

• From January 1 -st , 2006, the local tax on small business, the registration for the first time of the taxpayers is done after they are furnished from the local authorities with the License for Activity Exercise.

In the law No.8438, Dated 28.12.1998 "On the tariff of incomes" and in the law No.8978, Dated. 12.12.2002 "On local tax on small business" it was defined that all the subjects that paid these taxes would re-register every year near the tax authorities. With the 2005 Fiscal Package, these subjects are obliged to register only once in the beginning of their activity.

2.4 Direct tax levels on business

• Tax level on profit for the fiscal year that begins in January 1-rst 2005 – December 31-rst 2005 is 23%, and 20% for the coming years.

• Simplified tax on profit is 3% of the taxpayer gross incomes. For the tax basis on which this tax is calculated, no discounting expense is recognized .

• The local tax on small business is a fixed, annual and mandatory quota. Every business, whenever it is located, is taxed separately. Categories and their respective tax levels are given in the following table. The Municipality Council or the Communal Council of the territory where the business is located may increase or decrease the indicator level value by no more than 30%. Each increase or decrease equally applies to all business categories.

Indicator levels of local tax on small businesses (in '000 Lek)

No.	Type of Business	Cat. I	Cat. II	Cat. III
A	RETAIL SALE	60	20	15
B	Wholesale	60	20	15
C	Production	35	15	10
Ç	Services	20	10	10
D	Freelances	45	30	15
DH	Ambulant vendors in the area of trade and services	15	10	10
E	Transport:			
	1.Passenger transport:			
	Vehicles up to 5 seats (including driver)		35	
	Vehicles from 6 to 9 seats (including driver)		70	
	Vehicles with 10 to 25 seats (including driver)		80	
	Vehicles with 26 up to 42 seats (including driver)		90	
	Vehicles with over 42 seats (including driver)		95	
	2.Freight transport:			
	Vehicles up to 2 tons		55	
	Vehicles from 2,1 to 5 tons		80	
	Vehicles from 5,1 to 10 tons		95	
	Vehicles from 10,1 to 16 tons		100	
	Vehicles with over 16 tons		150	
	3.Water transport			
	Transport by sea within the country		110	

Transport by lake within the country	95
Cruise ships/boats	30

Under category I: Municipality of Tirana , and Durrësi

Under category II: Municipalities: Shkodra, Korça, Vlora, Saranda, Gjirokastra, Elbasani, Fieri, Lushnja, Pogradeci, Berati, Lezha and Kavaja

Under category III: All the other Municipalities

Indicator tax level in communes is 50% for each category.

2.5. Tax Exemption

- ***The following are exempted from tax on profit :***
- Units/institutions of central and local government;
- Bank of Albania .
- Legal entities which exercise activities of a religious, humanitarian, charity, scientific or educational character, whose wealth or profits are not used for profits by its leaders or members.
- Labor organizations (unions, confederates) chamber of commerce, industry or agriculture, and any other organization similar in function, which do not have profit purposes.
- International organizations and their representations in the Republic of Albania, agencies of technical cooperation and their representatives, who are acknowledged as such by the Albanian State on the basis of legal provisions, whose tax exemption has been envisaged by special agreements.
- Persons envisaged in international agreements ratified by the People's Assembly.
- Foundations and financial non-banking institutions founded or delegated with a decision of Council of Ministers, whose main objective have the support of government development politics through crediting.
- Picture studios, licensed and subsided from the National Center of Cinematography.

- ***The following are exempted from simplified tax on profits:***
- Ambulant vendors.
- Persons exercising individual transport.
- Individuals that gather waste of metals, glasses, paper and individuals who gather herbs and spices, etc.
- Individuals that produce fire wood, mountain stones, etc,

The new law No. 9326, Date 06.12.2004 "For some amendments and changes in the law "On tariff on incomes", predicts that all subjects that have an annual turnover less than 3 million Leks are no longer excluded from he simplified tax on profit.

2.6. Establishing the taxable profit

- ***For taxpayers of the tax on profits:***

The financial balance sheet and its annexes will provide the basis to establish the taxable profit for a certain tax period. The financial balance sheet must comply with law no. 7661, of 19.1.1993 " On Accounting " valuable till January 1-rst, 2006 , with the provisions of law no. 8438, of 28.12.1998 "On Income Tax" as well as other sub-legal acts issued by the Minister of Finance for purpose of calculating the taxable profit. After January 1-rst, 2006, will come into act the law No.9228, date, 29.04.2004, "On accounting and Financial Declarations". In principle, the taxable profit or net income, is the difference between total incomes (incomes from normal activity and extraordinary incomes), including the value of profits and advantages in nature, with effective and recognized expenditures, for the purpose of income realization and protection. Under recognized expenditures fall all those expenditures made for business purposes, that is, expenditures that intend to realize and secure incomes. In order to be recognized or deductible expenditures should meet these conditions:

- They must be made to the direct benefit of the economic activity out of which incomes are achieved or to have been related to the normal course of the taxpayer's activity.
- They must be effectively made or faced and based on legally recognized justifying documents.
- The must be reflected by an accounting action, reducing the net active.
- In any case the taxpayer must evidence expenditures with relevant legal documentation

- ***For taxpayers of Simplified Tax on Profits***

This category of taxpayers it is taxed for the gross incomes. So, every taxpayer must declare before 31-th of March of every year his gross incomes, for all his businesses that are objects of the Simplified Tax on Profit.

The taxpayer is obligated hold the books of purchase and sell, where the every day sales and buys are registered. These books are kept for every location of the activity.

2.7. Special provisions for Tax on Profits

2.7.1. Amortization

Amortization of assets is one of the major items of recognized, deductible business expenses.

Amortization of business assets is calculated by:

- Owner of assets
- Person who runs the risk, in the case of rented assets (usually long-term), with loans or leasing contracts;

Such assets as land, building grounds, works of art, artifacts, jewellery, precious metals or stones are not amortized.

The following are individually amortized and in a linear manner :

• Purchase or construction costs; building improvement, renovation and reconstruction costs, as well as costs of machineries and equipment with a utilization lifetime of above 20 years. The amortization norm of these assets is 5%. Similar amortization applies to water pipelines, oil pipelines, gas pipelines, the higher voltage transmission lines, and other similar assets;

• All the following business assets such as patents, trademarks, expenses for starting a business, "the good name" in cases when the latter is purchased etc. are amortized by a 10% permissible norm for fiscal effects.

The calculation basis for the amortization of both "a" and "b" categories of the above-mentioned activities is the initial value of the asset (historical cost) to which are added the asset's improvement, renovations and restructuring costs.

The following are amortized on a group basis:

• Computers, information systems, computer programs and all data protection software and equipment. The amortization norm on this asset category is 25%.

• All other assets which are not grouped under the above-mentioned "a", "b" and "c", such as production and service machineries and equipments, all means of transportation, are amortized with a permissible norm for fiscal effect at 10%.

The calculation basis for the amortization of categories "c" and "d" of above-mentioned assets is the remaining accounting value of the asset group (the initial value minus amortization), to which are added the improvement, renovation and reconstruction costs of group assets and from which the incomes from sales and compensations received are deduced.

2.7.2. Bad debts

"Bad debt" implies a payment request (debt obligation), which becomes an obligation that can be totally or partially unpaid because of the debtor's bad financial situation, his placement in bankruptcy or because of any other reasons not depending on the creditor.

A bad debt must meet the following conditions in order to be recognized as such during the activity year, i.e. to reduce the taxable profit:

• The total sum of this debt must be included previously in the taxpayer's incomes.

• All necessary legal efforts must have been made for its payment;

• When this debt has been deleted from accounting books;

2.7.3. Participations that are exempted from tax on profits

In order to avoid double tax, dividends and profit-shares gained by companies and Albanian resident partnerships (beneficiaries) are exempted from tax on profits, provided that these dividends be paid by an Albanian resident tax company or the profit be shared by an Albanian resident tax company (i.e. these dividends or profit-shares are distributed after tax on profits in

Albania has been paid) and the beneficiaries of dividends or distributed profit should possess no les than 25% of the stock or capital of the company or partnership making the distribution.

Hence, dividends and profit-shares made by a company or partnership (i.e. beneficiaries) are exempted from the tax on profits, when all three following conditions are met:

- The beneficiary is an Albanian tax resident;
- The payer (company or partnership making the distribution of dividends is an Albanian tax resident;
- The beneficiary owns no less than 25% of the payer's stock capital, right to vote, or initial capital (in the case of partnerships).

2.7.4. Recapturing losses

If taxable profit in a certain tax period turns out as negative, that is if expenses are bigger than incomes, the resulting losses may be covered by the profits of three consecutive years.

If a loss is not recaptured for three consecutive years in a row (and the entity results in losses again), it cannot be extended farther and thus affecting the results of other years, prior to the application of tax on profit.
The law prohibits the transfer of company loss, because allowing carriage of losses should be linked only with the taxpayer who suffers the loss. That is, if during a tax period the direct and /or indirect property of the core capital, or the rights to vote of a person changes by more than 25% in value or number, the right of loss transfer for that tax period and the preceding periods is lost.

2.7.5 Crediting foreign tax

Crediting foreign tax has to do with crediting and recognition of taxes that taxpayers residing in the Republic of Albania have paid in other countries (outside the territory of the Republic of Albania) on profits that they have made in those countries. But this reduction or recognition cannot exceed the Albanian tax level to be applied on those incomes if they had been made within the territory of the Republic of Albania .

2.8. Tax payment and its final calculation

- ***Tax on profits***

During the activity year the tax on profits is paid by the taxpayer one month in advance. To determine the monthly payment amount of tax on profit the law has foreseen a formula, which takes into account the tax on profit the taxpayer has paid in the last two preceding years.

During the coming tax period, the taxpayer pays the respective monthly tax on profit to the tax organ accounts no later than the 15 th of each month, accounting for the next month, according to the calculation formula described above.

The final calculation of the tax on profits is based on the factual data included in the tax declaration (Annex A) and other supporting documents, such as the balance sheet and its annexes, data from tax controls, as well as any other legal document that helps to determine the tax obligation.

If the tax declared on the basis of the annual income declaration is far bigger than the advance payments made during the year, the taxpayer is obliged to pay the difference at the moment he presents the declaration. If the advance payment amounts turn out to be far bigger than those declared in the annual income declaration, or those resulting from a tax control, the tax organs are obliged to recognize these sums for overdue payment of tax obligations or for the payment of future obligations, including the advance payment amount for the coming periods. Upon taxpayer's request, these sums could be returned to him within 60 days after receiving the tax declaration.

- ***Simplified tax on profits***

Taxpayers pay the rate of their annual obligation considering the estimation of the flows for the calendarian year. These rates are paid as follows:

- Not later than 20-th of April, 20-th of July and 20-th of October, respectively in the first, second and the third quarter of the year

- Not later than the 20-th of December for the fourth quarter of the respective year.

- Possible differences that are related with the changes of the turnover, are declared and paid in the moment of presentation of the tax declaration that cannot be submitted later 31-th of March of the coming year.

When a business starts during a taxable period, the calculation of rates is based in the estimated circulation according to the predicts that are made by the taxpayer and the estimations done by the tax authorities. The payment is done according to the deadlines specified above. When a business delivers e declaration for the close down of its activity, the payment of the tax is done not later than 10 days from the day of declaration delivery.

The gathered taxes are shell out in the state budget and are transferred to the municipalities or communes' budget, once a month, where the taxpayer is registered or has his activity going. Law No. 9326, Date 06.12.2004, "For some amendments and changes in the law "Tariff on Incomes", changed, predicts the payment of this tariff in four rates than two that were predicted in the old law. The new law approved with the new 2005 Fiscal Package does not put any limitation in the sum of payment. In case that the activity closes down, the taxpayer must pay the debt 5 days earlier than the deadline specified by the law.

- ***Local tax on small business***

Local tax on small business is paid in two equal rates. The first rate has to be paid within the 30-th of April and the one not later than the 20-th October of the respective year. The place and the way of tax payment it is defined with a special instruction.

If a taxpayer begins its commercial activity during the year, the taxes are paid for effective working months according to the Instruction of the Minister of Finances.

The law predicts the reduction of the tax level, if the taxpayers pay their obligation, before the deadlines stated below:

- If the taxpayer pays the whole sum of his annual obligation within the 1-rst of February, the sum that has to be paid is reduced by 5%

- If the taxpayer pays the whole sum of his annual obligation within the 1-rst of March, the sum that has to be paid is reduced by 3%

If the information given from the taxpayer is incorrect and if the fixed sum to be paid is more than the one paid, the authorities must notify the taxpayer. The taxpayer must pay his tax obligation within 15 days from the day that he was noticed. In the same way, if a business shuts down and the value of the tax obligation is lower than the value paid than the tax authorities must reimburse the difference within 30 days from the day the business shuts down.

The new law No. 9327, Date 06.12.2004, “For some changes and amendments in the law No.8978, Date 12.12.2002 “On local tax on small business” predicts a delay of the deadlines for the payment of the rates of this tax.

The old law predicted the reduction of the annual obligation, in different levels from the ones presented above; this reduction was related with the ending of the re-registration process and the gaining of the registration certificate from the taxpayers. With coming into act of the law No. 9327, Date. 06.12.2004, approved with the 2005 Fiscal Package, we see a unification in the reduction of the sum of annual obligation, based only in the above mentioned deadlines.

2.9. Record Keeping

For the purpose of determining the tax calculation basis, the registered taxpayers should keep the required legal records and documentation. Models of the basic documents that are used for the calculation of the tariffs are given in Annex B

- ***Taxpayers of tax on profit***

This taxpayer category is taxed on net incomes (that is on net profit). To this effect, they should keep accounting records, issue the balance sheet with its annexes, which should comply with the law “On accounting” and the provisions of the law “On incomes tax”.

Being subject to VAT, these taxpayers are obliged to abide by the rules of the law “On Value Added Tax” related to the tax bill and its use.

- ***Taxpayers of simplified tax on profit***

This taxpayer category is not obliged to keep accounting records and issue the balance sheet, since the tax object is not the net profit, but the realized turnover (gross incomes).

The taxpayer should keep a series of records and documentation regarding the activity. The taxpayer should keep the following records and documents:

- Purchase documents, which include the VAT bills, simple bills, and tax bills, as evidence of the purchases made;

- Sales documents, simple tax bills, tax bills, and daily summaries of registering cash box (for sales from cash boxes).

- Purchase book and sales book.

Small business taxpayers are obliged to issue the following documents for each sale of goods or services made:

- Tax coupon in cases when the taxpayer is equipped with a registering cash box. This coupon is given to the buyer for each sale made.

- Tax bill when the taxpayer is not equipped with a registering cash box;

• A simple tax bill issued only by taxpayers selling goods or services to clients who are not the final consumers of those goods or services but purchase them for the purpose of processing or re-sale, i.e. they are registered tax entities. • At the end of each day's work, the taxpayer should record in the purchase book the total of purchases made during that day, as well as other expenses made, such as rent, electricity, salary payment, etc.

• At the end of each day's work, the taxpayer should record in the sales book the total value of sales made by him, respectively grouping them as sales with simple tax bill, sales with cash box (the daily total of cash box) and sales with tax bill.

• **Tax on fortune games, casinos and hippodromes**

Taxpayers exercising an activity in the realm of fortune games, casinos and hippodromes, like all other taxpayers, are subject to tax legislation provisions. Like all other taxpayers, they pay all taxes and tariffs specified in fiscal laws (such as VAT, tax on profits, various national and local taxes, etc).

Except usual tax and tariffs, every person that benefits from the fortune games and casinos, pays a tariff equal to 20% of the earnings. This tariff is taken from the owner of the game or casino, whom is obliged to shell out within 24 hours near tax authorities.

2005 Fiscal Package, and respectively the law No.9326, Date 06.12.2004, "For some amendments and changes in the law No. 8483, Date. 24.12.1998 “On Tariff on Incomes”, predicts a reduce of tax level by 5%

2005 Fiscal Package, and respectively the law No. 9326, Date 06.12.2004, "For some amendments and changes in the law No. 8483, Date 24.12.1998, “On Tariff on Incomes” predicts a reduce of the simplified tariff on profit by 1%.

Letters “g“ and “h” are part of the exclusions from the tax on profit in the 2005 Fiscal Package according to the law No. 9326, Dated. 06.12.2004 “For some Changes and Amendments in the law No. 8583, Dated.28.12.1998 “On Tax on Incomes”.

BANKING SYSTEM

Albania is trying to develop a diversified modern financial system. The operators in the Albanian financial system can be classified as follows:

1. the central issuing bank
2. commercial banks including savings bank
3. stock market
4. investment funds
5. insurance and reinsurance companies
6. credit associations (co-operatives)

BANKS

Law NR. 7559, dated 22.4.1992 " On the Bank of Albania" and Law NR. 7560, dated 28.4.1992 transformed bank system from a centrally planned, single tier system, to a Western two-tier system with the Bank of Albania as the central bank and second level or commercial banks. Law NR 8076, dated 22.2.1996 and law NR. 8075 dated 22.2.1996 further developed the banking sector. The activities of the Bank of Albania have paralleled those of central banks in other market economies. The main principle behind the legislation is that banks should operate on a fully commercial base whether they deal with public or private sector.

BANK ESTABLISHMENT

Joint banks or totally private banks with Albanian or foreign capital can be established. The licence to establish and operate a bank is obtained upon written application at the Bank of Albania. In accordance with a form issued by the Bank of Albania, a list of documents must be presented together with the request for getting a license. Actually in Albania there are three state-owned commercial banks, two joint banks with participation of foreign capitals, three foreign private banks and the branch of the National Bank of Greece. Other foreign banks or branches of foreign banks have got the license and are in the process of establishment. There are programs for the privatisation of second level state-owned banks.

ALBANIAN BANK SYSTEM

The structure of the bank system in Albania at the end of the year `91 was typical of a centralised and planed economy. It included four state institutions: (i) Bank of the State of Albania, which applied at the same time the functions of the central bank and of the commercial bank: (ii) Bank for Agriculture and Development, which credited co-operatives and the state farms: (iii) Savings Bank, the holder of the almost individuals deposits: (iv) Albanian Commercial Bank, which performed the transactions of the foreign market. Bank of the State of Albania changed in Bank of Albania and has only the functions of a central bank.

The approving of the new law on Central Bank and of law on bank activity in April 1992 which brought the creation of the two level bank system.

On 1 January 1993 its commercial operations joint with Albanian Commercial Bank and created the National Commercial Bank of Albania.

In September of 1993, Bank for Agriculture and Development restructured and its deposits and good assets transferred in a new bank, Commercial Rural Bank. In Albania till at the end of the year 1993 existed: a central bank, three state owned bank and the Bank for Agriculture and Development without any activity. Bank of Albania estimated the important role that the foreign equity, management and technology can played in the modernisation of the bank system in Albania. At this stage an important forward step was the creation of the first common bank in country at the end of the year 1992.

At the end of the March 2005 the system bank of Albania presented as follows:

1 **National Commercial Bank of Albania (NCBA):** has a network from 7 branches in all around the country. The most part of its passives, the deposits of enterprises and an important part of its loan are for the enterprises of the private and state sector. It applies short-term loans for enterprises in supporting their production and commercial activity and long term loans for the most important investment projects.
NBCA has created relationships with 21 analogue banks - 19 in Europe and 2 in USA. Also it has ownership interests in the equity of the Italian - Albanian Bank and of Islamic Arab-Albanian Bank possessing 40% of the shares of each of them.

2 **Albanian Savings Bank:** has 33 branches in all the country and the biggest bank network in the Republic of Albania. Actually the deposits of the individuals firstly compose its passives. Its portfolio of the loans consists mainly I the short and middle term loans for the private sector. It issues Eurocard, MasterCard, travel cheques, American Express, Thomas Cook and Eurocheques. Both, National Commercial Bank and Savings Bank performs exchange money transactions with enterprises and individuals.

3 **Rural Commercial Bank:** is created as the result of the restructuring and the recapitalising

of the Bank for Agriculture and Development. RCB performed commercial bank commonly activity, especially in the agricultural sector. It didn't offer transaction of the exchange money, even it accepted deposits in foreign money by its clients. During the first three months of the year 2005 the RCB was devised I two parts. The good part represented by deposits and liquids was gathered with Savings Bank. The other resting part of actives and passives were been transferred into the Credit Treatment Agency to be liquidated.

4 **Ital. – Albanian Bank** is the first common bank. Its shareholders are National Commercial Bank of Albania holds 40% of the shares, Bank of Rome holds 40 % of shares and European Bank for Reconstruction holds 20 % of shares. This bank acts as an universal bank offering the performing of deposits, transfers, commercial credits and exchange money transactions.

5 **Islamic Arab- Albanian Bank** is also a common bank. NCBA holds 40% of the shares and the foreign banks and individuals hold the other shares. It doesn't offer credits and doesn't accept deposits with time limit. It operates according to the bank Islamic principles.

6 **Dardania Bank** is the first private bank in country and up to now has developed a simple bank activity.

7 **Bank of Tirana** begins its activity in Tirana on September 1996 with a paid equity of 2 million USD recently is growing to 4 million USD. Its main shareholder is the Bank of Pireu in Greece. This bank offers universal commercial bank transactions and operates as consulate.

8 **National Bank of Greece** begins its activity at the end of September 1996. Its insure an complete --- of the bank transactions.

During `97, the Albanian Bank System was growing with two other foreign private banks (International Commercial Bank and Alpha Credit Bank). These two banks begin their activity respectively in May `97 and in January 2005. Both are universal banks and sitting in the city of Tirana. At this stage the number of the banks is growing in seven and the general number of the banks that actually operate is nine.

BANK OF ALBANIA AS A MONETARY AUTHORITY

According to the Law NR. 8269, dt. 23.12.2004 "On Bank of Albania" , the Bank of Albania is responsibility for the monetary police and its implementation; the issuing of the domestic money; the administration of the foreign currency reserves; the adjustment of the commercial banks and their supervisory; the keeping of the government accounts, etc. The main aim of the monetary police in Albania is the holding of the inflation under the control and the stability of prices. The intermediate and operational objectives of the inflation control are: the control of the monetary offer and of the monetary base, superfluous reserves, net foreign assets, the real percentage of the interests and the credit limit for economy.

The main used instruments for the implementation of the monetary police are: the obligatory reserve, the limit of the credit for the commercial banks, the minimum of the interest percentage for the state owned banks, Lombard credit and of Refinancial, the agreements of buying again, the transactions of the secondary market.

CREDIT POLICY

Substantially all Albanian banks provide a full range of services and operations for their clients and operate in accordance with the private-sector banking practices. The majority of commercial banks generally lend their funds preferably to private persons although they can also finance major public works. The most common credits are of short and medium terms.

Indications on credit and deposit interest rates of some commercial banks (as per first quarter 1999)

Lending rates, Per annum in %

Short and Medium term credit	*in Lek*	*in USD*
The Ital.-Albania Bank	28%-30%	10.5%-12.5%
The Tirana Bank	28%	10%

Deposit rates, Per annum in %

	in LEK	*in USD*
Current deposits	12%-13.5%	1.5%-2.5%
6-M deposits	16.5%	2.255-4%
12-M deposits	18 %	4.1%

STOCK MARKET

Tirana stock exchange was established on May 1996 and is a relatively new institution. For the moment governmental bonds, treasury bills with 12month maturity and privatisation vouchers are traded. A National Stock Exchange Commission controls the activity of the stock exchange and co-operates in the development of its regulations

Indication on security rates, as per March 1999.

3-M Treasury bills	17.95%-19.0%
6-M Treasury bills	18.90%-20.5%
12-M Treasury bills	20.80%-21.3%

Government bonds

20 Years 1.5%

INVESTMENT FUNDS

Law no. 7979, dated 26.7.1995 ,regulates the establishment and operation of Investment Funds.

Investment Funds are joint stock companies involved in investment, reinvestment, hold or exchange of privatisation vouchers. The minimum capital requirement is the equivalent in lek of USD 20 000. Foreign entities and companies whose capital is partly owned by foreigners may subscribe no more than 50% of the basic capital of the Fund.

The Fund is managed by a licensed administrator in accordance with the management contract. The administrator must be a subject not employed in the investment fund. The investment fund must appoint a licensed depositor to carry out depositor's duties, as well as a certified public accountant. Normally the organisation of an Investment Fund follows the rules found in the company Law for joint stock companies, except for some specific rules and regulation as specified in the Investment Law

ADDRESSES

Institution	***Address (Tirana, Albania)***	***Tel (00355/42)***	***Fax (00355/42)***
Bank of Albania	Sheshi "Skenderbej" Nr. 1	22230, 22752, 22152, 22153, 23205,35565	23587, 23695
National Commercial Bank	Bulevardi "Zhan D`Ark"	35100, 23133, 35113, 35114, 35116, 35118	
Savings Bank	Rr. "Deshmoret e 4 Shkurtit", Nr. 6	245 40, 226 60	

National Bank of Greece, Tirana Branch	Qendra e Bisnesit "Veve", Bulevard "Deshmoret e Kombit", nr. 72	336 21, 336 22, 336 23, 336 24, 336 25	
Dardania Bank	Qendra e Bisnesit "Veve", Bulevard "Deshmoret e Kombit"	287 59 Telex: 2298 DB BANC AB	305 66
Islamic Arab- Albanian Bank	Rr."Deshmoret e Kombit", nr. 8, P.O. Box 128	274 08, 284 60	284 60
Italo- Albanian Bank	Rr. Barrikadave,	339 65, 339 66	
Bank of Tirana	Bulevard "Deshmoret e Kombit", nr. 55/1,	334 43,334 67,334 41, 334 92	334 17
American Bank of Albania	Rr. "Ismail Qemali" nr. 27 P.O.Box 8319, *E-mail: aba@icc.al.eu.org*	48753, 48754, 48755,48756	48762
FEFAD Bank	Rr. "Sami Frasheri", Tirana e Re, P.O. Box 2395	304 99, 33496 Telex: +355 42 21 51	334 81
Tirana Burs	Sheshi "Skenderbej", Nr.1 *E-mail: emeka@capmark. tirana.al*	355 68 ext. 179	23558
First Investment Bank (Bulgaria Bank)	Bulevard "Deshmoret e Kombit", nr. 64	564 23, 56424	56422

ECONOMIC & BUSINESS ENVIRONMENT

Albania is an unusual country even by the standards of other former communist bloc countries such as Poland, Hungary, Russia etc.. For the 15 years prior to its change from a centrally planned dictatorship to a democratic, free market economy, it was isolated from both the East and West. During this period the country relied on minimal trade with Comecon pact countries and attempted to maintain a self-sufficiency policy with the effects that can now been seen in everyday life in Albania.

In the West we take for granted the flow of new information, new skills, techniques and experience through training programs, television, newspapers and magazines. During this period in Albania there was no such flow of new information. So the skills and knowledge the people of Albania possess today are based upon things they learned over fifteen years ago.

During the fifty years of brutal rule by the Hoxha regime, the ability of the average person to take responsibility for his own decisions was removed and taken over by the state. The State decided where you lived, where you worked, what you ate, etc.. To expect the Albanian people to quickly come to terms with their new rights of individual freedom and choice, is frankly expecting too much. The majority of appointees given responsibility for senior posts within the government and civil service need time to consider that such responsibility means they must now take the decisions.

The basic education standards achieved in Albania are very good, however they are based on text book theory and not practical experience. Those Albanian's who have moved into the private sector are quickly learning the practical skills needed to operate in a free market economy. Those who have remained in the state sector are, at the moment, prevented by bureaucracy from developing the same skills, however the culture is slowly changing. This makes life particularly difficult for foreign investors because of the Governments active role in business activity in Albania. All business opportunities outside of service and retail must be negotiated with either a state body or institution.

DECISION MAKING IN ALBANIA.

For fifty years the vast majority of Albanians, and certainly all those currently working for the state, have had no basic right to make decisions. They have not experienced the role of taking responsibility for their own actions. It is therefore important for Western businessmen to understand the basis on which business is conducted in Albania today. Most decision making within the government and state institutions is based upon 90% politics & personalities and only 10% on commerce.

Therefore to gain a decision in your favour it is important to establish who the political players are and the key personalities you must influence. Under no circumstances should this approach ever be taken as the need to bribe or pay someone for their support. It is simply a question of identifying the people who will influence and make the decision on your proposal and convince them that the benefits and merits of it are genuine and in the interests of Albania.

It is going to take many years for the people of Albania to come to terms with the new working environment that they are creating. It must be the responsibility of western businessmen to encourage them to understand the merits of personal decision making and taking responsibility for the posts that they work in.

MAKING THE FIRST MOVE.

Once you or your company has decided to take a serious look at the business opportunities Albania has to offer, it is vital that you research the specific field of interest, prior to visiting the country. There are, within the United Kingdom, a number of sources of information that can assist you in this task.

Once you have completed your research and decided that you wish to visit Albania, you should establish contact with the Ministries, Institutions and private sector companies you wish to meet whilst on your visit. We would always recommend that the first visit be no shorter than 5 working days. The reason for this is that transportation, office facilities and scheduling meetings is very time consuming and delays can often occur.

Having established your program and the individuals you wish to meet with, you will then need to arrange your flight and accommodation for the visit. Failing this it is possible to arrange a room at a private apartment, sharing with a local family. This of course is the cheapest, and can often be the best way to learn about local culture and customs.

It is likely that your first visit to Albania will focus on Tirana, the Capital city. If this is the case then it is unlikely that you will need a car during your stay, as most offices and government buildings are within walking distance from the centre. You will however need to arrange for an interpreter to accompany you to meetings. Although many people speak good English, it is still advisable to take the interpreter with you.

If you hold a European Union, EFTA member country or United States of America passport, you are no longer required to obtain a visa for entry into Albania.

YOUR FIRST TRIP TO ALBANIA.

Most of the scheduled flights from the UK arrive in Albania, mid afternoon. Upon arrival at the passport control office you are required to pay a USD$5.00 entry tax, have your passport stamped and then move into the luggage collection room. Porters will hand carry the luggage into the collection room and you are then asked to pass through the customs section. Once you clear customs you must then exit the terminal. If this is your first visit then you should brace yourself for the crowds of people immediately outside the main entrance door. You will be barraged by taxi drivers offering their services and locals seeking to carry your bags to the vehicle. They are extremely persistent and can often make first time visitors feel very insecure, be firm if you do not wish them to assist you. If you have not arranged for someone to meet with you at the airport, then you will need to hire a taxi, the going rate for the journey to Tirana is USD$20.00.

If this is your first trip to Albania, then you should brace yourself for the journey from the airport to Tirana. The country is severely underdeveloped and what little infrastructure there is, has been poorly maintained. The majority of buildings appear to have fallen into disrepair, the roads are very poor quality and the streets are very dirty. However, in contrast there are huge tracks of untouched countryside offering some of the most beautiful scenery in Central Europe.

The law and order situation in Albania and particularly in Tirana and Durres is now firmly under the control of the local police force. As long as common sense prevails, it is as safe as any European city, if not safer. The culture that exists across Albania is one of the utmost respect for foreigners and as such it is very rare to hear of any incidents of crime against foreign nationals.

When you have completed your visit, it is advisable to arrive at the airport an hour prior to your flight departure. You are required to pay an exit tax of USD$10.00 once you have checked in. There is a duty free shop and drinks bar in the main departure lounge.

LOCAL CUSTOMS

- The Albanian's nod their heads for NO and shake their heads for YES.

This can get very confusing, especially as over recent years with western influence many people nod for Yes and shake their heads for No. Always try to check an individual's response with a verbal Yes or No. Albanian for Yes is Po and No is Jo.

- The Albanians are extremely nervous about dealing with foreign businessmen; it is very important that your credibility is established quickly with them. Demonstrate that you have real proven experience in the fields you are discussing and if proposing to go into a Joint Venture or Direct Investment establish financial credibility very early on in the negotiations.

- When dealing with foreigners it is considered impolite to refer to someone by their first name, they will always refer to you as Mr * and you will be expected to do likewise. Although again due to western influence this is becoming less common.

- Private ownership of cars has only been permitted during the last three years and it would appear that the Italian driving system has been copied. Albanian drivers have an irritating habit of sounding their horn at every opportunity and display no regard for the safety of pedestrians.

- The high number of unemployed means that the majority of the ever increasing number of private cafes and bars are full with locals. Espresso, Cappuccino and Turkish coffee are served in most cafes. Soft drinks such as Pepsi, Coca-Cola, 7 Up etc. are also readily available.

- Privately run restaurants have now sprung up all over the capital, the majority of high quality, however they are expensive by Albanian living standards. The most popular are Italian, French and Chinese, although it is worth seeking out the few traditional Albanian cuisine restaurants.

HOW TO MAKE CONTACTS WHILE IN TIRANA.

On your first visit to Albania it is important to establish as many new contacts as possible. There are a variety of channels in which this can be achieved. First stop should be the British Charge d'affaires Office, Ministry of Industry and Trade, then the Albanian Chamber of Commerce. In addition to this you should visit the Hotel reception desks, where it is possible to buy copies of the ATA (State Press) news bulletins and local information brochures.

FIXING APPOINTMENTS WITH MINISTERS.

As a businessman, it is becoming more and more difficult to arrange a direct meeting with Ministers in Tirana. The reason for this is very simple; for the first two years of the transition, Ministers were eager to talk to as many people form foreign companies as possible. Unfortunately a large number of unscrupulous businessmen took advantage of this hospitality and had photographs taken in order that they could return to their own country and claim they had a special relationship with the Minister.

The Prime Minister has now decreed that Ministers should only meet with businessmen at a time when a project proposal is coming to its final conclusion. This said, it is still possible to arrange a meeting if a formal letter is sent to the Minister explaining the reasons for the meeting and that it is in his interest to meet with you.

UNDERSTANDING THE BUREAUCRACY.

If at the end of your visit you anticipate that you will be making concrete business proposals either now or in the future, it is necessary to understand the administrative procedures that will effect your project's chances of success.

If your proposal is solely concerned with individuals or companies in the private sector, you should be able to proceed relatively quickly. However, foreign proposals that require some form of State approval can be long and time consuming. It is necessary to engage the services of an Albanian lawyer to advise you on the laws effecting your proposed project.

For fifty years the Albanian State has employed only one law, that of the constitution, established by Enver Hoxha. The constitution was effectively Hoxha's law for ruling Albania and was not to be questioned or interpreted. Since there was only one law, the need for lawyers and judges was limited. Since the transition period commenced the government has slowly but surely drafted and approved laws for all sectors of economic, political and social life.

Because the legal profession in Albania is so new and inexperienced there is no interpretation of law. Whatever is published as the law is taken as sacro- sanct and non-negotiable. Thus when it comes to negotiating a contract with a government body you will be told that the conditions under which they can agree are published in the Laws. For this reason it is necessary to obtain English versions of all the legislation that will have a bearing on your particular project.

The second reason for requiring local legal services is that all documentation relating to the proposal, must be presented in Albanian and the translation must be notarised by the local court.

Each Ministry and local authority has a series of administrative procedures through which your proposal must pass, before it can be agreed upon. In certain circumstances a proposal, once it has passed through these procedures, must be approved by the Council of Ministers. The Council of Ministers sits once a week and is responsible for approving projects that under the legislation are deemed to be of national importance. The problem is that, what you might consider a straight forward business proposal, may under Albanian legislation be considered not in the nations interests. An example of this is, when a foreign company wishes to lease a piece of land for a project. If it is under 5 hectares in size the local authority can approve the lease contract. If the site is larger than 5 hectares the Council of Minister must approve it and only then is the local authority allowed to sign the lease contract.

So it is very important that you establish as quickly as possible the administrative procedures that your proposal will be subjected to. Once this has been achieved and you have decided to proceed, you will need to establish a local company in order to present your final proposal.

MAINTAINING PROGRESS IN YOUR ABSENCE.

It is important that, as you embark upon the process of putting forward a business proposal to a State body, your interests are being looked after once you have left the country. The ideal approach to take is to stay in Albania until such time as the proposal is either agreed or rejected. However, this is a very costly exercise and cannot guarantee the desired result. It therefore makes sense to appoint a local person to take responsibility for your projects progress when you are out of Albania.

His task should be to maintain contact with those individuals involved from the state sector and ensure that documents are presented at the appropriate time. He should also be responsible for arranging meetings and local facilities when you return to Albania. Someone who has respect in the local community and is known in Government circles will be able to push your project through the system much quicker than you could on your own. If you fail to make use of a local person during your absence, you will find that your project has not progressed since you were last in Albania.

THE WORLD BANK IN ALBANIA

AGRICULTURE, RURAL DEVELOPMENT AND THE ENVIRONMENT

Albania is a relatively small, very mountainous country with a population of about 3.1 million people. Only 24 percent of its land is classified as agricultural land, while 36 percent is forests and 15 percent is pastureland. Yet, agriculture provides the income basis for most of the population and serves as an employment safety net. The rural population is estimated to comprise about 54 percent of the total population while more than 60 percent of the labor force works in agriculture and related fields.

The agriculture sector continues to play an important role in the economy, providing for 53 percent of the GDP. Initially, the agricultural sector experienced high growth rates, which are still around 5 percent annually. The rapid growth and recovery during the early stages of the transition resulted mostly form the ability of farmers to quickly adapt to the changes brought about through the privatization by modifying their production structures. However, production has sometimes taken place at the expense of long term sustainability. Production continues to take place with limited use of improved seeds, fertilizers, and other inputs.

Albania has some advantages for the development of its agriculture. Among these are (a) a favorable geographic location relative to the European Union, particularly Italy and Greece, (b) comparably low wage levels, (c) a relatively educated rural population, many of whom have worked in other European countries for some period of time, (d) creativeness among Albanian farmers in adapting rapidly to changing circumstances, and (e) fertile soils and favorable climate in some regions. Based on these advantages, the major opportunities for growth in the agricultural sector are in the production of higher value crops, livestock, processing, and some agricultural niche markets.

The World Bank continues to aid in the development of the agricultrual and rural sectors by addressing different areas through initiation, implementation, and evaluation of World Bank financed projects.

TRANSPORT

Albania inherited a poor road and highway system from the Communist period. Only nine percent of rural households own a car or truck or have access to one. Over the last several years the government has invested in national highways running East-West and North-South. However, there are not enough of these investments and the quality of existing roads makes travel slow and difficult.

The main objectives for the sector include: (i) establishing a modern infrastructure network for an effective transport system to facilitate growth; (ii) increasing efficiency of cost recovery in transport operations by reducing the demand on the state budget; (iii) streamlining of transport operations with an aim of increasing economic efficiency, road safety, and environment protection; and (iv) promoting cooperation with the private sector and the development in teh context of the Stability Pact.

Despite visible progress in improving parts of Albania's road network, major deficiencies remain. A Road Maintenance Project (2002) as well as a Supplemental Credit to Road Maintenance (2003) supports improved maintenance of national and rural roads through gradual contracting of routine road maintenance, also ensuring adequate policies for financing road maintenance. Through a proposed Transport Project, the World Bank is committed to the improvement of the Durres-Morine road. This investment is widely perceived as a critical investment for the growth of the impoverished northeastern Albania.

In addition to road improvements, the Bank is also supporting the port sector through the ongoing Durres Port Project. The ongoing Trade and Transportation Facilitation in South East Europe Project - a part of a regional program joining eight Balkan countries--aims to reduce non-tariff costs of trade and transport and reduce corruption and smuggling at border crossings. A planned Transport Strategy will take stock of overall transport sector issues and needs, especially in the context of Albania's alignment with EU structures.

ENERGY

Over the transition period from a centrally-planed to a market-based economy, the country of Albania, like most other transitional countries experienced deterioration in a number of sectors, including the energy sector. In an attempt to address the fundamental issues affecting the energy sector, the Government of Albania is initiating an action to reverse the deterioration in sector performance. Despite the encouraging start, however, the sector's problems are so deep-rooted that sustained efforts will be needed for a considerable period of time, supported by critically needed investments. It will take time to implement the legislative and regulatory framework needed to attract private investment to the sector. Consequently, donor assistance will be required for several years.

The World Bank has so far taken the lead role in the sector, and is well placed to continue this role. A Power Transmission and Distribution Project has approved in 1996, but suspended in 2004, mainly because the government failed to reduce illegal electricity use and improve collection of electricity bills. The Bank lifted the suspension of disbursements in June 2005, after the government and KESH met the first quarter of 2005 Action Plan targets. At the same time, the Bank decided to prepare a new operation to support the government's efforts to resolve the crisis.

A Power Sector Rehabilitation and Restructuring Project, which was approved in June 2002 supports technical assistance, procurement and installation of meter boxes, and rehabilitation of priority components of the transmission and distribution networks in the Durres, Elbasan, and Kucova regions. At the government's requests, the Bank will also support efforts to add critically-needed thermal generation capacity. A planned Thermal Power Project will finance part of the construction cost of a new 100 MW thermal power station. The Bank will help the government raise additional financing from other donors for the construction of the new thermal power plant and will continue to play a key role in sector dialogue.

PRIVATE AND FINANCIAL SECTOR DEVELOPMENT

A primary World Bank Country Assistance Strategy (CAS) objective is to promote sustainable sector growth, reflecting on the National Strategy for Socio-Economic Development's (NSSED) theory, which treats the private sector as the driving force behind growth. Relative political stability and commitment to reforms since 2005 have led to robust growth in private sector activity. However, to sustain private sector growth leading to poverty reduction, it is necessary to improve the business environment and complete the structural reform agenda (especially enterprise and financial sector privatization). A Foreign Investment Advisory Sector (FIAS) study identified poor governance and weak institutions as the overarching problem deterring foreign direct investments (FDI).

In an attempt to overcome such obstacles, the World Bank's CAS is geared towards the creation of more accountable and transparent institutions. The Bank Group is supporting the government's efforts to improve the institutional and legal framework by assessing administrative barriers to investment (FIAS) and subsequently streamlining administrative procedures (PRSC II, 2003); improving the legal framework for bankruptcy, resolution of debt, and commercial disputes through the ongoing Financial Sector Adjustment Credit, 2002 and PRSC I and II, 2002-2003, respectively; and establishing with the Multilateral Investment Guarantee Agency (MIGA) an investment promotion agency.

Microenterprises and small enterprises dominate Albania's economy. A number of donor initiatives, including Southeast Europe Enterprise Development (SEED) are specifically working to assist micro, small, and medium enterprises. The need for a business climate extends to rural areas, where many of Albania's poor live, highlighting the need for a sound rural strategy. Improving infrastructure, especially in rural areas is also essential for enabling business environment.

Although the necessity for growth and reform is evident in the enterprise sector, tangible progress continues in the financial sector reforms. Since 2004, the government has liquidated the insolvent state-owned Rural Commercial Bank, privatized the National Commercial Bank to an investor consortium that included the IFC and EBRD, and put the Savings Bank - the last remaining state-owned and Albania's largest - under a governance contract in preparation for its privatization, which is well advanced at this point. Close IDA-IFC cooperation has been instrumental in helping Albania move forward with financial sector privatization. The IFC is helping the government market the Savings Bank while planning to invest in it. The ongoing Financial Sector Institution Building Technical Assistance Project and the proposed Financial Sector Adjustment Credit (2002), which will be presented to the Board with the CAS, will also support the government in privatizing the Savings Bank as well as INSIG. Meanwhile, the government of Albania, IFC and EBRD are in the process of negotiations for acquiring up to 40 percent in the share capital of INSIG. Respective agreements for the final transfer of the shares will mark the first stage of pre-privatization of INSIG.

WATER SUPPLY AND SANITATION

Albania can be considered a water-abundant country. Its overall renewable resources amount to 41.7 billion cubic meters or 13,300 cubic meter per capita, out of which about 65% are generated within Albania and the remaining from upstream countries (namely, Serbia and Montenegro and FYROM). Resources are unevenly distributed throughout the country. The major water resource is surface water, and is found in rivers, lakes, and lagoons. The most important rivers are the Drin, the Mati, the Ishmi, the Erzeni, the Shkumbini, the Semani, the Vjose, and the Bistrica.

The lack of adequate monitoring system, the rapid changes in economic activities, and the continuous movements in population make it difficult to assess the use of water resources.

Available data suggests that irrigation and mining rely mostly on sufrace water, while households and industry on groundwater from aquifers. Domestic water demand is increasing not only because of population growth but also because of the increase in the level of water losses, estimated to be greater than 50 percent in all cities.

Albania's water sector is plagued by a variety of problems facing the power sector, such as high consumption, wastage and misuse, illegal connections, below-cost tariffs, inadequate revenue collection, and insufficient investment in physical infrastructure. Consequently, despite Albania's abundant water resources, water supply in urban areas is intermittent and less than half of the rural population has access to piped water. The lack of reliable water supply hampers private investment and endangers public health, especially that of the poor. Without sector reform and investment in physical infrastructure, the ongoing deterioration will lead to crisis situations in many urban and rural areas.

The Bank, in close cooperation with other donors, is taking the lead in helping the government tackle policy reforms, focusing on cost recovery and private sector and community participation. The government has prepared, with Bank assistance, a Water Supply Action Plan and a comprehensive Water Supply and Sanitation Strategy. The Municipal Water and Wastewater Project (January 2003) tests private sector participation in water supply and sanitation through a management contract for four cities - Durres, Fier, Lezhe, and Saranda. Alongside this project, the World Bank is also committed to a variety of other projects in support of water supply rehabilitation throughout the country.

GOVERNANCE, ADMINISTRATIVE REFORM AND ANTICORRUPTION

A merit-oriented, depolicized civil service plays an essential role in enabling the public sector to deliver services and limiting the spread of corruption. Through its analytical studies, policy dialogue and lending operations, the World Bank is helping governments in many countries in Europe and Central Asia to begin to instill the features of transparent and accountable civil service institutions.

One of the Country Assistance Strategy (CAS) objectives in Albania is to improve governance and strengthen institutions. The World Bank - in close coordination with other donors - has focused on building critical central capacities, including public administration and the civil service, public expenditure management, and legal and judicial institutions. The Bank will extend institution building efforts to selected priority sectors - education, health, power, water, and transport - through sector-specific operations. Bank operations are also designed to support Albania's decentralization process, and to build capacity at local levels.

Fighting corruption - both a symptom of and a contributor to weak institutions - remains a part of the the Bank's strategy in the country. Since 2005, as part of a broad governance and anticorruption agenda defined and supported by the Friends of Albania, the Bank has helped the government develop and implement its Anti-Corruption Plan (ACP), which includes 150 specific actions affecting economic policy, rule of law, public administration, public finance, customs administration, procurement, audit, and public awareness. The Bank has undertaken surveys of public officials in order to establish baseline measurements of the performance of the public administration and its constituent parts. Surveys continue to be implemented due to raised concerns of weak governance and poor business climate reflected in recent data from the second Business Environment and Enterprise Performance Survey (BEEPS), covering the period 1999-2002, which showed an increase in perceived administrative corruption and state capture in Albania compared to the first BEEPS, which covered the period 1996-1999. However, the overall remaining corruption suggests that long-term efforts are required. An April 2002 report produced under the guidance of the Southeast European Legal Development Initiative indicates once again that Albanians rank corruption as the country's top problem. As a result, the Bank intends to continue supporting anticorruption efforts through a number of operations (including PRSCs II and III) and nonlending acitvities. In particular, building on the NSSED process, the Bank's future operations will focus on increasing transparency and accountability as a means to strengthen institutions and reduce corruption.

In response, the Albanian Government has demonstrated commitment through an agreement to be resurveyed in the coming years in an attempt to systematically monitor medium-term improvements in the functioning of the public administration. The World Bank has also supported the Government of Albania undertake a survey of salaries in the public sector, the private sector and within the local offices of the donor community; a survey which has provided important information in designing salary reform measures in Albania.

The foundations for public administration reform are in place, following the adoption of the Civil Service Law in November 1999. The Bank is supporting better public expenditure management - essential to poverty reduction. The government is improving budget formulation by adopting a Medium-Term Expenditure Framework (MTEF), which adds a strategic focus to the budget process. The Bank is also supporting better budget execution and financial accountability by improving the treasury, accounting, and internal audit.

The fundamentals for legal and judicial reform are in place: the Constitution of November 2005 provides for judicial independence, strengthened through the 2005 Law on Judicial Organization, amended in 1999. However, there is a need for continued institutional strengthening. There is slow progress in law enforcement, including enforcement of property rights. Corruption and incompetence in the judiciary remain serious problems and major obstacles to economic growth.

HUMAN DEVELOPMENT

Over the past decade Albania has experienced expansionary as well as recessive economic trends, accompanied by changes in education, healthcare and social protection systems; during which time the World Bank provided support for improvement in the previously mentioned fields. The country program under the Human Development umbrella attempts to address the myriad of challenges that touch on the fundamental aspects of human capital development and households well-being.

An education trend during the transition consisted of a decline in gross enrollment rates for basic and secondary education. Overall basic education enrollments declined from over 90 percent prior to the transition to 88 percent in 2004. Secondary enrollment rates in 1989 were 79 percent, and they fell to roughly 40 percent by 2004. Albania, however, has joined the Education for All (EFA) Fast Track Initiative, being one of the 18 countries invited. Bank interventions in the education sector are grounded in a comprehensive education sector review. Albania's Education Sector: Problems and Promises (2000). The ongoing Education Reform Project (2000) aims to improve the capacity of the Ministry of Education and Science (MOES) to plan and manage the delivery of education services. The MOES is a pilot ministry for civil service reform, supported by the ongoing Public Administration Reform Project. Crucial reforms for improving planning and management and increasing the access of the poor to quality education are also supported by the PRSC program.

The Bank is helping the government translate its health goals into actions that protect the basic health needs of the most vulnerable population. Although Albania entered the transition with a relatively healthy population, life expectancy has since fallen, and infant and under-five mortality rates remain relatively high, especially in rural areas. The ongoing Health Recovery and Development Project (2005) is focused on the secondary and tertiary health care systems, while being adjusted during implementation to better align the project with National Strategy for Socio-Economic Development (NSSED) priorities.

The World Bank supports the government's efforts to create a fiscally sustainable social protection system that effectively targets the poor and vulnerable. The government's comprehensive pension reform program aims to create an affordable and equitable pension system while reducing reliance on budget subsidies. The PRSCs support the implementation of Albania's pension reform package, as well as improved targeting of cash economic assistance (ndihme ekonomike). The Bank also supports the government's development of a sustainable framework for community-based social services, which are primarily being developed under the ongoing Social Service Delivery Project (2005).

POVERTY REDUCTION AND ECONOMIC MANAGEMENT

Albania has enjoyed strong economic performance in the last five years, growing at an average of above 7 percent annually for most of the period. Inflation remained at levels of 4 percent less, exports and imports grew steadily, and both the current account and the domestically financed deficit improved significantly. Several structural reforms have also been carried out in the last five years, and have involved banking, land reform and privatization. Almost all small and medium enterprises have been privatized and significant progress has been made in the privatization of strategic sectors, like telecommunications. Regulation in the financial sector as well as core public sector functions has been strengthened, and the Government has adopted a new bankruptcy law and deposit insurance scheme. Significant steps have also been taken in the area of public administration, and a comprehensive civil service law has been adopted. Legal and judicial capacities have been strengthened, accountability rules have been tightened, and anti-corruption action plan is under implementation. Despite the impressive performance of the economy, poverty in Albania has remained high and per capita income, at around US$1,230 in 2002, one of the lowest among transition economies.

Poverty in Albania has marked spatial and regional dimensions, with rural areas in the Mountain region being consistently poorer than the rest of the country, according to all definitions of poverty. Poverty headcount in rural areas is 66 percent higher than in Tirana, and 50 percent higher than in other urban areas. Per capita consumption in rural areas, at 7,224 Leks, is about four-fifths of the consumption levels in urban areas. Households in the most remote districts in the Mountain region in the north and northeast of the country do not fare well in terms of poverty, and almost half of residents in this area are poor, and more than a fifth live in extreme poverty. Also, the depth of poverty in this area is much more pronounced than in any of the other regions, with a poverty gap index of over 11 percent. Average consumption in the mountainous region is two-thirds of consumption levels in Tirana, and about 20-30 percent lower than the rest of the country. Poverty rates and depth in all other regions are around or below the national averages.

The preparation of Albania's Poverty Reduction Strategy Paper, known in Albania as the National Strategy for Social and Economic Development (NSSED) was the first national development strategy that explicitly addressed poverty - outlining medium-term actions to reach long-term goals. THe NSSED, which was completed in November 2005, rests on two pillars: governance and strong economic growth. It also emphasizes policy interventions to improve education, healthcare, and infrastructure, while calling for stronger public accountability and increased public participation in decision making to empower the poor. The NSSED creates a better environment for advancing reforms and reducing poverty, by strengthening country onwership of the reform program; reinforcing a long-term vision; focusing on results; and encouraging partnerships.

Albania's prospects for growth, development and poverty reduction, however, are good, especially in view of a more favorable and stable political climate in Southeastern Europe and enhanced prospects for a closer association with the European Union. In the medium term, economic growth is projected to remian strong, with GDP growing by about 5 percent a year. An increase in exports and private sector activities is expected to lead growth in the next three years. Albania's strong growth should contribute to attracting more investment, generating income-earning opportunities and reducing poverty.

In support of Albania's NSSED, the World Bank has launched, implemented and continues to prepare projects geared towards poverty reduction and economic development.

TRADE AND CUSTOMS REGULATIONS: IMPORTANT INFORMATION

CUSTOMS CONTACTS

Address
Address : Directorate general of Customs, Rr.Durresi, "Laprake",TIRANE
Contact
Director General - e_mail : drejtoripergjithshem@dogana.gov.al

Technical Deputy Director - e_mail : zvdrejtorteknik@dogana.gov.al

Administrative Deputy Director - e_mail : zvdrejtoradministrativ@dogana.gov.al

Law Enforcement Deputy Director - e_mail : zvdrejtordoh@dogana.gov.al

Contacts of custom houses

TIRANE	tel:356145	fax: 356145
DURRES	tel:052-23134/24500	fax:052-24499
RINAS	tel: 371609,056460200	fax:056460200
ELBASAN	tel:05452483	fax:05453743
KORCE	tel :0824-3188/3828	fax:0824-3188
FIER	tel:03422009	fax:03422009
SHKODER	tel:0224-0245/0244	fax:0224-0245
LEZHE	tel:0281-2200/3593/2575	fax:0281-2200
BERAT	tel:032-30250/4239	fax:03234239
VLORE	tel:033-24627/9316	fax:033-24627
SARANDE	tel:0852-2565/4602/5609	fax:0852-2565
KAKAVIJE	tel:08467270/088490111	fax:08467270
KAPSHTICE	tel:0824-5658/2302	fax:0824-5658
KUKES	tel:0242-2369/2816	fax:0242-2816
BLLATE	tel:0292-20430/20431	fax:0292-20430
TRE URAT	tel:08132344	fax:08132344
Q. THANE	tel:0832-2466/3240/2240	fax:0832-2466

CUSTOMS PROCEDURES

Customs procedures with regard to storage are regulated by Law No.8449, dated 27/01/1999 "On the Customs Code of the Republic of Albania, articles 75-76, 108,111,121-135,136-156,157-164,165-179 (" Official Journal of the Republic of Albania" No. 4 dt.19/2/1999 page 51). Movement of goods in transit regime is subject to customs supervision, which is regulated in detail through DCM [1] No.205, dated 13/04/1999 "On the Approval of the Implementing Provisions of the Customs Code " as well as specific guidelines of the General Director of Customs.

Goods which enjoy the status of temporary admission , upon their entry to a customs warehouse or a free zone, change this status via the designation of a destination and within the deadlines provided for this purpose.

In order to operate, a customs warehouse (storage), should have an authorization issued by the Customs Administration (GCD) for facilities management. Authorization is issued pursuant to a written request submitted to the Customs Office, provided for as a regime supervisory office, proving that all conditions set forth in the Customs Law and other acts of legislation are met.

The Customs Law and its implementing provisions stipulate and regulate the manner of operation of free economic zones and free warehouses in the Republic of Albania. Operation or activity of the free zones and free warehouses is under customs supervision. The Customs Administration verifies and confirms if customs supervision conditions are met. The Free economic zone becomes operational, after receiving a permit from the Council of Ministers and the free storehouse becomes operational after the issuing of a permit by the Minister of Finance. After this, the Customs Administration approves the model records to be used. Entries and exits of physical individuals, vehicles of goods and transport, within and outside the free economic zone, are subject to customs supervision and control.
The Customs Law and its implementing provisions, provide for entire approximation of procedures implemented for regimes with economic impact and procedures for the free zones with procedures regulated under the of EC legislation.

There are no free zones approved, neither are there demands to this purpose. The number of demands and of the authorized individuals for the management of free warehouses is limited.

The authorized individual must apply the inward processing procedures, both for the system with reimbursement (with payment of the import duties), and for the system with suspension, on condition that they have received the authorization. The application for receiving an authorization is submitted to the Customs Administration (GCD) which is also the responsible authority for issuing the authorization. Applicants usually refer to the economic justification for using the regime, consequently a quantity and a relevant value of goods and relevant processing deadline, upon agreement with suppliers or foreign customers. Procedures that apply regarding the use and monitoring of this regime are extensively regulated.

The authorized also apply processing procedures under customs control. The application for authorization is submitted to the Customs Administration (GCD) which is also the competent authority for issuing the authorization. The number of requests for authorization and the number of the authorized individuals is small.

The outward processing procedure is also subject to an authorization issued by the Customs Administration (GCD), based on a written request submitted, to the Customs Administration, except for the cases when the goods are exported temporarily for repair, where the submission of customs declaration at the competent customs office should be considered as a request for goods outward processing and acceptance of the customs declaration by the customs offices is considered as authorization for this procedure. The number of requests and that of the authorized individuals is small. If necessary, and depending on the aforementioned procedure with economic impact, the customs debt that may be incurred is foreseen to be insured with the appropriate instrument of the guarantee. If a customs debt incurs or is caused by certain goods intended for the procedure with economic impact and by the designation of a destination other than the one foreseen, either for illegitimate financial benefits or not, the compensatory interest is calculated. Procedures with economic impact are largely harmonized with the regulated procedures within the Community.

The procedure for temporary admission (import) of goods is applied with complete or partial duty relief and they are subject to review of the economic need to use the regime. In the event of temporary admission with complete due relief, the submission of the customs declaration at the competent customs office is considered as a request for the approval of a procedure for temporary importation of goods with complete relief and the acceptance of this customs declaration by the customs office is considered as authorization to this procedure. The request for temporary admission with partial due relief, is submitted to the Customs Administration (GCD) which is the competent authority for issuing the authorization.

The Preferential Tariff Treatment (PTF), for goods which, due to their specific nature or use, have lower customs duty, is stipulated in Law no.8449 dated 27.01.1999 on "the Customs Code of the Republic of Albania", Articles 28, 105, 109 and 110 and DCM no.205, dated 13/04/1999 on "On the Implementing Provision of the Customs Code " Article 169 to 179.

Goods subject to PTF can be summarized in the following groups: goods because of denaturalization, seeds for planting, goods for the production of the pharmaceutical products, goods that undergo a specific process and goods that undergo a chemical transformation. These goods are subject to the issuance of an authorization by the General Customs Directorate on condition that they are used for the specific purpose intended within one year from the date on which the declaration for free circulation is admitted by the customs authorities. However, for cases when goods may be designated for repeated use, the General Customs Directorate extends the deadline by another year

EXPORT

Article 181

1. The export procedure shall allow Albanian goods to leave the customs territory of the Republic of Albania. Exportation shall entail the application of exit formalities including commercial policy measures and, where appropriate, export duties.

2. With the exception of goods placed under the outward processing procedure, all Albanian goods intended for export shall be placed under the export procedure.

3. The case in which and the conditions under which goods leaving the customs territory of the Republic of Albania are not subject to an export declaration shall be determined in the Implementing Provisions of this Code and provisions enacted by the Minister of Finance, if necessary.

4. The export declaration must be lodged at the customs office responsible for supervising the place where the exporter is established or where the goods are packed or loaded for export shipment. Derogation shall be determined in the Implementing Provisions of this Code, if necessary.

Article 182 Release for export shall be granted on condition that the goods in question leave the customs territory of the Republic of Albania in the same condition as when the export declaration was accepted.

IMPORT

Setting the goods in free circulation:

Customs legislation

Article 103

1. Release for free circulation shall confer on non-Albanian goods the customs status of Albanian goods.

2. It shall entail application of commercial policy measures; completion of the other formalities laid down in respect of the importation of goods and the charging of any import duties.
Article 104

Where a consignment is made up of goods falling within different tariff classifications, and dealing with each of those goods in accordance with its tariff classification for the purpose of drawing up the declaration would entail a burden of work and expense disproportionate to the import duties chargeable, the customs authorities may, at the request of the declarant, agree that import duties be charged on the whole consignment on the basis of the tariff classification of the goods which are subject to the highest rate of import duty.

Article 103

1. Putting in circulation gives non-Albanian goods the customs status of goods.

2. This brings the application of commercial policy measures, completion of other formalities provided for the importation of goods and payment of import duties.

Article 104

When a consignment consists of goods with tariff classification and treatment of each of them under the proper classification for the prepared statement causes a great deal of extravagance compared with import duties payable, the customs authorities, with request of the declarant may agree that the obligations paid on the import of all cargo on the basis of the tariff classification of goods that have the highest level of import duty.

Article 105

1. Goods placed in free circulation, with a reduced or zero import duty because of their special use, shall remain under customs supervision. This supervision ends when the conditions for the benefit of the reduced or zero rate of duty cease to exist when goods are exported or destroyed, or when use of the goods for purposes other than those provided for the implementation of the reduced or zero duty, provided that the relevant obligations are paid.

2. Articles 111 and 113 apply mutatis mutandis to the goods referred to in paragraph 1.

Article 106

Goods placed in free circulation of goods lose Albanian customs status when:

a) the declaration entering the goods for free circulation is invalidated after release of the goods, in accordance with Article 91, or

b) import duties payable on those goods are repaid or remitted:

i) under the inward processing procedure in the form of the drawback system; or

ii) in respect of defective goods, which do not meet the conditions of the contract under section 251, or

iii) in situations like those mentioned in section 252, the repayment or remission is conditional on the exportation or re-export of goods or the provision of an equivalent customs destination.

TRANSIT

Article 114 1. The transit procedure shall allow the movement from one point to another within the customs territory of the Republic of Albania of:

a) non-Albanian goods, without such goods being subject to import duties and other charges or to commercial policy measures;

b) Albanian goods, which are subject to measures involving their export to other countries and in respect of which the corresponding customs formalities for export, have been carried out.

2. Movement as referred to in paragraph 1 shall take place:

a) under the transit procedure; or

b) under cover of a TIR carnet (TIR Convention) provided that such movement:

i) began or is to end outside the customs territory of the Republic of Albania;

ii) relates to consignments of goods which must be unloaded in the customs territory of the Republic of Albania and which are conveyed with goods to be unloaded in another country; or

c) under cover of an ATA carnet (ATA Convention) used as a transit document; or

d) by post (including parcel post).

3. The transit procedure shall apply without prejudice to the specific provisions applicable to the movement of goods placed under a customs procedure with economic impact.

RESTRICTED GOODS

THE RED CHANNEL MAKING YOUR CUSTOMS DECLARATIOON RED OR GREEN CHANNEL ?

COMING THROUGH CUSTOMS DECLARE TO GOODS

THE GREEN CHANNEL ONLY ENTER THE CHANNEL IF YOU ARE SURE THAT YOU HAVE NO MORE GOODS THAN THE CUSTOMS ALLOWANCES, NO GOODS FOR COMMERCIAL USE AND NO PROHIBITED OR RESTRICTED GOODS. TRAVELLERS IN THE GREEN CHANNEL MAY BE STOPPED FOR EXAMINATION.

WARNING IF A TRAVELLER IS FOUND CARRYING DUTIABLE GOODS OVER THE CUSTOMS ALLOWANCES OR THE GOODS ARE CLEARLY SUBJECT TO IMPORT RESTRICTIONS OR INTENDED FOR COMMERCIAL PURPOSES, MAY BE CHARGED WITH COMMITTING A CUSTOMS OFFENCE. TRAVELLERS ARE STRONGLY RECOMMENDED TO CHOOSE THE RED CHANNEL IF YOU HAVE GOODS OVER THE ALLOWANCES OR ARE UNCERTAIN OF THE RULES TO BE APPLIED NOTHING TO DECLARE THE GOODS MAY BE SEIZED, PENALTIES ISSUEDOR THE TRAVELLER NEVER CARRY BAGS THROUGH CUSTOMS FOR ANYONE ELSE. DO NOT TRY TO HIDE ANY GOODS OR TO MISLEAD A CUSTOMS OFFICER. ANYTHING THAT IS NOT PROPERLY DECLARED, MAY BE CONFISCATED. SEVERE PENALTIES CAN BE IMPOSED ON ANYONE BREAKING COSTOMS REGULATIONS IF YOU ARE UNSURE ABOUT THE PROCEDURE OR THE REGULATIONS, PLEASE ASK A CUSTOMS OFFICER WHO WILL BE PLEASED TO PROVIDE FURTHER ADVICE.

DO NOT SMUGGLE DRUGS

THE CUSTOMS ALLOWANCES TRAVELLERS COMING TO ALBANIA FROM OTHER COUNTRIES ARE ALLOWED TO IMPORT THE FOLLOWING GOODS CONTAINED IN THEIR PERSONAL LUGGAGE FREE OF IMPORT DUTIES,PROVIDED SUCH GOODS ARE OF NON-COMMERCIAL NATURE

200 CIGARETTES OR

100 CIGARILLOS(MAX 3G EACH) OR

250 G SMOKING TOBACCO

1 LITRE SPIRITS,STRONG LIQUEURS OVER 22% OR

2 LITRES DISTILLED BEVERAGES AND SPIRITS,

APERITIFS WITH WINE OR ALCOHOLIC BASE,TAFIE,SAKE OR SIMILAR UNDER 22% VOLUME,

SPARKLING WINES AND 2 LITRE STILL WINE 50 G PERFUMES OR 0,25 LITRE TOILET WATERS

NO-ONE UNDER 15 IS ENTITLED TO TOBACCO ALLOWANCES.

NO-ONE UNDER 18 IS ENTITLED TO ALCOHOL ALLOWANCES

THE TOTAL VALUE OF OTHER GOODS,GIFTS,SOUVENIRS AND OTHER PERSONAL GOODS ARE ALLOWED TO THE MAXIMUM VALUE OF 30.000.00 LEK PER TRAVELLER.

THE AMOUNT IS REDUCED TO 15.000.00 LEK FOR A TRAVELLER UNDER 15 YEARS OF AGE.

COMMERCIAL IMPORTATION IS ALWAYS TAXABLE IMPORTATION IS NOT COMMERCIAL WHEN IT IS INCIDENTAL AND WHEN THE GOODS ARE INTENDED FOR PERSONAL OR FAMILY USE.

WHEN THE QUANTITY OR NATURE OF THE PRODUCTS IS SUCH THAT THEY CAN BE DEEMED TO BE INNTENDED FOR COMMERCIAL USE, THEY ARE LIABLE TO CUSTOMS DUTY AND TAXES.

MAY BE SUBJECT TO EXAMINATION.

TRAVELLERS IN THE RED CHANNEL YOU LEAVE CUSTOMS.

ORIGIN OF GOODS

Section 1

Non-preferential origin

Article 29

(Goods wholly produced in a certain country)

1. Goods originating in a country shall be those wholly obtained or produced in that country.

2. The expression “goods wholly obtained or produced in a country” means:

    a) mineral products extracted within that country;

    b) vegetable products harvested therein;

    c) live animals born and raised therein;

    d) products derived from live animals raised therein;

    e) products of hunting or fishing carried on therein;

f) products of sea fishing and other products taken from the sea outside a country's territorial sea by vessels registered or recorded in the country concerned and flying the flag of that country;

g) goods obtained or produced on board factory ships from the products referred to in subparagraph (f), originating in that country, provided that such factory ships are registered or recorded in that country and fly its flag;

h) products taken from the seabed or subsoil beneath the seabed outside the territorial sea provided that, that country has exclusive rights to exploit that seabed or subsoil;

i) waste and scrap products derived from manufacturing operations and used articles, if they were collected therein and are fit only for the recovery of raw materials;

j) goods, which are produced exclusively from goods, referred to in subparagraph (a) to (i) or their derivatives at any stage of production.

3. For the purposes of paragraph 2, the expression 'country' covers also the territorial waters of that country.

Article 30

(In production is involved more than one country)

Goods whose production involves more than one country shall be deemed to originate in the country where they underwent their last, substantial, economically justified processing or working in an undertaking equipped for that purpose and resulting in the manufacture of a new product or representing an important stage of manufacture.

Article 31

(Certificate of origin)

1. Customs rules may require that a document must be produced as proof of the origin of goods.

2. The Chamber of Commerce territorially competent where the goods are produced issues the certificate of non-preferential origin of the Albanian goods.

3. Notwithstanding the production of this document, the customs authorities, in case of serious doubts, require any additional proof to ensure that the indication of origin does comply with the rules laid down by the relevant legislation.

4. The rules of non-preferential origin determine the conditions that the goods must meet to be considered originating from a certain country. They serve to:

a) to implement the Customs Tariff of the Republic of Albania, excluding the measures referred to in Article 28(3) (d);

b) to implement different measures from these tariffs laid down in specific dispositions in the field of trade of goods.

The formalities regarding the issuance of the non-preferential origin certificate are laid down in the Implementing Provisions of this Code.

Section 2 **Preferential origin of goods**

Article 32 (Preferential origin of goods)

1. The rules on preferential origin shall lay down the conditions governing acquisition of origin which goods must fulfill in order to benefit from the preferential measures contained in agreements which the Republic of Albania completes with certain countries or groups of countries.

2. Customs authorities are entitled to issue the certificate of preferential origin of goods.

3. Rules regarding preferential origin as well as the formalities of issuance of the certificates of preferential origin are described in the Implementing Provisions of this Code.

ACTIVE PROCESSING

I. General Provisions

Article 136

1. Without prejudice to Article 137, the inward processing procedure allows goods mentioned below are used in the customs territory of the Republic, in one or more processing operations:

a) non-Albanian goods intended for re-export from the customs territory of the Republic of Albania in the form of compensating products, without being subject to import duties or trade policy measures;

b) goods in free circulation with repayment or remission of import duties payable on such goods if they are exported outside the customs territory of the Republic of Albania in the form of compensating products.

2. The following expressions mean: a) "suspension system": measures mitigating the inward processing procedure for re-export as provided in paragraph 1 (a), b) "drawback system": measures mitigating the inward processing procedure for re-export as envisaged in paragraph 1 (b) c) "processing operations": i) working of goods, including assembly, union, or

adaptation to other goods, ii) processing of goods;

iii) repair of goods, including repair and fix them, and

iv) the use of certain goods defined in the bylaws pursuant to this Code, which are not found in the compensating products, but which allow or facilitate the production of these products, even if they are wholly or partially used during the work;

d) 'compensating products' means all products resulting from processing operations;

e) "rate of exploitation": the amount or percentage of compensating products obtained from processing a given quantity of imported goods.

II. Giving of authorization

Section 137 authorization is issued at the request of the person who carries out processing operations or who arranges for them.

Article 138 Authorization granted only:

a) to persons established in the Republic of Albania. However, the authorization can be granted to persons located abroad, in respect of imports of a non-commercial nature;

b) without prejudice to the use of the goods mentioned in Article 136 (2) (c) (iv), the import goods can be identified in the compensating products;

c) where the inward processing procedure can help create more favorable conditions for export or re-export of compensating products, provided that the essential interests of Albanian producers are not affected (economic conditions).

III. Operation of the procedure

Article 139

1. The customs authorities shall specify the period within which the compensating products must be exported or re-exported or assigned another customs destination. This term takes into account the time required for processing operations and the availability of compensating products.

2. The period begins from the date when non-Albanian goods are placed under the inward processing procedure. Customs authorities, with a reasoned request by the holder of the authorization may delay this deadline.

Article 140

1. The customs authorities determine the rate of yield or the operation or, where appropriate, the method of determining this ratio. Rate of yield is determined by the actual circumstances in which the processing operation is performed or to be performed.

2. When circumstances require, and particularly in the case of processing operations traditionally performed in clearly defined technical conditions, for goods with the same essential features, and that as a result of manufacture of compensating products of uniform quality, in-laws pursuant to this code can be determined using standard ratio, based on real data previously ascertained.

Article 141

The cases and conditions under which goods in the unaltered or

considered that the compensating products are placed in free circulation,

can be determined by provisions issued by the Minister of Finance.

Article 142

1. Without prejudice to Article 143, where a customs debt, the amount of this debt is determined on the basis of the relevant elements of taxation on imported goods, the date of the declaration placing these goods under the inward processing procedure.

2. If, on the date referred to in paragraph 1 of the import goods meet

conditions to qualify for the tariff treatment

68

within preferential tariff quotas or ceilings, they receive any treatment

preferential tariff for goods identical effect on the date of accession

the declaration of free circulation. Article 143 By derogation from Article 142, compensating products: a) subject to import duties calculated in accordance with the rules applicable in the customs procedure in question or in free zones, when placed under suspension or in a free zone or free warehouse; However, i) the person concerned may request that duty be assessed under section 142; ii) in cases where the compensating products were assigned to one of the treatments mentioned above, other than processing under customs control, the amount of import duties and other charges that are levied, should be at least equal to the amount calculated under section 142. b) be subject to the provisions governing the issuance of obligations and are determined under the regime of processing under customs control where the import goods could have been placed under this regime, c) receive preferential tariff treatment because of special use, when treatment is provided for identical goods;

d) exempt from import duties in case of identical goods imported in accordance with Article 199, has a legal provision about this exception.

IV. Processing operations in a foreign country

Article 144 69

1. Some or all of the compensating products or goods in the unaltered state may be exported temporarily, in order to be processed further in a foreign country, whether customs authorities authorize a thing

2. Such, in accordance with the requirements of the outward processing provisions.

2. Where a customs debt relates to the re-imported products, should be charged the following:

a) import duties on compensating products or goods in the unaltered state referred to in paragraph 1, calculated under sections 142 and 143, and

b) import duties on products re-imported after processing in a foreign country, the sum calculated under the provisions related to outward processing procedure, the same conditions that would have applied had the products exported under this regime were placed in free circulation before such export took place.

V. Special provisions relating to the reimbursement system

Article 145

1. The drawback system may be used for all goods, except that the date of receipt of the declaration of free circulation:

a) are subject to quantitative import restrictions,

b) within contingents may receive preferential tariff measure or a measure suspending the autonomous meaning of Article 28 (3) (d) and (e).

2. Moreover, the drawback system may be used only if the date of receipt of the declaration placing the goods imported for free circulation, export refunds are not given to compensating products.

70

3. Permission to use the drawback system shall be granted only if the date of acceptance of the export of compensating for these products is not certain export refund.

Article 146

1. Goods declaration for free circulation should note that the refund is being used and give particulars of the authorization.

2. The authorization shall be attached to the declaration of free circulation. Article 147

The drawback system, Articles 141, 142 and 143 (c) shall not apply. Article 148

Temporary exportation of compensating products carried out under section 144 (1) shall not be regarded as export for the purpose of section 149, unless such products are not re-imported into the Republic of Albania within the deadline.

Article 149

1. The authorization holder may request reimbursement or remission of import duties, if he can convincingly argue the customs authorities that compensating products obtained from imported goods, the free circulation under the drawback system are :

a) exported, or

b) with the aim of being subsequently re placed under transit, customs warehousing procedure, under the temporary importation under inward processing procedure (suspension system), or in a free zone or free warehouse,

71 provided that all conditions for use of the procedure have also been fulfilled.

1. For the purpose of establishing a customs destination mentioned in the second case of paragraph 1 (b) products shall be considered as non-Albanian goods.

2. The period within which claims must be made for repayment, defined in the bylaws pursuant to this Code.

3. Compensating products placed under a customs procedure or in a free zone or free warehouse, in accordance with the provisions of paragraph 1, put into free circulation only when authorized by customs authorities, which, when circumstances require, may This authorization issue. In this case, and without prejudice to section 143 (a), the amount of import duties repaid or remitted shall be deemed to constitute the amount of customs debt.

Active Processing

Section 1 General Provisions

For the purposes of section 272 until 3251:

a) "main compensating products' means compensating for obtaining products of which is given authorization to use inward processing;

b) "secondary compensating products" means: the compensating products, other than size, that a necessary product of the processing operations;

c) "Loss (/ expected losses)" means the share of imported goods which are destroyed and lost during processing, particularly due to evaporation, desiccation, venting as gas or leaching;

d) "quantitative measurement method" means: calculation of the proportion of import goods incorporated in compensating various products in the quantity of imported goods;

e) "Methods of measurement on the basis of value" means: calculation of the proportion of import goods incorporated in the various compensating products in relation to the value of the latter;

f) "operator" means a person who carries out all or part of the processing operations;

g) "period for re-exportation" means the period within which products should be "assigned a customs-as described in section 112 of the Code;

Article 272

In accordance with Part IV, Chapter 2, section 3D of the Code, this chapter sets out provisions for the implementation of the inward processing procedure.

Article 273

Goods referred to in Article 136 (2) (c) of the Code, which can be used as additional products listed in Annex 38. Section 2 Granting of authorization

Article 274

1. Authorization for the suspension system only when the petitioner has given the intention of re-exporting the main compensating products from the customs territory of the Republic of Albania. In these cases, the use of the suspension system may be authorized for all goods to be processed.

2. Authorization to use the system of reimbursement is given only in the cases referred to in Article 145 of the Code, where opportunities exist to export outside the customs territory of the Republic of Albania, the main compensating products.

3. When the conditions for use of both systems, the applicant may request that authorization be provided as well as the suspension system for the drawback.

4. For the purposes of section 138 (b) of the Code, the customs authorities shall determine the means of identification of imported goods in the compensating products. Customs authorities shall use mainly the following ways as appropriate:

a) an indication or description of specific brands or manufacturers numbers, b) setting plumbcit, seals, couplings signs, c) the taking of samples, illustrations or technical descriptions; d) performance analysis, e) examination of stock records or documents other related support

transaction in question, which clearly show that the compensating products are manufactured by

1 See section 2 (8). This text is rewritten here for convenience the terms defined.

import goods.

Article 275

1. The economic conditions described in section 138 (b) of the Code shall be satisfied inter alia that:

a) the processing consists of one of the following actions with the relevant codes:

a) acts committed in the context of the paper under a contract concluded with a person who is located in another country. "Message Agreement" means any processing performed on the instructions and on behalf of a person established outside the customs territory of the Republic, usually only on payment of conversion costs of goods imported directly or indirectly placed at the disposal of authorization holders (code 6201);

ii) related to cargo operations with a non-commercial nature (code 6202);

iii) repairs, including repairs and capital controls (code 6301);

iv) usual forms of handling intended to preserve goods, improve their appearance or marketable quality or prepare them for distribution or resale (code 6302)

v) operations associated with the goods, whose value is based on the Code 8-digit CN, not exceeding 50 million leks for each applicant and each calendar year, regardless of the number of operators carrying out the processing operation. This value is the customs value of goods specified in the database of known and documents submitted at the time the application is lodged. This point may be waived on imported goods, determined by order of Minister of Finance (6400),

vi) processing operations performed in the free zone or free warehouse;

b) When in the Republic of Albania is not comparable goods produced "comparable goods" means goods classified in the same 8-digit code of the Combined Nomenclature, which represent the same commercial quality and have the same technical characteristics, compared the compensating products (code 6101);

c) comparable goods as defined in letter (b) are produced in the Republic of Albania in sufficient quantity (code 6102);

d) comparable goods as defined in letter (b) above may not be available to researchers by producers established in the Republic of Albania within a suitable time. Such goods shall not within a "suitable time" if the producers established in the Republic of Albania can not make them comparable goods available to the operator in time for the performance of commercial operation, despite a request having been done in time (6103);

e) comparable goods as defined in item (b) are produced in the Republic of Albania, but that can not be used because:

i) makes the price of their commercial operation economically impossible to predict, given the (6104):

-

on the one hand, before carrying out customs formalities, the relevant price of goods destined to undergo processing and the price of comparable goods produced in the Republic of Albania with domestic taxes refunded or refundable on exportation goods. For the above price comparison takes into account the conditions of sale, in particular payment terms and delivery terms for goods Albanian

-

On the other hand, the price obtainable for the compensating products on the market of a third country,

or

ii) have no qualities or characteristics required for the operator to produce the required compensating products (6105),

iii) do not match the needs expressed by the purchaser of the compensating products (6106);

iv) compensating products must be obtained from import goods in order to comply with provisions regarding the protection of industrial property rights (6107);

f) for a particular type of goods to be entered for the procedure within a certain deadline, the applicant's authorization:

i) tries to prevent supply problems for that type of goods, which have proven to the satisfaction customs authorities, and the proportion of supplies of goods produced in the Republic of Albania is 80% lower than its needs (7002);

ii) proves that the customs authorities take the necessary measures to obtain goods for processing in the Republic of Albania, but there is no response from the Albanian producer (7002);

2. The applicant shall indicate in his application the reasons for which the meaning of paragraph 1, the economic conditions are fulfilled.

Article 276

1. In exceptional circumstances, the applicant considers the economic conditions are fulfilled for reasons different from those listed above, it should present these reasons in the request (code 8000).

2. When the customs authorities consider that economic conditions are fulfilled in cases other than those mentioned above, the authorization granted for a limited period, not longer than 9 months. The customs authorities at the request of the holder of the authorization, extend the period of validity.

Article 277

1. Without prejudice to the simplified procedure, the application referred to Article 276 made in accordance with Section 234 and the model in Annex 27 and presented by the person to whom the authorization.

2. The application is submitted to the General Director of Customs.

3. For the purpose of the second sentence of section 138 (a) of the Code, "imports of non-commercial nature" means imports of goods under section 1 (5).

Article 278

1. Without prejudice to the simplified procedure for the authorization, the authorization issued by the Directorate General of Customs and compiled according to the model in Annex 32. He signed and dated. Authorizations become effective on the date of issuance. However, in exceptional cases, Director General of Customs may issue a retroactive authorization. However, the retroactive effect of such authorization may not go back beyond when the application was lodged. Authorizations may cover more than one entries for the procedure requested.

2. Each authorization must be accompanied by a form called Active Register Import Processing is an integral part of each authorization, the model of which appears in Annex 32. Each setting for the procedure must be recorded in this form in accordance with instructions issued by the Directorate General of Customs.

3. (A) to ensure proper application of provisions governing the procedure, the customs authorities may require the holder of the authorization to maintain or ensure the keeping of records of storage of goods, from now onwards will be called in February, "records the inward processing ", which indicates the quantity of imported goods determined under the procedure and the quantity of compensating products obtained, and all the particulars necessary for the control of operations and the exact calculation of import duties to be paid;

(B) "inward processing records" must be made available to the supervising customs office so that the latter can carry out the necessary controls to ensure proper implementation of the regime. When the processing operations performed in more than one enterprise, the stock records must show at any time information related to the implementation of the regime in any enterprise.

Article 279

Period of validity of the authorization decided by the General Department of Customs on the basis of economic conditions and specific needs of the applicant. When the period during which the authorization is valid is longer than three years, the conditions under which the authorization was issued shall be reviewed periodically at intervals specified in the authorization.

Article 280

1. When issuing the authorization, the General Directorate of Customs determines the period within which the compensating products must be re-exported in accordance with Article 139 of the Code, taking into account the time needed to perform processing operations specified in the authorization for a certain amount goods, the authorized amount of goods imported into the regime, and the time within which the compensating products were assigned to a customs should.

2. When the authorization holder makes a reasoned request for extension, the Directorate General of Customs may extend the time set for re-export.

Article 281

The period within which the compensating products must be re-starts from the date of receipt of the declaration placing the goods under the regime, or the drawback system, the receipt of the declaration placing the goods in free circulation.

Article 282

1. Coefficient of yield as defined in Article 136 (2) (e) of the Code or the method of determining such rate referred to in Article 140 of the Code determined as far as possible on the basis of production data and must be identifiable in the records of the operator.

2. Rate or method of determining its appointed pursuant to paragraph 1 and subject to later verification by the customs authorities.

Article 283

1. Standard rates of yield referred to in paragraph 2 shall apply only to import goods whose qualities are in accordance with quality standards set by the relevant Albanian lrgjislacioni.

2. When performing operations on the active processing of imported goods which are listed in column 1 of Annex 39, to give as a result of compensating products listed in columns 3 and 4, then as a standard rate of use will be those shown in column 5 of this Annex.

Article 284

1. A simplified authorization procedure can be followed for the following cases: a) operations involving goods of a non-commercial nature; b) repairs, including overhaul and repairs c) processing operations carried out in a free zone or free warehouse .

2. In these cases any customs office empowered by the Directorate General of Customs to grant authorizations using the simplified procedure allows a declaration for placing under the procedure

under the suspension system, or the declaration for circulation free with the drawback system in this case will play the role of the application for authorization. In such cases, acceptance of the declaration shall constitute the authorization.

3. Declarations presented under paragraph 2, except when these data can be entered in box 44 of the form used for self-declaration, accompanied by a document made by the declarant containing the following information:

a) name or business name and address of the applicant when the person applying to use a regime is not the declarant;

b) name and the name or address of the operator when the operator is not self applicant or declarant;

c) the nature of the processing operation;

d) the trade and / or technical compensating products;

e) the rate of yield provided and where appropriate, the manner in which this ratio should be calculated;

f) estimated time for re-export;

g) where thought to carry out the processing.

4. Filing a declaration under the simplified procedures for applications signed by the applicant must show that the person concerned wishes to use the customs procedure applied without prejudice to the possible application of penal legislation, according to law, the person is responsible for:

a) the accuracy of the statement;

b) the authenticity of the documents accompanying it, and

c) fulfillment of all obligations related to the customs procedure for which the request is made.

1. The customs authorities shall keep the declaration and its annexes, together with the authorizations issued.

2. When an authorization is granted, the application, annexes and authorization shall be kept by the customs authorities for at least 3 years from the end of the calendar year in which the authorization expires.

3. When an application is rejected or annulled or revoked authorization, and either the decision rejecting the application or authorization, as appropriate, and all fixtures are held by customs authorities for at least 3 years from the end of the calendar year in which the application was rejected or was canceled or revoked authorization.

Section 3

Provisions regarding the suspension system

Article 285

1. Declaration for goods for inward processing (suspension system) shall be deposited in one of the customs offices of the procedure specified in the authorization.

2. When using the simplified procedure, the declaration referred to in paragraph 1 shall be lodged at the customs office authorized for this purpose.

Article 286

1. Declaration for the goods under the inward processing procedure (suspension system) is in accordance with sections 121 to 161.

2. Without prejudice to the simplified application procedure, description of goods in the declaration referred to in paragraph 1 must comply with specifications given in the authorization.

3. Any import declaration must contain the code in the box 1 IM 5 of the declaration number and date of the authorization for inward processing in box 44. Form Register for inward processing, export as described in Annex 32 should be issued for any statement that goods to the procedure and is part of the copy of the declaration is held by customs authorities. All exports must be registered on this form in accordance with instructions issued by the Directorate General of Customs. A copy of the declaration of import customs holds together with all attached documents, will be held after the release of the shipment in a separate folder for each company authorized to use inward processing procedure.

4. For the purposes of Article 87 (2) of the Code, the documents accompanying it are provided for in section 145.

Article 287

1. Pursuant to Article 112 of the Code, the inward processing procedure (suspension system) is closed when the compensating products or goods in the unaltered state have been declared for a new destination and customs are respected all other conditions for use of the procedure.

2. In view of the closure of inward processing (suspension system), called the export from the customs territory of the Republic of Albania to send compensating products to persons granted relief from customs duty, under the Vienna Convention dated 18 April 1961 on Diplomatic Relations, Vienna Convention of 24 April 1963 on Consular Relations with other conventions and consular content, or the New York Convention of 16 December 1969 on Special Missions.

3. Discharge of the procedure performed either on the basis of the quantity of import goods which correspond to compensating products which were assigned one of the treatments referred to in paragraph 1 or 2, or on the basis of the quantity of goods in the unaltered state, which was assigned one of the destinations concerned.

4. The declaration to assign compensating products or goods in the unaltered state to one of the customs destination contains all the details needed to close the proceedings.

Article 288

1. When due to unforeseen circumstances or force majeure, the nature and / or technical features of imported goods due to undergo changes which can not be obtained compensating products for which authorization is issued an active processing (suspension system), the holder of authorization must immediately notify the supervising office as it happened.

2. In cases where a change in question could affect the maintenance of the authority or its essence, paragraph 1 is used only if not contrary to Articles 20 and 110 (2) of the Code.

3. This article shall apply mutatis mutandis to compensating products.

Article 289

1. Without prejudice to commercial policy measures applied to imported goods, putting on free circulation of goods in the unaltered state or main compensating products is allowed only when the person concerned is unable to assign those products or goods a destination Customs which allows the import customs duties not paid. In this case we establish the free circulation shall entail the goods subject to payment of compensatory interest.

2. "Compensatory interest" means interest referred to in Article 229 (3) of the Code, calculated in accordance with section 293.

Article 290

1. Compensating products or goods in the unaltered state, which should be assigned to a customs office presented the discharge, in order to undergo the customs formalities of customs destination in question under the general provisions applicable to the case .

2. Statement on the closure of a regime of inward processing (suspension system) shall be deposited in supervising office specified in the authorization.

Article 291

1. Statement on the closure of inward processing (suspension system) shall be made in accordance with the provisions governing the relevant customs destination.

2. Description of compensating products or goods in the unaltered statement of discharge must comply with the particulars of the authorization.

3. For the purposes of Article 87 (2) of the Code, the documents that accompany the closing statements, those documents, the presentation of which is required to place goods under the procedure requested.

Article 292

1. Import duties payable under section 141 (a) of the Code on import goods, under a preferential tariff treatment by reason of their special use, shall be calculated, although not requiring any special treatment authorization , the fee that corresponds to this treatment when the declaration for the procedure has been accepted, provided that they meet all requirements in connection with the award.

2. Paragraph 1 applies only when the goods have been put to use special qualifying them for favorable tariff treatment before the deadline set for this purpose by the provisions governing the conditions under which these goods can be given such treatment. The time limit begins from the moment of acceptance of the declaration for the procedure. It can be extended by customs authorities when goods have not been put to use in such special due to unforeseen circumstances, force majeure or unavoidable technical requirements of processing operations.

Article 293

In accordance with Article 143 of the Code, when the compensating products for free circulation, and the customs debt is calculated on the basis of the relevant elements of the taxation of imported goods, boxes 15, 16, 34 and 41 of the declaration shall refer to goods import.

Article 294

Destruction of compensating products under customs control is treated as export from the customs territory of the Republic of Albania.

Article 295

1. Where a customs debt on compensating products or goods in their immutable, compensatory interest shall be paid on the import duty applicable case n1.

2. Paragraph 1 shall not apply where:

a) customs debt is incurred as a result of preferential tariff treatment under an agreement between the Republic of Albania and one other country on imports into that country;

b) waste and scrap resulting from destruction under Article 197 of the Code, are placed in free circulation;

c) compensatory interest that is calculated under paragraph 4 does not exceed 2 000 leks for declaration of free circulation;

d) require the holder of the free circulation and provides evidence that under certain circumstances, which are not due to any negligence or hileje turn, make it impossible or uneconomic to export actions in terms that he had këkesë planned when he presented for authorization;

e) a customs debt incurred as a result of an application for free circulation under Article 149 of the Code, as long as the duties to import the products in question are not repaid or extinguished.

3. (A) the annual interest rate determined by the Minister of Finance based on the arithmetic average of representative short-term rates in the same 6 month previous year. They apply to all customs debts incurred during a period of 6 months. The level of interest should be published at least a month before it becomes enforceable.

(B)

Interest shall be applied monthly and for the period beginning on the first day of the month following the month in which the import declaration is accepted until the last day of the month in which the customs debt. Where under section 149 (4) of the Code is required for free circulation, the period taken into consideration is what starts the first day of the month following the month in which they were reimbursed or died respective duties until the last month in which the customs debt arose;

(C)

The amount of interest shall be calculated on the basis of import duties, based on the interest rate referred to above in paragraph (a), and according to the period referred to above in paragraph (b).

4. In special cases, the decision of the General Customs Directorate, the methods can be simplified at the request of the person concerned for the calculation and accounting of compensatory interest.

Article 296

1. When necessary to determine the import duties to be paid, calculated according to the part of those import goods incorporated in compensating products. This calculation is not done, when, inter alia, the amount of debt is determined solely under Article 143 of the Code.

2. Calculations are performed in accordance with the method or quantity, or the method of calculating value, or by other means that give the same result based on the examples set out in

Annex 40.

Article 297

The quantitative scale method (compensating products) used when the inward processing operations comes a kind of compensating product only. In this case, the quantity of import goods corresponding to the quantity of compensating products for which it was born to a customs debt, calculated by applying to the total quantity of goods in question, a coefficient which corresponds to the relationship between the quantity of compensating products for which has had a customs debt, and total quantity of compensating products.

Article 298

1. The quantitative scale method (import goods) shall apply when all the elements of the imported goods found in each compensating product.

2. To determine if this method is applied, do not count losses.

3. The quantity of import goods used in production of each compensating product, determined by applying in consecutive order on the amount of imported goods a coefficient, which corresponds to the report of the quantity of goods in question found in each type of compensating the The total quantity of such goods found in the compensating products as a whole.

4. The quantity of import goods which correspond to the quantity of compensating products in respect of which a customs debt is determined by applying the corresponding coefficient ratio of the quantity of compensating products in respect of which a customs debt is incurred, the amount of goods Imported used to manufacture the products in question calculated in accordance with the third paragraph above.

Article 299

1. When the measurement method does not apply quantitative methods applied in all cases the value scale.

2. In order to determine the quantity of import goods used in the manufacture of each kind of compensating product, successive coefficients corresponding to the ratio between the value of each compensating product to the total value of those products, calculated in accordance with paragraph 3, shall applied to the total quantity of import goods.

3. The value of each compensating product to be used for applying the measurement based on the value is:

a) the last sale price of identical or similar products in the Republic of Albania, provided that this has not been influenced by the relationship between buyer and seller, or,

b) when such price is not known,

c) recent ex-works price of the Republic of Albania, provided that this has not been influenced by the relationship between buyer and seller.

When the value can not be determined by the methods above, it is determined by the supervising customs office using any reasonable method.

4. The quantity of imported goods that corresponds to the quantity of compensating products in respect of which a customs debt has arisen shall be calculated by applying the coefficient found by the method of quantitative measurement of compensating products, the quantity of imported

goods that are used to manufacture the products in question, calculated in accordance with paragraph 2.

Article 300

1. The holder of the authorization shall supply the supervising office of discharge.

2. Log discharge among other things should contain:

a) references to the authority;

b) the quantity of each type of import goods and reference particulars of the declarations entering them for the procedure;

c) the combined nomenclature code to import goods;

d) the customs value of imported goods and the level of import duties on the goods concerned;

e) the rate determined to yield;

f) nature and quantity and destination customs compensating products have been given, together with references to the statements according to which the compensating products have been given an appropriate destination customs;

g) the value of compensating products, whether used for discharge measurement method based on the value;

1. Discharge document is sent to the supervising office within 30 days of the expiry of the deadline for re-export.

2. The supervising office may agree that the discharge document to be made by computer or in any other form that the relevant office.

Article 301

The supervising office shall annotate the document of discharge on the basis of verification conducted by informed, if necessary, the holder of the authorization for the outcome of the verification, and maintains the discharge document and related documents for at least 3 calendar years from the date on which it was drawn up.

Article 302

1. Where import goods have been assigned to a regime through the same authorization but under several declarations, the compensating products or goods in their unaltered state, which was given a customs considered derived from the import goods entered for regime on the basis of the first statement.

2. Paragraph 1 shall not apply where the authorization holder is able to show the import goods which are obtained by compensating products or goods in the unaltered state referred to in paragraph 1.

Article 303

When the request for authorization for the subject goods which are subject to commercial policy measures, it is not necessary to show any license, authorization or other similar document at the time the application is lodged.

Article 304

1. When the Albanian legislation provides for special measures of commercial policy:

a) placing the goods in free circulation, such measures will not apply on the goods inward processing, as long as the goods remain under the procedure;

b) goods brought into the customs territory of the Republic of Albania, measures shall apply when the import goods under the inward processing.

1. Where paragraph 1 (a) is not necessary to present a license, authorization or other related document at the time of the procedure.

2. Without prejudice to commercial policy measures applying to export of goods that originate in the Republic of Albania, Albanian or re-export of goods placed under the regime does not entail application of commercial policy measures related to export of goods in the unaltered state or products compensating.

Article 305

Setting the free circulation of imported goods, as in the form of goods in their unaltered state, and in the form of compensating products subject to enforcement by the customs authorities, any measure of commercial policy measures in force for goods at the time of import declaration was accepted for entry of goods in free circulation.

Article 306

1. When the compensating products or goods in their unaltered state are placed in a free zone or free warehouse, enabling the inward processing procedure, the box 31 of the single administrative document, in addition to the information laid down by the regime in question, contain the following indication: "Goods for inward processing, suspension," written in red.

2. Where import goods entered for the procedure using the suspension system are subject to commercial policy measures and such measures continue to be applicable at the time when the goods in their unaltered state or in the form of compensating products, janëvendosur under a customs regime or in a free zone or free warehouse, the note referred to in paragraph 1 should be followed by the note: "Trade Policy," written in red.

3. The office of discharge shall be satisfied that the records of whom refer to paragraphs 1 and 2 have been entered as appropriate on any documents issued to replace or discharge the documents referred to in those paragraphs.

Article 307

1. Customs authorities may permit compensating products or goods in the unaltered state to be transferred by the holder of an authorization to the holder of an authorization, provided that the transfer is recorded in the inward processing of the first holder.

2. Responsibility for transferred goods or products of the holder of the authorization passes the second time when he receives the goods or products in question, and enters them in the inward processing records.

3. Such entry in the inward processing records have the effect of placing the goods or products under the procedure again in the name of the holder of the second authorization.

Article 308

The authorization holder is responsible for customs authorities to send advance notice of transfer to be performed, in the form and manner determined by the customs authorities.

Section 4

Provisions applicable to the reimbursement system

Article 309

Declaration for entry of goods in free circulation under the drawback system shall be deposited in one of the offices specified in the authorization for placing the goods inward processing procedure.

Article 310

1. Declaration for entry of goods in free circulation under the drawback system shall be made in accordance with sections 121 to 161.

2. Without prejudice to the simplified application procedure, description of goods given in the statement referred to in paragraph 1 shall correspond to the explanation of the authorization.

3. For the purposes of Article 87 (2) of the Code, the documents that accompany the declaration shall be those provided for in section 145.

4. Any import declaration must contain the code in the box 1 IM 5 of the declaration and the number and date of authorization for inward processing in box 44. Inward processing record form for export, whose model is presented in Annex 32 shall be issued for each statement that goods to the procedure and forms an integral part of the copy of the declaration is held by customs authorities. All exports must be registered on this form in accordance with guidelines to be issued the General Directorate of Customs. Import declaration together with all attached documents shall, upon release of the consignment to be stored in a separate folder for each of the companies authorized to use inward processing procedure.

Article 311

For the purpose of discharge of inward processing (drawback system) is treated as export of compensating products from the customs territory of the Republic of Albania to send compensating products to benefit from duty exemptions, according to the Vienna Convention dated April 18, 1961 on Diplomatic Relations, the Vienna Convention of 24 April 1963 on Consular Relations with other conventions or consular content, or the New York Convention of 16 December 1969 on Special Missions.

Article 312

1. Declaration or application to assign compensating products or goods, if need be capable of a customs unchanged as referred to in Article 149 of the Code should contain all the particulars necessary to support the request for reimbursement.

1. Any statement on the closure of the inward processing procedure shall include in box 44 and the date of authorization number of active processing.

Article 313

Each product compensatory and, if need be, goods in the unaltered state which should be assigned to one of the treatments referred to in Article 149 of the Code should be submitted to the customs office of discharge and are subject to the relevant customs formalities customs destination in question in accordance with the general provisions that apply.

Article 314

1. Declaration assigning the compensating products and, if need be, goods in the unaltered state, one of the treatments referred to in Article 149 of the Code, filed with the customs office of discharge as indicated in the authorization.

2. Declaration assigning the compensating products or goods in their unaltered state of a customs made in accordance with the provisions laid down for the treatment or use concerned.

3. Description of compensating products or goods in their unaltered state in the declaration of discharge must comply with the specifications in the authorization.

4. For the purposes of Article 87 (2) of the Code, the documents that accompany the closing statement shall be those documents whose submission is required for entry of goods under the procedure requested.

Article 315

1. When necessary to determine the import duties to be repaid or remitted, calculated that part of the import goods incorporated in compensating products. No Such calculation is performed when all the compensating products were assigned to one of the treatments referred to in Article 149 of the Code.

2. The calculation is performed in accordance with the method or methods of quantitative measurement on the basis of value or any other method gives the same results, according to the examples in Annex 40.

Article 316

The quantitative scale method (compensating products) shall be used when from inward processing operations obtained only one kind of compensating product. In this case, the quantity of import goods corresponding to the compensating products which may be required repayment or remission of customs duties, calculated by applying on the entire quantity of goods in question, a corresponding coefficient ratio quantity of compensating products , for which reimbursement may be requested or remission of customs duties, the total quantity of compensating products.

Article 317

1. The quantitative scale method (import goods) shall be used when all elements of the goods placed in free circulation, found in each compensating product.

2. In deciding whether to apply this method, do not count losses.

3. Volume of goods imported under the drawback system, which are used in the fabrication process of each compensating product, determined by applying in consecutive order, for all the quantity of import goods a coefficient corresponding to the quantity ratio goods in question, found in each compensating product to the total quantity of such goods found in the compensating products in general.

4. Volume of goods imported under the drawback system, which corresponds to the quantity of compensating products for which reimbursement may be requested or remission of customs duties, determined by applying the corresponding coefficient ratio of the amount of products for which compensation is sought refund or remission, the total quantity of compensating products to the quantity of import goods used in the manufacture of products in question, calculated in

accordance with the third paragraph.

Article 318

1. When you can not apply quantitative methods of measurement, using methods on the basis of value.

2. In order to determine the quantity of import goods used in the manufacture of each kind of compensating product, successive coefficients corresponding to the ratio between the comparable value of each compensating product, calculated in accordance with paragraph 3 shall apply to all amount of imported goods.

3. To be used for value-based method, the value of each compensating product consists of:

a) price of the last in the Republic of Albania is identical or similar products, provided that this price is not affected by the relationship between buyer and seller, or when it is not known,

b) the most recent price ex works in the Republic of Albania, provided that is not influenced by the relationship between buyer and seller.

When the value can not be ascertained using the methods above, determined by the supervising customs office, through any other reasonable method.

4. The quantity of import goods corresponding to the quantity of compensating products for which the refund or remission of customs duty, calculated by applying the coefficient found by quantitative measurement method (compensating products) to the quantity of import goods used in the production in question, calculated in accordance with paragraph 2.

Article 319

Repayment or remission shall be subject to filing by the holder of the authorization, the supervising office, a request that hereinafter referred to as the "repayment claim / Inward Processing."

Article 320

1. The period referred to in Article 149 (3) of the Code, within which requests must be submitted for reimbursement / processing asset is maximum 6 months from the date on which the compensating products were assigned one of the customs destinations referred to in Article 149 (1) of the Code.

2. When circumstances so warrant, the Directorate General of Customs may extend the deadline referred to in paragraph 1, after it has expired.

Article 321

1. Requests for reimbursement / processing active among others should include the following:

a) references to the authority;

b) the amount of each type of import goods for which the refund or remission of customs duties;

c) code of imported goods in the Combined Nomenclature;

d) the customs value of imported goods and the level of import duties to be paid for goods at the date of receipt of the declaration placing the goods in free circulation under the drawback system, as ascertained by the customs authorities;

e) the date on which the free circulation of goods imported under the drawback system;

f) references to declarations under which the goods were placed in free circulation under the drawback system;

g) the type and quantity of compensating products and the customs that have been assigned or to which they should be appointed;

h) the value of compensating products, whether for the purpose of discharge is used on the value scale method;

i) coefficient of yield;

j) references to the declarations under which the compensating products or, if need be, goods in their unaltered state were placed in one of the treatments referred to in Article 149 of the Code;

k) the amount of import duties to be repaid or remitted and any compensatory interest collected, taking into account inter alia the import duties on other compensating products.

Article 322

1. The supervising office may allow claims to omit some of the particulars, if it does not affect calculation of the amount to be repaid or remitted.

2. The supervising office may allow the repayment claim / deduct passive done by computer or in such other form as the said office.

Article 323

The supervising office shall annotate the repayment claim / active processing on the basis of the verification carried out and shall inform the holder of the authorization of the result of verification, it shall keep the application and related documents for at least 3 calendar years from the end of the which took the decision on the claim.

Article 324

1. When the compensating products in the drawback system are placed in one of the destinations referred to the customs of the second paragraph of Article 149 (1) of the Code, allowing reimbursement in this manner, the box reserved for the description of goods in the documents used for establishing these goods in the regime, in a free zone or free warehouse shall përmabajë note: "Inward Processing / Goods refunded" in red.

2. The office of discharge shall satisfy itself that the notes, which refers to paragraph 1, lo] s made] of each of the documents issued to replace or discharge the documents referred to in that paragraph.

Article 325

Directorate General of Customs may issue guidelines for practical implementation of the inward processing regime.

VALUATION

CHAPTER 3 VALUE OF GOODS FOR CUSTOMS PURPOSES

Article 33

(Scope of this chapter)

The provisions of this Chapter shall determine the customs value for the purposes of applying the Customs Tariff of the Republic of Albania and non-tariff measures laid down by other provisions governing specific fields related to trade of goods.

Article 34

(Transaction value as customs value)

1. The customs value of imported goods shall be the transaction value, which is the price actually paid or payable for the goods when sold for export to the customs territory of the Republic of Albania, adjusted, where necessary, in accordance with Articles 37 and 38, provided:

a) that there are no restrictions as to the disposal or use of the goods by the buyer, other than restrictions which:

i) are imposed or required by a law or by the public authorities in the Republic of Albania,

ii) do not substantially affect the value of the goods;

b) that the sale or price is not subject to some condition or consideration for which a value may not be determined with respect to the goods being valued;

c) that no part of the proceeds of any subsequent resale, disposal or use of the goods by the buyer will accrue directly or indirectly to the seller, unless an appropriate adjustment may be made in accordance with Article 37; and

d) that the buyer and seller are not related, or, where the buyer and seller are related, the transaction value is acceptable for customs purposes under paragraph 2.

2 a) In determining whether the transaction value is acceptable for the purposes of paragraph 1, the fact that the buyer and the seller are related shall not in itself be sufficient grounds for regarding the transaction value as unacceptable. Where necessary, the circumstances surrounding the sale shall be examined and the transaction value shall be accepted provided that the relationship did not influence the price. If, in the light of information provided by the declarant or otherwise, the customs authorities have grounds for considering that the relationship influenced the price, they shall communicate their grounds to the declarant and he shall be given a reasonable opportunity to respond. If the declarant so requests, the communication of the grounds shall be notified in writing;

b) In a sale between related persons, the transaction value shall be accepted and the goods valued in accordance with paragraph 1 wherever the declarant demonstrates that such value closely approximates to one of the following occurring at or about the same time:

i) the transaction value in sales, between buyers and sellers who are not related in any case, of identical or similar goods for export to the Republic of Albania,

ii) the customs value of identical or similar goods, as determined under Article 35 (2) (c);

iii) the customs value of identical or similar goods, as determined under Article 35 (2) (d).

In applying the foregoing criteria, due account shall be taken of demonstrated differences in commercial levels, quantity levels, the elements enumerated in Article 37 and costs incurred by the seller in sales in which he and the buyer are not related and where such costs are not incurred by the seller in sales in which he and the buyer are related.

c) The criteria set forth in subparagraph (b) are to be used at the initiative of the declarant and only for comparison purposes. Substitute values may not be established in the meaning of the said subparagraph.

3.a) The price actually paid or payable is the total payment made or to be made by the buyer to or for the benefit of the seller for the imported goods and includes all payments made or to be made as a condition of sale of the imported goods by the buyer to the seller or by the buyer to a third party to satisfy an obligation of the seller. The payment need not necessarily take the form of a transfer of money. Payment may be made by way of letters of credit or any negotiable instrument and may be made directly or indirectly.

b) Activities, including marketing activities, undertaken by the buyer on his own account, other than those for which an adjustment is provided in Article 37, are not considered to be an indirect payment to the seller, even though they might be regarded as of benefit to the seller or have been undertaken by agreement with the seller, and their cost shall not be added to the price actually paid or payable in determining the customs value of imported goods.

Article 35

(Alternative methods)

1. Where the customs value may not be determined under Article 34, it is to be determined by proceeding sequentially through subparagraphs (a), (b), (c) and (d) of paragraph 2 to the first subparagraph under which it may be determined, subject to the provisions that the order of application of subparagraphs (c) and (d) shall be reversed if the declarant so requests; it is only when such value may not be determined under a particular subparagraph that the provisions of the next subparagraph in a sequence established by virtue of this paragraph may be applied.

2. The customs value determined under this Article shall be:

a) the transaction value of identical goods sold for export to the Republic of Albania and exported at or about the same time as the goods being valued;

b) the transaction value of similar goods sold for export to the Republic of Albania and exported at or about the same time as the goods being valued;

c) the value based on the unit price at which the imported goods for identical or similar imported goods are sold within the Republic of Albania in the greatest aggregate quantity to persons not related to the sellers;

d) the computed value, consisting of the sum of:

i) the cost or value of materials and fabrication or other processing employed in producing the imported goods,

ii) an amount for profit and general expenses equal to that usually reflected in sales of goods of the same class or kind as the goods being valued which are made by producers in the country of exportation for export to the Republic of Albania,

iii) the cost or value of the items referred to in Article 37 (1) (e).

3. Any further conditions and rules for the application of paragraph 2 above shall be determined in the Implementing Provisions of this Code.

Article 36

(Fall-back method)

1. Where the customs value of imported goods may not be determined under Articles 34 or 35, it shall be determined on the basis of data available in the Republic of Albania, using reasonable means, in accordance with:

a) the agreement for the application of Article 7 of the General Agreement on Tariffs and Trade;

b) Article 7 of the General Agreement on Tariffs and Trade;

c) dispositions of this Chapter.

2. No customs value shall be determined under paragraph 1 based on:

a) the selling price in the Republic of Albania of goods produced in the Republic of Albania;

b) a system which provides for the acceptance for customs purposes of the higher of two alternative values;

c) the price of goods on the domestic market of the country of exportation;

d) the cost of production, other than computed values which have been determined for identical or similar goods in accordance with Article 35 (2) (d);

e) prices for export to another country ;

f) minimum customs values; or

g) arbitrary or fictitious values.

Article 37

(Elements to be added)

1. In determining the customs value under Article 34, there shall be added to the price actually paid or payable for the imported goods:

a) the following, to the extent that they are incurred by the buyer but are not included in the price actually paid or payable for the goods:

i) commissions and brokerage, except the buying commissions,

ii) the cost of containers which is treated as being one, for customs purposes, with the goods in question,

iii) the cost of packing, whether for labor or materials;

b) the value apportioned as appropriate, of the following goods and services where supplied directly or indirectly by the buyer free of charge or at reduced cost for use in connection with the production and sale for export of the imported goods, to the extent that such value has not been included in the price actually paid or payable:

i) materials, components, parts and similar items incorporated in the imported goods,

ii) tools, dies, molds and similar items used in the production of the imported goods,

iii) materials consumed in the production of the imported goods,

iv) engineering work, development, artwork, design work, and plans and sketches undertaken elsewhere than in the Republic of Albania and necessary for the production of the imported goods;

c) royalties and license fees related to the goods being valued that the buyer must pay, either directly or indirectly, as a condition of sale of the goods being valued to the extent that such royalties and fees are not included in the price actually paid or payable;

d) the value of any part of the proceeds of any subsequent resale, disposal or use of the imported goods that accrues directly or indirectly to the seller;

e) to the place of introduction into the customs territory of the Republic of Albania:

(i) the cost of transport and insurance of the imported goods, and

(ii) loading and handling charges associated with the transport of the imported goods,

2. Additions to the price actually paid or payable shall be made under this Article only based on objective and quantifiable data.

2/1 No additions shall be made to the price actually paid or payable in determining the customs value except as provided in this Article.

3. For the purpose of this Chapter, the term 'buying commission' means fees paid by an importer to his agent for the service of representing him in the purchase of the goods being valued.

4. Notwithstanding, paragraph 1 (c):

a) charges for the right to reproduce the imported goods in the Republic of Albania shall not be added to the price actually paid or payable for the imported goods in determining the customs value, and

b) payments made by the buyer for the right to distribute or resell the imported goods shall not be added to the price actually paid or payable for the imported goods, if such payments are not a condition of the sale for export to the Republic of Albania of the goods.

Article 38

(Element to be deducted)

Provided that they are shown separately from the price actually paid or payable for the imported goods, the following shall not be included in the customs value:

a) charges for the transport of goods after their arrival at the place of introduction into the customs territory of the Republic of Albania;

b) charges for construction, erection, assembly, maintenance or technical assistance, undertaken after importation of imported goods such as industrial plant, machinery or equipment;

c) charges for interest under a financing arrangement entered into by the buyer and relating to the purchase of imported goods, irrespective of whether the finance is provided by the seller or another person, provided that the financing arrangement has been made in writing and where required, the buyer may demonstrate that:

i. such goods are actually sold at the price declared as the price actually paid or payable, and

ii. the claimed rate of interest does not exceed the level for such transactions prevailing in the country, where, and at the time when, the finance was provided;

d) charges for the right to reproduce imported goods in the Republic of Albania;

e) buying commissions;

f) import duties or other charges payable in the Republic of Albania because of the importation or sale of the goods.

Article 39

(Customs value of information carrier media)

Specific rules to determine the customs value of carrier media for use in data processing equipment and bearing data or instructions are laid down in the Implementing Provisions of this Code.

Article 40

(Determination of exchange rate)

1. The provisions of this Chapter shall be without prejudice to the specific provisions regarding the determination of the value for customs purposes of goods released for free circulation after being assigned a different customs-approved treatment or use.

2. The customs value of perishable goods usually delivered on consignment may, at the request of the declarant, be determined under simplified rules without being subject to the evaluation criteria established in Articles 34, 35, and 36.

3. When there is a need to determine the customs value of imported goods and it is expressed in a currency other than Albanian Lek, the following procedure shall be used:

a) New exchange rates shall be determined each month , with the exception mentioned in paragraph 3(d);

b) Exchange rates shall be valid from the 6 of a month to the 5 of the following month;

c) The rate of exchange to be used shall be the exchange rate published by the Bank of Albania on the last working day of the month before the period mentioned in paragraph 3(b);

d) Where a rate of exchange published by the Bank of Albania differs by 5% or more from the rate decided in accordance with paragraph 3(c) for use in accordance with paragraph 3(b), it shall replace the latter rate and enter into use from the second working day following its publication as the rate to be used for the application of Article 27 for the rest of that period.

UNTAXABLE LIMIT

Section 5

Consignments of negligible value

504.

504.1. Subject to Point 505, any consignments made up of goods of negligible value dispatched direct from another country to a consignee in the Republic of Albania shall be admitted free of import duties.

504.2. Â“Goods of negligible valueÂ” means goods the intrinsic value of which does not exceed a total of 10 000 Lek per consignment.

505. The relief shall not apply to the following:

a) alcoholic products;

b) perfumes and toilet waters;

c) tobacco or tobacco products.

Section 6

Goods contained in travellers' personal luggage

506.

506.1. Subject to Points 507 to 510, goods contained in the personal luggage of travellers coming from another country shall be admitted free of import duties, provided such imports are of a non-commercial nature.

EXPORTING USING ATA CARNET

Article 428

In accordance with Part IV, Chapter 2, Section 4 of the Code, this chapter sets out provisions for the implementation of the export regime.

Article 429

1. The exporter, in terms of section 181 (4) of the Code, the person named in the name of or on behalf of which the export declaration is made and who is the owner of the goods or has similar right of disposal over them at the time when the accepted statements.

2. Where ownership or a similar right of disposal over the goods belongs to a person located abroad as a result of a contract in which the export is based, the exporter is considered to be the contracting party established in the Republic of Albania.

Article 430

Where administrative reasons, the first sentence of Article 181 (4) of the Code can not be applied, the declaration may be lodged with any customs office competent for the operation in question.

Article 431

When there is reason to duly justified and accepted by the Customs, an export declaration may be accepted at a customs office different from that referred to the first sentence of Article 181 (4) of the Code.

Article 432

Reasons duly justified means eg the customs office responsible for supervising the place where the exporter is established not in the direction of movement of goods and located farther than 30 km from the exporters premises. In these cases the exporter may submit an export declaration at the customs office first located on the border.

Article 433

1. The export declaration is based on the Single Administrative Document and copies 1, 2 and 3 of the form. Customs office where the export declaration is lodged (customs office of export) shall stamp Box A and complete box D. After release of the goods, it shall retain copy 1, send copy 2 to the statistical office and return copy 3 to the person concerned.

2. Before releasing the goods, as a general rule, identification of the goods provided by the sealing.

3. Must be sealed:

a) space where the transport vehicle containing the goods, when the conveyance is approved under other rules or recognized by the customs office of export as suitable for sealing;

b) each package, in other cases.

4. Means of transport may be suitable for sealing on condition that:

a) seals can be easily and effectively on them;

b) are constructed in such a way that no goods can be removed or introduced without leaving visible signs of damage or breaking the seal;

c) no concealed spaces where goods may be hidden, and

d) the space reserved for the load can be easily controlled by the customs authorities.

5. The customs office of export may dispense with sealing if, having identified other opportunities, description of goods in the export declaration makes it easily identifiable goods.

Article 434

1. Copy 3 of the Single Administrative Document and the goods released for export shall be presented to the customs office of exit.

2. "Customs office of exit" means:

a) in the case of goods exported by rail, postal, air or sea, the customs office competent for the place where goods are taken over by a single transport contract for transport to another location by the railway companies, the postal authorities, by companies airline or shipping companies;

b) in the case of goods exported by pipeline and in the case of electricity, the office designated by the General Directorate of Customs;

c) in the case of goods exported by other means or in circumstances not covered by paragraph (a) and (b), the last customs office before the goods leave the customs territory of the Republic of Albania.

3. Customs office of exit shall satisfy itself that the goods presented correspond to those declared and shall supervise the emergence of physical departure from the territory of the Republic of Albania. Normal indication that the goods presented correspond to the goods

declared that sinker is located are not affected and there is no sign of damage. Office in question, confirms the emergence of the goods through the confirmation on the reverse of the copy no. 3 and gives the copy the person who filed. Confirmation is made by a stamp showing the date and name of the office. Copy 3 of the export declaration, confirmed in accordance with this paragraph, at the request of other public authorities, can be used to test the goods to which it belongs are exported from the customs territory of the Republic of Albania. However, under paragraph 8, No. 3 return a copy of the featured person is not conducted before the close of the transit regime.

4. When the customs office of exit establishes that goods are missing, without prejudice to the criminal case, it shall note the copy of the declaration presented and inform the customs office of export.

5. When the customs office of exit establishes that goods are in excess, without prejudice to the criminal case, refuse exit to these goods until the formalities are fulfilled.

6. When the customs office of exit establishes a discrepancy in the nature of the goods, without prejudice to the criminal case, the goods shall refuse exit until the export formalities are completed and shall also inform the customs office of export.

7. In the cases referred to in paragraph 2 (a), the customs office of export shall endorse copy 3 of the declaration in accordance with paragraph 3. The transit should be used if the goods are unloaded or transhipped to another port, airport or railway station.

8. When the export goods are sent to a customs office of exit under a transit procedure, the office of departure the endorsement "Export" in red on all copies of the transit. The customs office of exit controls in the goods.

9. The customs office may require exporters to provide evidence that goods have left the customs territory of the Republic of Albania.

Article 435

1. Goods not subject to prohibition or restriction and with no value greater than 100 000 ALL per consignment and per declarant may be declared at the customs office of exit. This provision does not apply when the person making the export declaration acts as a professional customs agent on behalf of others.

2. Oral statements may be made only at the customs office of exit.

Article 436

Without prejudice to the export of used products of fisheries and other marine products, when goods leave the customs territory of the Republic of Albania without an export declaration filed as a result of errors or omissions or other special circumstances of involuntary, This declaration can be lodged retrospectively by the exporter at the customs office competent for the place where it is located. Acceptance of this declaration is performed when the exporter presents to the customs office concerned, of evidence concerning the nature and quantity of the goods concerned and the circumstances under which they left the customs territory of the Republic of Albania. That office shall also endorse copy 3 of the Single Administrative Document. Retrospective acceptance of the declaration does not preclude the imposition of sanctions in force.

Article 437

Where goods released for export do not leave the customs territory of the Republic of Albania, the exporter shall immediately inform the customs office of export. Copy 3 of the statement in question is returned to the office.

CHAPTER 2

Exports of fishing products and other products taken from the sea of Albanian fishing vessels without appearing in the Republic of Albania

Article 438

In the case of fisheries products and other products taken from the sea exported to the Republic of Albania without appearing there, used the following procedure:

a) return to the Republic of Albania, the master shall file an export declaration. This statement filed with the customs office competent for the place where it is located. Acceptance of this declaration shall be the driver submits to the customs office concerned, of evidence concerning the nature and quantity of the goods in question;

b) such evidence should consist of an authorized copy of the declaration filed in the country of destination;

c) the competent customs office shall endorse copy 3 of the Single Administrative Document in accordance with Article 433 (3).

CHAPTER 3

Temporary Exportation of using ATA Carnet

Article 439

1. An ATA Carnet can be used for export where the following conditions:

a) ATA carnet must be issued in the Republic and confirmed and guaranteed by an association established in the Republic which is part of an international guarantee chain;

b) ATA carnet Albanian applies only to goods on which no request for reimbursement;

c) should present the documents referred to in Article 221. The customs authorities may require the submission of the transport document;

d) is intended to be re-imported goods.

2. Where goods covered by an ATA Carnet are presented for the purpose of temporary exportation, the customs office of export shall carry out all formalities following:

a) verify the information given in boxes A to G of the exportation voucher against the goods covered by the carnet;

b) complete, where appropriate, the box cover of the carnet headed 'Certificate by customs authorities '';

c) complete the counterfoil and box H of the exportation voucher;

d) enter its name in box H (b) of the reimportation voucher;

e) retain the exportation voucher.

3. If the customs office of export is not the office of exit, customs office of export shall carry out the formalities referred to in paragraph 2, but not complete box 7 of the exportation counterfoil, which must be completed by the customs office of exit.

4. The time limit for reimportation of the goods designated by the customs authorities in box H (b) the exportation voucher may not exceed the validity of the carnet.

Article 440

When the goods leave the customs territory of the Republic of Albania under ATA Carnet is not intended to be reimported, the customs office of export is presented an export declaration containing the particulars referred to in Annex 37. Presentation of the carnet in question, it shall endorse copy 3 of the export declaration and shall invalidate the reimportation voucher and counterfoil.

Article 441

Directorate General of Customs may lay down guidelines for practical application of the export.

TRADE REGULATIONS, CUSTOMS AND STANDARDS

IMPORT TARIFFS

Albania enjoys a liberal trade regime. Foreign trade was liberalized in 1990 and follows guidelines set by the European Union and World Trade Organization. Albania has been a member of WTO since 2000.

The Directorate General of Customs is the institution responsible for the management of customs in the Republic of Albania. DG Customs is under the Ministry of Finance and conducts its activity pursuant to law no.8449 dated 27.01.1999 "Customs Code of the Republic of Albania" and its respective bylaws. The Albanian Custom Code's design is based on the Instruction of the Council of Europe EEC No. 2913/92 dated on 12 October 1992.

The general legal framework mainly consists of:

• Law no.8449 of 27.01.1999 "Customs Code of the Republic of Albania" which is in line with Regulation 2913/92/EEC "The Community Customs Code".

• Law no.8474 of 14.04.1999 "On the Combined Nomenclature of Goods" based on Regulation 2263/2000/EC which amended Annex I of Regulation EEC 2658/87. The nomenclature of goods in Albania changes every year as a result of the fulfillment of WTO requirements and Free Trade Agreements.

• Decision of Council of Ministers No 205 dated April 13, 1999, "On the Implementation of Provisions of the Customs Code", based on Regulation 2454/1993/EC.

• Free Trade Agreements (SAA, CEFTA ,FTA with Turkey)

The Stabilization and Association Agreement (SAA) with Albania, signed on 12 June 2006, entered into force almost three years later, on 1 April 2009, following ratification by EU member countries. The part of the Stabilization and Association Agreement (SAA) which is considered the Free Trade Agreement (FTA) between Albania and the EU was separated from the general agreement under the title "Interim Agreement" and entered

into force on December 2006. The SAA supersedes the Interim Agreement which is now an integral part of the SAA. It guarantees the:

* Establishment of a free trade area according to the commitments of Albania under the agreements signed with the World Trade Organization (WTO) and in concordance with article XXIV of the General Agreement on Tariffs and Trade (GATT) 1994;

* Implementation of a transitional period, which establishes a free trade area between the two parties, over a period of ten years, divided in two five year periods. The first period foresees: (i) tariff reduction for sensitive industrial products, agricultural products, processed agricultural products and fish products; (ii) different transitional periods for further liberalization of trade in services, public procurement, technical barriers to trade, etc. The provisions of the second period are subject to negotiations at the end of the first phase;

* Elimination of all quantitative trade restrictions, or other measures with a similar effect;

* Gradual elimination of custom tariffs, to ensure the complete liberalization of imports of industrial products, as well as a more balanced liberalization policy for the import of agricultural goods at the end of the transitional period;

* Convergence and harmonization of trade legislation with EU legislation, leading to a contemporary and appropriate legal framework with respect to: protective mechanisms, anti□dumping, provisional protective measures, technical trade barriers, sanitary and phytosanitary measures, protection of intellectual property, etc;

* Elimination of fiscal discrimination resulting from tariffs and taxes which are applicable in both parties' territories.

Tariff levels applied by the Albanian Customs vary from zero to fifteen percent based on the type of goods.

Albania has a Value Added Tax (VAT) of 20 percent. For imports into Albania, the VAT is assessed on the CIF (cost, insurance and freight) value of the goods plus the duty. Import regulations are generally not available in English. In order to learn about customs duties, taxes, and quality requirements for a specific product, U.S. exporters can contact freight forwarders or business consultants in Albania. For machinery and equipment imported for investment in the production, construction, transport, and telecommunications industries and in the energy sector, a VAT deferral payment system is applied. According to this system, VAT is not paid at customs points upon importation, but when the VAT Declaration is submitted at the tax office where the taxpayer is registered.

Goods placed in the transit regime, goods in active processing, and those which fall under the Temporary Allowance regime are exempt from VAT. The Decision of the Council of Ministers dated August 16, 2006 defines rules and specifics of products and services that are exempt from VAT.

Albanian exports are exempt from VAT. The Export Declaration serves as proof of export. The Export Declaration is designed according to the Unique Excise duty and applies to all of the following categories of products:

* Coffee

* Beer, wine, alcoholic drinks and other spirits

* Tobacco and its by-products

* Oil and its by-products

* different packaging materials i.e. plastic, glass and mixed packaging,

* new and used pneumatic tires,

* primary cells and batteries and electric accumulators.

For imported goods, excise is calculated on the basis of the CIF price plus duty.

During the last couple of years excise taxes have been the subject of frequent changes with most of the excises increasing. The last change was in 2010. For customs tariffs and excise tax levels please see the Customs Administration website at http://www.dogana.gov.al and the Tax Administration's website at www.tatime.gov.al . For certain items, taxes are levied based on a government-determined fair market price (reference price) or the global market price regardless of the actual price paid.

TRADE BARRIERS

Tariffs for exporting to Albania include customs duties, VAT and excise taxes. There are no significant non-tariff trade barriers. However, administrative bureaucracy can delay the movement of goods and increase costs. In addition, the application of "market prices" often referred to as "reference prices" in calculating customs dues and other taxes are becoming a concern and are being considered as a barrier for many businesses involved in trade activity.

IMPORT REQUIREMENTS AND DOCUMENTATION

The following are the main documents required for imports and exports:

1. Certificate of the quality of goods
2. Certificate of the analysis of goods
3. Certificate of the origin of goods
4. Original Purchase invoice (sales contract for the goods is optional)
5. Transportation documents (CMR, BL, AWB)
6. VAT number of Importer
7. Import Authorization for certain goods

It is obligatory to describe the sanitary characteristics of food or medical products.

IMPORT PROCEDURE

Importers should fill out a Declaration Form of Goods through a licensed customs agency for selling goods in Albania. The customs officers examine this form and then accept the Declaration Form. Payment of customs duties is made for the amount calculated by the customs authority. Customs officials might carry out a physical inspection of the merchandise prior to releasing it.

Import licenses are required for specific commodities with restricted circulation within the country, such as military or strategic goods, radioactive materials, psychotropic substances, and drugs. Import licenses can be obtained from the Ministry of Defense (military or strategic goods) or the Ministry of Health (drugs and psychotropic substances).

U.S. EXPORT CONTROLS

Most technology can be exported from the United States to Albania under general export licensing, but some equipment requires validated export licenses from the Bureau of Industry and Security (BIS), formerly the Bureau of Export Administration (U.S. Department of Commerce). Generally, military products and equipment such as optical equipment and software that may have dual usage require an export license. Export licenses can be obtained from the Bureau of Industry and Security. BIS coordinates the licensing process with the Departments of State and Defense.

The need for an export license depends on the product's Export Commodity Control Number (ECCN), available from the manufacturer, or from BIS by calling (202) 482-3332 or - 4811.

Albania has also approved a new law on the "State control over import-export of dual use military goods and commoditites/technologies."

Starting in June 2009, any company, public or private, dealing with import-export, transit, transshipping, transfer, exhibition of dual use military goods and commodities/ technologies or that serves as broker for these goods, included in the EU list of control, approved with the decision of the Council of Ministers No. 569, dated November 19, 2008, are legally bound to get licensed or authorized prior to the start of procedures by the State Export Control Agency in compliance with the Albanian legislation in force.

For more information please visit the State Export Control Authority web page: http://www.akshe.gov.al

TEMPORARY ENTRY

Albania is not a party to the Customs Convention on Carnet (ATA) for Temporary Import of Goods.

The Albanian customs regime is structured as follows:

Free circulation regime – Import or release of goods into free circulation, as a category of customs regime, means the permanent placing of goods in the territory of Albania. Products set under such a regime are subject to all trade policy measures, such as custom duties and other related payments.

Export – Export regime is applied on all Albanian products destined for export, outside the Albanian customs territory.

Active processing (Fason Regime) - The active processing regime implies that foreign goods undergo operations of transformation or processing on Albania's customs territory without the application of measures of economic policy, except for the customs processing fees, provided resulting products are exported.

Processing under customs control – This regime allows goods to be imported from outside Albania for processing operations, which change their nature or state, without being subject to import duties or other trade policy measures. Duty becomes payable when the finished product is put on free circulation. The duty is then payable on the finished product as if it had been imported directly.

Temporary Permit Regime – Under such a regime, non-Albanian goods destined for re-export can be used in the Albanian customs territory being completely or partially exempted from import duties and any trade policy measures if they are not experiencing any change except depreciation. The maximum period for goods to be under such regime is one year. After this period they should be re-exported.

Passive Processing - Albanian products are allowed to be exported temporarily outside the Albanian customs territory, so they can be processed and products gained from these operations may be placed in free circulation (re-imported) with complete or partial exception from import duties.

Transit regime - Transit of goods and vehicles means movement of goods and/or vehicles between foreign countries through the territory of Albania without application of economic policy measures thereof. Goods transported through the territory of Albania are exempt from customs duty, VAT, and excise taxes.

Temporary Warehouse regime – Products are considered to have the status of temporary storage from the moment they are present in the customs office until the time their destination is determined. Such goods are hold in specific areas approved by customs authorities.

LABELING AND MARKING REQUIREMENTS

According to the regulation for labeling of food products approved in 2006, labels must contain information that conforms to international standards. Labels for food products intended for end-consumers must be printed in Albanian and should include: name of the product, ingredients, quantity of special ingredients or categories of ingredients, details of the country of origin, net quantity/weight/volume, expiration date, manner of storage, pertinent consumer warnings, full address of the importer, the instructions for use if the appropriate use of the product is not possible without these instructions, and for drinks that contain more than 1.2 percent alcohol it should list the volume of alcohol.

Labels for non-food products destined for end consumer must have printed in Albanian language the information necessary for the identification and use of the product.

PROHIBITED AND RESTRICTED IMPORTS

There are no prohibited imports. Special Import Provisions are enforced for strategic sectors, such as weapons and munitions and dual-use items.

CUSTOMS REGULATIONS AND CONTACT INFORMATION

The General Directorate of Customs is responsible for the management, organization, and control of customs activity in Albania. The customs value of goods includes the price of the goods as well as transport and insurance expenses. For certain items, taxes are levied based on a government-determined fair market price or prices on the stock exchange regardless of the actual price paid.

For more information about customs regulations in Albania you can contact:

Mr. Flamur Gjymishka
General Director
General Directorate of Customs
Rr. Sami Frasheri
Tel: ++ 355 42 234499
Fax: ++ 355 42 243914
http://www.dogana.gov.al

STANDARDS

Albania has standardization, conformity assessment, accreditation and product certification bodies. In certain areas, such as processed foods, beverages and pharmaceutical products, individual ministries or agencies issue sector-specific standards and certificates.

Albania, in large part, has adopted standards regimes developed in other Western countries. ISO and EN are the primary standards-making bodies. Albania is a correspondent member without the right to vote in the International and European Organization for Standards (ISO, CEN & CENELEC) and, since April 2009, is an associate member to the IEC with a limited vote right.

Application of Albanian standards is mainly voluntary unless specifically provided otherwise in law. Aside from standards concerning products for human ingestion, most standards are not enforced by legislation. Standards are developed or adopted by Technical Committees composed of interested parties from different sectors and industries. The work of the committees is then passed on to the national standards organization -- the General Directorate of Standardization (DPS). DPS is the official local inquiry point for issues relating to Technical Barriers to Trade (TBT) and from July 2009, the obligations under WTO/SPS Agreement are passed to Ministry of Agriculture, Food and Consumer Protection sanitary and phyto-sanitary measures (SPS).

STANDARDS ORGANIZATIONS

The Ministry of European Integration (www.moi.gov.al) is responsible for the technical management and coordination of Albania's integration process in the European Union, through the approximation of national legislation to that of the Community, the development of integration policies, and the coordination of financial assistance and public information on this process.

General Directorate of Standardization (DPS) (www.dps.gov.al) is a non-profit public institution acting as the National Standards Body of the Republic of Albania, except for the telecommunication field. DPS reports to the Ministry of Economy, Trade and Energy and represents the Republic of Albania at European and International Organizations dealing with standards like CEN, CENELEC, ISO, IEC. DPS serves as a liaison to WTO officials.

In February 2008, the Albanian Parliament approved the new law on standardization, no. 9870. The objective of this law is to establish rules and procedures for the development of all national standardization activities and the establishment and functioning of the General Directorate of Standardization, as the National Standards Body in Albania. The law also aims to improve the existed legal framework in the field of standardization including the development of Albanian standards, and their publication and implementation.

DPS is responsible for developing, adopting, approving, implementing, amending, withdrawing, and publishing the Albanian Standards and to publish European and international standards. The price for an Albanian standard varies from USD 12 to 260 and, in general, their price is approximately 30% of the international standards. The most requested standards in Albania are construction, diesel and gasoline S SH EN 590 and S SH EN 228 and the standards for quality management and laboratory accreditation S SH ISO 9001 and S SH ISO 17025.

Ministry of Agriculture and Food and Consumer Protection: Albania follows WTO agreements on Sanitary and Phyto-Sanitary Procedures. To import food and agricultural products, companies must receive a license from the Food Quality and Inspection Directorate at the Ministry of Agriculture. When applicable, products also must pass sanitary, psychopathologic or veterinary control. Additional information on sanitary requirements can be obtained from the Ministry of Agriculture (www.mbumk.gov.al)

National Center for Drug Control –NCDC (www.qkkb.gov.al) represents an institution specialized in the analysis, control, and registration of drugs. It operates under the Ministry of Health and works in accordance with WHO principles. NCDC is the licensing authority for drug imports and maintains the drug registry in Albania. In June 2008, the government streamlined the import of the pharmaceutical products by lifting some document requirements.

NIST NOTIFY U.S. SERVICE

Member countries of the World Trade Organization (WTO) are required under the Agreement on Technical Barriers to Trade (TBT Agreement) to report all proposed technical regulations that could affect trade with other member countries. Notify U.S. is a free, web-based e-mail subscription service that offers an opportunity to review and comment on proposed foreign technical regulations that can affect your access to international markets. Register online at Internet URL: http://www.nist.gov/notifyus/

CONFORMITY ASSESSMENT

The conformity assessment body is the General Directorate of Metrology (GDM) www.dpmk.gov.al which operates under the responsibility of the Ministry of Economy, Trade and Energetic (METE) in accordance with the Law no. 9875 dated 14.02.2008, "On metrology". GDM implements the metrology policy in Albania in the three categories: scientific, industrial and legal metrology.

The GDM policy is to develop the national metrology system, in line with European standards fulfilling the country needs and requirements and to harmonize technical procedures for the conformity of measurements in order to avoid technical barriers to trade and enhance the quality of life of Albanian citizens. Its mission is to create, maintain and use the national measurement standards and references, to control measuring instruments in the fields of official and trade transactions, health care, environmental protection and technical safety as well as the quantity control of prepackaged goods and to offer calibration services to producers and users of measuring instruments

PRODUCT CERTIFICATION

Product certification is done on a voluntary basis, unless specifically provided otherwise under law. Most legal product certifications concern sanitary characteristics of foodstuffs and medicine.

As of today, Albania does not have any Mutual Recognition Agreements with any foreign organizations. However, in 2009, DPS signed cooperation agreements with its counterparts from Macedonia, Montenegro, Russia and Turkey.

ACCREDITATION

The Albanian Accreditation Directorate (DA) is recognized by the Albanian Government as the single national accreditation body to assess, in concordance with

internationally agreed standards, organizations that provide certification, testing, and inspection and calibration services. DA is a public authority under the Minister of Economy, Trade and Energy and exercises its activity pursuant to Law no.9024 dated on 06/03/2003 "On Accreditation of testing and calibration laboratories, certification and inspection bodies in Republic of Albania". DA operates a management system in line with the requirements of S SH ISO/IEC 17011 (Conformity Assessment General Requirements for accreditation conformity assessment bodies). DA also provides advice to the State Administration in matters concerning accreditation and other assessments and approvals of competence for carrying out conformity assessment procedures, and maintains updates and provides information on the status of accreditation of the accredited bodies.

Accreditation of laboratories is not compulsory for every sector. Accreditation is, however, mandatory for laboratories dealing with safety and health issues.

PUBLICATION OF TECHNICAL REGULATIONS

Approved technical regulations are published in the Official Gazette which can be found at the following address www.qpz.gov.al . Also each agency publishes its own publications. GDS publishes a quarterly standards bulletin (in Albanian) and the annual Catalogue of Albanian Standards. GDS is, according to the law, the National Authority for Notifications and a reference for draft standards, technical rules and procedures for conformity assessment.

Proposed technical regulations are not easily accessible to the public. With proposed regulations, however, the DPS notifies WTO officials in order to solicit comments.

LABELING AND MARKING RETURN TO TOP

According to the law on food, all food products destined for end consumers must have labels in Albanian. In 2008, the GOA passed legislation requiring that products destined for end consumers have labels in the Albanian language with all the info necessary for the identification and use of the product.

CONTACTS

General Directorate of Standardization
Mr. Bashkim Mucaj
Director
Rruga "Mine Peza", Nr. 143/3,
Tirana, Albania
Phone: + 355 4 224 7176 / 222 6255
Fax: + 355 4 224 7177 / 224 7177
http://www.dps.gov.al

National Food Authority
Mr. Genc Juka
Director
Ministry of Agriculture and Food
Deshmoret e Kombit, Blvd. No. 2
Tirana, Albania
Tel.: ++355 4 225 2658
Mobile: ++355 67 203 3171
http://www.mbumk.gov.al

Accreditation Directorate
Mr. Gezim Karapici
Director
Ministry of Economy and Energy
"Jean D'Ark," Blvd, No. 1
Tirana, Albania
Tel: ++355 4 234 0364 / 236 2566
E-mail: info@albanianaccreditation.gov.al
http://www.albanianaccreditation.gov.al

General Directorate of Metrology
Director
Rruga " Sami Frasheri" Nr.33
TIRANE ALBANIA Tel: 00 355 4 223 3174 Fax: 00 355 4 223 3462

E-mail: metrology@dpmk.gov.al
http://www.dpmk.gov.al

Point of Contact at the U.S. Embassy are
Ms. Margo Pogorzelski
Economic & Commercial Officer
United States Embassy
Rruga Elbasanit, 103
Tirana, Albania
Tel. +355 4 224 7285 x 3319
Fax: +355 4 223 2222
E-mail: PogorzelskiML@state.gov

Ms. Edi Jacellari
Commercial Assistant
United States Embassy
Rruga Elbasanit, 103
Tirana, Albania
Tel. +355 4 224 7285 x 3116
Fax: +355 4 223 2222
E-mail: JacellariE@state.gov

Mr. Frank Nikolla
Economic Assistant
United States Embassy
Rruga Elbasanit, 103
Tirana, Albania
Tel. +355 4 224 7285 x 3065
Fax: +355 4 223 2222
E-mail: NikollaF@state.gov

TRADE AGREEMENTS

Albania joined the World Trade Organization in 2000 and applies WTO rules on import licensing. From October 1999 to December 2006, Albanian exports to EU countries have benefited from an asymmetric regime, in the form of autonomous measures. Therefore, Albanian exports are subject to various reductions and discounts on duties when accessing the EU market. The regime was applicable both to agricultural and industrial goods.

On June 12, 2006, Albania signed the Stabilization and Association Agreement with the European Union after a prolonged period of negotiations. As an important achievement toward eventual EU integration, the Stabilization and Association Agreement includes the establishment of a free trade area between Albania and the EU in a 10 year time frame. The Interim Agreement (the FTA part of the SAA) entered into force on December 1, 2006. This liberalizes trade relations between the EU and Albania in terms of tariff barriers for both agricultural and industrial goods. The SAA was ratified on April 2009 and supersedes the Interim Agreement which is now an integral part of the SAA.

Trade with neighboring countries has improved since 2003, when the first bilateral Free Trade Agreement entered into force. On December 19, 2006, all of Albania's bilateral trade agreements with countries in the region were transformed into a multilateral one, the Central European Free Trade Agreement (CEFTA), which includes eight countries (Albania, Macedonia, Montenegro, Kosovo, Moldova, Croatia, Serbia and Bosnia and Herzegovina). CEFTA officially came into effect on July 26, 2007. Since CEFTA replaced all the bilateral FTAs its member states had signed with one another and created one regional FTA, it has not created new trade incentives that did not already exist. Albania's trade with its neighbors is seeing modest growth, but it starts from a low base and is constrained by poor infrastructure such as roads and ports.

Albania has also a free Trade Agreement with Turkey (signed in 2006 and entered into force on May 2008.) On June 2009, Albania also signed an FTA with the European Free Trade Association (EFTA.) Following ratification of the EFTA-Albania Free Trade Agreement by Liechtenstein, Switzerland and Albania, the Agreement entered into force between these three parties on 1 November 2010. For Iceland and Norway, it will become effective after completion of the respective ratification procedures. EFTA member states are Iceland, Liechtenstein, Norway and Switzerland.

WEB RESOURCES

http://www.mete.gov.al
http://www.dogana.gov.al
http://www.dps.gov.al
http:/www.dpmk.gov.al
http:/www.albanianaccreditation.gov.al
http://www.mbu.gov.al
http://www.acit-al.org
http://www.moh.gov.al
http://www.qkkb.gov.al

INVESTMENT CLIMATE

OPENNESS TO FOREIGN INVESTMENT

Albania has put in place a liberal foreign investment regime and increasing FDI is a top priority for the Albanian government. The government has taken measures to improve the business climate by streamlining business procedures through e-government reforms and has also undertaken a comprehensive structural reform to improve the legislation in many sectors. Although FDI has increased during the last couple of years, it still remains among the lowest in the region with a good part of it coming from privatizations. Despite progress in reforms, the major factors hindering FDI seem to remain the same: widespread corruption, weak law enforcement, insufficiently defined property rights, lack of developed infrastructure, government bureaucracy and frequent changes in the legal framework.

The legal framework to encourage investment is already in place. Law 7764 "On Foreign Investment," dated November 2, 1993, was designed to create a favorable investment climate for foreign investors in the country. The law offers considerable guarantees to all foreigners (either physical persons or legal entities) willing to invest in Albania. Such provisions include:

* No prior government authorization is needed and no sector is closed to foreign investment.

* There is no limitation on the percentage share of foreign participation in companies - 100 percent foreign ownership is possible.

* Foreign investment may not be expropriated or nationalized directly or indirectly, except for designated special cases, in the interest of public use and defined by law.

* Foreign investors enjoy the right to expatriate all funds and contributions in kind of their investments.

* Most favorable treatment for investors according to international agreements is provided under Albanian law.

In addition, in September 2010 the parliament approved some amendments to this law, introducing special protection for foreign investments in the public and tourism infrastructure, energy and agriculture sectors. The state special protection is not granted *a priori* but is granted only after occurrence of the dispute through a decision of the Council of Ministers following the request presented by the respective minister and the foreign investor.

According to Law 10316 "On some amendments to the law on foreign investments", special protection of the state is granted to investments related to a concession agreement based on the Albanian Concession Law; or an immovable property, made available to the foreign investor by the Albanian state; or an immovable property over which the foreign investor has rights based on a valid, legal, public document or act issued by a competent state-entity or public authority, where such investment exceeds or is foreseen to exceed the value of EUR 10 million. Under the special state protection, the foreign investor is substituted in the judiciary process by the Albanian state and any injunction order issued by the court shall be executed over state properties.

There are limited exceptions to this liberal investment regime - most of which apply the purchase of real estate: agricultural land cannot be purchased by foreigners, but may be rented for up to 99 years; and commercial property may be purchased, but only if the proposed investment is worth three times the price of the land. There are no restrictions on the purchase of private residential property.

Investors in Albania are entitled to judicial protection of legal rights related to their investments. Foreign investors have the right to submit disputes to an Albanian court. In addition, parties to a dispute may agree to arbitration. Provisions regarding domestic and international commercial arbitration are incorporated into the Albanian Code of Civil Procedure.

Albania's tax system does not discriminate against foreign investors and no distinction is made between foreign and domestic investors. The on-going reform in the sector aims at increasing the efficiency of the tax administration and reducing corruption.

The key piece of legislation that addresses the activities of companies and establishes the type of legal structure under which companies may operate is the new law 9901 of 2008 "On Entrepreneurs and Commercial Companies," which replaced the law of 1992. The new law brings Albanian legislation in line with the EU's acquis communitaire and reflects amendments of other Albanian legislation like the Civil Code, the Law on National Business Registration Center, Labor Law, Law on Securities and others. The most common type of organization for foreign investors is a limited liability company. Other forms of business entities allowed under the current law are joint stock companies, joint ventures, unlimited partnership, limited partnership and sole entrepreneur enterprises.

The National Business Registration Center, functional since September 2007, serves as a one-stop-shop for business registration. Starting a business became easier with online publishing of forms and procedures, reduction of registration costs, and the consolidation of tax, health insurance, and labor registration into a single application. Licensing for businesses has also been streamlined with the opening of the Business Licensing Center in July 2009. As a result, many licenses were abolished and a broad simplification of licensing procedures has been completed in many sectors.

Albania improved public procurement procedures by approving a new law and introducing e-procurement. The new law approved in 2006 takes into account the principles of non-discrimination, equal treatment, transparency, and legal protection of interests of bidders on public contracts. Direct tendering has been abolished and criteria to identify abnormally low bids have been introduced. The latest amendments of the law mostly enabled the establishment of the Public Procurement Commission (PPC) transferring the claims-reviewing function from the Public Procurement Agency to the Commission. (Previously the PPA was responsible for both policymaking and implementation of the law as well as with the reviewing of the claims.) The Public Procurement Advocate established in 2008 performs functions similar to an ombudsman, safeguarding the rights and interests of suppliers against acts or omissions by contracting authorities. Regardless of legal improvements, companies continue to experience issues with transparency in specifications and communication in competing for public tenders. Overall, the improvements in the public procurement legislation are advancing while the proper enforcement of the law is still a work in progress.

The law "On Concessions," No. 9663, dated December 18, 2006, established the necessary framework for promoting and facilitating the implementation of privately financed concessionary projects enhancing transparency, fairness, efficiency and long-term sustainability in the development of infrastructure and public service projects. One of its major amendments includes a better regulation for unsolicited proposals and of public-private partnerships in general. The law applies to a wide range of sectors, including:

a) transport (railway system, rail transport, ports, airports, roads, tunnels, bridges, parking facilities, public transport);

b) generation and distribution of electricity and heating;

c) production and distribution of water, treatment, collection distribution and administration of waste water, irrigation, drainage, cleaning of canals, dams;

d) collection, transfer, processing and administration of solid waste;

e) telecommunication;

f) education and sport;

g) health;

h) tourism and culture;

i) prison infrastructure;

j) recycling projects, rehabilitation of land and forests, in industrial parks, housing, governmental buildings, service of maintenance of IT and data base infrastructure;

k) natural gas distribution; and

l) management contracts or provision of public services including those related to sectors specified above.

In order to promote investments in priority sectors the GOA may offer concessions to local or international investors for the symbolic price of one Euro. The GOA, with the approval of the Minister of Economy, authorizes concessions in other sectors besides those listed above. The law does not apply to concessions that require a separate operating license unless that is included in the framework of the concession agreement.

The privatization process of the past 20 years has almost come to an end with only a few large privatizations remaining. The privatizations are carried out by open international tender or auction. The GOA has announced its intention to continue with the privatization of 100 percent of the state-owned insurer INSIG, privatization of Albpetrol, the state-owned company that manages all the existing gas and oil fields in Albania and enjoys the right to sign Petroleum Agreements for the existing oil-fields, as well as privatization through auction of the 16.7 percent of state owned shares on the fixed line monopoly Albtelecom and its constituent Eagle Mobile, and privatization of real estate owned by military. Recently, the Minister of Economy has announced that the Albanian government will consider privatizing four existing Hydropower Plants (HPPs): Ulza 25 MW, Shkopet 24 MW, and Bistrica I and Bistrica II with 22MW and 2MW installed respective capacity.

The GOA does not screen foreign investments and the United States enjoys a popular image in Albania. Both business community and public generally welcome American firms and their products. Companies interested in entering the Albanian market should contact Albanian Investment and Development Agency (AIDA.) AIDA provides direct assistance to investors, promotes SMEs, Albanian exports and FDI.

AIDA Albanian Investment and Development Agency (former ALBINVEST)
Blv. "Gjergj Fishta", Pall. Shallvareve, Tirana, Albania
tel: +355 4 252 886; fax: +355 4 222 341
e-mail: info@albinvest.gov.al
www.albinvest.gov.al

Corruption perception Index, Doing Business 2011, Heritage Economic Freedom Scorecard by MCC and Moody evaluation

	2011	2010	2009	2008	2007
TI Corruption Index	n/a	3.3	3.20	3.40	2.90
Heritage Economic Freedom	n/a	66	63.70	63.30	61.38
World Bank - Ease of Doing Business (rank)	82	81.00	86.00	135.00	120.00
MCC Government Effectiveness	n/a	0.08	0.00	-0.15	-0.33
MCC Rule of Law	n/a	-0.24	-0.22	-0.20	-0.47
MCC Control of Corruption	n/a	0.09	-0.12	-0.30	-0.34
MCC Fiscal Policy	n/a	-4.20	-3.60	-3.98	-4.41
MCC Trade Policy	n/a	85.80	75.80	63.20	57.40
MCC Regulatory Quality	n/a	0.60	0.24	0.01	-0.01
MCC Business Start Up	n/a	0.98	0.97	0.97	0.39
MCC Lands Rights Access	n/a	0.87	0.81	0.73	n/a
MCC Natural Resource Management	n/a	97.29	79.65	79.43	n/a

MCC median score is zero and reports are for fiscal year noted.

In June 2007, Moody's Investors Service assigned Albania its first-ever sovereign rating of 'Ba1' for foreign-currency bonds and an issuer rating of 'B1' for debt obligations of the government. In April 2010, Standard & Poor's assigned Albania B+ long-term foreign and local currency sovereign credit ratings. S&P also assigned B short-term foreign and local currency ratings to the country. As of December 6, 2010 Moody's rated GOA debt for both foreign and domestic currency as B1 and forecasted a stable outlook for the future. Albania successfully issued a five year term 300 million Eurobond in late 2010 with an interest rate of 7.5 percent.

CONVERSION AND TRANSFER POLICIES

The Bank of Albania (BOA) formulates, adopts and implements the foreign exchange policy of Albania and maintains a supervisory role in foreign exchange activities in accordance with the Law On the Bank of Albania No. 8269 dated 1997 amended in July 2002, the Banking Law No. 9662 dating December 2006 which regulates the operation of commercial banks, and the Regulation on Foreign Exchange Activities (FX Regulation).

As a general rule, the Banking Law does not impose any restrictions on the purchase, sale, holding, or transfer of monetary foreign exchanges. However, the Law on the BOA authorizes it to temporarily restrict the purchase, sale, holding, or transfer of foreign exchanges if the BOA so decides, in order to preserve the foreign exchange rate or its official reserves. In practice, the BOA has not used such measures in an overly restrictive manner and aims to achieve European standards for banking systems. In 2009, BOA temporarily tightened supervision rules over liquidity transfers by domestic banks to their foreign mother banks due to the financial global crisis, the widespread lack of liquidity in the international banking sector and its negative effects over the domestic market

The Albanian currency, the lek, follows a floating free regime and is freely convertible at banks and exchange bureaus. The Albanian foreign investment law guarantees the right to transfer and repatriate any funds associated with an investment from Albania into freely usable currency, at a market-clearing rate. To repatriate profit, evidence of the settlement of tax liabilities and establishment company act should be presented. In the case of joint ventures, the company should present evidence of distribution of profits to shareholders and proof of joint stock company membership. Banks might also ask additional information in the framework of the Anti Money Laundering law.

Under the FX Regulation, foreign exchange transactions are those involving the exchange, purchase or sale of foreign currency in cash through a personal account or that of a third party, including the repayment of a loan in a currency different from the one in which the loan was granted or accepted.

Foreign exchange transfers abroad can only be carried out by licensed entities (domestic banks, foreign bank branches and foreign exchange offices) that are required

to report their foreign exchange activities to the BOA regularly. These entities are also obliged to complete and keep all documentation required for transfers abroad.

Although the FX Regulation provides that residents and non-residents may transfer capital within and into Albania without any restrictions, capital transfers out of the territory of Albania are subject to certain documentation requirements. Physical persons must submit a request indicating the reasons for the capital transfer, the amount of capital transferred outside the territory of Albania, and the address to which the capital is to be transferred. Such persons must also submit a declaration on the source of the funds to be transferred. Legal entities must submit a request setting forth the reason for the capital transfer, the source of the funds, the amount to be transferred, and the address to which the capital is to be transferred; a document from the foreign entity explaining this transfer (if such a document exists); the decision by the legal entities' relevant decision-making body on carrying out the capital transfer; the legal entities' registration decision; and, a certificate issued by the tax office certifying that the legal entities has settled its tax obligations toward the tax authorities.

In May 2008, Parliament passed a new law "On Money Laundering and Terror Financing," which lowers the threshold for reporting financial transactions to the Financial Investigation Unit (FIU) from the current US$ 20,000 to US$ 15,000 for cash transactions (thereby ensuring compliance with EU standards). Both Albanian and foreign citizens entering or leaving the country must declare assets in excess of Lek 1,000,000 (approximately US$ 10,000) in hard currency and/or precious items. Failure to declare such assets is considered a criminal act and punishable by confiscation of the assets and detention.

EXPROPRIATION AND COMPENSATION

The Albanian constitution guarantees the right of private property. According to Article 41 of the Albanian Constitution, expropriation or limitation in the exercise of a property right can be done only in the public interest and with fair compensation. In the post-communist period, expropriation has been limited to land needed for projects in the public interest, mainly infrastructure projects including but not limited to roads, energy infrastructure, water works, airports, etc. However, compensation has generally been below market value and some owners have complained publicly about the slow compensation process and unfair compensation.

There are many on-going disputes for properties confiscated during the communist regime. The restitution and compensation process that started in 1993 has been slow and marred by corruption. The process is still on-going and many U.S. citizens have long-running disputes with the government regarding restitution of property. Cases that end up in the courts tend to drag on for years without a final decision, forcing many to take the case to the Strasburg Human Rights Court.

The GOA has presented three methods of compensation for expropriation claims: 1) restitution, 2) compensation of property with similarly valued land in a different location, and 3) cash settlement/financial compensation. However, the process is not expected to complete in the near term because of large number of requests, the large financial cost associated with it and the slow pace of compensation with similarly valued property.

DISPUTE SETTLEMENT

The Government of Albania has made efforts to handle investment disputes in an appropriate manner but issues continue to hamper effective resolution of disputes. The judicial system is viewed by the business community to be slow and inefficient in its handling of investment disputes. Albania has signed major arbitration agreements and is legally obligated to enforce international and domestic arbitration agreements.

Legal System

Albania has a civil law system similar to that of most other European countries. The Albanian Constitution provides for a clear separation of legislative, executive and judicial branches, thus sanctioning the independence of the judiciary. Civil Procedure in Albania is governed by the Civil Procedure Code enacted in 1996. The civil court system consists of District Courts as the first instance courts, appellate courts as the second instance courts, and the Supreme Court, as the third instance court. Outside of the court system, there is another special court, namely the Constitutional Court which, upon request, reviews whether laws or subsidiary legislation are in compliance with the Constitution and also protects and enforces the constitutional rights of citizens and legal entities. The District Courts are organized in special sections for adjudication; family disputes, commercial disputes and the section for administrative disputes. Parties may appeal the judgment of the first instance courts within 15 days while the Appellate Court judgments might be appealed within 30 days to the Supreme Court.

As Albania does not have a commercial code, legislation is encapsulated in a series of commercial laws. Relevant laws include: Foreign Investment Law, Commercial Companies Law, Bankruptcy Law, Environmental Law, Corporate and Municipal Bonds, Transport Law, Maritime Law, Secured Transactions Law, Employment Law, Taxation Procedures Law, Banking Law, Insurance and Reinsurance Law, Concessions Law, Mining Law, Energy Law, Water Resources

Law, Waste Management Law, Excise Law, Oil and Gas Law, Gambling Law, Telecommunications Law, Value Added Law, and Sports Law.

Albania has enacted and introduced laws and subsidiary legislation in respect to property rights and contract rights. The courts and the court bailiffs are the authorities empowered by law to (i) issue the writ of execution and (ii) enforce in practice the claims of parties described in the writ of execution. According to the Albanian Civil Procedure Code, foreign court judgments are recognized and enforced by the Court of Appeal in a summary proceeding.

Bankruptcy: Bankruptcy is governed by Law 8901, dated May 23, 2002, "On Bankruptcy" amended in May 2008. It is similar in organization to German bankruptcy law. The Bankruptcy Law, as amended, aims at finding a proper solution through the reorganization or liquidation of insolvent businesses. It sets out non-discriminatory and mandatory rules for the repayment of the obligations by a debtor in a bankruptcy procedure. The new insolvency law established time limits during insolvency, professional qualifications for insolvency administrators, and an Agency of Insolvency Supervision to regulate insolvency administrators. A simplified insolvency procedure for small businesses was introduced as well. In reality, the law on the bankruptcy has reportedly never been utilized and there have been no bankruptcy procedures so far. Generally, there exists only a voluntary liquidation procedure.

Arbitration: The Government of Albania accepts binding international arbitration clauses in specific investment agreements, and in many cases it has been a party to arbitration disputes in foreign or international arbitration tribunals, as agreed in investment agreements. Albania has signed and ratified the New York Convention. In order to have a settlement recognized, a case must be brought before the Court of Appeals and have the order to enforce directed to the court bailiffs. This is necessary because winning parties cannot directly communicate with bailiffs to enforce settlements/awards.

A new law on commercial arbitration is still in draft form and aims at regulating all domestic and international arbitration procedures and transposes the provisions of UNCITRAL Model law, which in turn incorporates the New York Convention provisions. This means that to date international proceedings arbitration can be conducted based on the aforementioned ratified international conventions. Domestic arbitration continues to be governed by the provisions on the Civil Code Procedure which is more or less in line with UNCITRAL arbitration. There is a private arbitration centre (MEDART), which is a service center established under a World Bank funded legal and judicial reform project in 2001.

An alternative to the dispute settlement via the courts is private arbitration or mediation. Parties can engage in arbitration when they have agreed to arbitrate according to a dispute resolution clause integrated in the original agreement, through a separate arbitration agreement or by mutual agreement at any time when the dispute is evidenced. Legislation distinguishes arbitration of international disputes from arbitration of domestic disputes in that the parties involved in an international dispute may agree to settle through either a domestic or foreign arbitration tribunal. Under the Albanian Constitution, ratified international agreements prevail over the domestic legislation. Albania has signed and ratified the 1966 Convention "On the Settlement of Investment Disputes" between States and Nationals of Other States (Washington Convention) as well as the Convention of 1958 "On the Recognition and Enforcement of Foreign Arbitral Awards" (New York Convention). It has also ratified the 1927 Convention and the European Convention on Arbitration (Geneva Convention).

PERFORMANCE REQUIREMENTS AND INCENTIVES

Albanian law generally does not establish performance requirements or detailed incentives for foreign investors except for a few cases. One important exception concerning performance requirements is the investment requirement relating to the purchase of commercial property by foreigners. Such a purchase can be made only if the investor plans to improve the value of the property by three times the purchase price. Another recently approved incentive has to do with the state special protection related to a concession agreement based on the Albanian Concession Law; or an immovable property, made available to the foreign investor by the Albanian state or an immovable property over which the foreign investor has rights based on a valid, legal, public document or act issued by a competent state-entity or public authority, where such investment exceeds or is foreseen to exceed the value of EUR 10 million. Under the special state protection, the foreign investor is substituted in the judiciary process by the Albanian state and any injunction order issued by the court shall be executed over state properties.

The GOA applies a liberal foreign investment regime offering equal treatment of foreign and domestic investors. Albania has also signed bilateral agreements on the promotion and protection of reciprocal investments and has signed double taxation treaties with many countries. Some other incentives include: tax exemption of dividends designated for investments; importers of machinery and equipment are eligible for VAT deferral if the machinery and equipment will solely serve its taxable economic activity; apparel producers are exempt from VAT on raw materials as long as the finished product is exported; subsidized leases of state-owned premises. (On a case by case investors are eligible to lease state-owned property such as land or buildings at rents below market rates. In the case of production activities, the level of rent reduction will be made according to the level of investment made and the number of new jobs created. This is based on the decree of the Council of Ministers, No. 315, dated April 24, 2006 "On the leasing of state enterprises and institution's property.")

During the last couple of years, Albania has reduced the corporate income tax from 20% to 10% and has reduced the fiscal burden of social security contributions payable by employers to 15%. Incentives are regulated by Law 9374, dated April 21, 2005, "On State Aid," for the implementation of important projects, to facilitate the development of specific economic activities, and to promote national culture and heritage conservation. "On State Aid" applies to all sectors of manufacturing and services and all measures undertaken by central and local government, as well as other entities acting on behalf of the state that confer benefits to particular enterprises, except those acting in the agriculture and fisheries sectors. Energy Sector Incentives: The government ensures the sale of electricity generated from new hydro power plants with less than 15MW installed capacity for a period of 15 years with favorable prices approved annually by the Energy Regulator. The law on concessions established the necessary framework for promoting and facilitating the implementation of privately financed concessionary projects. The law regulates the unsolicited proposals and the public-private partnership in general and applies to a wide-range of sectors.

There are no excessively onerous visas, residence, or work permit requirements, or any similar requirements inhibiting foreign investors' mobility. There are no discriminatory or preferential export policies and import policies affecting foreign investors. There are no requirements in Albania for foreign investors to purchase from local sources or to export a certain percentage of the output. One of the non-tariff barriers, which reportedly is one of the major concerns of the business community, are reference prices (alternately called market prices) that are used for the calculation of custom dues of imported goods and salaries (for the purpose of calculating personal income tax, social and health contributions.) However, the Albanian government claims the use of reference prices in customs is limited.

RIGHT TO PRIVATE OWNERSHIP AND ESTABLISHMENT RETURN TO TOP

Albanian law permits private ownership and establishment of enterprises and property. Foreign investors do not need additional permission or authorization to do so over and above that required of domestic investors. Albania applies restrictions only on the purchase of real estate; agricultural land cannot be purchased by foreigners, but may be rented for up to 99 years; commercial property may be purchased, but only if the proposed investment is worth three times the price of the land. There are no restrictions on the purchase of private residential property. Both foreign and domestic investors

continue to experience significant issues in resolving property disputes arising from unclear or incomplete documentation.

Foreigners can acquire concession rights on natural resources and on resources of the common interest, as defined by the law on concessions. For some business operations, licenses are needed. The National Licensing Center (NLC) became functional in July 2009 and the center serves as a one-stop-shop for business licenses. More information on the types of licenses and application procedures can be found at www.qkl.gov.al

Based on the Law No. 9723, dated 03.05.2007 "National Registration Center" and following the opening of the National Registration Center for Businesses (NRC) in September 2007, business entities can be registered in a single place, in one day, for one Euro. More information on NCR can be found at www.qkr.gov.al . Both NLC and NRC were established with assistance from the Millennium Challenge Corporation Albania Threshold Program, as e-government initiatives, and save investors valuable time in establishing and carrying out business operations, while also increasing transparency and reducing opportunities for corruption.

Foreign and domestic investors have numerous options available for organizing business operations in Albania. According to the new Law No. 9901, dated April 14, 2008 "On Entrepreneurs and Commercial Companies" ("Commercial Law") and Law No. 9723, dated 03.05.2007 "On National Registration Center", the legal types of business entities that can be registered with NRC are as follows: Sole Entrepreneur, Unlimited Partnership, Limited Partnership, Limited Liability Company (Shpk), Joint Stock Company, Branches and Representative Offices and Joint Ventures. More details can be found by visiting NLC at www.qkl.gov.al

PROTECTION OF PROPERTY RIGHTS

Albanian law protects copyrights, patents, trademarks, stamps, mark of origin, and industrial designs but in general, IPR rules are poorly enforced in Albania. Albania has ratified the following international treaties and conventions:

On Copyright

* Berne Convention on the Protection of Literary and Artistic Works, since 1994.

* Universal Copyright Convention, since 2003

* Rome Convention for the Protection of Performers, Producers of Phonograms and Broadcasting Organizations, since 2000

* Convention for the Protection of Producers of Phonograms Against Unauthorized Duplication of Their Phonograms, since 2001

* WTO TRIPS Agreement on Trade Related Aspects of Intellectual Property Rights, since 2002

* WIPO Copyright Treaty (WCT), since 2005

* WIPO Performances and Phonograms Treaty (WPPT), since 2002

On intellectual property

* Convention Establishing the World Intellectual Property Organization (WIPO Convention) since 1992.

* Paris Convention for the Protection of Industrial Property, since 1995.

* Madrid Agreement Concerning the International Registration of Marks, since 1995, and the Protocol relating to that Agreement, since 2003.

* Patent Corporation Treaties (PCT) 1970, since 1995.

* Extension Agreement between the Government of Albania and the European Patent Organization on the cooperation in the field of Patents

* Nice Agreement Concerning the International Classification of Goods and Services for the purposes of the registration of Marks, since 2003.

* Budapest Treaties on the International Recognition of the deposit of Micro organisms for the purposes of patent procedure, since 2003.

* Hague Agreement and Geneva Act Concerning the International deposit of Industrial Design, since 2007.

* Strasbourg Agreement Concerning the International Patent Classification, since 2007.

* TRIPS Agreement since 1994

In 2010, Albania became a contracting party to the WIPO Patent Law Treaty and a full member of the European Patent Organization.

Albania has been updating the legal framework for the protection of Copyrights and Intellectual and Industrial Property Rights and the main institutions involved in enforcing the legislation on IPR are: Albanian Copyright Office (ACO); the General Directorate of Patents and Trademarks (GDPT); the General Directorate for Customs; Tax Inspectorate; Prosecutor's Office; police and the courts.

The Albanian Copyright Office, established in 2006 is the main institution responsible for monitoring and implementing the law on copyright approved in 2005. However, the ACO lacks administrative and institutional capacity and law enforcement on copyrights remains incomplete and violations of copyrights are common. The number of cases of violation of copyright law brought to court remains low. The ACO sanctions are not effective as the level of fines is low and collection rate is insignificant. In 2010, a law on administrative contraventions was adopted aiming to improve collection of fines for infringements of copyrights.

The Directorate General for Patents and Trademarks (GDPT) is responsible for registration and administration of patents, commercial trademarks and service marks, industrial designs and geographical indications. In 2008 the Albanian government approved the Industrial Property Law and a number of by-laws and implementing regulation are already in place. Further capacity strengthening and additional human resources are needed for GDPT.

The General Directorate of Customs includes a directorate for the protection of the IPR and has the powers to act *ex officio.*

Overall, the copyright and IPR protection are weak and the effects of the national strategy for the enforcement of copyrights and intellectual and industrial property rights approved in 2010, aimed at strengthening the administrative capacity, improving inter-institutional coordination and raising the awareness of the benefits of IPR, remain to be evaluated in the future. Meanwhile, U.S. companies are advised to consult an attorney

experienced in IPR issues and to diffuse as much IPR risk as possible by establishing solid commercial relationships and drafting tight contracts.

Immovable Property Rights

Large-scale property confiscation during communist rule and the subsequent nationalization of the economy completely altered Albania's economic landscape. Following the fall of communism in the early 1990, GOA undertook property reform re-establishing private immovable property, introducing civil law principles and transactions and acknowledging ownership rights to those who had been expropriated during communism.

The property restitution and compensation process started in 1993 and is still on-going with no set date for finalization on the horizon. The property registration process has begun but has only been completed partially. More lucrative land in high value coastal areas has not yet been fully registered due to existing disputes over property title. The legalization process that started in 2006, aiming to address the large scale illegal construction, which is considered a major impediment to secure property titles, is still on-going. The number of informal buildings is estimated to be 350,000 and the surface occupied is estimated to be 320,000 hectares.

Despite some progress, immovable property rights (land rights) are still far from well defined. The legislation was developed in a piecemeal and uncoordinated way, often resulting in overlapping property titles leading to a large number of legal conflicts. The numerous agencies operating in an uncoordinated fashion contributed to the already complex property issue. In addition, the improper functioning of the land registry system, large presence of illegal construction and widespread corruption further contributed to what is considered today one of the most complex issues that needs to be addressed properly by the Albanian government.

Currently, enforcement of property rights is pursued in the civil court system. An overwhelmingly large number of civil cases in the Albanian courts involve property issues while many property disputes linger for years before reaching a final ruling. This has caused the courts to suffer from a backlog of property issues. Also, the lack of the enforcement of court decisions is another issue of concern re property issues. Those have led an escalating number of citizens to file suit with the European Court for Human Rights in Strasbourg against the GOA over property claims.

Generally, despite progress, unresolved property issues have undermined efforts to develop a functional land market and have hindered FDI in the country. To address the negative impact that the lack of clear property titles and legal uncertainty over property titles have on foreign investors, the Albanian government recently approved a law that grants special protection to investments related to a concession agreement based on the Albanian Concession Law; or an immovable property, made available to the foreign investor by the Albanian state; or an immovable property over which the foreign investor has rights based on a valid, legal, public document or act issued by a competent state-entity or public authority, where such investment exceeds or is foreseen to exceed the value of EUR 10 million. Under the special state protection, the foreign investor is substituted in the judiciary process by the Albanian state and any injunction order issued by the court shall be executed over state properties.

Overall, despite progress clear property title and legal certainty over property titles continue to remain an issue of concern for investors and hamper the functioning of a land market.

TRANSPARENCY OF REGULATORY SYSTEM

Albania's regulatory system has improved over the years and doesn't specifically discriminate against foreign investors. However, frequent changes in legislation, lack of transparency in developing legislation and regulations, improper enforcement of the legislation and bureaucracy are a burden for the business community.

According to the World Bank Doing Business 2011 report, which measures business regulation across nine indicators, Albania ranked 82 out of 183 countries up from 136 out of 178 countries in 2008 and down one place from its 2010 ranking. The significant ranking improvement over the last couple of years reflects major improvements in starting a business, paying taxes, protecting investors, enforcing contracts, obtaining credit and registering property.

Albania has adopted the necessary legislation and has established the necessary agencies aimed at ensuring transparent rules and regulations in order to foster competition and attract investment. The law on Protection of Competition was approved in 2003 and amended several times with the Agency for the Protection of Competition becoming functional in 2004. The law seeks to secure "clear game rules" however, the operational independence and administrative capacity of the Competition Authority need to be strengthened to enforce the legislation efficiently.

Other independent agencies and bodies, including the High State Audit, Energy Regulator, Telecom Regulator and other major institutions that operate to ensure transparency in different sectors. New legislation on public procurement introduced e-procurement and contributed in increased transparency in public procurements. Business registration and licensing are streamlined through the once stop shop centers for registration and licensing. A new company law approved in 2008 includes rules on disclosure requirements, formation, maintenance and alteration of capital, mergers and divisions, takeover bids and shareholders' rights, as well as corporate governance principles. The law on accounting and financial statements includes reporting provisions according to which large companies will apply International Financial Reporting Standards, while small and medium businesses will apply National Financial Reporting Standards.

Proposed laws and regulations are sometimes not published in draft form for public comment. Businesses have difficulty obtaining copies of laws and regulations especially in their draft form. There has been modest improvement in this area recently as several state agencies operate well-organized websites which are updated regularly. Some agencies have undertaken steps to consult with business, civil society and affected groups about issues in proposed laws and regulations. Although Albania has taken some steps forward to improve business advocacy by establishing the Business Advisory Council, business participation in the legislative processes remains limited

EFFICIENT CAPITAL MARKETS AND PORTFOLIO INVESTMENT

The banking sector in Albania remains sound, profitable and well supplied with liquidity. It has, in general, been spared from the global financial turmoil, primarily due to the low amount of loans relative to total deposits and a lack of a housing/real estate bubble. In fall 2008, the sector suffered from a significant reduction of about 15% of deposits which created some liquidity concerns which were promptly managed by Central Bank which played an active role in monitoring the sector and ensuring enough liquidity in the banking sector.

After summer 2009, a stable increase of bank deposits took place and by the end of 2009 the system fully recovered and deposits reached their pre-crisis level. In November 2010, banks deposits were 16% higher than one year ago. That said, commercial banks remain cautious in their lending policies which has been reflected in a lower rate of growth credit of the economy.

This is also a result of increasing non performing loans in November 2010 at 14.4% of the total loans compared to just 4.3% before the eruption of the financial crisis.

GOA has adopted policies and regulations stipulating the free flow of financial resources in an attempt to promote foreign investments in Albania. The Bank of Albania is legally entitled to restrict temporarily the transfer of foreign exchange for current transactions in order to protect the level of the exchange rates or its official reserves. However, such restrictions can only be introduced for a period not exceeding twelve months, and can only be extended for another similar period. In 2009, following global financial meltdown BOA restricted the distribution of the domestic banking sector profits in order to maintain sufficient liquidity in the sector. The restriction was lifted in July 2010.

In the absence of a stock market, the banking sector remains the main channel for business financing. It is totally dominated by commercial banks with private shareholders. Currently, 16 banks are operating in country – two with Albanian shareholders while the rest are foreign including Raiffeisen, Intesa San Paolo, Societe General, Alfa Bank, Piraeus Group etc. The performance of the financial sector in channeling savings towards productive investment has substantially improved and is quickly reaching Western standards.

The credit market is quite competitive but interest rates can be high; under some circumstances, between 10 and 15% in the domestic currency. Most mortgage and commercial loans are denominated in euros. There are no additional conditions to foreign investors to get credit from the banks operating in Albania. Commercial banks have improved the quality of services they offer including credit instruments. The private sector has widely benefited from the expansion of these instruments varying from the traditional letter of credit to bank drafts, etc for clearing business payments. Still, businesses report that high interest rates, distrust of the banking system, high operating costs of banks and poor business/project proposals remain concerning issues which affect access to credit in Albania;.

While portfolio investments remain limited mostly to company shares, government bonds and real estate, the government has undertaken different measures to render investing in Albania attractive to foreign investors. It has adopted a 10% flat rate on both corporate and personal income taxes while interest rates in domestic currency are more than double of those in dollars. In 2010, the GOA successfully launched its debut

Eurobonds in international markets with an interest rate of 7.5% which was regard as quite positive considering the current global financial situation.

Total assets of the banking sector at the end of November 2010 are estimated at about US$ 10 billion consisting mostly of bank deposits. The degree of market concentration remains fairly high as the largest five largest banks dominate the market with about 80 percent of total assets. There is enough liquidity to transfer out sizable positions but must conform to rules like advance notification. The banking network has extended to most parts of Albania and developments in this respect are promising. In September 2010, there were 554 branches, up from 127 in 2005. Also the number of debit/credit cards, ATM and Point-of-Sales terminals is growing rapidly.

There do not appear to be "cross-shareholding" or "stable shareholder" arrangements to restrict foreign investment in private firms through mergers and acquisitions. The Albania law On Entrepreneurs and Companies does not limit the percentage of shares that joint-stock companies may own in cross-shareholding. The law recognizes the company as "parent" if it has at least 30% of votes at the general meeting of the other which is considered as its subsidiary.

Hostile takeover is not known in Albania. Domestic legislation does not specifically deal with hostile takeovers especially in the total absence of publicly-traded firms. The law On the Takeover of Companies with Public Offer applies to publicly announced offers issued by a public company as well as foreign public companies listed on the stock exchange in Albania. The law on Entrepreneurs and Companies requires that a person or company that acquires or sells shares of a joint stock company from 3 to 75% must notify the National Registration Centre in writing of that acquisition or sale within 15 days.

COMPETITION FROM STATE OWNED ENTERPRISES

The privatization process of SOEs in Albania is nearing completion and SOEs are active only in few sectors (mainly utilities). SOEs are present is energy generation (KESH), insurance (INSIG), water supply, ports, railway and extraction and sale of oil (Albpetrol.)

In general, there is no discrimination between public and private companies operating in the same sector but there have been instances of allegations by businesses that believe state-owned companies were granted preferential treatment in government contracts. SOEs operate as commercial companies in compliance with the law on “Entrepreneurs and Commercial Companies.” SOEs have the executive director and a Supervisory Board whose members are proposed: one third from the Ministry of Finance, one third from the Ministry of Economy, Trade and Energy and one third by the ministry or institution the company reports to. For water supply and sewage companies the proposal is done based on their statute. Under procedure, the SOE supervisory board report directly to the government. SOEs are required to submit annual reports and are also required to undergo independent audits. Albania doesn’t have a major Sovereign Wealth Fund.

CORPORATE SOCIAL RESPONSIBILITY

In general, there is little awareness of corporate social responsibility among producers and consumers with the exception of large companies, mostly foreign companies, which try to employ social corporate responsibility principles. The laws and legislation related to CSR exist in Albania and if implemented fully could constitute a strong base for further development of CSR practices in Albania. Even academic instruction on CSR in Albania is in a very early stage of development. Corporate Governance courses, Environmental Engineering and Business Ethics curricula have only been introduced in the past several years at some universities. The UNDP Global Compact and Corporate Social Responsibility project launched in 2007 has organized a number of educational events aimed at informing all stakeholders, government and media in particular, on their role in raising overall awareness of Corporate Social Responsibility in Albania and increasing knowledge and engagement of business communities in CSR practices.

POLITICAL VIOLENCE

There have not been any incidents of politically-motivated damage to commercial or government projects and the overall level of political violence is low. However, a political demonstration led by the opposition Socialist Party turned violent on January 21, 2011. Four protesters were shot and killed with many injured, including police, protesters and bystanders. An investigation into the events surrounding the violence is ongoing. Albania held parliamentary elections on June 28, 2009. The new government was formed with a coalition between the ruling Democratic Party (DP) and the formerly left-opposition party Movement for Socialist Integration (LSI). The Socialist Party (SP) has at times boycotted parliament since it convened in September 2009 and has called for investigations into alleged electoral fraud in the June 28 elections. Small crime, specifically incidents of extortion, theft and robbery, continue to be of some concern to the business community. Nonetheless, the domestic climate has been steadily improving and the violent crime rate has substantially decreased. Albania is a steady source of stability in the region and relations with neighboring countries are friendly.

CORRUPTION

Corruption, including bribery, raises the costs and risks of doing business. Corruption has a corrosive impact on both market opportunities overseas for U.S. companies and the broader business climate. It also deters international investment, stifles economic growth and development, distorts prices, and undermines the rule of law.

It is important for U.S. companies, irrespective of their size, to assess the business climate in the relevant market in which they will be operating or investing, and to have an effective compliance program or measures to prevent and detect corruption, including foreign bribery. U.S. individuals and firms operating or investing in foreign markets should take the time to become familiar with the relevant anticorruption laws of both the foreign country and the United States in order to properly comply with them, and where appropriate, they should seek the advice of legal counsel.

The U.S. Government seeks to level the global playing field for U.S. businesses by encouraging other countries to take steps to criminalize their own companies' acts of corruption, including bribery of foreign public officials, by requiring them to uphold their obligations under relevant international conventions. A U. S. firm that believes a competitor is seeking to use bribery of a foreign public official to secure a contract should bring this to the attention of appropriate U.S. agencies, as noted below.

U.S. Foreign Corrupt Practices Act: In 1977, the United States enacted the Foreign Corrupt Practices Act (FCPA), which makes it unlawful for a U.S. person, and certain foreign issuers of securities, to make a corrupt payment to foreign public officials for the purpose of obtaining or retaining business for or with, or directing business to, any person. The FCPA also applies to foreign firms and persons who take any act in furtherance of such a corrupt payment while in the United States. For more detailed information on the FCPA, see the FCPA Lay-Person's Guide at: http://www.justice.gov/criminal/fraud/

Other Instruments: It is U.S. Government policy to promote good governance, including host country implementation and enforcement of anti-corruption laws and policies pursuant to their obligations under international agreements. Since enactment of the FCPA, the United States has been instrumental to the expansion of the international framework to fight corruption. Several significant components of this framework are the OECD Convention on Combating Bribery of Foreign Public Officials in International Business Transactions (OECD Antibribery Convention), the United Nations Convention against Corruption (UN Convention), the Inter-American Convention against Corruption (OAS Convention), the Council of Europe Criminal and Civil Law Conventions, and a growing list of U.S. free trade agreements. This country is party to [add instrument to which this country is party], but generally all countries prohibit the bribery and solicitation of their public officials.

OECD Antibribery Convention: The OECD Antibribery Convention entered into force in February 1999. As of December 2009, there are 38 parties to the Convention including the United States (see http://www.oecd.org/dataoecd/59/13/40272933.pdf). Major exporters China, India, and Russia are not parties, although the U.S. Government strongly endorses their eventual accession to the Convention. The Convention obligates the Parties to criminalize bribery of foreign public officials in the conduct of international business. The United States meets its international obligations under the OECD Antibribery Convention through the U.S. FCPA. [Insert information as to whether your country is a party to the OECD Convention.]

UN Convention: The UN Anticorruption Convention entered into force on December 14, 2005, and there are 143 parties to it as of December 2009 (see http://www.unodc.org/unodc/en/treaties/CAC/signatories.html). The UN Convention is the first global comprehensive international anticorruption agreement. The UN Convention requires countries to establish criminal and other offences to cover a wide range of acts of corruption. The

UN Convention goes beyond previous anticorruption instruments, covering a broad range of issues ranging from basic forms of corruption such as bribery and solicitation, embezzlement, trading in influence to the concealment and laundering of the proceeds of corruption. The Convention contains transnational business bribery provisions that are functionally similar to those in the OECD Antibribery Convention and contains provisions on private sector auditing and books and records requirements. Other provisions address matters such as prevention, international

cooperation, and asset recovery. [Insert information as to whether your country is a party to the UN Convention.]

OAS Convention: In 1996, the Member States of the Organization of American States (OAS) adopted the first international anticorruption legal instrument, the Inter-American Convention against Corruption (OAS Convention), which entered into force in March 1997. The OAS Convention, among other things, establishes a set of preventive measures against corruption, provides for the criminalization of certain acts of corruption, including transnational bribery and illicit enrichment, and contains a series of provisions to strengthen the cooperation between its States Parties in areas such as mutual legal assistance and technical cooperation. As of December 2009, the OAS Convention has 33 parties (see http://www.oas.org/juridico/english/Sigs/b-58.html) [Insert information as to whether your country is a party to the OAS Convention.]

Council of Europe Criminal Law and Civil Law Conventions: Many European countries are parties to either the Council of Europe (CoE) Criminal Law Convention on Corruption, the Civil Law Convention, or both. The Criminal Law Convention requires criminalization of a wide range of national and transnational conduct, including bribery, money-laundering, and account offenses. It also incorporates provisions on liability of legal persons and witness protection. The Civil Law Convention includes provisions on compensation for damage relating to corrupt acts, whistleblower protection, and validity of contracts, inter alia. The Group of States against Corruption (GRECO) was established in 1999 by the CoE to monitor compliance with these and related anti-corruption standards. Currently, GRECO comprises 46 member States (45 European countries and the United States). As of December 2009, the Criminal Law Convention has 42 parties and the Civil Law Convention has 34 (see www.coe.int/greco.) [Insert information as to whether your country is a party to the Council of Europe Conventions.]

Free Trade Agreements: While it is U.S. Government policy to include anticorruption provisions in free trade agreements (FTAs) that it negotiates with its trading partners, the anticorruption provisions have evolved over time. The most recent FTAs negotiated now require trading partners to criminalize "active bribery" of public officials (offering bribes to any public official must be made a criminal offense, both domestically and trans-nationally) as well as domestic "passive bribery" (solicitation of a bribe by a domestic official). All U.S. FTAs may be found at the U.S. Trade Representative Website: http://www.ustr.gov/trade-agreements/free-trade-agreements . [Insert information as to whether your country has an FTA with the United States: Country [X] has a free trade agreement (FTA) in place with the United States, the [name of FTA], which came into force. Consult USTR Website for date: http://www.ustr.gov/trade-agreements/free-trade-agreements.]

Local Laws: U.S. firms should familiarize themselves with local anticorruption laws, and, where appropriate, seek legal counsel. While the U.S. Department of Commerce cannot provide legal advice on local laws, the Department's U.S. and Foreign Commercial Service can provide assistance with navigating the host country's legal system and obtaining a list of local legal counsel.

Assistance for U.S. Businesses: The U.S. Department of Commerce offers several services to aid U.S. businesses seeking to address business-related corruption issues. For example, the U.S.

and Foreign Commercial Service can provide services that may assist U.S. companies in conducting their due diligence as part of the company's

overarching compliance program when choosing business partners or agents overseas. The U.S. Foreign and Commercial Service can be reached directly through its offices in every major U.S. and foreign city, or through its Website at www.trade.gov/cs .

The Departments of Commerce and State provide worldwide support for qualified U.S. companies bidding on foreign government contracts through the Commerce Department's Advocacy Center and State's Office of Commercial and Business Affairs. Problems, including alleged corruption by foreign governments or competitors, encountered by U.S. companies in seeking such foreign business opportunities can be brought to the attention of appropriate U.S. government officials, including local embassy personnel and through the Department of Commerce Trade Compliance Center "Report A Trade Barrier" Website at tcc.export.gov/Report_a_Barrier/index.asp .

Guidance on the U.S. FCPA: The Department of Justice's (DOJ) FCPA Opinion Procedure enables U.S. firms and individuals to request a statement of the Justice Department's present enforcement intentions under the anti-bribery provisions of the FCPA regarding any proposed business conduct. The details of the opinion procedure are available on DOJ's Fraud Section Website at www.justice.gov/criminal/fraud/fcpa . Although the Department of Commerce has no enforcement role with respect to the FCPA, it supplies general guidance to U.S. exporters who have questions about the FCPA and about international developments concerning the FCPA. For further information, see the Office of the Chief Counsel for International Counsel, U.S. Department of Commerce, Website, at http://www.ogc.doc.gov/trans_anti_bribery.html . More general information on the FCPA is available at the Websites listed below.

Exporters and investors should be aware that generally all countries prohibit the bribery of their public officials, and prohibit their officials from soliciting bribes under domestic laws. Most countries are required to criminalize such bribery and other acts of corruption by virtue of being parties to various international conventions discussed above.

Anti-Corruption Resources

Some useful resources for individuals and companies regarding combating corruption in global markets include the following:

* Information about the U.S. Foreign Corrupt Practices Act (FCPA), including a "Lay-Person's Guide to the FCPA" is available at the U.S. Department of Justice's Website at: http://www.justice.gov/criminal/fraud/fcpa .

* Information about the OECD Antibribery Convention including links to national implementing legislation and country monitoring reports is available at: http://www.oecd.org/department/0,3355,en_2649_34859_1_1_1_1_1,00.html . See also new Antibribery Recommendation and Good Practice Guidance Annex for companies: http://www.oecd.org/dataoecd/11/40/44176910.pdf

* General information about anticorruption initiatives, such as the OECD Convention and the FCPA, including translations of the statute into several languages, is available at the Department of Commerce Office of the Chief Counsel for International Commerce Website: http://www.ogc.doc.gov/trans_anti_bribery.html .

* Transparency International (TI) publishes an annual Corruption Perceptions Index (CPI). The CPI measures the perceived level of public-sector corruption in 180 countries and territories around the world. The CPI is available at: http://www.transparency.org/policy_research/surveys_indices/cpi/2009 . TI also publishes

an annual *Global Corruption Report* which provides a systematic evaluation of the state of corruption around the world. It includes an in-depth analysis of a focal theme, a series of country reports that document major corruption related events and developments from all continents and an overview of the latest research findings on anti-corruption diagnostics and tools. See http://www.transparency.org/publications/gcr .

* The World Bank Institute publishes Worldwide Governance Indicators (WGI). These indicators assess six dimensions of governance in 212 countries, including Voice and Accountability, Political Stability and Absence of Violence, Government Effectiveness, Regulatory Quality, Rule of Law and Control of Corruption. See http://info.worldbank.org/governance/wgi/sc_country.asp . The World Bank Business Environment and Enterprise Performance Surveys may also be of interest and are available at: http://go.worldbank.org/RQQXYJ6210 .

* The World Economic Forum publishes the *Global Enabling Trade Report*, which presents the rankings of the Enabling Trade Index, and includes an assessment of the transparency of border administration (focused on bribe payments and corruption) and a separate segment on corruption and the regulatory environment. See http://www.weforum.org/en/initiatives/gcp/GlobalEnablingTradeReport/index.htm .

* Additional country information related to corruption can be found in the U.S. State Department's annual *Human Rights Report* available at http://www.state.gov/g/drl/rls/hrrpt/ .

* Global Integrity, a nonprofit organization, publishes its annual *Global Integrity Report*, which provides indicators for 92 countries with respect to governance and anti-corruption. The report highlights the strengths and weaknesses of national level anti-corruption systems. The report is available at: http://report.globalintegrity.org/ .

Corruption in Albania

Under the Albanian criminal code both active and passive corruption, abuse of office and undue influence are considered criminal offences. In addition to basic corruption offenses, there are specific criminal provisions addressing active and passive corruption by persons exercising public functions, high state officials and locally elected persons, judges, prosecutors and employees of the judicial bodies and the private sector. There are also provisions addressing trading in influence.

Active corruption in private sector (Art, 164/a of Criminal Code) is punished with a term of three months up to two years and a fine of from approximately USD 2,000 - 10,000 while passive corruption (Art. 164/b) is sentenced from six months up to three years of imprisonment and a fine from USD 3,000 - 10,000. Active corruption by high state public

officials (Art. 245) is punishable from one up to five years of imprisonment and a fine from USD 5,000 -20,000 while passive corruption of the above mentioned officials (Art 259) is punishable from four to twelve years of imprisonments and a fine from USD 10,000 - 50,000. Active corruption of persons exercising public functions (Art 244) is punishable from six months up to five years of imprisonment and a fine from USD 5,000 - 20,000, while passive corruption (Art 259) is punishable with a prison terms from two up to eight years and a fine from USD 5,000 - 30,000. The exercising of unlawful influence on public officials (Art 245/1) for the receiver of the irregular benefits as a result of this influence is punishable from six months to two years of imprisonment and a fine from USD 3,000 - 10,000 and for the exerciser of such influence with a prison term from six months to four years and a fine from USD 5,000 -20,000. Abuse of office (Art. 312), when it doesn't constitute another criminal offense is punishable up to seven years of imprisonment and a fine of USD 3,000 -10,000. Active corruption of judges (art 319), prosecutors and other officials of the justice bodies is punished with a prison term of one to four years and a fine from USD 4,000-20,000 while passive corruption of the above is punishable with a prison term from three to ten years and a fine from USD 8,000 – 40,000.

However, gaps exist and cases of bribery by foreign public officials are not covered by the Criminal Code. Based on GRECO recommendations GOA has prepared the necessary amendments to the Criminal Code addressing cases of active and passive corruption by foreign public officials, of a judge or official of international courts, local and foreign arbitrator and member of a foreign jury. The amendments are currently awaiting approval by the parliament. However, the question of jurisdiction on criminal acts committed abroad by Albanian citizens is still unresolved even with the current proposed amendments that are awaiting parliament's approval.

Albanian legislation has been amended and changed frequently in recent years to strengthen the framework dealing with corruption and organized crime in order to bring the Albanian legislation in line with civil and criminal conventions of the European Union. There has been some progress in reducing corruption, mainly through reducing opportunities for corruption, automating government processes and streamlining the procedures for business registration, payment of taxes, licensing and increasing transparency in public procurements. However, corruption remains a serious problem in Albania and the judiciary, health sector, property rights and funding of political parties remain areas of particular concern. Government procurements, despite considerable improvements, continue to be an issue of concern for businesses. Despite that the number of corruption cases that have been investigated and prosecuted is increasing the conviction rates remain very low. Furthermore, there is little track-record of investigation, prosecution and conviction in high-level corruption cases. Overall, Albania is improving but falls short on law enforcement in the fight against corruption. Perception of corruption, despite some slight improvements, continues to be high and in 2010 TI Corruption Perception Index Report Albania scored 3.3, ranking 87 out of 178 countries.

Albania has ratified several international treaties and conventions relating to corruption and is member of some of the major international organizations and programs dealing with corruption and/or organized crime. Albania has ratified The Civil Law Convention on Corruption (Council of Europe), The Criminal Law Convention on Corruption (Council of Europe), The Additional Protocol to Criminal Law Convention on Corruption (Council of Europe), and the United Nations Convention Against Corruption (UNCAC). Albania has also ratified a number of key conventions in the broader field of economic crime,

including the Convention on Laundering, Search, Seizure and Confiscation of the Proceeds from Crime (2001) and Convention on Cybercrime (2002). Albania has been a member of the Group of States Against Corruption (GRECO) since the ratification of the Criminal Law Convention on Corruption in 2001 and is also a member of the Stability Pact Anti-Corruption Network (SPAI). Albania is not a party to OECD Convention on Combating Bribery of Foreign Public Officials in International Business Transactions.

Main institutions involved in combating corruption include the Inter-Ministerial Anti-Corruption Task Force headed by the Prime Minister. This structure serves as a coordinating body for anti-corruption initiatives, namely anti-corruption strategy which is drafted every year. The Anti-Corruption Task Force is supported by the Department of Internal Administrative Control and Anti-Corruption (DIACA) which has relatively wide-ranging powers to investigate allegations of irregularities by public officials. DIACA serves as an Inspectorate for all central executive public institutions and is mandated to investigate allegations of procedural irregularities and irregularities in the handling of public finances. It reports to the Prime Minister. The High Inspectorate for the Declaration and Audit of Assets (HIDAA), established in 2003, collects and audits the annual declaration of assets and properties of mid-high level public officials in central and local executive agencies as well as politicians, and supervises the prevention of conflicts of interest situations.

Police authorities and the Prosecutor General's Office are in charge of criminal investigations and law enforcement, while the State Audit Commission and internal auditing units within different state institutions, inspect, assess, and report alleged cases of corruption. Joint Investigative Unit against corruption and economic crime was established in 2007 in the Tirana District Prosecution Office. The unit is a multi-agency taskforce composed of police staff from the prosecutor's offices, the state, customs and tax police and other relevant institutions, working together on specific investigations. Based on the first unit model, six more units were established in regions throughout Albania to prosecute corruption and economic crimes outside Tirana. The High State Control is the highest institution of economic and financial control. It supervises the economic activity of state institutions and other state juridical persons as well as the use and preservation of state funds by the central and local government institutions. It is subject only to the Constitution and laws, and the Head of the High State Control is appointed and dismissed by the Assembly upon proposal of the President. In the Judiciary, the High Council of Justice is in charge of appointment and removal of judges and prosecutors in the first and second instances. Specialized inspectors investigate allegations of misconduct of judges and the High Council of Justice then takes the relevant disciplinary measures, including removal.

Transparency International Albania is the main international non-governmental watchdog organization in Albania. There are also other non-governmental organizations that perform watchdog functions re corruption.

BILATERAL INVESTMENT AGREEMENTS RETURN TO TOP

A bilateral investment treaty between the United States and Albania was signed in 1995 and entered into force on January 3, 1998. This treaty, inter alia, ensures that U.S. investors receive national or most-favored-nation treatment and provides for dispute settlement. As of December, 2010, Albania has concluded bilateral investment protection agreements with the following countries:

Agreements in force:

Austria, Belgium, Bosnia &Herzegovina, Bulgaria, China, Croatia, Czech Republic, Denmark, Egypt, Lithuania, Finland, France, Germany, Greece, Hungary, Israel, Italy, Kosovo, Kuwait, Macedonia, Malaysia, Moldavia, Montenegro, Netherland Antilles, Netherlands, OPEC Fund for International Development, Poland, Portugal, Republic of Korea, Romania, Russia, Serbia,

Slovenia, Spain, Sweden, Switzerland, Turkey, Ukraine, United Kingdom and USA

Signed Agreements:

Tunisia

Albania has also signed agreements for the avoidance of double taxation and the prevention of fiscal evasion with respect to taxes on income and on capital with many countries, which have priority over Albanian domestic laws. The following are countries with which Albania has signed and ratified treaties for the avoidance of double taxation:

Poland, Romania, Malaysia, Hungary, Turkey, Czech Republic, Russia, Macedonia, Croatia, Italy, Bulgaria, Sweden, Norway, Greece, Malta, Switzerland, Moldava, Belgium, China, France, Egypt, Netherlands, Kosova, Serbia, Montenegro, Austria, Slovenia, Latvia, South Korea, Bosnia and Herzegovina, Ireland, Luxemburg, Spain and Kuwait.

Agreements negotiated, awaiting signature: Slovakia, Germany, Estonia, Lebanon, Ukraine, Singapore, Kuwait, Spain and India.

Agreemetns in process: Qatar, Pakistani, Thailand, Singapore, Mexico, Indonesia, Australia, Marocco, Vietnam, United Arab Emirates and Syria.

OPIC AND OTHER INVESTMENT INSURANCE PROGRAMS

The U.S. Overseas Private Investment Corporation (OPIC) and Albania signed a bilateral agreement on November 19, 1991. Albania has also ratified MIGA Convention, which established the Multilateral Investment Guarantees Agency (MIGA). MIGA provides investment guarantees against certain non-commercial risks (i.e., political risk insurance) to eligible foreign investors for qualified investments in developing member countries. MIGA's coverage is against the following risks: currency transfer restriction, expropriation, breach of contract, war, terrorism, and civil disturbance and non-honoring of sovereign financial obligations. It provides insurance against risks similar to that offered by OPI; MIGA and OPIC can work together on projects.

In 1998, OPIC supported the Southeast Europe Equity Investment Fund, which invested heavily in southeastern Europe. OPIC supported its successor, SEEF II managed by Bedminster Capital. SEEF II has invested in the Albanian health sector and IT. For more information on OPIC please visit http://www.opic.gov

Overseas Private Investment Corporation
1100 New York Ave., NW Washington, DC 20527
Tel: 202-336-8400
Email for general business inquiries to: info@opic.gov

LABOR

Labor relations between employee and employer are regulated by individual employment contracts pursuant to Law "On the Status of the Civil Employee and the Labor Code. Albania was an ILO member from 1920-1967 and has been ILO member from 1991 onwards and adheres to all basic international labor organization (ILO) conventions protecting worker rights. The GOA has established the National Council of Labor, composed of government officials, trade unions and employers associations. Its major goal is to improve social dialogue between the government, management and employees. The institutions that deal with the labor market are: Ministry of Labor and Social Affairs, National Employment Service, State Labor Inspectorate and other private actors like Private Employment Agencies, and Private Vocational Training Centers.

Employers and employees have the right to form trade unions (Labor Code, article 176). Trade unions are organized at the national level (according to industrial sector) and at the company level. The right to strike is sanctioned by Law no. 7458 (January 12, 1991) and by the Labor Code. Trade unions have the right to negotiate wages, working conditions, etc., and the employment contracts are applicable both to union and to non-union workers. Two main national-level trade unions, both affiliated with the ITUC (International Trade Union Confederation) are the Confederation of Trade Unions (KSSH) and The Union of the Independent Trade Unions of Albania (BSPSH). Employment contracts can be for a limited or an unlimited period, but as a general rule, employment contracts are signed for an unlimited period if the duration is not specified properly in the contract.

The labor force in Albania is about 1.06 million and the official unemployment rate during the third quarter of 2010 stood at 13.52%. Almost 55% of the population is considered self-employed in the agricultural sector. Almost 1.2 million Albanians emigrated to Italy and Greece during the last two decades. A high proportion of Albanians under-40 speaks two languages, generally Italian and English. Due to the large number of emigrants in neighboring Greece, Greek is also spoken. While some members of the labor force are highly skilled, many work in low-skill industries or have out-of-date technological skills. However, Albanians are a young population (median age

31) and have adapted to modern market practices quickly and often display impressive entrepreneurship.

Albania has a tradition of strong secondary education which prepares students to enter the labor market. Elementary education is compulsory and a large percentage of those who finish elementary school continue to high school. Sixty two percent of high school graduates go on to college. The GOA has opened new public universities in Albania which, along with the new private universities, represent impressive growth in this sector. In addition, the number of students who receive graduate degrees abroad has increased significantly, establishing a generation of skilled professionals which the government is trying to lure back to Albania through the Brain Gain Project (a UNDP program offering financial incentives to Albanians educated abroad to return to Albania to work). In 2007, the GOA established the Excellency Fund which aims to promote and financially reward youngsters and students during their studies.

The average salary in public administration during the third quarter of 2009 amounted to 44,700 lek (about US$ 440) monthly. In July 2010, the GOA increased the minimum monthly wage applicable for both the public administration and the private sector to 19,000 lek (about US$ 190), which is still among the lowest in the region. However, since 2008, to counter informality in the labor sector due to under reporting of revenue by businesses, the government is using minimum reference salaries (MRS) for the private sector. The MRS establishes a standard wage depending on job code for all employees and is used to calculate both the personal income tax and the rate of contributions for social and health insurance. It is not necessarily the actual salary an employee receives.

FOREIGN-TRADE ZONES/FREE PORTS

The GOA approved Law 9789, dated July 19. 2007 “On the Establishment and Functioning of Economic Zones,” abolishing Law 8636, dated July 6, 2000, "On Free Zones." The current legislation regulates the establishment of economic zones and related matters and makes the establishment and the functioning of such zones more efficient. It anticipates the establishment of free trade zones and industrial parks near ports, airports or at the crossroads of international transport. Economic zones are proposed by the Ministry of Economy and approved by the Council of Ministers on a case-by-case basis. The latter has the power to define the status of the zone (either a free zone or an industrial park), areas and boundaries, the economic activities to be performed within the zones, the period of the zone functioning, the method of granting the permission (lease, concession, etc.) and the procedures for the selection of the “developer.” The selection of the "developer" of the economic zones is based on the criteria defined in the law 9663, dated December 18, 2006 “On Concessions.”

Following the approval of the new law in 2007, the GOA approved the construction of several industrial parks: Shengjin, Koplik, Vlore, Elbasan, Lezhe, Shkoder and the industrial and energy park in Spitalle, Durres (the largest, with 850 hectares). Four of these parks are located near the main ports of Albania - Durres, Vlore, Shengjin and Lezhe. Industrial zones may be used for production, manufacturing, agro-processing, export-import and supporting activities. To date none of these projects have moved significantly forward.

In 2009, Albanian government approved the first free economic zone adjacent to the approved container port in Vlore. On March 2010, following an open international tender Albanian government selected Zumax AG as the developer of the zone (Zumax AG has also the concession for the container port in Vlore.)

FOREIGN DIRECT INVESTMENT STATISTICS

Although FDI has increased over the years, fueled in large part by privatizations, it still remains among the lowest in the region. Cumulative FDI in Albania is also among the lowest in the region and Albania's investments abroad are insignificant. Strategic privatizations, once the major source of FDI, are shriveling with only a few ones left. Although the Albanian government has focused on promoting FDI in the country and has

signed a large number of projects in several sectors including energy, oil and mining only a few projects have materialized during 2009-2010.

The Bank of Albania reports the following figures for foreign direct investment in Albania. FDI during the first nine months of 2010 dropped slightly from US$ 788 million in 2009 to US$ 742 in 2010 reflecting the global economic downturn. In 2009, the FDI was 7.8 % of GDP.

Years	2004	2005	2006	2007	2008	2009	2010*
FDI in million USD	324	258	315	647	888	942	742

Source: Bank of Albania

*BoA estimate for the first three quarters of 2010

Leading investor nations in Albania include: Italy, Greece, Turkey, Austria, Czech Republic, Canada, Austria, Germany, Spain and the U.S. Foreign investment focuses on financial sector, oil, telecommunications, mining, metallurgy, energy, manufacturing and cement production.

Some of the large foreign companies that have invested in Albania are:

Bankers Petroleum Canada Oil and Gas Production

Vodafone Greece Telecommunications

AMC Greece Telecommunications

Kurum Turkey Metallurgy

Edil Centro Italy Manufacturing

Consortium Artemon s.a – Roder & Blackwell Consulting Greece Energy

Titan Cement Group – Antea Cement Sh.a Greece Cement Manufacturing

Calik (Albtelecom) Turkey Telecommunications

Verbund – Austria - Energy Ashta Hydro Power Plant

Raiffeisen Bank Austria Banking

SanPaolo Imi – Italian Abnking

Credit Agricole – France Banking

Interalbanian (Aspis Group) / (Acquisition) Greece Insurance

Sigal (Uniqa Group)/ (Acquisition) Austria Insurance

Kirchberger, Albania - Wood Sanitary Materials

Airport Partners (Hotchtief) Germany Infrastructure

Alumil Greece Manufacturing

Deco-Terwingo (Austria-Russian) Mining

There are no available statistics regarding FDI breakdown by country of origin, by industry destination or by company.

TRADE AND PROJECT FINANCING

METHODS OF PAYMENT

Trade financing options for imports to Albania have improved in recent years due to the growing financial sector which has found ways to accommodate trade financing requirements. Most commonly used payment mechanisms are available to facilitate international transactions.

Bank-to-Bank trade finance alternatives can be structured with or without a letter of credit. A considerable number of larger importers regularly receive goods under a short-term supplier credit agreement. Importers are free to arrange payments through long-term supplier loans when they make larger purchases. For transactions abroad, the most preferred forms of payment are letters of credit or payments in advance.

U.S. EXIM Bank provides insurance policies to U.S. exporters to allow more flexible payment terms.

BANKING SYSTEM

The financial system in Albania consists of the Central Bank or Bank of Albania (BOA), commercial banks, non banking and micro credit institutions, insurance companies and pension institutions. The Tirana stock exchange remains a non functioning institution as there no companies listed and all the attempts to boost its activity have not succeeded. Law No. 8269, "On the Bank of Albania," dated December 1997 amended in July 2002, establishes the targets, tasks, relationships with the banking system and the state, organization and management, ownership on the capital, financial statements and profit allocation. The BOA compiles, approves and implements the monetary policy of the country and employs appropriate monetary instruments to achieve the monetary policy targets.

The BOA has the exclusive right to issue and circulate the national currency and banknote , keeps and administers the foreign reserve of the Republic of Albania, compiles, adopts and implements the foreign exchange regime and the exchange rate policy, licenses or revokes a license on exercising banking activity and supervises the banking activity to ensure banking system stability, acts as banker and advisor to, and as fiscal agent, of the Government of the Republic of Albania and serves as the banker to second-tier banks.

The banking commercial sector is regulated by the Law No.9662 "On banks in the Republic of Albania," dated December 2006. The banking law stipulates the core principles in conducting banking activity in Albania as well as rules and procedures to ensure a sound banking system, management and administration methods for banks and branches of foreign banks. According to the Banking Law, banks are obligated to observe the principles of profit maximization, liquidity, safety and profitability. A bank can be founded as a stock company, by domestic and foreign legal entities and individuals, for receiving deposits, credit payment operations domestically and abroad, and other banking-related activities.

Also, a foreign bank can establish a branch either as a legal entity or as a representative office. Since 2005 the founding capital for the bank license amounts to lek 1 billion (US$ 10 million). Despite some requests, BOA has not issued any new bank license since 2006 mainly due to the difficult situation and the unclear outlook following the global financial sector crisis. The banking sector is dominated by commercial banks entirely owned by private shareholders. Currently, 16 banks are operating in country - two with domestic shareholders Credins and Union Bank and 14 foreign, Raiffeisen Bank (Austria), Intesa San Paolo (Italy), National Bank of Greece, United Bank of Albania, Procredit Bank, Societe Generale Albania (French), First Investment Bank (Bulgaria), Alpha Bank (Greece), Emporiki Bank (Greece), National Commercial Bank (Turkey), Veneto Banca (Italy), Tirana Bank (Greece), the International Commercial Bank (Malaysia) and Albanian Bank of Credit (Kuwait). The degree of market concentration remains fairly high as the group of the five largest banks dominates the market with about 80% of total assets as of December 2010.

The banking sector in Albania remains sound, profitable and well supplied with liquidity. It has, in general, been spared from the global financial turmoil, primarily due to the low amount of loans relative to total deposits and a lack of a housing/real estate bubble. In fall 2008, the sector suffered from a significant reduction of about 15% of the deposits which created some liquidity concerns which were promptly managed by Central Bank which plays an active role in monitoring situation and ensuring enough liquidity in the banking sector. BOA, whose primarily goal is to focus on inflation targeting, in July 2010, reduced the key interest rate to its lowest level of 5% due to lower inflationary pressure and to promote credit growth

After summer 2009, a stable increase of bank deposits took place and by the end of 2009 the system fully recovered and deposits reached their pre-crisis level. In November 2010, banks deposits were 16% higher than one year ago. That said, commercial banks remain cautious in their lending policies which has been reflected in a lower rate of growth credit of the economy. This is also a result of increasing non performing loans in November 2010 at 14.4% of the total loans compared to just 4.3% before the eruption of the financial crisis. For 2010, sector overall profit recouped to about US$ 70 million, almost the double of one year ago.

The credit market is quite competitive but interest rates can be high; under some circumstances, between 10 and 15% in the domestic currency. Most mortgage and commercial loans are denominated in euros. There are no additional conditions to foreign investors to get credit from the banks operating in Albania. Commercial banks have improved the quality of services they offer including credit instruments. The private sector has widely benefited from the expansion of these instruments varying from the traditional letter of credit to bank drafts, etc for clearing business payments. Still,

businesses report that high interest rates, distrust of the banking system, high operating costs of banks and poor business/project proposals remain concerning issues which affect access to credit in Albania.

Total assets of the banking sector at the end of November 2010 are estimated at about US$ 10 billion consisting mostly of bank deposits. The degree of market concentration remains fairly high as the largest five largest banks dominate the market with about 80 percent of total assets. There is enough liquidity to transfer out sizable positions but must conform to rules like advance notification. The banking network has extended to most parts of Albania and developments in this respect are promising. In September 2010, there were 554 branches, up from 127 in 2005. Also the number of debit/credit cards, ATM and Point-of-Sales terminals is growing rapidly.

The regulatory framework for banking supervision is, following its recent comprehensive overhaul, well-developed and continuing the process of alignment with international practice. The BOA has tightened supervision rules over second tier banks, especially in the framework of the global financial crisis. The Regulation Law on credit risk management was amended, establishing higher capital requirements for banks that record credit growth exceeding the set benchmarks, and control over cash transfer to the mother companies abroad tightened. Also, the new banking law provides the principal conditions for the establishment of banks and financial institutions, granting and revoking of licensing, requirements on capital, conditions for carrying out lending and the criteria for banking supervision. The credit information bureau, established in January 2008, has enhanced system transparency and improved its image, especially to retail customers. Its main responsibility is to track consumers' credit histories. The regulatory, governance and supervisory framework for the non-bank financial sector is in progress as the Financial Supervision Authority in charge of supervising insurance, pensions and capital markets builds human and technical capacities.

In April 2010, Standard & Poor's assigned Albania B+ long-term foreign and local currency sovereign credit ratings. S&P also assigned B short-term foreign and local currency ratings to the country. S&P rating came just after Albania's second rating from Moody's which rated Albania at B1 for the debt obligations of the government, with a stable outlook. In October 2010, Government successfully launched its debut Eurobonds worth Euro 300 million on international markets with an interest rate of 7.5% which was regard as quite positive considering the current global financial situation.

In addition to the main banks, in Albania operate 13 nonbank financial institutions, 135 savings and loans associations and 2 unions of savings and loans associations. Their activity is targeting mainly small and medium businesses not serviced by banks. The amount of loans they offer ranges in general from US$ 1,000 to US$ 500,000. A detailed list is in the following address: http://www.bankofalbania.org/web/Commercial_Bank_Register_50_2.php

FOREIGN-EXCHANGE CONTROLS

There are no foreign exchange controls in Albania. The Bank of Albania is entitled to impose exchange restrictions for the making of payments and transfers for capital account transactions. However, such restrictions can only be introduced for a period not

exceeding twelve months, and can only be extended for another similar period. In September 2009, the BOA amended the Regulation of Foreign Exchange Controls which does not include any restriction over international financial remittances. Exporting of hard currency by commercial entities, including juridical persons and sole traders must be done through bank transfer. When the amount of funds to be transferred abroad is large enough to negatively impact Albania's balance of payments abroad the Central Bank reserves the right to break it down into smaller amounts. In 2009, following the global financial meltdown the BOA restricted the distribution of the domestic banking sector profits in order to maintain sufficient liquidity in the sector. The restriction was lifted in July 2010

Repatriation of income (dividends, royalties and consultancy services) is allowed if no tax liabilities are outstanding in Albania. Transfers for current international payments (imports of goods and services, transportation, interest and principal payments and other purposes defined in the regulation) must be supported by documentation such as invoices, certificates, or transport documents, to the transferring bank.

U.S. BANKS AND LOCAL CORRESPONDENT BANKS

There are no American banks present in Albania. However, many banks in Albania may have different U.S. correspondent banks and some U.S. banks may have correspondent relations with more than one bank in Albania. As banking relationships can change quickly, the best source of current information on correspondent banking arrangements is the banks themselves. Contact information for all banks in Albania can be found on the Bank of Albania website

http://www.bankofalbania.org

PROJECT FINANCING

In the absence of a stock market, the banking sector remains the main channel for project financing. The entrance of large European banks during the last few years has strengthened the market competition and has improved the role of the banking system as a primary developer of the economy. After a spectacular expansion during 2005-07 with growth rates of 74% in 2005, 56 % in 2006 and 50% in 2007, mostly due to the very low starting base credit growth has slowed down considerably after the global financial meltdown. Since 2009, banks have restricted their lending policies and become more cautious in crediting especially for individuals. In 2010, the stock of outstanding loans grew by 9% mostly in the private sector. At the end of 2010 loans constituted 49.5% of total banking assets compare to 25% at the end of 2005 and 50.3% one year ago. Corporate loans represent almost 70% of banks' credit portfolio.

The cost of borrowing locally is relatively high, characterized by mid-term loans and high interest rates. While companies from Albania are free to borrow from foreign banks without restrictions, the inflow of foreign capital for this purpose has been minimal. Domestic banks have limited financial ability to issue credit, which has led some of them to use corporate loans for certain large-scale commercial projects.

U.S.-based financing

U.S. Export-Import Bank:

Ex-Im Bank is an independent U.S. Government agency that helps finance the overseas sales of U.S. goods and services. Ex-Im Bank will finance the export of all types of goods or services including commodities as long as they are not military-related (certain exceptions exist). In 2005, Ex-Im Bank provided a US$ 47.6 million long-term loan guarantee to support the sale by Lockheed Martin of an air traffic control navigation system to upgrade Albania's air navigation system.

Major programs of Ex-Im Bank are:

* working capital guarantees that cover 90 percent of the principal and interest on commercial loans to creditworthy small and medium-sized companies that need funds to buy or produce U.S. goods or services for export;

* export credit insurance policies to protect against the political and commercial risks of a foreign buyer defaulting on payment;

* guarantees of commercial loans to foreign buyers of U.S. goods or services that cover 100 percent of principal and interest against both political and commercial risks of non-payment; and

* direct loans that provide foreign buyers with competitive, fixed-rate financing for their purchases from the U.S.

U.S. Trade and Development Agency (USTDA)

USTDA is an independent U.S. government agency, which promotes American private sector participation in developing and middle-income countries, with special emphasis on economic sectors that represent significant U.S. export potential. Through funding of feasibility studies, orientation visits, specialized training grants, and various forms of technical assistance, USTDA helps U.S. businesses compete for infrastructure projects in emerging markets. USTDA assists in building mutually beneficial partnerships between American companies and local project sponsors, which result in increased U.S. exports, and the completion of high quality, successful projects in host countries. In Albania, USTDA has financed projects to study airports, roads, ports, railroads, and the energy sector, as well as increased activities in supporting private sector projects.

Contact: Ms. Jamie Merriman Country Manager, European Region 1621 N. Kent Street #200 Arlington, VA 22209-2131 USA Tel: (703) 875-4357 Fax: (703) 875-4009

Web site: www.tda.gov

Overseas Private Investment Corporation (OPIC):

OPIC is a self-sustaining U.S. Government agency that sells investment services to small, medium and large American businesses expanding into emerging markets around the world. OPIC's three main activities are risk insurance, project finance and

investment funds. OPIC financing through the investment guaranty program and the direct loan program is limited to US$ 200 million. OPIC has established the Southeast Europe Equity Investment Fund (SEEF) I and II that is managed by Bedminster Capital Management. This fund is capitalized at US$ 320 million and operated in South East Europe and Turkey. It does equity investments in communications, healthcare, consumer and financial service industries.

Overseas Private Investment Corporation Information Officer, Office of External Affairs 1100 New York Avenue, NW Washington, D.C. 20527 info@opic.gov

Financing from International Institutions

World Bank (IBRD):

Albania became a member of the World Bank in 1991 and has since received assistance across a broad range of sectors. The World Bank provides technical assistance, analytical and policy advice. The World Bank lending in Albania totals US$1.4 billion comprising 68 projects. Out of this, US$ 791 million have been disbursed. Commitments under the current portfolio consists of 14 operations totaling US$263 million in IBRD/IDA loans and credits, US$180 million in co-financing loans and credits, and US$35 million of recipient-executed Trust Funds, amounting to US$480 million of investments under implementation. The bank is investing in social sectors, in energy, transport, and water, business environment reform including property registration, and agriculture, environment and community development.

In 2008, on account of its strong achievements in economic growth, Albania has achieved middle income status and graduated from IDA concessional flows to IBRD lending, sending a positive signal to investors and the financial markets about the economic prospects of the country. The basis for the World Bank's activities in Albania is the Country Partnership Strategy. The current one (2011-2014) approved in July 2010 guides the World Bank's program and has been agreed in consultation with the Government and other stakeholders, including the civil society.

World Bank Resident Office Kseniya Lvovsky,
Resident Representative
Deshmoret e 4 Shkurtit, no. 34
Tirana, Albania
Tel: +355 (4) 2280 650/1
Fax: +355 (4) 2240 590

International Finance Corporation (IFC):

The IFC, the private sector "window" of the World Bank, offers a full array of financial products and services to companies in its developing member countries: long-term loans, equity investments, quasi-equity instruments (subordinated loans, preferred stock, income notes), guarantees and standby financing, and risk management (intermediation of currency and interest rate swaps, and provision of hedging facilities).

IFC established its field office in Tirana in December 1997 (at the World Bank premises). Albania became a shareholder and member of IFC in 1991. As of 31 July 2010, IFC's portfolio in Albania stands at $79.7 million. IFC's advisory services in Albania aim to improve the investment climate, performance of private sector companies, access to finance, and to attract private sector participation in development of infrastructure projects

IFC Tirana
Ms. Elira Sakiqi, Program Manager
Deshmoret e 4 Shkurtit, 34
Sky Tower 8/1
Tirana, Albania
Tel: + 355 4 231 401

Multilateral Investment Guarantee Agency (MIGA):

MIGA provides investment guarantees against certain non-commercial risks (i.e., political risk insurance) to eligible foreign investors for qualified investments in developing member countries. MIGA's coverage is against the following risks: currency transfer restriction, expropriation, breach of contract, and war and civil disturbance. It provides insurance against risks similar to that offered by OPIC; MIGA and OPIC will work together on a project. MIGA offers long-term (15 to 20 years) political risk insurance coverage to eligible investors for qualified investments.

MIGA can insure new cross-border investments originating in any MIGA member country, destined for any developing member country. New investment contributions associated with the expansion, modernization, or financial restructuring of existing projects are also eligible, as are acquisitions that involve the privatization of state-owned enterprises. MIGA insures investments in a wide range of industries. Types of foreign investments that can be covered include equity, shareholder loans, and shareholder loan guarantees, provided the loans have a minimum maturity of three years. Other forms of investment, such as technical assistance and management contracts, and franchising and licensing agreements, may also be eligible for MIGA guarantees.

Investors may choose any combination of the four types of coverage. Equity investments can be covered up to 90 percent, and debt up to 95 percent, with coverage typically available for up to 15 years, and in some cases, for up to 20. MIGA may insure up to US$ 200 million and, if necessary, more can be arranged through syndication of insurance.

So far, MIGA has issued its first two guarantees for projects in Albania. The first guarantee, US$ 1.6 million issued in February 2000 covers an Italian investment in a tourism project and the second guarantee US$ 7 million issued in June 2001 covers the

Commercial Bank of Greece for its investment in the Intercommmercial Bank. As of June 2009, MIGA's total outstanding guarantee exposure for Albania is US$ 1.56 million.

Multilateral Investment Guarantee Agency 1818 H. Street, N.W. Washington, D.C. 20433 Tel. (202) 458-9292 Fax. (202) 522-2630 Internet: www.miga.org

European Bank for Reconstruction and Development:

The European Bank for Reconstruction and Development (EBRD), whose largest shareholder is the U.S. Government, has a number of programs available to U.S. investors. The Bank makes loans as well as takes equity stakes in infrastructure projects. It will be increasingly focusing on private-sector development in Albania. It also mandates open competitive tenders in procurements, which give U.S. companies opportunities to supply goods and services.

As a guideline, the standard minimum involvement for the Bank is five million euro, though this may be reduced if the project has fundamental benefits for the country. The EBRD has established links with a variety of financial intermediaries to provide financing for projects that are too small to be funded directly. This allows the Bank to support SMEs, which are vital for generating a strong private sector. The EBRD is uniquely positioned and fully committed to provide direct support to the country in the development of the private and financial sector, as well as in the rehabilitation and development of infrastructure as a key factor to the promotion of foreign direct investments.

Overall the Bank has committed to date around US$ 800 million for 52 projects in various sectors of the country's economy, mobilizing additional investments of close to €1 billion. EBRD portfolio is divided between infrastructure, energy, financial sector and corporate sector. In general a total of 54% of total investments are in the private sector.

The US Commerce Department is represented at EBRD headquarters. For more information please contact:

Mr. William Center
Advisor/Senior Commercial Officer
Office of the U.S. Executive Director
European Bank for Reconstruction and Development
Tel: +44 (0)20 7338 7493
http://www.buyusa.com/ebrd

For EBRD in Albania, please contact
Mr. Fabio Serri,
Head of Office
European Bank for Reconstruction and Development, Albania
Drini Tower, 4th Floor
Tirana, Albania
Tel: +355 (4) 2235 204/2230 580
Fax: +355 (4) 2230 580

WEB RESOURCES

Export-Import Bank of the United States: http://www.exim.gov
Country Limitation Schedule: http://www.exim.gov/tools/country/country_limits.html
OPIC: http://www.opic.gov
Trade and Development Agency: http://www.tda.gov/
SBA's Office of International Trade: http://www.sba.gov/oit/
USDA Commodity Credit Corporation: http://www.fsa.usda.gov/ccc/default.htm
U.S. Agency for International Development: http://www.usaid.gov

CUSTOM LEGISLATION

The Customs Legislation consists mainly of the Customs Code and the Decision on Implementing Provisions of the Customs Code, the international legislation regarding the Conventions where the Republic of Albania accedes to, the sublegal acts pursuant to the Customs Code, as well as a series of other legal acts and sublegal acts as follows:

The law adopted by the Parliament of Albania, No.8449, dated 27.01.1999, "The Customs Code of the Republic of Albania", as amended, entered into force on 06.03.1999 and started its implementation after the one month transitory period (Article 297), (Official Journal No. 4, dated 19.02.1999, p. 51.). The Customs Code of the Republic of Albania was drafted based on the Regulation of the European Council KEE No. 2913/92, dated October 12, 1992, "Community Customs Code", 31992R2913, (Official Journal no. 302, Series L, dated 19/10/1992, p. 1-50.) It should be noted that the Customs Code of the Republic of Albania is a partial (almost complete) approximation of this Regulation of the European Council.

The "Harmonised Goods Classification System" have been in force in Albania since 1992. The main body of legal acts concerning customs is comprised by: Law nr. 7599, dated 2.9.1992 " On Custom Code" Law nr. 7609, dated 22.9.1992 " On Custom Duties", and a series of amendments updating it as well as a number of Council of Ministers Decisions and Circulators of the Ministry of Finance .According to the Custom Code, the management, organisation and the control of the custom activity in Albania is realised by the General Directory of the Customs.Normally the custom value includes the price of the good, and transport and insurance expenses.

In beginning of 1999 the New **Custom Code** went out.

The Custom Legislation *is composed by: Custom Code International Custom Legislation linked with conventions in which the Republic of Albanian is adhered.*

- *Legal acts in performance of the Code*
- *Others legal acts according to the custom activities.*

IMPORTANT LAWS AND REGULATIONS

KEY BUSINESS LEGISLATION

- Company Legislation
- Tax and Customs Legislation
- Public Procurement and
- Other relevant Business Legislation *(e.g. Labour Code, Small and Medium Enterprises Law, Law on Accounting, Law on Securities and Stock Market etc...)*

In view of the constantly changing legal framework this information will be kept under regular review.

COMPANY LEGISLATION

- Law No. 7638, dated 19.11.1992 "On Business Companies" *(Basic Law)*

TAX AND CUSTOMS LEGISLATION

- Law No. 7758, dated 12.10.1993 "On documenting and keeping of the accounts for the taxes"
- Law No. 7928, dated 27.4.1995 "On Value Added Tax"
- Law No. 8438, dated 28.12.1998 "On tax income"
- Law No. 8560, dated 22.12.1999 "For tax procedures in the Republic of Albania "
- Law No. 8636, dated 6.7.2001 "On free zones"
- Law No. 8701, dated 1.12.2001 "On gambling, casinos and hippodromes"
- Law No. 8976, dated 12.12.2002 "On excise tax"
- Law no. 8977, dated 12.12.2002 "On tax system in the Republic of Albania "
- Law No. 8978, dated 12.12.2002 "on local tax on small business in Albania "
- Law No. 8982, dated 12.12.2002 "On local tax system in Albania "
- CUSTOMS CODE – Law No.8449, dated 27.1.1999
- Instruction No. 12, dated 14.7.1995 "on organizing and functioning of tax police in centre and in districts"
- Instruction No. 5, dated 20.9.2001 " On provision of tax payers with registration cash desk and issue of tax invoice"
- Instruction No. 4, dated 11.2.2002 "On Value Added Tax"
- Supplement instruction no.3, dated 10.4.2003 "on value added tax"
- Instruction No. 3, dated 11.2.2002 "On the income tax"
- Instruction No. 1, dated 8.1.2003 "On exclusion from paying the direct tax of veterans and persons with disabilities...
- Instruction No. 2, dated 8.1.2003 2On tax system in the Republic of Albania
- Instruction No. 3, dated 27.1.2003 "On simplified profit tax"
- Instruction No. 4, dated 27.1.2003 "On local tax on small business"
- Instruction No. 5, dated 27.1.2003 2 "On cooperation between central and local government tax units"
- Instruction No. 6, dated 4.2.2003 "On building tax"
- Instruction No. 7, dated 4.2.2003 2 "On agricultural land tax"
- Instruction No. 8, dated, 4.2.2003 "on transferring of the properties right on immovable properties"
- Instruction No. 9, dated 4.2.2003 " On annual tax registration of road transportation vehicles"
- Instruction No. 10, dated 4.2.2003 "On local taxes"

- Instruction No. 2, dated 10.4.2003 "on tax procedures"
- Instruction No. 7, dated 16.6.2003 "On excise tax"
- Supplement Instruction No. 2, dated 1.8.2003 "On tax procedures"

PUBLIC PROCUREMENT LEGISLATION

- Law No. 7971, dated 26.7.1995 "On public procurement"
- Instruction No. 1, dated 1.1.1995 "On public procurement"
- Instruction No. 3, dated 19.2.1996 "On low prices buying"
- Instruction No. 1, dated 30.12.2003 "On using the budged funds"
- Decision No. 335, dated, 23.6.2000 "On public procurement rules"
- Decision no. 675, dated 20.12.2002 "On using the public funds, programmed for goods, services and constructions".

OTHER RELEVANT BUSINESS LEGISLATION

- Law No.8957, dated 17.10.2002 "On small and medium enterprises"
- Penal Code – Acts against property in the economic field
- Labour Code – Law No. 7961, dated 12.7.1995
- Law "On Accounting"
- Law nr. 7941 "On Food", dated 31 may 1995, *(Framework law on food production, processing, storage, distribution, controll and commerce in the interest of consumer health and safety)*
- ***Legislation on Securities and Stock Exchange***
    - Law No. 8080, dated 1.3.1996, "On securities"
    - Statute of the Tirana Stock Exchange
    - Tirana Stock Exchange – Instruction No. 2, dated 8.11. 1999 "Listing in the Tirana Stock Exchange"

LAW ON FOREIGN INVESTMENT

ARTICLE 1 GENERAL DISPOSITIONS

For the purpose of this law:

1. "Territory" is understood to mean the territory under the sovereignty of the Republic of Albania, including water courses, sea zones and the continental shelf, upon which the Republic of Albania, in accordance with international norms, exercises its rights of legal sovereignty.

2. "Foreign investor" is understood to mean:

a)every physical person that is a citizen of a foreign country; or
b)every physical person that is a citizen of the Republic of Albania but who has always resided outside the country; or
c)every legal entity founded according to the laws of a foreign country, which directly or indirectly seeks to carry Out or is carrying out an investment in the territory of the Republic of Albania in accordance with its law; or has carried out investment in accordance with laws that have taken effect since 31.7.1990 to the present.

3. "Foreign investment" is understood to mean every kind of investment in the territory of the Republic of Albania under the direct or indirect ownership of the foreign investor, which consists of:

a) movable or immovable assets, tangible or intangible assets or any other kind of possession;
b) a company, stock shares in a company and any form of participation in a company;
c) loans, financial obligations or obligations in an activity that has economic value and that is connected with an investment;
c) intellectual property, including literary, artistic, scientific, technological, audio recording, invention, industrial designs, semiconductor mask works, know-how.
d) every right given by law or contract, and every license or authorization given in accordance with the laws.

4. "Foreign dispute investment" is understood to mean every disagreement or pretense that is caused by a foreign investment or that is associated with one.

5. "Revenue" is understood to mean the amount of money that arises from or related to an investment, including profit, dividends, interest, recapitalization, management fees, technical assistance fees, or other fees or contributions in-kind.

ARTICLE 2 AUTHORITY AND TREATMENT

1. Foreign investment in the Republic of Albania is not subject to prior authorization. It is permitted and treated based on conditions not less favorable than those that apply to domestic investment in similar circumstances, excluding ownership of land, which is regulated by a special law.

2. In all cases and at all times investments have equal and impartial treatment, and full security.

3. In all cases foreign investment is treated no less favorably than that secured by general norms, accepted by international law.

ARTICLE 3 THE RIGHT TO EMPLOY

A company with foreign investment, has the right to employ Albanian and foreign citizens.

ARTICLE 4 EXPROPRIATION AND NATIONALIZATION

Foreign investments will not be expropriated or nationalized neither directly nor indirectly and will not be subject to any measure or similar action, except for public purposes determined by law. Foreign investments will be treated in a nondiscriminatory manner and paid immediately, in a fair and effective manner, and in accordance with due process of law.

ARTICLE 5 COMPENSATION FOR EXPROPRIATION AND NATIONALIZATION

1. The compensation will be equivalent to the fair market value of the expropriated investors.

2. The compensation will be paid without delay and include interest at the commercial market rate from the date of the expropriation; the compensation is fully transferable and convertible at the market rate of exchange on the date of the expropriation.

3. A foreign investor has the right to request an immediate review of an expropriated action or compensation, through the appropriate legal or administrative institutions, according to article 8 of this law.

ARTICLE 6 WAR AND ARMED CONFLICTS

Foreign investors, whose investments suffer losses due to war, armed conflicts, state of national emergency or other similar events, will be treated no less favorable than the treatment accorded to Albanian investors regarding measures adopted in relation to such losses.

ARTICLE 7 TRANSFERS

1. Foreign investors have the right to transfer out of the territory of the Republic of Albania all assets related to a foreign investment, including as follows:

a) revenues
b) compensation
c) payments as a consequence of an investment disagreement;
c) payments made under a contract, including loan and interest payments according to a loan agreement;
d) revenues stemming from the sale or the payment of any or all part of an investment;
dh) return of shareholders' equity, resulting from the reduction of capital when the company has decreased its capital according to Albanian legislation.

2. Foreign investors will have the right to make transfers out the territory of the Republic of Albania to a freely convertible currency calculated at the prevailing market rate on the date of the transfer, with respect to spot transactions in the currency to be transferred.

3. The Republic of Albania may limit the right of transfer through the equal and nondiscriminatory manner of the laws of general application, including laws regarding the payment of taxes and the satisfaction of claims and court decisions.

ARTICLE 8 DISPUTE SETTLEMENT

1. If a foreign investment dispute arises between a foreign investor and either an Albanian private party or an Albanian state enterprise or organization, which cannot be settled amicably, then a foreign investor may choose to submit the dispute for resolution to any applicable, previously agreed upon dispute settlement procedure. If no dispute settlement procedure has been agreed upon, then a foreign investor may submit the dispute for resolution to an authorized court or arbitrator of the Republic of Albania, according to laws of Albania.

2. If a foreign investment dispute arises between a foreign investor and the state administration of the Republic of Albania, and this disagreement cannot be settled amicably, then a foreign investor may choose to submit the dispute for resolution to an authorized court or arbitrator of the Republic of Albania according to the laws of Albania. In cases when the dispute arises out of, or relates to expropriation, compensation for expropriation, discrimination or transfers according to article 7 of this law, then a foreign investor may submit the dispute for resolution and the Republic of Albania hereby consents to the submission thereof, to the International Center for Settlement of Investment Disputes ("Center"). established by the Convention on the Settlement of Investment Dispute between States and Citizens of Other States, approved in Washington. D.C., in March 1965.

3. Any award of international arbitration according to this article is final and binding on the parties to the dispute. The Republic of Albania must carry out, without delay, dispositions of any such award and provide for its enforcement within the territory of Albania.

ARTICLE 9 THE STATUS OF THIS LAW

1. Law no.7549, date 4.8.1992 "On foreign investments" and all other clauses within laws or decisions of the Council of Ministers contrary to this law are repealed.

2. In the event that this law does not conform with any other international agreement or treaty ratified by the Parliament to which the Republic of Albania or the Government of Albania is member, the latter will prevail, to the extent that they provide greater rights or protection to a foreign investor than those provided by this law.

ARTICLE 10 NATIONAL SECURITY

There is nothing in this law that will prevent the application by the Republic of Albania of measures necessary for preserving public order, satisfaction of international obligations of Albania relating to preservation and restoration of international peace or security, protection of its own national security or defense interests.

ARTICLE 11 PUBLICATION OF LAWS

The Republic of Albania will publish all laws, rules and procedures concerning foreign investment.

ARTICLE 12 COMING INTO FORCE

This law comes into force 15 days after publication in Fletorja Zyrtare.

Proclaimed with decree no.687, date 10.11.1993 of the President of the Republic of Albania, Sali Berisha.

LAW ON CONCESSIONS

CHAPTER 1 GENERAL PROVISIONS

Article 1 PURPOSE OF LAW

The purpose of this law is to create a favorable framework for promoting and facilitating the implementation of privately financed Concession Projects enhancing transparency, fairness, efficiency and long-term sustainability, in development of infrastructure and public service projects.

It aims at further developing the general principles in the award of contracts by public authorities through the establishment of specific procedures for the award of Concession Projects.

Article 2 DEFINITIONS

In this law, the following terms shall mean:

1. "Bidder" or "Bidders", means legal entities, including groups thereof, that intend to participate or participate in a selection procedure concerning a Concession.
2. "Competitive Selection Procedure", means the procedure for the selection of the Concessionaire in accordance with Articles 10 to 21 of this law.
3. "Concession", means the agreement, not withstanding the term, between the Contracting Authority and the concessionaire which provides for requirements and conditions in terms

of which the Concessionaire:

(a) Carries out an economic activity which would otherwise be carried out by Contracting Authority related to a concession project, management contract or other public services;

(b) Assumes all or substantial part of risks related to such economic activity;

(c) Receives a benefit by way of:

(i) Direct payments paid by or on behalf of contracting authority;

(ii) Tariffs or fees collected from users or customers;

(iii) A combination of such direct payments and tariffs.

1. "Concessionaire" is a legal person, Albanian or foreign, with or without local or foreign participation, that enters into a concession contract with the contracting authority.
2. "Concession register", means the appropriate record of information pertaining to the Concession selection and award procedure to be kept by the contracting authority and which at the end of the process is filed with the Public Procurement Agency. Form and method of filing shall be determined by this Agency.
3. "Contracting Authority", means a public authority that has the power to enter into a Concession Contract.
4. "Infrastructure Facility", means physical assets and systems that directly or indirectly provide services to the public.
5. "Concession project", means each of the following activities or any combination such as: the design, construction and development of new infrastructure facilities, rehabilitation, modernization, expansion of existing infrastructure facilities; administration, expansion or other services pertaining to new or existing infrastructure facilities.
6. "License" means an administrative act which is issued by a relevant public authority to exercise an activity based on objective qualification criteria.
7. "Local Concessions" are concessions for those economic activities which according to the legislation in effect in the Republic of Albania fall under the competence of local government units.
8. "State Concessions", means Concessions for those economic activities, which based on the legislation in effect in the Republic of Albania, fall under the competence of the central government.
9. "Unsolicited Proposal" means any proposal undertaking concession projects that is not submitted in response to a request issued by the Contracting Authority within the context of a Competitive Selection Procedure.
10. "Private Investment" means the proposal, financed and implemented fully by private sector where the public sector does not participate directly or indirectly. For the purpose of this law, any kind of guarantees, financial or other guarantees, given by public sector, will be considered as participation of public sector in private investment.
11. "Public Procurement Agency is the agency created and operating according to Law no. 9643, dated 20.11.2006 "On Public Procurement".

12. "Procurement Advocate" is the institution established and operating according to law no 9643, dated 20.11.2006 "On Public Procurement.

13. Temporary union of companies" is an agreement in writing between two or more legal entities, the scope of which is the accomplishment of a certain activity, whereby the role of each party is defined and where one party is the main company that represents the union in signing the contract and in each initiative.

14. Value for money, is a term, which is used to determine whether a contractual authority has gained the maximum profit from goods or services, which it receives and/or provides for use within the limits of resources it possesses. This term is not only used to measure the value of goods or services, but assesses the quality, cost and utilization of resources, compliance with the purpose, time and possibility to decide that all of these together constitute the best economic value.

Article 3 SCOPE OF LAW

This law defines conditions, modalities, criteria and procedures for granting concession in the Republic of Albania.

Article 4 SECTORS FOR APPLICATION OF CONCESSIONS

1. This law is implemented for granting of concessions by contractual authorities for the economic activities in the following sectors:

a) transport (railway system, rail transport, ports, airports, roads, tunnels, bridges, parking, public transport);

b) generation and distribution of electricity and heating;

c) production and distribution of water, treatment, collection distribution and administration of waste water, irrigation, drainage, cleaning of canals, dams;

ç) collection, transfer, processing and administration of solid waste;

d) telecommunication;

dh) education and sport;

e) health;

ë) tourism and culture;

f) prison infrastructure;

g) recycling projects, rehabilitation of land and forests, in industrial parks, housing, governmental buildings, service of maintenance of IT and data base infrastructure;

gj) natural gas distribution;

h) management contract or provision of public services including those related to sectors specified above.

1. Council of Ministers, upon the proposal of the Minister responsible for economy, authorizes Concessions to be implemented in other sectors.

2. In particular instances, for the promotion of investments pointed out in point 1 of this Article or for other priority sectors for the economic development of the country, in line with the strategic objectives, Council of Ministers may offer to local or international investors concessions for the symbolic price of 1 EURO. Council of Ministers, upon the proposal of the Minister responsible for economy, approves the list of assets that will be given on concession, to the effect of applying this point.

3. This Law shall not apply to grant of licenses, except to the extent that a license is issued within the framework of a Concession Contract.

4. This Law shall not apply to public procurement of services, goods and constructions, as well as for private investments.

Article 5 CONTRACTING AUTHORITY

1. The contracting authority is the ministry or the local government unit, which in compliance with the legislation in effect is responsible for the economic activity for which the concession is granted.

2. The contracting authority for local concessions is the responsible authority of the local government units.

3. Council of Ministers shall identify the contracting authority for each concession after the identification of potential concessions, according to Article 11 of this law.

4. Council of Ministers approves the evaluation regulations and granting of concessions, to the effect of achieving the purpose and applying the provisions of this law, as well as standard documents in concession field.

Article 6 SUPERVISION OF APPLICATION OF CONCESSIONARY PROCEDURES

1. Supervision of application of the concession procedures and administrative review of complaints against them shall be performed by the Public Procurement Agency.

2. Exercising the concession functions, Public Procurement Agency has the following competencies:

a) it requires from the contracting authorities periodic reporting, once in 6 months regarding the concessions situation;

b) it verifies the application of concessionary procedures, in compliance with this law and other acts stemming from its implementation, while requesting from the concession authorities all the necessary information;

c) it proposes disciplinary measures and imposes penalties to the extent defined in the procurement legislation, in the instances when it observes violation of the procedures of this law.

ç) it conducts the administrative review of complaints from bidders regarding concession procedures.

d) it decides and announces the debarment from concession procedures of bidders who have, during a concessionary procedure, deposited forged documents or declared false information;

dh) it provides to Council of Ministers its opinion regarding the procedure followed for concessions.

Article 7 REPRESENTATION OF LEGAL INTERESTS OF BIDDERS

1. Monitoring of the implementation of this law and the bylaw acts, stemming from it and for its implementation, during the conduct of the concessionary procedures, in protection of the legitimate interests of the bidders, is done by the Procurement Advocate.

2. Exercising the functions under this law, the Procurement Advocate has the following competencies:

a) reviews complaints of interested persons relating to acts or omissions on the side of the contracting authority;

b) institutes administrative investigation upon finding out that the cases consists a violation of this law;

c) upon completion of the administrative investigation, informs the contracting authority and Public Procurement Agency about the results of the investigation.

1. The Procurement Advocate notifies, within 5 days from the beginning of the investigations, the interested parties and the Public Procurement Agency about this fact.

2. In the course of exercising his functions for the investigation of administrative procedure, the Procurement Advocate may:

a) inspect on the spot acts and documents relating to the investigation case;

b) seek information and explanation from public administration or interview any person with regard to the case under investigation, as well ask for expertise from third parties.

c) recommend changes in the law and the acts issued for its implementation, upon observing that the content of these acts possibly causes the violation of concessionary procedures.

Article 8 CONCESSION TRATMENT UNIT

The Concession Treatment Unit shall be under the Minister responsible for economy, to promote and assist the contracting authority in evaluation and negotiation of concessions.

CHAPTER II IDENTIFICATION OF POTENTIAL CONCESSIONS AND SELECTION OF THE CONCESSIONNAIRE

Article 9 IDENTIFICATION OF POTENTIAL CONCESSIONS

1. Identification of Potential Concessions shall be done by competent ministries or local government authorities, in cooperation with the Concession Treatment Agency.

2. Potential Concessions may also be identified by a proponent through unsolicited proposals, in compliance with the procedures set forth in Article 23 of this law.

2. Competent ministries or the Local Government units, in cooperation with the Concession Treatment Unit, shall carry out a viability and bankability analysis to decide whether a potential concession should be implemented. This analysis shall be based upon the principles of value for money, alignment of potential Concessions with the national strategic objectives, as well as with sector strategic objectives, the technical and commercial feasibility of the potential Concession and its ability to attract potential Concessionaires and private financing.

Article 10 SELECTION STAGES

1. The Concessionaires are selected through a pre-qualification procedure, accompanied by a request for proposal foreseen in Articles 11 through 21 of this law. An exception to this rule shall constitute concessions granted according to point 2 of this Article and Article 23 of this law.

2. Notwithstanding the definition contained in point 1 of this Article, the Contracting Authority shall be entitled to request proposals from all potential bidders, without a pre-qualification procedure, if it deems that in this case the conduct of prequalification procedure is not necessary.

Article 11 PRE-QUALIFICATION PROCEDURE

1. The Contracting Authority shall prepare the invitation for participation in the pre-selection procedure and the pre-qualification documents with a view to identifying bidders that are suitably qualified to implement the concession.

2. The invitation to participate in the pre-qualification procedure shall be published in the Public Announcements Bulletin, as well as in the international and local press.

3. The invitation to participate in the pre-selection procedure shall include the following data:

a) A brief description of the infrastructure facility;

b) indicators of other essential elements of the concession, such as the services to be delivered by the concessionaire, ways of financing the concession envisaged by the contracting authority (for example, funds to be used, whether they will be entirely financed by user fees or payments or whether public funds shall be provided to the concessionaire, such as direct payments, loans or guarantees);

c) where appropriate, a summary of the main terms of the concession contract to be entered into;

ç) manner and place for the submission of applications for pre-qualification and the legal deadline for the submission, expressed as a specific date and time, allowing sufficient time for bidders to prepare and submit their applications;

d) manner and place of receiving the pre-qualification documents.

Article 12 PRE-QUALIFICATION DOCUMENTS

In the pre-qualification criteria, there are at least included: a) pre-qualification criteria in accordance with Article 13 of this law; b) participation of the temporary union of companies, in line with Article 12 of this law; c) any requirement for the necessity to create a legal entity for the wining bidder, according to the legislation in effect.

Article 13 PRE- QUALIFICATION CRITERIA

1. In order to participate in the selection procedure, interested bidders must meet some objective criteria, which the Contracting Authority considers appropriate in the particular procedure.

The criteria shall at least include:

(a) professional and technical qualifications, human resources, equipment and other physical facilities as necessary to carry out all the phases of the concession project, including design, construction, operation and, where appropriate, maintenance;

(b) Sufficient ability to manage the financial funds of the project and capability to finance the project;

(c) Appropriate managerial and organizational capability, reliability and experience in operating similar projects.

2. Interested qualified bidders are qualified to participate in a selection procedure when:

(a) they are not subject to proceedings of bankruptcy, liquidation or controlled administration or termination of activity or of any other related situation, which according to the effective laws, brings about proceedings of the same character;

(b) they have not been found guilty of producing false documents.

Article 14 PARTICIPATION OF TEMPORARY UNION OC COMPANIES

1. The contracting authority shall, prior to inviting the bidders into the selection phases, allow them to form temporary bidding unions of companies. Unless otherwise stated in the pre-qualification documents, the information required from members of temporary bidding unions of companies to demonstrate their qualifications in accordance with provisions of this article, shall relate to the temporary union of companies as a whole as well as to its individual members in particular.

2. Each member of a temporary union of companies may participate, either directly or indirectly, in only one temporary union of companies at a time. A violation of this rule shall cause the disqualification of the temporary union of companies and of the individual member of this union of companies.

Article 15 PRE-QUALIFICATION DECISION

The contracting authority performs the qualification of each bidder that has submitted an application for pre-qualification, in accordance with the criteria set forth in the pre-qualification documents. The contracting authority shall publish the list of pre-qualified bidders in the Public Announcements Bulletin within 30 days from taking the decision. All pre-selected bidders shall be invited to submit proposals in accordance with provisions of Articles 16 through 21 of this law.

Article 16 PROCEDURES FOR SOLICITED PROPOSALS

1. The procedures for solicited proposal shall take place in 1 or 2 stages.

    1. The contracting authority provides, against payment of a fee that might be applied, the pre-qualified bidders with the request for proposal and related documents, in compliance with Article 5 of this law, or any other document if deemed necessary. If the pre-qualification

    2. procedures are not implemented, the request for proposal shall be issued to all potential bidders.

2. Notwithstanding the above, the contracting authority may use a two-staged procedure to request proposals from Bidders, if elements of the concession project such as project specifications, performance indicators, financial arrangements or contractual terms can not be described in the request for proposal in a manner that detailed or accurate that would allow the bidders to submit their final proposals.

3. Where a two-staged procedure is used, the following provisions apply:

a) The initial request for proposals shall call upon the bidders to submit, in the first stage of the procedure, initial proposals relating to project specifications, performance indicators, financing requirements or other characteristics of the project, as well as to the main contractual terms proposed by the contracting authority;

b) The contracting authority may convene meetings and hold discussions with any of the bidders to clarify questions concerning the initial request for proposals or the initial proposals and accompanying documents submitted by the bidders. The contracting authority shall prepare minutes of any such meeting or discussion on this issue. (The minutes contain the questions raised and the clarifications provided by the contracting authority.)

c) Following examination of the proposals, the contracting authority may review and revise the initial request for proposals by deleting or modifying any aspect of the initial project specifications, performance indicators, financing requirements or other characteristics of the project, including the main contractual terms, and any criterion for evaluating and comparing proposals and for ascertaining the successful bidder, as well as by adding characteristics or criteria to it. The contracting authority shall indicate in the concession register, the justification for any revision to the request for proposals. Any such deletion, modification or addition shall be contained in the invitation to submit final proposals;

ç) In the second stage of the procedure, the contracting authority shall invite the bidders to submit final proposals with respect to a single set of project specifications, performance indicators or contractual terms in accordance with Articles 17 through 21 of this law.

Article 17 CONTENT OF THE REQUEST FOR PROPOSALS

The request for proposals, prepared by the contracting authority, shall include in the least the following data:

a) general information as may be required by the bidders in order to prepare and submit their proposals;

b) project specifications and performance indicators, as appropriate, including the contracting authority's requirements regarding safety and security standards and environmental protection;

c) contractual terms proposed by the contracting authority, including an indication of non-negotiable terms;

ç) criteria for evaluating proposals and the thresholds, if any, for evaluating the proposals, the relative importance of each criterion and the manner in which the criteria and thresholds are to be applied in the evaluation and disqualification of proposals;

d) requirements pertaining to bid security.

Article 18 CLARIFICATIONS AND MODIFICATIONS

1. The contracting authority may, whether on its own initiative or upon a request for clarification by a bidder, review and, as appropriate, revise any element of the request for proposals in compliance with article 17 of this law.
2. Each change shall be communicated promptly to all candidates having purchased the documents. If the contracting authority deems it necessary to change the documents, and when this is done within less than 1/3 of the number of days defined for the preparation of bids, it shall postpone the deadline for bid submission by the same period.

2. The contracting authority shall, in the case set forth in point 1, indicate in the concession register the justification for any revision to the request for proposals. Any such deletion,

modification or addition shall be communicated to the bidders in the same manner as the request for proposals.

Article 19 EVALUATION CRITERIA

1. The criteria for the evaluation and comparison of the technical proposals shall include at least:

a) technical soundness;

b) compliance with environmental standards;

c) operational efficiency;

ç) quality of services and measures to ensure their continuity;

d) social and economic development potential offered by the proposals.

2. The criteria for the evaluation and comparison of the financial and commercial proposals shall at least include, as appropriate:

a) present value of the proposed tolls, unit prices and other charges over the concession period;

b) present value of the proposed direct payments by the contracting authority, if any;

c) costs for design and construction activities, annual operation and maintenance costs, present value of investments and operating and maintenance costs;

ç) extent of financial support, if any, expected from a public authority of the Republic of Albania; and

d) soundness and viability of the proposed financial arrangements.

3. Council of Ministers determines, in line with implementation of point 3 of Article 4 of this law, additional criteria which will be taken into account in the bid evaluation process. These criteria are based on the sector importance of the development of economy, investment amount, and employment level, priorities for the development of particular areas of the country, other sector specific indicators, as well as the proposed price or fee. Council of Ministers determines in this case the weight of each criterion in the bid evaluation.

Article 20 COMPARISON AND EVALUATION OF PROPOSALS

1. The contracting authority shall compare and evaluate each proposal in accordance with the evaluation criteria, the relative weight accorded to each such criterion and the evaluation process set forth in the request for proposals.

2. For the purposes of point 1 of this Article, the contracting authority may establish minimum thresholds with respect to quality, technical, financial and commercial aspects. Proposals that fail to achieve these minimum thresholds shall be regarded as non responsive and disqualified.

Article 21 DETERMINATION OF THE SUCCESSFUL BIDDER AND FINAL NEGOTIATIONS

1. The contracting authority shall rank all responsive proposals on the basis of the evaluation criteria and notify about this the bidders. Upon notification, all bidders have the right to present any claims in compliance with provisions of CHAPTER III of this law. Upon expiry of the complaining period, the contracting authority shall invite for final negotiations the bidder that has attained the best rating.

2. Final negotiations shall not concern those contractual terms that were stated as nonnegotiable in the final request for proposals.

3. If it becomes clear to the contracting authority, within a time period set by Council of Ministers, that the negotiations with the bidder invited will not result in a concession contract, the contracting authority shall terminate the negotiations with such bidder and invite for negotiations the other bidders in the order of their ranking until it signs a concession contract or rejects all remaining proposals. The contracting authority shall not resume negotiations with a bidder with which negotiations have been terminated pursuant to this point.

4. Following completion of concession contract negotiations, the Concession Treatment Agency shall, within 45 days, issue an opinion on the terms thereof. Following such opinion and the signature of the Concession Contract, it shall be submitted to Council of Ministers for approval.

5. The contracting authority shall publish in the Public Notification Bulletin the name of the concessionaire and essential terms of the concession contract within 30 days after the approval in line with the provision of point 4 of this Article.

Article 22 NEGOTIATION OF CONCESSION CONTRACTS WITHOUT SELECTION PROCEDURES

1. Contracting authority may conduct the negotiation of concession contracts without using the selection procedure, only with the approval of Council of Ministers, where:

(a) the project affects national security. The cases where national security is affected, as a consequence of implementation of selection procedure, shall be approved upon the decision of National Security Council;

(b) the concession contract has been terminated due to a serious violation by the concessionaire and where there a selection procedure is not possible to be implemented, due to the urgent need to ensure continuation of activity.

1. The duration of a concession contract signed according to letter (b), point 1 of this Article shall not exceed 12 months.

2. No concession contract shall be concluded pursuant to letter (b), point 1 of this Article, unless the contracting authority has initiated a competitive selection procedure for the selection of a concessionaire, in accordance with the contract terms set forth in point 2 of this Article or when it has decided not to grant a concession following expiry of such contract term.

3. When a concession contract is negotiated pursuant to this article without using the Selection Procedure, the contracting authority shall determine reasonable evaluation criteria for the requirements of the projects, based on which there shall be evaluated and ranked the proposals.

4. The contracting authority shall publish in the Public Announcements Bulletin the name of the concessionaire and essential terms of the concession contract within 30 days after the

approval of the Concession Contract by the Council of Ministers, excluding the cases determined in letter "a", point 1 of this Article.

Article 23 UNSOLICITED PROPOSALS

1. The contracting authority is authorized to review and accept unsolicited proposals pursuant to the procedures set forth in this article, provided that such proposals do not relate to a project for which selection procedures have been initiated or announced.

2. Procedures for determining the admissibility of unsolicited proposals are the following:

a) within 90 days of receipt and review of such unsolicited proposal, the contracting authority shall determine whether the project is considered to be in the public interest, and to this end informs the proponent.

b) if the concession project is considered to be in the public interest, the contracting authority shall invite the proponent to submit additional data, to make an evaluation of the proponent's qualifications and the technical and financial feasibility of the project;

c) within 120 days of the invitation from the contracting authority, the proponent has to submit a technical and financial feasibility study (including but not limited to a financial model and a project financing plan), an environmental impact study and satisfactory information regarding the concept or technology contemplated in the proposal.

ç) in course of reviewing the unsolicited proposal, the contracting authority shall respect the intellectual property, trade secrets or other exclusive rights contained in, arising from or referred to in the proposal. The contracting authority shall not make use of information provided by or on behalf of the proponent in connection with its unsolicited proposal without the consent of the proponent, for a period of 12 month from its receipt.

3. Initiation of a Selection Procedure shall be done as follows:

(a)the contracting authority shall, within 6 months of receipt of the documentation in compliance with letter "b" of point 2 of this Article, decide to accept or reject the potential concession project derived from the unsolicited proposal. If the unsolicited proposal is accepted by the contracting authority, the contracting authority shall initiate a competitive selection procedure in accordance with Articles 11 through 21 of this law, while when the proposal is refused and the parties do not agree differently, the contracting authority shall return to the proponent the original documents and the submitted copies of documents;

(b)the proponent shall be invited to participate in the competitive selection procedure initiated pursuant to letter (a) of point 3 of this Article, and upon decision of the Council of Ministers, it shall be awarded a bonus on its technical and/or financial score during the competitive selection procedure up to a maximum of 10% of the points. The identity of the proponent and the existence and amount of the bonus shall be indicated in the competitive selection procedure documents.

Article 24 CONFIDENTIALITY

The contracting authority shall preserve the confidentiality of all the technical, economic, financial and other data of the proposals done by the bidders. Unless provided for by law or court decision or request for proposals, no party to the negotiations shall disclose to any other person any technical, price or other elements with regard to discussions, communications and negotiations, pursuant to the aforementioned provisions without the consent of the other party.

CHAPTER III ADMINISTRATIVE REVIEW PROCEDURES

Article 25 COMPLIANT PROCEDURES

1. Each bidder may request an administrative review of the selection processes, when he

deems that an action undertaken by the contracting authority is in violation of the provisions of this law or other legal or bylegal acts on the concession procedures.

2. The complaint shall be submitted to the Public Procurement Agency within 5 calendar days from the date of the publication of the announcement of the pre-qualified candidates or announcement of the ranking of the bidders by the contracting authority.

3. Upon receipt of the complaint, the Public Procurement Agency notifies within 5 days the contracting authority regarding suspension of concession procedures and institution of administrative review procedures.

    1. Public Procurement Agency does not suspend the concession procedure when: a) from the preliminary review it results that the complaint has no legal grounds.

    2. b) suspension would be in conflict with the public interest or would be to the detriment of the contracting authority or other bidders.

4. During the review of the complaint, until the moment of entering into the contract, Public Procurement Agency shall be entitled to:

a) cancel partially or wholly decisions or acts of the contracting authority.

b) guide the contracting authority to rectify the violation prior to proceeding with the concession procedures.

1. The Public Procurement Agency shall, during the procedures of administrative investigation, have all competencies set forth in the law no 9643, dated 20.11.2006 “On public procurement” and in the bylaw acts issued for its implementation.

2. The complaint with the Public Procurement Agency is done by the relevant form, which includes the name and address of the petitioner, the reference to the concrete procedure, the legal basis and the description of the violation. The above mentioned elements are indispensable for the review of the complaint. The Public Procurement Agency reviews the complaint, in compliance with this legislation, bylaw acts issued for its implementation, as well as with the Administrative Procedures Code.

3. Public Procurement Agency concludes the administrative review within 20 calendar days from the submission of the complaint and notifies the contracting authority and the petitioner about the decision.

9. The decision of Public Procurement Agency constitutes a final administrative act.

Article 26 COMPLAINT IN THE COURT

The petitioner is entitled to take an appeal against the decision of the Public Procurement Agency within 30 days since the notification to the effect of having the administrative conflict tried at the Court of Tirana Judicial circle (Administrative Section).

The court shall carry out the judicial review in line with the procedures and time periods established in the provisions of the Civil Procedures Code, chapter II, “Adjudication of administrative disputes”.

The review of such a complaint in the court does not suspend continuation of the concession procedures.

CHAPTER IV CONCESSION CONTRACTS

Article 27 CONTENT

Concession contracts shall provide for such issues as the parties deem appropriate, such as:

a) nature and scope of works to be performed and services to be provided by the concessionaire;

b) concession contract duration, which shall be adjusted to the specific requirement of the relevant concession and shall not exceed 35 years, and conditions, if any, to its extension;

c) assistance that the contracting authority and the concession treatment agency may provide to the concessionaire in obtaining licenses and permits necessary for the concession;

ç) any requirements relating to the establishment and minimum capital of a legal entity to be established by the successful bidder in accordance with the effective laws, and prohibition of transfer of shares or part of the capital of this company without prior consent of the contracting authority;

d) ownership on assets related to the concession project and the obligations of the parties, as appropriate, concerning the acquisition of the concession project site and any necessary facility;

dh) remuneration of the concessionaire, regardless whether it consists of tariffs or fees for the use of the infrastructure facility or the provision of services; the methods and formulas for the establishment or adjustment of any such tariffs or fees; payments, if any, that may be made by the contracting authority or other public authority; as well as whether there is any obligation of the concessionaire to make payments to the contracting authority;

e) procedures for the review and approval of engineering designs, construction plans and specifications by the contracting authority, as well as the procedures for testing and final inspection, approval and acceptance of the infrastructure facility, rules and standards based on which the concession projects are designed, which should ensure the application of best practice, developing the market through sensible risks allocation;

ë) extent of the concessionaire's obligations to ensure, as appropriate, the modification of the service so as to meet the actual demand for the service, its continuation and its provision under essentially the same conditions for all users; mechanisms to deal with eventual costs related thereto;

f) right of contracting authority, or of another public authority to monitor the works to be performed and services to be provided by the concessionaire and the conditions and extent to which the contracting authority may order variations in respect of the works and conditions of service. The right of contracting authority to take such other reasonable actions as they may find appropriate to ensure that the infrastructure facility is properly operated and the services are provided in accordance with the applicable legal and contractual requirements, as well as the right to monitor mechanisms to deal with eventual costs related thereto;

g) concessionaire's obligation to provide the contracting authority, or other public authority, as appropriate, with reports and other information on its activity;

gj) any restrictions or conditions applicable to the assignment of rights and obligations of the concessionaire under the concession contract;

h) Any restrictions or conditions related to the transfer of a controlling interest at the concessionaire;

i) definition and consequence of force majeure, change in law and other changes in circumstances (including any right of the parties to seek compensation or revision of concession contract);

j) eventual liabilities, if any, of the relevant public authorities or contracting authority;

k) circumstances under which the contracting authority has the right to temporarily take over the operation of the infrastructure facility for the purpose of ensuring the effective and uninterrupted delivery of the service in the event of failure by the Concessionaire to perform its obligations and to rectify the breach of contract;

l) any rights of the contracting authority to review and approve the main contracts to be entered into by the concessionaire, in particular with the concessionaire's own shareholders or other legal entities where the concessionaire is participating or vice versa;

ll) guarantees of performance to be provided and insurance policies to be maintained by the concessionaire in connection with the implementation of the concession;

m) remedy procedures available in the event of breach of contract by any of the parties;

n) conditions and procedure for amendment and/or termination of contract; rights and obligations of the parties upon the expiry of time period or termination of contract (including mechanism of transfer of assets, technology, compensation, training and support services to be provided by the concessionaire);

nj) applicable law and the mechanisms for the settlement of disputes that may arise between the contracting authority and the concessionaire;

o) rights and obligations of the parties with regard to confidential information.

Article 28 TERMINATION OF THE CONCESSION CONTRACT

1. Unless otherwise provided for in the concession contract, the contracting authority may terminate the concession contract when:

(a) tt has a reason to believe that the concessionaire can no longer be expected to perform its obligations, owing to insolvency, serious breach or other cases which hinder or do not allow the continuation of concession contract;

(b) concessionaire fails to ensure the financing of the project within 12 months as of signing the concession contract.

2. Either party shall, unless otherwise provided for in the concession contract, have the right to terminate the Concession Contract, when:

(a) performance of its obligations is rendered impossible by circumstances beyond either party's reasonable control;

(b) there is serious breach by the other party, and that party fails to rectify such breach within the time period and in the manner established in the concession contract.

3. The parties shall also have the right to terminate the concession contract upon mutual consent.

CHAPTER V FINANCING

Article 29 FINANCIAL ARRANGEMENTS

1. The Concessionaire shall have the right to charge, receive or collect tariffs or other incomes for the use of the facility or the services provided by it, in accordance with the concession contract, which shall provide for methods and formulas for the establishment and adjustment of those tariffs or payments.

2. The contracting authority shall have the power to make direct payments to the concessionaire as a substitute for, or in addition to, tariffs or payments for the use of the facility or services provided by it.

CHAPTER VI SETTLEMENT OF DISPUTES AND APPLICABLE LAW

Article 30 APPLICABLE LAW

1. The concession contract shall be governed by the laws of the Republic of Albania.

2. The concessionaire, its shareholders and other business partners shall be free to choose the law governing their relations.

Article 31

DISPUTES BETWEEN THE CONTRACTING AUTHORITY AND THE CONCESSIONAIRE

1. Any disputes between the contracting authority and the concessionaire shall be settled through the dispute settlement mechanisms agreed by the parties in the concession contract, including procedures of international arbitration.

2. The concessionaire, its shareholders and other business partners shall be free to choose the appropriate mechanisms for settling disputes among themselves.

CHAPTER VII FINAL PROVISIONS

Article 32 REPEAL

The Law No .7973, dated 26.7.1995 "On concessions and the participation of the private sector in public and infrastructure services" as amended, shall be repealed.

Article 33 TRANSITION PERIOD UNTIL THE ESTABLISHMENT OF THE CONCESSION TREATMENT AGENCY

Until the establishment of the Concession Treatment Agency in accordance with Article 8 of this law and it becoming fully operational, its responsibilities and powers shall be exercised by the ministry responsible for economy.

Article 34 EXISTING AND SECTOR SPECIFIC LAWS

1. In case of incompatibility with the existing laws, this law shall prevail over all other existing laws on concessions.

2. All sector specific laws shall regulate concessions in accordance with this law.

Article 35 CONCESSION CONTRACTS ALREADY SIGNED

This law shall not apply to the concession contracts already signed prior to the date of this law. The contracts may never be renewed or extended, except in compliance with this law.

Article 36 ENTRY INTO FORCE

This law shall enter into force 15 days after its publication in the Official Gazette.

Promulgated by the Decree no 5179, dated 12.01.2007 of the President of the Republic of Albania. Alfred Moisiu

LAW NO. 9572, DATE 3.7.2006 ON THE FINANCIAL SUPERVISORY AUTHORITY

In line with articles 78 and 83 paragraph 1 of the Constitution of the Republic of Albania, with the proposal of the Council of Ministers,

THE PEOPLE'S ASSEMBLY OF THE REPUBLIC OF ALBANIA

DECIDED:

CHAPTER I GENERAL PROVISIONS

ARTICLE 1 SCOPE OF LAW

The scope of this law is to define the rules concerning the establishment, tasks and functions of the Financial Supervisory Authority, which hence is going to be referred to as the Authority

Article 2 Scope of activity of the Authority

The scope of activity of the Authority is the regulation and supervision of:

a. the securities market and the activity of the securities market, including the activities of other subjects included in this market;

b. The insurance market and the activities of the insurance market, which includes all activities of insurance, re-insurance, brokerage and operations that derive from these activities;

c. The supplementary pensions market and the activity of supplementary pensions market, which includes all activities of insurance of supplementary pensions offered by private supplementary pensions institutions;

ç. and other activities related to financial leasing, factoring, mortgage and other non-banking financial activities according to the definitions provided by the relevant legislation, which are going to be referred to as "non-banking financial markets".

CHAPTER II THE STATUS, STRUCTURE AND ADMINISTRATION OF THE AUTHORITY

ARTICLE 3 THE STATUS OF THE AUTHORITY

The Authority is a public legal person independent with the residence in Tirana specialized in the regulation and supervision of the activity of the subjects engaged in one or more of the activities mentioned in article 2 of this Law.

The Authority for the activity it exercises in line with this law reports to the Assembly.

Article 4 The Board of the Authority

The Board is the decision-making body of the Authority. The Board comprises of 7 members, namely: one Chairman, two Vice Chairmen, and four other members.

Article 5 Requirements for appointment of members of the Board

Members of the Board are:

1. Albanian citizens;
2. university degree in economics, or law, or actuarial science;
    1. at least 3 years professional experience in at least one of the following fields:
        1. finance -accounting;
        2. administration of trade companies
        3. legal counseling of trade companies;

ç. drafting of legislation;

d. Actuarial science

e. Social insurance and pensions

1. enjoy moral and professional integrity;
2. do not exercise any high ranking functions in a political party.
3. Have not been found criminally indicted through a court decision of final verdict
4. Meet the legal provision requirements regarding the conflict of interest.

The Chairman and the vice chairmen of the Board do not exercise other paid activities, except for lecturing, research and scientific activities or participation in local or international organizations related to the activity of the Authority.

The four other members of the Board may be full time employee in other institutions, but can not be members of more than one The Board or decision-making body of any other supervisory Authority.

Each member of the Board has the obligation to declare to the Speaker of the Parliament related to the circumstances anticipated in this article.

Article 6 Appointment of the members of the Board

The members of the Board get appointed by the Parliament.

The chairman, two Vice chairmen, and two of the members of the Board are appointed by the Parliament with the proposal of the Council of Ministers.

One member of the Board is appointed by the Parliament with the proposal of the Laws, Public Administration and Human Rights Parliamentary Commission.

One member of the Board is appointed by the Parliament with the proposal of the Economy and Finance Parliamentary Commission.

The Minister of Finance, Supervisory Board of the Bank of Albania, and the National Accounting Council each are entitled to propose to the Council of Ministers one candidate as member of the Board of the Supervisory Authority. The candidate proposed by the BoA, should not be a member of BoA's Board. The candidate proposed by the NAC should not be a member of the NAC Board. The Council of Ministers based on its two candidates and the candidates proposed by the Minister of Finance, the Supervisory Board of the Bank of Albania, and the National Accounting Council drafts the proposals for the Parliament.

The proposal defines the functions that candidates will have/exercise in the Board of the Authority. In the case of the Vice Chairmen, the proposal also defines which will be the department that each will run.

The Parliament, in the decision for the appointment of each of the Vice Chairmen also determines the department that will be run by each of them.

Article 7 The mandate of the Members of the Board

The mandates of the Chairman, Vice Chairmen and other members of the Board are 5 years. In the instances, when the mandate of the chairman, vice chairmen or The Board's member has terminated, each will continue to exercise their duties until the appointment of the new members. One month before the termination of the mandate of each of the members, the Authority notify in a written form the Parliament, which starts the procedure for the appointment of the new member.

The individuals that have been once appointed as members of the Board of the Authority are entitled to be re-appointed only once. The individual who has been appointed once as Chairman of the Board of the Financial Supervisory Authority can not be re-appointed as Chairman.

At the end of his/her mandate, the member of the Board can not be employed for a period up to two years or be directly or indirectly paid from any of the subjects supervised by the Authority.

Individuals who held the position of either the chairman or of the Vice Chairmen of the Board, after their release from office, when is unemployed are entitled to one year of remuneration in the amount of the salary that they have had while in their position. The individual who has been re-appointed as member of the Board and the individual that is released from the duty based on article 8 of this Law are not entitled to this right.

Article 8 Release from duty of the members of the Board

The Parliament decides on the release from duty of any of the members of the Board, before the termination of the mandate provided for in the first paragraph of article 7 of this Law in the following cases:

a. the individual resigns;

b. the individual becomes physically incapacitated to accomplish the assigned task for more than 3 months;

c. due to new circumstances the provisions envisaged in points 5 and 6 of the first paragraph of article 5, and the conditions foreseen in paragraphs 2, 3, and 4 of article 5 of this law are no longer respected;

d. in case of absence, without proper ground, in more than three consecutive meetings;

e. during exercise of his/her functions acts in violation of the obligation for maintaining confidentiality;

f. Because of professional incapacity or negligence causes damages/detriment to the Authority or to the image of the Authority as an independent institution

g. Lost of Albanian citizenship

The proposal for the release from duty for any of members of the Board is submitted to the assembly from each of the institutions that enjoy the right for the proposal of members of the Board and from other public institutions, whose function is related to that of the Authority. The proposal also should define the reason thereof and evidence related to the case. The Parliament may decide suspension from office of a given member until the end of the process of verification and until decision making. The Parliament, after the review takes a decision regarding the proposal for the release from duty, while approving or refuting the proposal.

In case of release from office before the deadline of any of the members of the Board, the other member is appointed via the same procedure as the member who is being released for the period until the completion of the deadline of the member who is released.

Article 9

Competencies for the approval of the structure and salaries of the Authority

The monthly salary of the chairman of the Board, of the vice chairmen and remuneration for the other members who do not carry out executive functions in the Authority are approved by the assembly, with the proposal of the Board of the Authority.

The structure of the Authority is approved by the Parliament with the proposal of the Board of the Authority.

The Authority, in addition to other units is composed of two main Departments. The name of these departments and other units of the Authority are determined related to the structure of the Authority.

The Board approves its regulation, related to the structure, specific functions and responsibilities of the departments and directorates, procedures for communication among them, and the duties of the civil servants and other employees.

Article 10 Meetings of the Board

The meetings of the Board are summoned with the initiative of the chairman of the Board or upon the request of each of its members sent to the Chairman. The Board meets at least once a month to discuss and decide regarding the agenda.

The meetings of the Board are chaired by the chairman, and in his absence according to his delegation of Authority, by one of the vice chairmen.

The meetings of the Board are considered valid when have participated at least 4 members of the Board.

The decisions of the Board are considered valid when at least four members of the Board have voted “in favor”.

Abstention in not allowed in voting.

Minutes are kept for each meeting. The minutes are signed by all the members who have been present. The decisions of the Board are signed by the chairman and the responsible vice chairman for the issue for which the decision has been taken. In case the decision is of general nature, it is signed by the chairman and by both Vice chairmen.

The Board approves the regulation regarding the operation and maintenance of minutes of the meeting.

Article 11 Transparency in the activity of the Authority

The Board publicly announces the policies and practice it follows in the implementation of the legal and by-legal provisions, as well as the ground for their change/amendment.

The policies that the Board follows for the implementation of provisions according to the first paragraph of this article include also the means selected by the Authority and used independently from it in the course of fulfillment of the objectives of this law.

The Authority approves the regulations for the procedures of making available to the public its documentation and the deadlines and terms for maintaining/keeping certified copies of this documentation.

The Board approves regulations regarding the type of publications, deadlines for their publication, and formulation and operation of the web page of the Authority.

CHAPTER III THE OBJECTIVES, THE COMPETENCIES OF THE AUTHORITY AND THE RIGHTS OF THE BOARD

Article 12

The objectives of the Authority

In carrying out its functions and competencies foreseen in this law, the Authority has the following objectives:

1. To protect the interests of investors and insured persons;
2. To promote sustainability and enhance transparency and credibility of non-banking financial markets;
3. To ensure respect of law.

Article 13

The aim of the Authority's activity

The Authority and its structures aim to:

1. to regulate the activity of the supervised subjects via drafting of by laws foreseen by this law, as well as to publish guidelines and explanatory notes/materials;
2. To ensure public supervision on the securities market, insurance market, and supplementary pensions schemes, which are regulated and function in line with the relevant legislation

In the exercise of the competencies foreseen in article 2 of this law, the Authority, enjoy full rights regarding:

a) approval, issuing or rejection of licenses for subjects that wish to exercise activities in one of the non-banking financial markets;

b) oversight and organization of the supervision of subjects that request to exercise activities in one of the non-banking financial markets; The subjects, either individuals or physical or legal persons, that exercise the activities mentioned in Article 2 of this law, are called " supervised subjects".

c) Follow up the implementation of this law and its by-laws issued on its base and sectoral laws and their by-laws, and enforcement of the restringing measures.

Article 14 The competencies of the Board

The Board has the following competencies:

1. in line with the structure, the Board drafts rules regarding the job descriptions and the scope of work;
2. drafts and approves the basic principles of its activity;
3. drafts and approves rules and instructions envisaged in the law;
4. disseminates written instructions regarding interpretation and enforcement of laws that regulate the area of activity, and the by-laws for their implementation;
5. approves the format of licenses issued for the exercise of activities supervised by the Authority;

6. Issues, rejects, bring to a close, or revoke the licenses or permits to exercise activities in one of the non-bank financial markets supervised by the Authority. In line with this competency, the Board: a) in compliance with the deadlines, terms and procedures foreseen in the Albanian legislation for securities approves or refutes the prospects for public offers or for the registration of new emissions for sale according to the rules of the regulated securities market; b) supervise the enforcement of temporary or final decisions regarding publication of public bids of shares;

c) approves licenses for individuals or companies that wish to exercise activities in the securities market, including activities as security markets, registrars, depositories, brokers or investment advisors and other subjects involved in the market;

ç) approves licenses of companies that wish to exercise activities as administrators of investment funds, as well as licenses for the exercise of activities as investment companies;

d) endorse the statute and changes/amendments to the statute of the companies that wish to exercise activities in the securities market;

dh) in line with the legislation that regulates that the activity of insurance, reinsurance and brokerage in insurance and re-insurance approves licenses for the exercise of the activity of insurance, and for the exercise of the activity of insurance brokerage and operations that directly stem from these activities;

e) reviews requests for expansion of the activities from subjects that exercise activities in the insurance market;

ë) reviews requests for exercise of activities outside the territory of the Republic of Albania, as well as for opening representation offices of foreign companies that exercise related activities with the objective of Authority's function;

f) reviews requests for the transfer of portfolio, and for undertaking some of the functions of the insurance company;

g) approves the merger or split of insurance companies (licensed);

gj) approves high management bodies, approves the statute of the insurance companies (licensed), and the changes to the statute before they are submitted for approval to the general assembly of shareholders;

h) reviews the requests for influential participation in the insurance companies, and the capital investments of the insurance companies;

i) approves volunteer liquidation, and decides on the start of procedures for bankruptcy of the insurance company;

j) approves high management bodies, approves the statute and the changes to the statute of the companies that wish to exercise activities as private pensions institutions prior to court registration;

k) undertakes appropriate corrective measures and on time when the insurance or re-insurance companies do not reach the required level of payment capacity or in case there is an observation of cases of failure to meet the payment capacity as determined in the legislation in effect in the area of insurance and re-insurance;

l) approves methodological guidelines, the format of the insurance contracts, lists, types of notes and other documents related to the activities of private pensions institutions;

ll) approves the regulations of private supplementary pensions, as well as the changes to these regulations, and controls their implementation;

m) approves the type, format and content of the reports submitted to the Board by the licensed subjects;

n) approves the transfer of the takeover of the supervised subjects.

1. restricts or suspends investments of the insurance and re-insurance company when it is certified that these investments are not in compliance with the established regulatory and when they put at stake the financial position of the company;
2. within a month from the submission of the request, reviews the general and specific terms of the insurance contract, that the insurance company wants to put in the market;
3. approves the financial statements of the insurance and re-insurance companies;
4. approves and disseminates accounting standards, and the financial reporting formats mandatory for implementation by the licensees;

11.approves the list of the accounting experts who may exercise this function for the companies that operate in the non-banking financial markets;

12.in the instances spelled out in the legislation takes a decision for the start of the bankruptcy procedures for the supervised subjects, and when spelled out in the law, it also appoints the liquidator;

13.approves the policy for wages and remuneration of staff and other employers of the Authority;

14.in line with the activity of the Authority, it takes decisions for signing memorandums of understanding and exchange of information with authorities within and outside the country;

15.it discusses on periodical terms the reports related to the main activity of the main departments of the Authority; 16.approves the draft budget and the Annual Report of the Authority; 17.within June of each year, it approves the Industry Report regarding the status

and perspective of the market supervised by the Authority; 18.in the regulations for internal administrative procedures, it approves the

deadlines for submission of issues/cases for review; 19.approves the inspection manuals; 20.defines the policies on supervising and control of supervised subjects and the

development of non-banking financial market; 21.decides on purchase of the counseling service from experts of the area; 22.approves rules on employment and resignation of the employees of the Authority

23. other competencies spelled out in this law or in other legislation of the area.

The decisions are reasoned and are subject of appeal to a court.

The administrative decisions of the Board are published in the forms decided by the Board for the publication of official notifications.

Article 15

The competencies of the Chairman of the Board

The chairman of the Board is also the general executive director. The chairman runs and administers the activities of the Authority and its administration, except for the activities which are the competencies of the vice chairmen of the Board or of the other members spelled out in this law or in any other act.

The chairman of the Board is in charge of:

1. representing the Authority;
2. calling and chair the meetings of the Board;
3. to coordinate the work of the two vice chairmen;
4. propose the ratio of salaries of staff and other employees of the administration;
5. organizing, run and control the activities of the administration;
6. organizing the work for the preparation and submission for approval by the Board of the draft budget;
7. organizing the work for the implementation of the budget, closure of the financial year, and of the financial report, and submit them for approval by the Board.
8. signs for criminal investigation in the instances of discovery of actions or failure of action that constitute a criminal act.
9. exchanging information with the Bank of Albania, other governmental institutions and agencies, local authorities and administration, NGOs that exercise their activity in the financial non-bank markets supervised by the Authority, and with the supervised subjects;
10. in cooperation with the Bank of Albania, through a joint order instructs and orders carrying out of inspections in the depository banks regarding the activities of the subjects licensed by the Authority, and which exercise activities in one of the financial non-banking

financial markets supervised by the Authority.

11. requesting the Bank of Albania to exercise inspections within a given scope in the banks of this level, in compliance with the law "On second tier (commercial) banks in the Republic of Albania", and to be informed about the results of the control.
12. establishing advisory committees that support him in the exercise of his functions.

Article 16 The competencies of the Vice Chairmen

The competencies of the Vice Chairmen are determined in the rules of the job description prepared by the Board.

The Vice chairmen of the Board, according to the definition of the decision for their appointment are each managers of one of the two main departments of the Financial Supervisory Authority. Within the legal competencies, the vice chairmen organize, run and are responsible for the work of the relevant departments.

Article 17

Competencies of the members that do not hold executive functions

The four members of the Board, who do not have managerial functions in the Authority, in cases of a request for the review of a special case related to deficiencies or law violations during the Authority's activity operate as the Audit Committee. The Members of the Board review the documentation and prepare detailed reports which they submit to the Board. In case of observation of violations or gaps, the report contains recommendations for the measures that need to be taken.

The audit committee appoints one of its members as a reporter who reviews the appeals and claims against the decisions of the Board and its bodies.

The rapporteur enjoys all rights to carry out a full-fledged inspection regarding the matter. For the appealed decisions, the rapporteur prepares detailed reports and submits them to the Board. In case of observation of violations or gaps, the report contains recommendations regarding the measures that need to be taken regarding the improvement of the situation.

The Board reviews the submitted report and decides regarding the proposed measures, if any.

The Parliament decides, if it is necessary the external auditing of the Authority.

Article 18

The procedures for the execution of the rights of the Board and of the structures of the Authority

In the exercise of the rights of the Board and all other structures of the Authority, members of the Board and the appointed employees with supervisory functions enjoy these rights in compliance with the procedures spelled out in this law, and with the duty that they are in charge of delivering:

1. to request from the supervised subjects and other subjects as well who have been acting in violation of the provisions of this law or other legislation that regulate the markets of the area, written explanation, documentation, including certified copies of documents, data, information and other data, and verify the documentation and the reporting. The documentation and written information shall be in Albanian;
2. to obtain data regarding funds, assets, including securities and other assets in the ownership of supervised subjects;

3. to inspect the accounts, trade/commercial documents, and other documentation related to the performed transactions;

4. to lead the third party inspections, which will include the review of that part of the documentation of the third party's activity, related to the issue that the supervised subject is inspected.

5. request from third parties information, and documentation including certified copies of documents, statement of accounts, and other necessary data for the process of verification;

6. to attend the meetings organized by the managerial and control structure of the supervised entities.

In order of the implementation of the exercise of the supervisory procedures, the vice chairman in charge can for a supervised subject ask from the Board the appointment of external experts, in compliance with the specific requests approved by the Board. In this particular instance, the incurred expenses shall be paid by the supervised subject.

Upon the request of the chairman of the Board, the banks for the supervised subjects by the Authority must provide information regarding the existing or closed account numbers and codes alongside with the data of the latest transaction.

All data and documents related to violation of this law, which contain the name of the individual in charge of their drafting, are submitted to the third parties by the chairman of the Board, only with the preliminary approval/consent of the above mentioned individual, except when the law foresees otherwise.

The police authorities, prosecutor's offices and all other state authorities shall within their competencies assist the work of the Authority and of its staff during the course of the exercise of their supervisory functions.

In the context of the exercise of the competencies of this law, the Authority may carry out general inspections, in cooperation with the tax authorities.

The members of the Board of the Authority and the other staff of the administration are not financially liable for damages caused in the course of the exercise of their inspection activity, except when they have committed a crime or have been acting wrongly on purpose.

Article 19

The Inspection

The inspection is exercised by the staff of the Authority according to the definition of the Order signed by the chairman or one of the Vice chairmen. The inspection takes place with prior notification or without.

The staff appointed according to paragraph 1 of this article inspects the following:

1. respect of the legal and by-legal provisions of the legislation that regulates the activities of the non-banking financial markets;

2. prevention and identification of violations.

In the course of the exercise of the inspection, the supervised subject shall have to ensure normal working conditions, and provide documentation or any other written information in Albanian.

The staff of the administration of the Authority shall have to introduce themselves at the outset of the inspection procedures, by presenting the order spelled out in the first paragraph of this article.

The supervised subject shall assist the Authority and its administration, and to this end it:

a) provides them with the necessary means for inspection if so requested, and responds to the questions in the facilities of the Authority; b) from its staff appoints the contact persons that will help out in the process of inspection; c) ensures free access in the building;

ç) makes available all the accounts, commercial documentation, and any other necessary documentation to determine the facts and circumstances related to the case for which the inspection is taking place;

d) after a preliminary request, ensures and makes available photocopies of the accounts and other documents, putting in writing in capital letters: "the same with the original" and the date and signature of the person authorized by the inspected subject.

The final report for each inspection is prepared in two copies, and is signed by the staff of the Authority in charge with the inspection, and is submitted for countersignature to the person that represents the supervised subject.

CHAPTER IV THE ADMINISTRATION OF THE SUPERVISORY AUTHORITY

ARTICLE 20 ORGANIZATION AND OBLIGATIONS

The activity of the Authority is supported by an administration which operates in compliance with the internal regulation of the job description of the administration of the Authority, and the other regulations related to the operation of the administration, which are approve by the Board in line with the proposal of the chairman.

The working relations with the personnel of this administration are regulated according to the Labor Code. The following individuals can not be employed in the structures of the Authority: a) have been criminally charged with a decision of the court of the final instance; b). they are shareholders in supervised subjects; c) have been members of executive or control entities of the supervised subjects during the last 2 years;

ç) have family links with the individuals spelled out in letter "c" of this article, with members of the Board, or with other staff of the administration who have hierarchical relations;

d) work part-time or full time in the supervised subjects;

dh) do not have a good reputation and have violated previously the ethics.

Article 21 Remuneration of the administration

The internal rules regarding the level of salaries, monthly salary of staff of the Authority, and remuneration are established by the Board with the proposal of the chairman, in accordance with the regulatory framework of the field.

CHAPTER V DECLRATION OF CONFLICT OF INTEREST

Article 22

Conflict of interest

The Members of the Board and the staff of the Authority shall declare their assets at the moment of the start of their duty, and further on in line with the legal provision in effect.

The Members of the Board do not participate in the procedures of discussion, voting and decision making in the cases when they have a direct or vested interest in the matter in discussion, which makes him/her bias in the official position.

The staff of the Authority does not participate in inspections of the supervised subjects if they have direct or vested interests in the matter for which the inspection is taking place, and which makes him/her biased in the official positions.

The Members e The Board and the staff of the Authority, in case they observe that they are in a situation spelled out in the second and third paragraphs of this article they declare this in written and withdraw from the review of the case.

In case there is an observation that even though they have been faced with a case spelled out in the second and third paragraphs of this article, and have not made the relevant declaration and consequently have not withdrawn from the review of the case, the individuals are either released from duty or fired. This measure does not have an impact on the decisions taken up until that moment.

CHAPTER VI CODE OF ETHICS, PROFESSIONALISM AND CONFIDENTIALITY

ARTICLE 23 CODE OF ETHICS AND PROFESSIONALISM

The members of the Board and the other employees of the Authority in the exercise of their activity implement the code of ethics and the professional standards approved by the Board, according to the proposal of the chairman.

In those instances when there is an observation of the violation of the code of ethics disciplinary measures are taken up to release from duty or firing.

Article 24 Confidentiality

The information which is made available to the Authority, in the course of the exercise of the supervisory activity of the institution, and the dissemination of which might infringe the commercial interest or the good name of the supervised subject is classified under confidential information.

Commercial information which has been obtained by the supervised subject, and the obligation for the publication of which is spelled out in this law or other legislation is not considered confidential information. Classification of information is done through internal regulations approved by the Board.

Members of the Board, the staff and the other employees of the Authority shall preserve and not distribute confidential information.

In those instances when there is a verification of the violation of the terms spelled out in this article, administrative measures are taken up to the release from duty of the members of the Board, or firing of other staff of the Authority.

Article 25 Termination of treatment as confidential information

Information which falls under the confidential category is no longer regarded as such 3 years from the moment it has become available to the Authority. This deadline may be prolonged with a decision of the Board.

Exceptions regarding the respecting of the deadline spelled out in the first paragraph of this article are the cases when:

1. it is requested by the court authorities according to legal requirements ;
2. requested by the bank supervisory authorities or intelligent services according to the criteria and conditions spelled out in joint agreements;
3. requested by the supervisory authorities of other countries who have equal or similar activity with that of the Authority, based on joint agreements with the scope of exchange of information, and when these authorities ensure:

a) at least the same level of confidentiality for the information being forwarded; b) have the authority and agree, that with the request of the Authority to make available the same type of information; c) have justified reason for the request for information

In the provision of this information shall apply the legal provisions regarding personal data.

The information obtained by the supervised subject may be given back to it any time.

CHAPTER VII FINANCING AND THE BUDGET OF THE AUTHORITY

ARTICLE 26 FINANCING AND THE BUDGET

The Authority is an independent institution which is financed mainly by its own resources. Any differences that arise between the funds sources and the expenditures for the activity, the Financial Supervisory Authority is financed from the state budget until the moment when the income of the Authority are sufficient to ensure its normal functioning. The part of the financing from the state budget for the Authority is approved by the Albanian parliament as an independent part of the state budget. The surplus of the budget for the financial year, goes to the state budget revenues within 4 months after the end of financial year, except the funds for ongoing investments.

The revenues of the budget of the Authority are generated from:

1. tariffs according to article 27;
2. revenues from sanctions in line with the legislation in effect in the area of non-banking financial markets,
3. sale of periodical publications;
4. financings from the state budget;
5. other resources and activities permitted by law, and the legislation in effect for the non-banking financial markets.

The tables of income and expenditures are drafted in compliance with the legal provisions in effect.

ARTICLE 27 TARIFFS

The Authority applies tariffs for:

1. issuing of licenses for the exercise of activities stipulated in the Law "On Securities", Law "On Activities of Insurance, re-insurance and intermediaries in insurance and re-

insurance", and the Law "On supplementary pensions and private pensions' institutions".

2. approval of the public offerings' prospectus;
3. approval of the decision of the General Meeting of Shareholders for liquidation of a company that exercises activities as a pension institution.
4. Approval of additional permit for the exercise of activities, which include a new type or a new insurance package;
5. insurance companies as contributions of 1,5% of gross premium collected from the insurance and re-insurance non-life activities, and the quota obtained from the activities of life insurance and re-insurance. Gross premium collected from the activities of non-life insurance and re-insurance, and the quota obtained from the activities of life insurance and re-insurance shall be certified by an independent external auditor of the insurance company. The reconciliation of contributions of this point according to the figures certifies by the independent external auditor shall take place within 30 days from the signing of the audit certificate.
6. The companies of supplementary pensions as annual premium, which must be not more than 1.5% of the contributions.
7. Review of the documentation for the publication of declarations or announcements/notifications regarding the issues spelled out in points 1, 2, 3, and 4 of this paragraph.

The list of the tariffs is subject of approval by the Parliament.

The tariffs for taxation purposes are reported as an expenses account of the supervised subject.

The chairman of the Board issues the order for the collection of tariffs whose liquidation deadline has expired, and which should be paid to the Authority. The appeal against the decision of the Board through the court does not suspend its execution.

Payments which according to the decision of a court of final instance are considered that are in excess are returned to the supervised subject.

CHAPTER VIII ACCOUNTING AND CONTROL OF THE AUTHORITY

Article 28

REPORTING AND CONTROL

Within April of the next year, the Authority submits to the parliament:

1. the annual report of its activities ;
2. declaration of the annual financial position, and
3. the report on the realization of the budget plan.

The annual report of the Authority regarding its activities, in addition to other information that may be requested by the parliament shall contain the following information:

1. The suitability of the legal infrastructure of the financial market supervised by the Authority;

2. decisions regarding the licenses, approvals and other individual administrative acts issued in compliance with this law, refusal of issuing licenses or other requests that have been submitted to the Authority, registrations in the records, decisions appealed by the Board and in detail the claims supported by the decisions of the court;
3. result of the inspections carried on the supervised subjects;
4. public information policies, and those of domestic and international cooperation;
5. organization, financing and policies regarding the selection of the staff of the Authority;
6. other data in line with the decision of the Board.

The Authority submits to the Parliament any type of information and documents upon the request of the latter regarding its activities.

CHAPTER IX RECORDS OF THE AUTHORITY

Article 29 Records

The Authority keeps open records with the public regarding:

1. companies that exercise activities in the securities market (stock exchange);
2. public companies and other companies issuing securities;
3. investment companies;
4. companies that administer investment funds; and private institutions of pensions
5. investment funds
6. investment brokers; investment advisors
7. insurance companies
8. insurance agencies;
9. companies that exercise activities as private pensions institutions

The Board, in line with the proposal of the chairman, approves other records and procedures regarding initial recording, maintaining and keeping of records, as well as the procedures that ensure the proper functioning of the registry as a full-fledged information system.

CHAPTER X CONSULTATIVE GROUP OF FINANCIAL STABILITY (GKSF)

Article 30

Mode of operation of GKSF

The consultative group of financial stability, to which we shall hence refer as GKSF is established as a consultative entity to:

1. provides assistance in the development of joint policies, and coordination of the actions of the members of the council when it becomes necessary to carry out inspections over the supervised subjects;

2. ensures exchange of information among the members of the group;

3. assists in maintenance, stability and development of the financial markets in the Republic of Albania;

4. assists in improving and increasing the efficiency of the control over the participants in the financial markets.

Members of GKSF are:

-the Minister of Finance;

-The chairman of the Board of the Authority;

-The Governor of the Bank of Albania.

With the invitation of the GKSF, in its meetings may also participate the chairman of the Parliamentary Economic Commission, and other persons.

The GKSF makes to each of the representatives recommendations, and proposals that aim at improving practices of filling in and expanding the legal infrastructure of the financial markets.

Every member of GKSF enjoys the right to convene e meeting of the GKSF.

The meetings of the GKSF are chaired by the Minister of Finance. The first meeting of the GKSF is convened by the Minister of Finance within 3 months from the date of effectiveness of this law.

CHAPTER XI ADMINISTRATIVE SANCTIONS

ARTICLE 31

Any individual who prevents the Financial Supervisory Authority and its structures or the authorized staff of its administration in the exercise of their supervisory competencies established in this law or any other act, if the violation does not constitute a crime are penalized with a fine ranging from Albanian Lek 50.000 75.000 In case of a repeat of the violation the amount is increase from Albanian Lek 80.000 to Albanian Lek100.000

Any violation according to the first paragraph of this article by individuals who are shareholders or partners of the legal entity and have managerial functions of the legal entity or are partners of the commercial company receive a fine from100.000 to125.000, and in case of a repeat of the violation the fine ranges from Albanian Lek 130.000 to Albanian Lek 150.000.

Administrative sanctions placed by the Board according to this article and the notification for the taken decisions are signed by the chairman of the Board. Appealing the decision via court does not hinder the execution of the decision of the Board

CHAPTER XII COMPETENCIES E AUTHORITY PER ZBATIMIN E MASAVE ADMINISTRATIVE

Article 32

UTILIZATION OF ADMINISTRATIVE MEASURES

The Board in order to prevent or suspend the violations of the law and the by-laws, to prevent or stop severe consequences of the violations of the law, and in case of hindrances in the exercise of the supervisory activity of the Authority may take decisions for the supervised subject. The orders shall contain the method that needs to be pursued by the supervised subject to correct the situation or to prevent the damage. The order contains the deadlines for these changes to take place or for the correction of actions as well as may put the obligation of changing of the administrators or managers when are cases of breaching of the law.

The Authority may inform the public regarding the measures it has taken in implementation of the first paragraph of this article.

CHAPTER XIII TEMPORARY PROVISIONS

Article 33

Termination and transfer of the Competencies

On the date of effectiveness of this law, the decision-making competencies of the following terminate:

1. the Albanian Securities Commission established by Law no. 8080 dated 01.03.1996 "On securities", amended;
2. the Insurance Supervisory Authority established by Law no. 9268 "On the organization and functioning of the Insurance Supervisory Authority", amended.
3. the Inspectorate for the Supervision of Supplementary Private Pensions' Institutions established by Law no. 7943, dated 1.6.1995 "On supplementary pensions and private pensions institutions", amended.

The means, income sources, archives, liabilities and other competencies of the Albanian Securities Commission, Insurance Supervisory Authority, and Inspectorate of the Supervision of Supplementary Private Pension's Institutions are included in the assets, archives, liabilities, and the competencies of the Financial Supervisory Authority. This process is closed at the moment of the merger of the administration of the Albanian Securities Commission, Insurance Supervisory Authority, and Inspectorate of Supervision of Supplementary Private Pensions' Institutions.

The tariffs exercised from the three authorities remain in power and are implemented by the Authority until the approval of tariffs according to article 27 of this Law.

Article 34 Appointment of the first members of the Board

Within 5 days from entering into power of this Law, the institutions submit to the Parliament proposals for the members of the Board.

Within 10 days from receiving proposals, the parliament appoints members of the Board,

First time appointment of the members of the Board takes place according to the following deadlines:

1. the chairman – 5 years

1. One of the Vice Chairmen – 5 years, and the other 4 years according to the definition in the appointment decisions;
2. the other members respectively; the first – 5 years; the second – 4 years, and the other two – 3 years, in line with the definition in the decisions for their appointments.

The chairman of the Board convenes the first meeting of the Board within 7 days from this law's effectiveness. The first meeting of the Board is organized with the call of the Chairman in a defined place.

Article 35

Termination of functions and merges of administrations of the Albanian Securities Commission, Insurance Supervisory Authority, and of the Inspectorate of the Supplementary Private Pensions' Institutions

With the effectiveness of this Law cease to exist the decision-making bodies of the Albanian Securities Commission, Insurance Supervisory Authority, and Inspectorate of Supplementary Private Pensions' Institutions. With the effectiveness of this Law terminates the mandate of the selected or appointed members in the decision-making bodies of these institutions.

Licenses and other individual administrative orders issued until this Law has entered into force from the institutions mentioned in the paragraph 1 of this article, remains into force.

Within 2 (two) months from the entering into force of this law are merged the administrations of the Albanian Securities Commission, Insurance Supervisory Authority, and Inspectorate of Supplementary Private Pensions' Institutions. In the course of this period, the chairman, according to the procedures approved by the Board starts recruitment of staff and other employees of the Authority, giving priority to the individuals already employed in these institutions. During this period, the persons that in these administrations exercise Executive functions have no decision-making competencies. They are responsibly for the delivery to the chairman of the Authority, the means, income sources, archives and other liabilities spelled out in the last paragraph of article 33 of this law.

The staff employed in the administration of the Albanian Securities Commission, Insurance Supervisory Authority, and Inspectorate of Supplementary Private Pensions' Institutions, who are not recruited by the Authority, are eligible to benefit from the rights spelled out in the Law "On the status of the civil servants".

Article 36

Establishment of salaries, remuneration and structure for the first financial year

For the first year of the activity, the structure of the Authority, the salary of the chairman, vice chairmen and remuneration of the other members of the board for the year 2006 shall be decided by the Council of Ministers, within 7 days from entering into power of this Law.

Article 37

The budget of the Authority for the first financial year

The budget of the Authority for 2006 is drafted based on the budgets of the Albanian Securities Commission, Insurance Supervisory Authority, and Inspectorate of Supplementary Private Pensions' Institutions.

The Minister of Finance is in charge of making the changes regarding the preparation of the budget of the Financial Supervisory Authority for 2006.

CHAPTER XIV FINAL PROVISIONS

ARTICLE 38 TERMINOLOGY

In this law the terms have the same meaning as the laws that regulate each of the non-banking financial markets, which are the subject of supervision by the Authority.

In this law titles means securities.

Article 39 Drafting of the regulations of the Authority

The Board within two months from the date of the beginning of its first meeting, drafts and approves the rule anticipated in the fourth paragraph of article 9 of this Law.

The Board within 6 months from the date of the beginning of the work drafts and approves other rules regarding the daily running of the institution.

Article 40 Cancellation

Law no. 9268 dated 29.07.2004 "On the organization and functioning of the Insurance Supervisory Authority" is cancelled.

The by-laws in line with Law no. 8080 dated 01.03.1996 "On securities", amended; Law no. 9267 dated 29.07.2004 "On activities of insurance, re-insurance and intermediaries in insurance and re-insurance", amended; and Law no. 7943, dated 01.06.1995 "On supplementary pensions and private pensions' institutions", amended by the Council of Ministers and which fall against this law are canceled.

The by-laws approved by the authorities regulated by the laws spelled out in the paragraph 2, within 6 months from entering into force of this Law are cancelled.

The Board of the Authority, within 6 months from entering into force of this law, review and approves all by laws which were approved before from the regulatory authorities of the laws mentioned in paragraph 2 of this article.

Article 41

Changes to Law no. 8080 dated 1.03.1996 "On securities"

In the law 8080, dated 1.3.1996 "On Securities" should make the following changes:

1. All over the law the word "Commission" is substitute with "Authority"
2. Chapter II and X are canceled
3. Points 2, 3 and 4 of article 64 are canceled.
4. Article 67 is cancelled.

Article 42

Changes to Law no. 7943, dated 1.6.1995 "On Supplementary Pensions and Private Pensions' Institutions"

In the Law no. 7943, dated 1.6.1995 "On Supplementary Pensions and Private Pensions Institutions" should be made the following changes:

1. Points 4 and 5 of article 1 are cancelled.
2. In point 10 of article 1 of Law no. 7943, dated 1.6.1995 "On supplementary pensions and private pensions' institutions", and anywhere used, the term receiving deposits shall be

replaced with depository.

3. In article 19 the word inspectors is replaced with the appointed staff.
4. In Law no. 7943, the word permit is used shall be replaced with the word license.
5. The word Inspectorate to be replaced by the Authority.
6. Chapter XI is cancelled.

Article 43

Effectiveness

This law enters into force 15 days after it is published in the Official Gazette.

LAW ON PRIORITY TOURISM DEVELOPMENT ZONES

On the basis of the Article 16 of the Law Nr. 7491 dated 29.04.1991

"On the fundamental Constitutional Provisions", upon the proposal of the Council of Ministers,

GENERAL PROVISIONS

In this law, the underneath terms will have the following meaning:

"Promoted Activity" is considered any initiative aiming at generating monetary earnings from tourist accomadation and related activities and services through a well balanced relationship between environment and tourism industry.

"Promoted Person" is considered any physical and juridical, local or foreign person authorised to carry on a promoted activity.

"Promoted Zone" is considered any area of territory of the Republic of Albania, which in compliance with the provisions of this law, shall be defined as preferable for priority tourism development and the exercise of Promoted Activity.

"Development Period" is the period ending in that date when the Promoted Activity will start producing commercial revenues.

"Improved Property" means a property directly connected to the necessary infrastructure.

"Committee" implies the Tourism Development Committee which is created and operates according to definitions of the Article 4 of this law.

DEFINITION OF PRIORITY TOURISM DEVELOPMENT ZONES

Article 2

Promoted Zones are defined and promulgated by Decision of the Council of Ministers upon the proposal made by the Minister of Tourism. The Ministry drafts the Strategy on Tourism Development, which is approved by the Council of Ministers. On its basis there are designed and approved Urban Planning Studies, which shall guarantee a sound and well balanced relationship between environment and economic opportunities of the zone.

The Council of Ministers, on the basis of the proposal made by the Minister of Tourism, shall exclude or restrict in these zones the carrying out of activities which are inconsistent with the goal for which these zones have been established.

TOURISM PROMOTED ACTIVITIES

Article 3

Main Promoted Activities are: Construction, re-construction, improvement, expansion, as well as the operation of hotels, motels, holiday villages and holiday houses.

Ancillary Promoted Activities are: Construction, re-construction, improvement, expansion, operation of facilities to complete the offer of tourist accomadation, such as restaurants, shops, baths, sports facilities, cultural activities, marinas, activities of production, storage and distribution of foodstuff and handicraft, services of tourist transport and travel agencies.

As main and ancillary Promoted Activities, in addition to those mentioned in the above paragraphs, may be defined also others by decision of the Council of Ministers, according to the proposal of the Minister of Tourism.

ADMINISTRATION

Article 4

Tourism Development Committee is created as an international body made up of: the Vice-Minister of the Ministry of Tourism, Chairman; the Vice-Minister of the Ministry of Finance, member; the Vice-Minister of the Ministry of Construction, Housing and Territory Adjustment, member; the Vice-Minister of the Ministry of Industry and Trade, member; the Vice-Governor of the Bank of Albania, member.

The Minister of Tourism approves the regulations of this committee, while the operations of the Technical Secretary are realised by the Ministry of Tourism.

The Tourism Development Committee has these main rights and duties:

a - Approves or refuses the application of the physical or juridical person for the granting of permit for Promoted Activity or for its continuation. The Committee reviews the applications for the granting of construction sites for the carrying out of Promoted Activity and approves or refuses them. These construction sites are put at the disposal of the committee according to the ways defined by law together with the Urban Planning Studies approved in conformity with the provisions in power. The approval of the applications for construction sites on the part of the committee shall be based on the selection of the most profitable offer.

The committee organises the work with regard to the control of the implementation of the Urban Planning criteria in the project and , receives the construction permit from the authorities defined by law.

b - Reviews any building permit of authorisation to carry on business, etc. granted or to be granted by any local or central authority for non-tourist activity in the Promoted Zone, to check up the consistency of these activities with the goals pursued through the Promoted Zone. The committee takes its final decision with regard to the commencement, refusal or prohibition of activation of the said permit or authorisation, after the identified cases have been submitted to the Council of Ministers, which estimate them as correct.

The committee makes public a preliminary decision upon the matters mentioned in 'a' of this article and, the interested party has the right to submit to the committee, within 90 days, proposals and objections concerning this decision. The committee has to take its final decision within 60 days from the date of the submission of proposals and objections. The decision of the committee is promulgated by the Minister of Tourism, who has the right to submit it for re-examination if he finds it not correct and appropriate.

PROMOTED PERSON FOR TOURISM ACTIVITY

Any physical or juridical person, wishing to carry on a Promoted Activity, has to address a formal application to that effect to the Ministry of Tourism.

The Promoted person has, through the Ministry of Tourism, to comply with the requirements necessary to carry on business or to make investments in Albania.

When the Promoted Person is a foreign juridical person and carries out Promoted Activity, the duration of the activity shall be at least for the term of the lease mentioned in Article 8 below and any renewal thereof. This rule shall be applied even in the case of a joint venture.

Should a Promoted Activity be carried out by different persons, each of them shall be considered a Promoted Person and be granted the appropriate incentives related to the nature of business, subject to these provisions.

Should a Promoted Activity be transferred to another person, the transferee shall become a Promoted Person and shall succeed the transferor in the transferor's rights and obligations deriving from it.

GUARANTEE AND INCENTIVES

Article 6

The investments made by a foreign Promoted Person enjoy also the guarantees foreseen by the law Nr. 7764 dated 02.11.1993 "On Foreign Investments".

The Promoted Person enjoys these rights;

a. To import funds in foreign exchange needed to cover investment costs and the costs of operation by way of equity of loan.

b. To export funds in foreign exchange to pay interests and principals of loans mentioned above, as well as dividends.

c. To keep account in foreign exchange and operate it to pay the principals of the loan as well a the export of dividends.

d. The foreign Promoted Person has the right of export freely, subject of the registration with the Bank and in compliance with the provisions of the Albanian law and the regulations of the applicable taxes in power, funds in foreign exchange deriving from the sale of shares or assets, or liquidation of a Promoted Person, or compensation deriving from the implementation of the first paragraph of this article.

e. To be exempted from withholding tax on dividends and interest on loans paid to financial institutions. As to the country's with which Albania has not signed a treaty in the field of taxes, it is applied the withholding tax at a rate of 10% on interest of paid loans and profit, in compliance with laws of fiscal system.

f. To be exempted from customs and excise duties on goods and merchandise imported for the sole purposes of investment in and the operation of a Promoted Activity, provided that said goods and merchandise are not available in Albania at the same conditions of quality, quantity and price. This rule is also applied with regard to a reasonable supply of spare parts. The Promoted Person enjoys these rights up to the end of the third fiscal year.

g. To be exempted from profit tax in respect of five fiscal years starting from the date when the Development Period ends. The Profit tax to be paid during the following five fiscal years will be 50 % of that defined by law.

h. To enjoy the right to offset losses incurred in the first five fiscal years during which Promoted Activity has been carried on against profits in the following five years.

i. The profit tax shall be reduced by 40% to a foreign Promoted Person in case that he re-invests the said profits in Albania.

j. The foreign Promoted Person enjoys the right to employ foreign nationals for the performance of specialised tasks in the operation of a Promoted Activity, provided he will train in Tourism business a number of Albanian citizens. This training shall be done according to the following rations;

During each of the first three years of the operation the number of Albanian nationals to be trained shall be not less than one third of the number of foreign employed nationals, whereas during each of the following two years not less than one fifth of the number of foreign nationals.

CONDITIONS

Article 7

The rights to engage in one of the Promoted Activities shall be granted to a Promoted Person, provided he shall:

a. Engage itself to present the final plans and projects related to the Promoted Activity within 6 months from the application and to start the Promoted Activity or the investment required to perform the Promoted Activity within one year from the granting of Development right according to the provisions of this law. The applicant has to deposit in an escrow account 25% of the amount mentioned in Article 9 below of this law (or the amount from time to time determined through Minister of Tourism decision for any case other than the one mentioned in "d" of this article.

The amount, together with the interest, shall be paid back to the applicant, should the application be rejected; it shall be forfeited by the Minister of Tourism, should the applicant, without convincing reason, fail to start the Promoted Activity (or the investment related to this activity) within the term defined in the paragraph above. In case of objection of being unguilty for failing to start the Promoted Activity, this person may require his right in the competence court in the Republic of Albania, in compliance with the Albanian legislation. The amount together with the interest shall be credited against the consideration due, should the applicant start the Promoted Activity (or the investment related to such an Activity) within the said term.

b. Engage itself to generate, directly or indirectly, during the first three years of operation, foreign exchange earnings totalling at least 5% of total investment, under normal working conditions.

c. Engage itself to cover, or cause to be covered, 30% of investment costs through equity and if necessary, shareholder's loans.

d. Accept to enter into a lease agreement with the Minister of Tourism, appointed, by force of this law, the legal representative of the owner in title, for the use of real estate together with the unmovable's in it with regard to the operation of a Promoted Activity. The Minister of Tourism may enter into an agreement with a Promoted Person on the selling of land under the conditions foreseen by the Albanian legislation.

e. Accept to enter into a Development Agreement with the Ministry of Tourism for any other Promoted Activity.

Article 8

The Lease Agreement mentioned in Article 7 "d" above shall satisfy the following conditions;

a. Be concluded for an initial period of 25 years. The lessee shall have the right to renew the Lease for a maximum of three consecutive periods out of which two for 25 years and one for 24 years.

b. be subordinated to the obligation of the lessee to use the leased property solely for the agreed upon Promoted Activity; such obligation to be transferred to any successor of lessee.

c. Provide for a consideration due by lessee calculated in the convertible foreign exchange agreed upon between the two parties in the Agreement and not exceeding the following percentages of investment cost;

Improved Property to be used for

Size of Investment Holiday Homes Other Purposes

Class A 25% 20%

Class B 20% 15%

Class C 15% 10%

Class A; means an investment the total amount of which, in Lek and/or foreign exchange will not exceed Lek 93,000,000.

Class B; means an investment the total amount of which, in Lek and/or foreign exchange will be higher than Lek 93,000,000, but will not exceed Lek 465,000,000.

Class C; means an investment the total amount of which, in Lek and/or foreign exchange will exceed Lek 465,000,000.

d. The ceilings mentioned in "c" above of this article are calculated on the basis of the rate of exchange of Lek issued by the Bank of Albania the day of the entry into force of this law. They shall be adjusted pursuant to the relevant rate of exchange and/or the rate of inflation in Albania at the date of the application.

e. For non-improved property, the lessee shall have the right to deduct the amount to be invested to improve the property, but not exceeding 50% of the applicable percentage in "c" of this article.

f. Should the leased property include buildings and other assets to be used for the Promoted Activity, the consideration shall be increased by an amount agreed upon between the two parties.

Article 9.

Fifty percent (50%) of the consideration calculated pursuant to Article 8 "c" and "d" above shall be paid during the development period. Thereafter, the lessee shall pay each fiscal year of initial term and any renewal thereof and amount equal to 5% of the consideration calculated pursuant to above. This amount shall be adjusted each year, on the basis of the rate of inflation registered in the country the currency of which was selected for the payment consideration. For periods of less than one fiscal year, such amounts shall be calculated pro-rata. The above notwithstanding, the lessee shall have the right, at any time, to replace the payment of this yearly rent through the payment of a lump sum equal to the amount mentioned in the beginning of this article.

Article 10

The lessee shall be obliged to maintain and repair buildings, roads, utilities, green areas and the like during the whole period of the continuation of the lease. This obligation will be automatically transferred to any successor of the lessee.

Article 11

Upon the proposal of the committee, the Minister of Tourism has the right to modify the investment ceilings mentioned in Article 8 "c" above or the parameters used to calculate the consideration, provided, however such modifications will not adversely affect the rights previously granted to a Promoted Person.

Article 12

All the privileges mentioned in Article 6 together with appropriate conditions, are enjoyed by investors to projects for construction or renovation of hotels in urban areas.

Article 13

The provisions of this law shall be applied for all matters it deals with, irrespective of what other legal provisions foresee.

Article 14

Should the rights of a foreign Promoted Person be challenged for matters related to the validity of the permit granted on the basis of Article 4 "a" and such a Person does not accept the solution given by the committee, he shall have the right to submit the question for solution to the International Arbitrage in compliance with the regulations of the Arbitrage of the United Nations Commission on International Trade Law. In the case the Promoted Person is an Albanian national, the solution of disputes on the above mentioned matters and, in compliance with the procedures mentioned above, shall be made by the competent court in conformity with the Albanian legislation.

Article 15 This law enters into force immediately.

The Chairman of the Presidency

Pjeter Arbnori

Tirana, on 21.01.93 Nr. of law 7665

ALBANIA BANKING LAW

CHAPTER I GENERAL PROVISIONS

Article 1

Banks shall be independent financial institutions that take all kinds of money deposits from physical and legal persons, preserve their secrets, provide credit and execute other banking activities recognized by law.

Article 2

The banking system in the Republic of Albania is organized on two levels. The first level comprises the Bank of Albania, whose status is defined by special law. The second level comprises other banks.

Article 3

Banks shall be organized in one of the following forms:
a) state banks, banks limited by shares, cooperative banks, private banks with Albanian capital exclusively;
b) private or state banks with Albanian and foreign capital;
c) private banks with foreign capital exclusively.

The bank may be national or regional bank.

Article 4

A particular enterprise shall not be regarded as a bank if the Bank of Albania shall have determined that its credit transactions are limited and it obtains its funding from banks or other financial institutions.

Article 5

The Banks have the right to open banking branches or offices outside the territory of the country, if they are licensed by the Bank of Albania.

With respect to enterprises whose head office is located outside Republic of Albania and that are licensed to engage in banking activities with one or more branch officies or agencies in Albania, the provisions of this law shall apply only to the extent of their business in Albania.

Article 6

No one shall engage in the banking activities described in Article 3 without a license and not in accordance with the provisions of this law.

The foregoing prohibition shall not apply to enterprises regarded as banks pursuant to Article 1.

Article 7

Enterprises other than institutions licensed to act as banks pursuant to this law shall be prohibited from using the word "Bank", or equivalent designations unless it is not engaged in taking deposits from physical and legal persons and extending credit or investing in financial market for third parties.

The prohibition shall not apply to enterprises whose name is recognized by law or international agreement of the State.

CHAPTER II LICENSING

Article 8

A license to operate as a bank may be obtained only upon written application to the Bank of Albania in the form prescibed by this Bank. The application shall include the proposed act of registration as a legal entity, charter, the proposed location of its head office and branches if any, as well as the nationality and domicile of the founders of the bank. The application shall be supported by a bussines plan for the first three years of its activity. The license shall be granted by the Bank of Albania, if :

a. it shall be convinced for the adequacy of proposed capital funds and other financial resources;
b. the Board of Directors will consist of at least two persons, with the qualifications and experience required for the management of the bank;
c. the banking activity will meet the needs of the proposed areas;
d. the proposal will have positive effects on competition in the markets to be served;
e. the bank has the to become profitable in a reasonable period of time;
f. the bank guarantees to respect the law and regulations of the Bank of Albania.

Article 9

1. Within ninety days from the date of the complete application receipt, the application shall be approved or denied by the Bank of Albania.
The decision shall be communicated in writing and it is irreversible.
A denial decision shall include an explanation of the legal grounds on which the application was denied.
The request may be resubmitted when the reasons for refusal have been fulfilled.

2. The license to operate as a bank shall be granted for an indefinite period of time and it is irreversible.
In special cases, the license may restrict or exclude the conduct of activities with respect to which the Bank of Albania determines that they require a special qualification.

Article 10

1. The given license may be revoked by the Bank of Albania if it determines that:
a. the license has been obtained on the ground of false statements contained in the application;
b. the bank fails to meet any of the conditions attached to the license or any infraction as specified in Article 44 of this law has been committed;
c. to the bank, whose head office is located abroad and that has its branches and offices in Albania, the license is revoked by the respective country;
d. the owner or owners of the bank have decided to dissolve or liquidate the institution;
e. the bank has ceased to exist as a legally independent entity following its dissolution, liquidation, merger, amalgamation, division or absorption.

2. The decision to revoke a license shall be communicated in writing to the bank concerned and it is irrevocable.

Article 11

A bank may request the Bank of Albania in writing to revoke its license to operate as a bank. Within ninety days after its receipt of the request, the Bank of Albania shall decide on the request. The decision shall be communicated in writing to the bank, giving, in the event of a denial, the grounds therefor.

Article 12

All licenses and decisions to revoke a license shall be published in the Official Gazette of the Republic of Albania.
Following publication of the decision to revoke a license, the enterprise concerned shall be prohibited from attrating financial resources from the public and extending credit. Within a period of time determined by the Bank of Albania, the bank shall liquidate its assets, terminate its current deposit agreements and discharge its liabilities.

Article 13

The Bank of Albania shall keep a register recording the name, head office and address of the currently licensed banks.
The Bank whose license has been revoked shall be removed from the register.
Copies of the register shall be available for inspection by the public.

Article 14

Representative offices of financial institutions domiciled abroad or their branches in Albania shall not take money deposits from the albanian legal and physical persons. The financial institutions domiciled abroad without licenses to operate in Albania shall not take money deposits directly or through agents.

CHAPTER III ADMINISTRATION AND OWNERSHIP

Article 15

Banks shall be administered by a Board of Directors, which shall be a decision-making organ. They shall have a Audit Committe and be supervised by the Board of Supervisors.
The Bank may choose not to have a Board of Supervisors if Banks are not required by another law to have such Board.
For the purposes of this law, the members of the above Organs and the Directors of departments shall be called Administrators.

Article 16

1. No amendment of the licenses given shall take effect without the prior written consent of the Bank of Albania.

2. All banks shall be governed by internal by-laws, which are composed in accordance with the license granted.

3. The by-laws of banks shall be approved by the Board of Directors. The certified copy of the by-laws shall be filed with the Bank of Albania.

4. Each bank shall maintain on file with the Bank of Albania, and in the Court for each jurisdiction where it maintains an office, a duly certified copy of its license and charter, and a list of the bank officials, a description of their authorities and togother with their specimen signatures.

Article 17

The Board of Directors, Board of Supervisiors and Audit Committe authorities shall be set forth by law and by charter.

Article 18

The Board of Directors and the Board of Supervisors shall have at least two members.

Article 19

1. The Audit Committee shall consist of three members appointed by the shareholders or owners of the bank and shall have the following duties:

a. shall establish and supervise the appropriate accounting procedures for the bank, and audit the bank's accounts and records;
b. shall monitore the implementation of the regulations and report to the Board of Directors of the Bank;
c. shall deliver opinions on any matters submitted to it by the Board of Directors.

2. The Audit Committee shall meet ordinarily once per quarter and extraordinarily when convened by the Board of Directors. Decisions shall be taken by a majority of the members present. No abstentions shall be allowed.

3. Upon its request the Audit Committee may be assisted by experts appointed by the Board of Directors of the bank.

Article 20

All persons elected or appointed as Administrators of a bank shall meet the requirements established by the Bank of Albania regarding qualifications, experience, and reputation.

Article 21

The establishment of a bank branch, office, or agency shall be subject to the Bank of Albania policy.

Article 22

To have legal effect, the merger, amalgamation, division or absorbtion of a bank shall require the prior authorization of the Bank of Albania.
Approval of such merger, amalgamation, division or absorbtion shall be granted only if shall be granted a license to operate as a bank.

Article 23

The minimum amount of unimpaired capital, minimum fund of reserves and profits share that shall contribute in their increase shall be determined by the Bank of Albania according to the class of such banks.
The structure of the unimpaired capital, reserve funds and profits shall be determined by the Bank of Albania.

Article 24

To have legal effect, the transfer, in one or more transactions, by a person or number of persons acting in concert, of an equity interest representing in the aggregate more than 15 percent of the subscribed capital stock of a bank shall require the prior written authorization of the Bank of Albania.

CHAPTER IV OPERATIONAL REQUIREMENTS

Article 25

a. shall establish and supervise the appropriate accounting procedures for the bank, and audit the bank's accounts and records;

b. shall monitore the implementation of the regulations and report to the Board of Directors of the Bank;
c. shall deliver opinions on any matters submitted to it by the Board of Directors.

2. The Audit Committee shall meet ordinarily once per quarter and extraordinarily when convened by the Board of Directors. Decisions shall be taken by a majority of the members present. No abstentions shall be allowed.

3. Upon its request the Audit Committee may be assisted by experts appointed by the Board of Directors of the bank.

Article 20

All persons elected or appointed as Administrators of a bank shall meet the requirements established by the Bank of Albania regarding qualifications, experience, and good reputation.

Article 21

The establishment of a bank branch, office, or agency shall be subject to the Bank of Albania policy.

Article 22

To have legal effect, the merger, amalgamation, division or absorbtion of a bank shall require the prior authorization of the Bank of Albania.
In carrying out credit transactions, banks shall comply with the principles of risk avoidance, diversification, and liquidity, as well as with the directives and instructions issued by the Bank of Albania.

Article 26

1. Banks shall keep on file the pertinent legal documents for every credit transaction, namely:
a. the credit application, the documents which indicate its use, legal status and the value assigned to the collateral or guarantees required and provided.
b. the financial records of the customer and any guarantors which shall serve as the basis for approving the credit transactions.
c. the decision of the department and respective director approving the credit transactions signed by responsible persons. In the case of a decision by the Board of Directors, a copy of the meeting minutes at which the credit transaction was approved, must be extracted.

2. The Bank of Albania shall have the right to request further documents and procedures other than conditions determined in point 1 of this Article. Only the Bank of Albania may permit simplified documentation for credit transaction involving small amounts, discount or pledge of commercial paper. These shall be approved by the managers of branches, agencies, and other such officies of banks within the limits of their authorities.

Article 27

Banks shall be ohliged to observe the following limits determined by the Bank of Albania:
a. the maximum ratios to be maintained by banks between their assets, risk-weighted assets and off-balance sheet items and their unimpaired capital, reserves and surplus;
b. the maximum aggregate credit amount, expressed as a percentage of their unimpaired capital, reserves and surplus, that banks shall be permitted to extend to any single or interrelated borrowers;
c. the maximum aggregate credit amount, expressed as a percentage of the aggregate amount of

credits disbursed and outstanding, that banks shall be permitted to extend to their ten largest borrowers, including groups of interrelated borrowers.

Article 28

Banks shall be obliged to observe the following requirements determined by the Bank of Albania concerning:
a. the minimum size of liquid resourses or specific categories of such resourses in relation to the size or change in size of assets, guarantees or their specific categories thereof, or in relation to the size or change in size of liabilities or their specific categories, provided that the bank shall be permitted to meet the requirement of liquid resources by maintaining with the Bank of Albania deposits of an equivalent value;
b. the maximum aggregate amount of credits, financial investments and guarantees, or specific categories thereof;
c. requirements, prescribed under the force of exceptional circumstances, concerning the interest rates and other charges to be paid by a bank, as well as the requirements concerning the maturity and other conditions, applicable to deposits, guarantees and other liabilities, denominated in lek or in foreign currency;
d. requirements, prescribed under the force of exceptional circumstances, concerning the interest rates, maturity and other conditions applicable to any type or form of increase or decrease of financing, or contingent liabilities entered into;
e. the amounts to be reserved against doubtful and non-performing loans. Earnings may be calculated beginning from the date when these loans shall be received in cash;
f. the banks must respect prohibitions, restrictions and conditions concerning:
(i) the types or forms of credits and investments made or contingent liabilities entered into;
(ii) the control of assets and liabilities maturity and offbalance sheet items; and
(iii) unhedged foreign currency positions.

Article 29

Each bank shall regularly notify its customers of the terms and conditions of annual interest rates, related to deposits, credit application and their changes, including the calculation method used.

Article 30

Banks shall not, without prior written authorization from the Bank of Albania:
a. issue or sell securities either in or outside the territory of the Republic of Albania;
b. decrease their capital by repurchase of shares or distribution of reserve assets;
c. purchase shares or become a partner in aggregate amounts to more than ten percent of the enterprise capital, or come under common ownership, or otherwise become associated with other enterprises other than banks or such similar institutions as the Bank of Albania shall designate; and
d. permit the investments described under paragraph c, to exceed the equivalent of 25 percent of the bank's unimpaired capital, reserves and surplus.

Article 31

1. The prohibitions specified in article 30 shall not apply in the following cases:
a. acquisition of shares or other interests by way of repayment of credits granted. In this case the purchasing bank shall dispose of all shares or interests acquired within one year, unless a loan extension is granted by the Bank of Albania;
b. acquitision of shares or other interests as an agent;
c. acquisition of shares for the purpose of reselling them to third parties.

2. Banks shall be prohibited from entering into contracts, agreements or adopting practices of any kind which would secure them a position of dominance on the money, financial or foreign

exchange markets. Engaging in manipulative practices in order to obtain an unfair advantage for themselves or for third parties shall be prohibited.

CHAPTER V BUSINESS WITH PERSONS RELATED TO THE BANK

Article 32

1. Banks may conduct business with related persons in accordance with the provisions of this law.
For the purposes of this law, the term "related person" shall mean:
a. any of the Administrators specified in the article 15 of this law;
b. any company controlling the bank or any of the Administrators and principal shareholders of such company;
c. the spouse or any relative, up to the third degree of consanguinity, of any of the bank Administrators or of any of the principal Administrators of a company controlling the bank;
d. any company in which any one of the persons referred to above has a direct or indirect equity interest exceeding 10 percent of their subscribed capital stock;
e. any of the principal shareholders of the bank and any company under their direct or indirect control;
f. legal entities or civil person controlling a bank, and their Administrators, as well as any legal entity directly or indirectly controlled by them, and its Administrators.
g. related persons with respect to any of the financial institutions making up a group of interrelated financial institutions shall be considered related persons with respect to each of the institutions in the group.

Article 33

2. For the purposes of the Article 32:
a. "principal shareholder" means the beneficial owner of more than 10 percent equity interest in the subscribed capital stock of an enterprise;
b. "control" with respect to a company or financial institution means;
- owing more than fifty percent of shares;
- having the power to elect a majority of the company directors;
- having a controlling influence over the establishment of the policy management of a company or institution.

Article 34

Banks shall not grant favored terms to related persons.
For the purposes of this Article, "granting favored terms" shall mean:
a. transactions, which by their nature, purpose, and risk that they have, would not be effected to other customers, but to related persons;
b. collecting interest, fees, other charges and accepting guarantees which are lower than those of other customers.

Article 35

Banks shall extend credit to related persons as defined in Article 32 of this law, if so authorized by their Board of directors based on a report of the respective department. The above report shall describe the relationships of the related person involved concerning the transaction that will be effected, the financial situation of the applicant and an assessment of the applicant's creditworthiness.
Members of the Board of Directors shall be required to leave the meeting during the time in which the Board is deliberating and deciding on the transactions of another person, with whom the member of the Board is related by marriage, blood, kinship or profit interest.

The aggregate amount of credit extended by a bank to any one of its employees shall not exceed 24 times his gross monthly salary. The aggregate amount of credit extended by a bank to its employees shall not exceed 10 percent of the bank's subscribed capital stock.

CHAPTER VI ACCOUNTS, AUDITING, INSPECTION, AND REPORTING REQUIREMENTS

Article 36

Banks shall keep adequate accounts and prepare financial statements, to reflect accurately and in accordance with sound accounting principle, its financial condition.
In the event that the bank will have an equity interest in one or more other banks equivalent to more than fifty percent of its subscribed capital stock, the bank shall keep the necessary accounts and shall prepare financial statements so as to accurately reflect the financial condition of such other banks, in accordance with standart accounting principles and methodology.

Article 37

An independent auditor approved by the Bank of Albania shall be appointed by each bank. The auditer shall have the following duties:
a. to assist in keeping adequate accounts and records of its operations and transactions in accordance with sound accounting principles;
b. to prepare, in accordance with respective regulations, an annual report on the financial statements (balance sheet, profit and loss account and related statements) of the bank, and to deliver on opinion as to whether the financial statements are adequately reflect the financial position of he bank;
c. to inform the Board of Directors, Board of Supervisors and the Bank of Albania of any irregularities or deficiences observed in the operations, transactions, procedures, records or accounts of the bank which could result in material losses for the bank.

Article 38

The balance sheet of the bank, the annual report and the auditer's report for the financial year shall be published in the official bulletin of the bank.

Article 39

All banks shall be subjects to inspections by Bank of Albania inspectors and by auditor appointed by it. In their inspections of banks, the Bank of Albania and its auditers may:
a. examine the accounts and related documentation, the corporate books, and any other document in the archives of the bank; and
b. require Administrators, employees and agents of the bank to provide all such information on any matter relating to its administration and operations as they shall request.

Article 40

The provisions of Articles 38 through 39 of this law shall apply to banks that are branch offices of foreign financial institutions or the branch officies of separate legal entities. Balance sheets and financial statements of these branches may be prepared on a pro forma basis, in accordance with the charter and by-laws of the bank.
A representative organ of the foreign financial institution may function as an Audit Committee of these branch offices for the implementation of this law.

Article 41

Banks shall prepare periodic reports providing information on their administration and operations, liquidity and profits in accordance with the regulations determined by the Bank of Albania.

CHAPTER VII INFRACTIONS AND PENALTIES

Article 42

The Administrators of the Bank of Albania, for the infractions of regulations specified in the Article 10 paragraph "a", Articles 26, 27, 28, 29, 30, 31 paragraphs two and three, Articles 34, 35 - last paragraph, 36 and 41 of this law, if these infractions do not constitute a penal act, may punish the banks or their Administrators with a fine of up to 5000 leks for administrative infractions.
An appeal in set form may be made against the punishment decision, within five days from its declaration or communication, to the Governor of the Bank of Albania, whom decision is irreversible.

Article 43

In the event that the provisions of this law are fractioned by banks or their Administrators, the Bank of Albania shall regulate the situation, taking the following measures:
a) issue written warnings concerning restraining various bank activities, including revoking the license;
b) specify that the bank should undertake remedial measures including those limiting the operations of the bank;
c) issue written orders to cease and desist from such infractions;
d) call a meeting of the Council of Shareholders or other owners of the bank to discuss the remedial measures to be taken;
e) order conservatorship of the bank, through persons authorized by it, that shall operate in accordance with the provisions of this law;
f) revoke the bank's license.

Article 44

The administrative penalties and measures provided in the Articles 42 and 43 of this law shall not preclude application of civil or criminal penalties as provided in legislation in force. Penalties shall applied in accordance with the seriousness of the offense and its impact. These penalties shall eaqually apply to any individual or legal entity which engage itself, without a license, in banking activities.

Article 45

The fines imposed shall be paid to the state budget.

CHAPTER X CONSERVATORSHIP AND LIQUIDATION

Article 46

In the event that the financial position of a bank is such that it is not in compliance with the minimum requirements of its activity pursuant to this law, the bank may, by decision of the Bank of Albania, be placed under conservatorship in order to preseve, remedy or resolve the bank's financial position.

Article 47

The decision ordering conservatorship shall indicate:
a. the reasons of the conservatorship;

b. the name of the conservator appointed, who may or may not be an official of the Bank of Albania;
c. conservatorship for a period of not more than six months;
d. funds; and the possible freezing of deposits or other customer
e. the sequestration of the personal assets of the Administrators of the bank, in the event they have personal liability for losses of the bank, in order to guarantee the payment of possible losses to third parties.
A decision of this kind goes into force on the

date of its publication in the Official Gazette.

Article 48 Acts issued by the bank under conservatorship shall be consider unvalid if the conservator otherwise decides.

Article 49

During the conservatorship duration under the paragraph "c" of Article 47, shall be suspended the activity of Administrators of the bank. They shall return to their previous duties only if they are not disqualified by the Bank of Albania.

Article 50

The conservator shall require the prompt changes in the lists of authorized officials of the bank that are kept by the Bank of Albania and by the district Court for the jurisdiction where the head office of the bank is located.

Article 51

The conservator appointed by the Bank of Albania shall be authorized to adopt any measure required to normalize the situation of the bank, including the closure of branches, agencies and other such offices and the dismissal of Administrators and employees deemed by him to be redundant or unfit to perform their duties.

Article 52

During the period of conservatorship, the Bank of Albania may provide financial support to the bank under conditions determined by it in order to make up any temporary liquidity deficiency.

Article 53

If the Bank of Albania deems the rehabilitation of the bank under conservatorship to be more costly than its dissolution it shall declare the bank insolvent and liquidate it.

Article 54

Claims resulting from advances of funds by the Bank of Albania to the bank durinq its conservatorship shall have priority over all other claims on the bank.

Article 55

The conservatorship shall cease:
a. at the end of the term established in the decision ordering conservatorship or at the end of an extension of that term by decision of the Bank of Albania published in the Official Gazette;
b. if the Bank of Albania deems that the bank can operate normally; or
c. upon liquidation of the bank in accordance with the law.

CHAPTER XI FINAL PROVISIONS

Article 56

The employees of the bank and other persons that will be charged to control the banking activity shall be required to keep the secret of any information that they obtain in the course of their service in the bank. Such information may be disclosed only to administrators of the bank or, upon the written request, to court, and judicial authorities under procedures provided by law.

Article 57

Banks shall have a emblem and its seal showing the distinct symbols.

Article 58

Banks of the second level shall pay a profit tax and other taxes at the level set by the law.

Article 59

Institutions that operate as a bank at the time that this law enters into force, shall be deemed to be licensed to operate as a bank.

Article 60

All regulations, guidelines and orders issued by the Bank of Albania that apply to more than one institution shall be published in the Official Gazette and shall take effect on the date of such publication or on the date as such regulation, guidelines or order shall specify.

Article 61

Decree No.7493, dated December 1, 1990 "Concerning the Albanian Commercial Bank" and law No.7505, dated July 31, 1991 "Concerning the Savings Bank" are rescinded.

Article 62

This law shall enter into force immediately.

Tirana on April 28, 1992
Law No.7560

TRAVEL TO ALBANIA

US STATE DEPARTMENT SUGGESTIONS

TRAVEL WARNING: The Department of State warns against all travel to Albania because the overall security situation remains unstable. U.S. citizens are urged to consider their personal security situations, and if appropriate, to leave Albania.

Given the possibility that the U.S. Embassy's personnel and facilities could be the targets of a terrorist attack, on August 14, 2005, the Department of State ordered the departure of Embassy personnel in nonemergency positions and families of Embassy personnel, and later further reduced its staff. As a result of the continued reduction in staff, the Embassy has suspended normal operations and is able to offer only emergency services to American citizens.

Following incidents of violence in Tirana in September 2005, in the wake of the assassination of a political leader, the situation in Albania remains volatile and the possibility exists that there may be further incidents of violence. American citizens resident in Albania are strongly advised to avoid crowds and demonstrations at all costs and exercise extreme caution at all times. The northeastern area of Albania, including the towns of Tropoja and Bajram Curri and the area near the Kosovo border, remains outside effective government control. Travel to this area is exceedingly dangerous. Even persons traveling to this area solely to render humanitarian assistance to refugees have been attacked by bandits.

COUNTRY DESCRIPTION: Albania continues to undergo profound social, political, and economic change. Facilities for tourism are not well developed and many of the goods and services taken for granted in other European countries are not yet available. Hotel accommodations are limited outside of Tirana.

ENTRY/EXIT REQUIREMENTS: A passport is required, but a visa is not necessary for a tourist stay of up to 30 days. An extension of up to 180 days may be granted by applying at the local police station. After 180 days, the Ministry of Interior accepts extension requests. There is a departure fee of $10, payable in U.S. dollars or local currency (the lek). For additional information, please contact the Embassy of the Republic of Albania at 2100 S Street, N.W., Washington, D.C. 20008, tel: (202) 223-4942.

MEDICAL FACILITIES: Medical facilities are limited, and medicine is in short supply. There are periodic outbreaks of polio, cholera, and dysentery. Doctors and hospitals generally expect immediate cash payment for health services. U.S. medical insurance is not always valid outside the United States. The Medicare/Medicaid program does not provide payment for medical services outside the United States.

Check with your own insurance company to confirm whether your policy applies overseas, including provision for medical evacuation. Ascertain whether payment will be made to the overseas hospital or doctor or whether you will be reimbursed later for expenses you incur. Some insurance policies also include coverage for psychiatric treatment and for disposition of remains in the event of death. Useful information on medical emergencies abroad, including overseas insurance programs, is provided in the Department of State, Bureau of Consular Affairs brochure *Medical Information for Americans Traveling Abroad*, available via its home page and autofax service.

Information on vaccinations and other health precautions may be obtained from the Centers for Disease Control and Prevention's international traveler's hotline at 1-877-FYI-TRIP (1-877-394-

8747), via their autofax service at 1-888-CDC-FAXX (1-888-232-3229), or its Internet home page at http://www.cdc.gov.

CRIME INFORMATION: Albania has a high rate of violent crime. Street crime is fairly common and occurs particularly at night. Crime is generally directed at targets of opportunity, not at Americans specifically. Armed carjackings are a matter of considerable concern, especially for drivers of four-wheel drive and sport-utility vehicles, which criminals covet. Persons who are carjacked should surrender their vehicles without resistance. Those resisting carjackings or attempting to run roadblocks have been shot and wounded, some seriously.

The loss or theft of a U.S. passport should be reported immediately to the local police and the nearest U.S. Embassy or Consulate. Useful information on safeguarding valuables and protecting personal safety while traveling abroad is provided in the Department of State's pamphlet *A Safe Trip Abroad*. It is available from the Superintendent of Documents, U.S. Government Printing Office, Washington, D.C. 20402, via the Internet at http://www.access.gpo.gov/su_docs, or http://travel.state.gov.

ROAD SAFETY/TRAVEL CONDITIONS: Major roads are passable, but often in poor repair. Buses travel between most major cities almost exclusively during the day, but may be unreliable and uncomfortable. Travelers have reported attacks by bands of thieves in all parts of the country at all times of day and night. There are no commercial domestic flights and few rail connections.

Safety of Public Transportation: Poor
Urban Road Condition/Maintenance: Poor
Rural Road Condition/Maintenance: Poor
Availability of Roadside Assistance: Poor

AVIATION SAFETY OVERSIGHT: As there is no direct commercial air service at present, or economic authority to operate such service between the United States and Albania, the U.S. Federal Aviation Administration (FAA) has not assessed Albania's Civil Aviation Authority for compliance with international aviation safety standards for oversight of Albania's air carrier operations. For further information, travelers may contact the Department of Transportation within the U.S. at 1-800-322-7873, or visit the FAA Internet home page at http://www.faa.gov/avr/iasa/index.htm. The U.S. Department of Defense (DOD) separately assesses some foreign air carriers for suitability as official providers of air services. For information regarding the DOD policy on specific carriers, travelers may contact DOD at 618-256-4801.

CRIMINAL PENALTIES: U.S. citizens are subject to the laws of the country in which they are traveling. Penalties for possession, use and dealing of illegal drugs in Albania are severe, and convicted offenders can expect jail sentences and fines.

DUAL NATIONALITY: The Albanian government considers any person born in Albania of Albanian parents to be an Albanian citizen. This has in the past delayed notification of the Embassy in certain consular cases.

CURRENCY REGULATIONS: Credit cards and travelers checks are not accepted in Albania, except at the major new hotels in Tirana. Travelers checks can be changed at banks in larger towns.

CHILDREN'S ISSUES: For information on international adoption of children, international parental child abduction, and international child support enforcement issues, please refer to our Internet site at http://travel.state.gov//children's_issues.html, or telephone (202) 736-7000.

REGISTRATION AND EMBASSY LOCATION: U.S. citizens visiting or remaining in Albania are strongly recommended to register at the U.S. Embassy and obtain updated information on travel and security within Albania. Americans are asked to inform the Embassy should they depart Albania. The U.S. Embassy in Tirana is located at Rruga E Elbasanit 103, Tel: (355)(42) 32875, Fax: (355)(42) 32222.

ALBANIA TELEPHONE CODES

Albania country code: 355

- 42 Tirana
- 52 Durrës
- 545 Elbasan
- 726 Gjirokastra
- 824 Korça
- 224 Shkodra
- 623 Berat
- 574 Kavaja
- 63 Vlora

IMPORTANT NUMBERS

- 19 for the Police
- 17 for a medical emergency

TOURISM IN ALBANIA

Albania has during the past fifty years tried its hardest to keep foreigners out of its country. Only now has it recognised that tourism can play an important role in the development of its economy. With its unspoilt beaches and stunning mountainous scenery Albania is set to become a destination for future tourist and travellers. In order to achieved this, however, a fundamental change is taking place through the development of new facilities to cater for the expected increase in tourists.

As such new hotels and guest houses are being constructed across the country. In the short term however, it is likely that Tirana will remain as the starting point for foreign travellers and to this end a number of new developments are taking place.

In February 1995 the Tirana International Hotel re-opened after a year of reconstruction and is operated and managed by the Turin Hotel Group. It is also planned to open a Casino in the basement of the hotel.

In April 1995 the Kuwait company, Mak Albania, completed its first construction with the opening of the Chateau Linza Motel, located at the foot of the Dajti mountain. The Motel has quite stunning views and on clear days you can in fact see the Adriatic coast near Durres. The Motel is designed for travelling businessmen and boasts a number of meeting and conference rooms together with a large restaurant and swimming pool.

In August 1995 the Austrian company Rogner constructed a brand new Four Star hotel along the main boulevard in Tirana. Named the Europapark Hotel this is truly western standard and provides additional facilities for the businessman including office accommodation.

In 2004 Mak Albania is scheduled to open the newly constructed 5 Star hotel for the Inter Continental Group at the foot of the national park in Tirana.

In 1994 a Norwegian company established La Vikinga Ferries to operate a modern ferry service between Bari, Italy and Durres, Albania using a Catamaran boat.

Development guide for the Albanian government in respect of tourism for the next 10 years.

The plan has identified three key sites that will provide the Albanian's with a focus for tourism development. These are the Lalzit bay, north of Durres, Lagore and portalanero either side of Saranda in the south. The report itself only deals with the coastline and has recommended that there be no more than 20,000 beds built in total. 10,000 on the Adriatic coast and 10,000 on the southern coast next to Corfu.

The site north of Durres has been identified as having no more than 1,500 to 2,000 beds and that they must be tourist villages. Each village must have no more than 200/300 beds and be no higher than 2 - 3 storeys.

HOTEL INFORMATION

Rozafa Hotel - 2hrs 30mins from Tirana
Situated in Shkoder. It is a six storey building not in good condition. It needs modernisation and refurbishment. It has two dining halls, a bar, a souvenir shop etc. The hotel is near the Albanian-Yugoslav border post of Hani I Hotit, about a forty five minute drive.

The Hunting Lodge - 2hrs from Tirana
Situated in Lezha, about 4 miles west of the town. It is a one storey high building made of timber. It was set up in the early forties, commissioned by Count Ciano Mussolini's son-in-law. Very few foreigners go there for the night because there are not many rooms with showers or bathrooms, though some still retain the old furniture, which is nice. This hotel is daily frequented by foreigners as the food there is generally very good. It has two dining halls decorated with trophies of wild life. One of the halls is a recent addition but the old one is more comfortable and better furnished. In the past this lodge was frequented by wild fowl's as there is a water-bird reservation nearby along with a fazanry. The hotel is near by the Adriatic sea but the water there is polluted by the waste water of the paper factory of Lissus (the ancient name of Lezha).

The New Hotel - 8 Hrs from Tirana
Situated in Kukes. This is a new hotel built in the last year and is open to foreigners. The hotel is about 1 hour drive from the Albanian-Yugoslav border post of Qafe Morina.

Gjergj Kastrioti - 40 Mins from Tirana
Situated in the town of Kruja. It is a small hotel which badly needs modernisation. It has two dining halls and a bar.

DURRES.

Durres is the ancient Dyrrachium, a Greek colony of the sixth century B.C. It is also the main harbour of Albania and is some forty minutes from Tirana Airport.

The Adriatic Hotel - 45mins from Tirana
Situated in the harbour town of Durres this is the biggest hotel in the area and in the past was generally considered the best in the country. It was built in the fifties. It is a 4 storey building that has most of its rooms facing the sea, which is no more than 20 metres away. It has a nice spacious dining hall, a bar, a tavern, a souvenir shop, a book shop with books in foreign languages. There are two tennis courts behind the hotel.

The Durres Hotel and The Apollonia Hotel - 45 mins from Tirana
Situated in Central Durres, these hotels are adjoining and share the same dining hall.

Blue Moon - Durres
Probably one of the best small hotels in Albania today. This villa was purchased from the state by a Kuwaiti businessman who wanted a secure rest place on the beach. Situated in the former Government Bloc, the building was totally refurbished with the finest possible fixtures and fittings

in 1994. It was then sold onto an Albanian businessman who turned it into a small hotel with 8 rooms. Service is excellent, private facilties with all bedrooms and secure parking.

The Butrinti Hotel - 45mins from Tirana Also situated in central Durres, this hotel is generally frequented by locals.

Tirana Hotel

Situated in Tirana the capital of Albania. Recently re-opened following a refurbishment program undertaken by Turin Hotel Group of Italy. It is the tallest building ever constructed in Albania. Most of the rooms face "Skanderbeg" Square, the main square of the capital. It has a big dining room, 2 smaller ones, 3 bars, where coffee and light refreshments are served, a tavern, a spacious lobby, a souvenir shop. There is a money exchange desk at the reception together with access to telephone and fax facilities. It is about a 30 minute drive from Tirana Airport.

Dajti Hotel
Also situated in the capital, it is the oldest hotel in Albania, mainly frequented by businessmen and diplomats from abroad. The rooms are bigger than in other hotels. There are two dining halls, a bar, a tavern, a souvenir shop. There are also two other duty free shops belonging to the French. This Hotel takes American Express.

Europapark Hotel
Recently opened Four star hotel in the centre of Tirana, offering western standard accommodation, service and food.

Arberia Hotel
Also situated in Tirana, this is mainly frequented by local people.

Apollonia Hotel - 3hrs from Tirana
Situated in Fier. This is a small hotel not in very good condition and is rarely used by foreigners.

Ardenica Monastery - 2hrs 30mins from Tirana
Situated in the district of Fier, this has recently been converted into a small hotel with a capacity of only 32 beds.

Korabi Hotel - 7hrs from Tirana
Situated in Peshkopia, this is a very small hotel.

Skampa Hotel - 1hr 30mins from Tirana, 100 rooms.
Situated in Elbasan which is in the centre of Albania. Elbasan is an historical region and possess the country's only Hot Springs.

Tomori Hotel - 2hrs 30mins from Tirana
Situated in the town of Berat, again this is a small hotel.

Guri I Kuq Hotel - 3hrs 20mins from Tirana, 120 rooms.
Situated in Pogradec on the shores of Lake Ohrid. In terms of location the is probably one of Albania's most idyllic positions for tourism. With a similar environment to that of the lakes in Switzerland. It is about 40 minutes from the Albanian-Yugoslav border post of Struga.

Illiria Hotel - 4hrs from Tirana
Situated in the town of Korca. This is a large hotel however has not been maintained very well and needs extensive modernisation. It is some 45 minutes from the Albanian border post of Kapashtica.

Cajupi Hotel - 5hrs 30mins from Tirana, 50 rooms
Situated in the town of Gjirokastra, considered to be the worst hotel in the country for management and service. The town of Gjirokastra is an area of vast historical interest and is said to be one of the most picturesque regions in the country. This hotel is near the Albanian-Greek border post of Kakavia, some 30 minutes away.

Vlora - 3hrs 30mins from Tirana
The Hotel "Adriatik" is located in central Vlore and can be booked by Telephone 355.42.10 (Tirana central) ext. 2415. It has 38 rooms with 81 beds. It also has a bar, restaurant, and parking available.

Butrinti Hotel - 7hrs from Tirana
Situated in the Adriatic coastal town of Saranda. This hotel is in good condition with most of the rooms facing the sea front. Corfu Island is less than 4 miles away.

SUPPLEMENTS

LAW FIRMS

Durres

Tivari & Harecari1

Address: Rr. Sulejman Kadiu, L. 2 2001 Durres, Albania

Contact: +355(0)52227085 (tel) +355(0)52227085 (fax) info@studioligjore.info; info@lawfirmalbania.com www.studioligjore.info; www.lawfirmalbania.com

Services: Certified Translations. Notary Services.

Attorneys: 1 . 2 . Mr. Idlir Tivari Ms. Elda Harecari

TIRANA

Boga & Associates2

Address: Rr. Ibrahim Rugova (P.O. Box 8264) Tirana, Albania

Contact: +355(0)42251050 (tel) +355(0)42251055 (fax) www.bogalaw.com

Services:

Attorneys: 1 . 2 . Mr. Genc Boga Mr. 3 . 4 . Gerhard Velaj Mr. Sokol 5 . Elmazaj Ms. Alketa Uruci Ms. Renata Leka

Celibashi & Associates3

Address: Rr. Egnatia, Don Bosko P. 9, 5th Floor, H. 3 (Near Tring TV) Tirana, Albania

Contact:

Services: Certified Translations. Notary Services.

Attorneys: 1 . Mr. Aurel Celibashi

CLO Legal Solutions 4

Address: Blvd. Bajram Curri P. Palma e Arte, 5th Floor Tirana, Albania

Contact: +355(0)44314122 (tel) +355(0)44314122 (fax) www.cenameri.com

Services: Certified Translations.

Attorneys: 1 . Mr. Bledar Cenameri

Duraj Law Firm 5

Address: Blvd. Gjergj Fishta P. Gora 1, Kt. 2 Tirana, Albania

Contact: +35544532512 (tel) +35544532512 (fax) info@durajlaw.com www.durajlaw.com

Services:

Attorneys: 1 . Mr. Alban Duraj

6 Fatmir Braka Partners & Associates

Address: Rr. Ismail Qemali P. 11/1, Apr. 1 Tirana, Albania

Contact: julian.mertiri@studiobraka.com www.studiobraka.com

Services: Certified Translations. Notary Services. **Attorneys:** 1 . Mr. Fatmir Braka

7 **Hakani & Associates**

Address: Rr. Vaso Pasha P. 13/1, Katui i Zyrave, Apt. 4 Tirana, Albania

Contact: +355(0)42240200 (tel) +355(0)42253422 (fax) www.hakani-attorneys.al

Services: Court Reporter/Stenographer. **Attorneys:** 1 . Mr. Arben Hakani

8 **Haxhia & Hajdari**

Address: Blvd. Deshmoret e Kombit Twin Towers, 2, Suite 9/1 & 2 Tirana, Albania

Contact: +355(0)42280170 (tel) +355(0)42280171 (fax) venerajaupllari@lawfirmh-h.com.al www.lawfirmh-h.com.al

Services: Certified Translations. Notary Services. **Attorneys:** 1 . 2 . 3 . 4 . Mr. Artan Hajdari Mr. Envi Hicka Mr. Maksim R. Haxhia Ms. Eris Hysi

9 **Hoxha, Memi & Hoxha**

Address: Rr. Nikolla Tupe P.O. Box 48 Tirana, Albania

Contact: +35542274558 (tel) +35542244047 (fax) info@hmh.al www.hmh.al

Services: Certified Translations. Notary Services. **Attorneys:** 1 . 2 . Mr. Shpati Hoxha Ms. Eris Hoxha

10 **Isufi International & Associates**

Address: Rr. Ismail Qemali Kulla Fratari, Nr. 27 Tirana, Albania

Contact: +355(0)662100000 (tel) +355(0)4226935 (fax) info@isufilaw.eu www.isufilaw.eu

Services: Certified Translations. Notary Services. **Attorneys:** 1 . Mr. Naim Isufi

K & H Lawfirm Address: Rr. Petro Nini Luarasi,
Nr. 51 Tirana, Albania Contact: +355(0)42237064 (tel) +355(0)4240893 (fax) info@kh-lawfirm.com www.kh-lawfirm.com 11 Attorneys: Services: Mr. Andi Mani 1 . Kalo & Associates Address: G-Kam Business Center Rr. Kavajes,
4th Floor Tirana, Albania Contact: +355(0)42233532 (tel)
www.kalo-attorneys.com
12 Attorneys: Services: Certified Translations.

Mr. Perparim Kalo 1 . Kushe Law Firm Address: Rr. Barrikadave P.
118, Kt. 3 Tirana, Albania Contact: +355(0)42247561 (tel) info@kushe.al www.kushe.al
13 Attorneys:
Services:
Certified Translations.
Notary Services. Mr. Muharrem Kushe 1 . LLF Legal & Tax Address: Rr. Gjin Bue Shpata Tirana, Albania Contact: www.llf-al.com
14 Attorneys:
Services: Certified Translations.

Mr. Erjon Lena 1 . Puto, Topi & Partners Address: Rr. Gjin Bue Shpata, Nr. 3/2 1006 Tirana, Albania Contact: +355(0)44529797 (tel) +355(0)44529797 (fax) www.putopartners.com
15 Attorneys:

Services:
Certified Translations.
Notary Services.
Court Reporter/Stenographer. Mr. Erlir Puto 1 . Tonucci & Partners Albania Address: Rr. Abdi Toptani Torre Drin, 2nd Floor Tirana, Albania Contact: +355(0)42250711/2/4 (tel) +355(0)42250713 (fax) www.tonucci.com 16 Attorneys: Services: Certified Translations. Notary Services.

Court Reporter/Stenographer. Mr. Artur Asllani 1 .
VLORE Zoto Law Office
Address: Blvd. Ismail Qemali P. 538 Vlore, Albania Contact: +355(0)33227262 (tel) +355(0)33227262 (fax) zotosoffice@gmail.com www.studiozoto.al 17

Services: Certified Translations. **Attorneys:** 1 . Mr. Ilir Zoto

http://tirana.usembassy.gov/list_of_attorneys.html Page 3 of 3

ATTORNEYS

2015

The U.S. Embassy in Tirana, Albania, assumes no responsibility or liability for the professional ability or reputation of, or the quality of services provided by, the following persons or firms. Inclusion on this list is in no way an endorsement by the Department of State or the U.S. Embassy. Names are listed alphabetically, and the order in which they appear has no other significance. The information in the list on professional credentials, areas of expertise and language ability are provided directly by the lawyers. You may receive additional information about the individuals on the list by contacting the Albanian National Chamber of Advocates (http://www.dhka.org.al/).

HARECARI, ELDA (MS.)

Law Firm:	Tivari & Harecari		
Address:	Rr. Sulejman Kadiu, L. 2	Contact:	+355(0)52227085 (tel)
	2001 Durres, Albania		+355(0)52227085 (fax)
			+355(0)684055889
			info@studioligjore.info; info@lawfirmalbania.com
			www.studioligjore.info; www.lawfirmalbania.com

Cases:

Adoptions; Aeronautical/Maritime; Auto/Accidents; Child Custody; Child Protection; Civil Law; Commercial/Business Law; Contracts; Criminal Law; Damages; Estates; Family Law; Foreign Claims; Foreign Investments; Government Relations; Insurance; Labor Relations; Marketing Agreements; Marriage/Divorce; Narcotics; Parental Child Abduction; Patents/Trademarks/Copyrights; Taxes; Transportation Law;

TIVARI, IDLIR (MR.)

Law Firm: Tivari & Harecari

Address: Rr. Sulejman Kadiu, L. 2
2001 Durres, Albania

Contact: +355(0)52227085 (tel)
+355(0)52227085 (fax)
+355(0)684055889
info@studioligjore.info; info@lawfirmalbania.com
www.studioligjore.info; www.lawfirmalbania.com

Cases:

Adoptions; Aeronautical/Maritime; Auto/Accidents; Child Custody; Child Protection; Civil Law; Commercial/Business Law; Contracts; Criminal Law; Damages; Estates; Family Law; Foreign Claims; Foreign Investments; Government Relations; Insurance; Labor Relations; Marketing Agreements; Marriage/Divorce; Narcotics; Parental Child Abduction; Patents/Trademarks/Copyrights; Taxes; Transportation Law;

ELBASAN

3 GJORGA, MERITA (MS.)

Law Firm: Individual

Address: L. Aqif Pasha, P. 31/1
Elbasan, Albania

Contact: +355(0)684051156
meritagjorga@yahoo.com;

Cases:

Adoptions; Auto/Accidents; Child Custody; Child Protection; Civil Law; Commercial/Business Law; Contracts; Criminal Law; Damages; Family Law; Insurance; Labor Relations; Marriage/Divorce; Narcotics; Parental Child Abduction; Taxes;

TIRANA

4 ASLLANI, Artur (Mr.)

Law Firm: Tonucci & Partners Albania

Address: Rr. Abdi Toptani Torre Drin, 2nd Floor Tirana, Albania

Contact: +355(0)42250711/2/4 (tel)
+355(0)42250713 (fax) +355(0)682093083
www.tonucci.com

Cases:

Aeronautical/Maritime; Auto/Accidents; Banking/Financial; Civil Law; Collections; Commercial/Business Law; Contracts; Corporations; Criminal Law; Damages; Estates; Family Law; Foreign Claims; Foreign Investments; Government Relations; Immigration; Insurance; Labor Relations; Marketing Agreements; Marriage/Divorce; Patents/Trademarks/Copyrights; Sports; Taxes; Transportation Law;

5 BOGA, Genc (Mr.)

Address: Law Firm: Rr. Ibrahim Rugova (P.O. Box 8264) Tirana, Albania Boga & Associates

Contact: +355(0)42251050 (tel) +355(0)42251055 (fax) +355(0)682020481
www.bogalaw.com

Cases:

Aeronautical/Maritime; Banking/Financial; Civil Law; Commercial/Business Law; Contracts; Corporations; Estates; Foreign Investments; Government Relations; Immigration; Insurance; Labor Relations; Marketing Agreements; Patents/Trademarks/Copyrights; Sports; Taxes; Transportation Law;

6 BRAKA, Fatmir (Mr.)

Law Firm: Fatmir Braka Partners &

Address: Rr. Ismail Qemali P. 11/1, Apr. 1 Tirana, Albania

Contact: +355(0)684066838 julian.mertiri@studiobraka.com www.studiobraka.com

Cases:

Aeronautical/Maritime; Auto/Accidents; Banking/Financial; Civil Law; Collections; Commercial/Business Law; Contracts; Corporations; Criminal Law; Damages; Estates; Family Law; Foreign Claims; Foreign Investments; Government Relations; Immigration; Labor Relations; Marketing Agreements; Marriage/Divorce; Narcotics; Sports;

CELIBASHI, AUREL (MR.)

Law Firm: Celibashi & Associates Address: Rr. Egnatia, Don Bosko Contact: +355(0)693082255; +355(0)672011401
P. 9, 5th Floor, H. 3 (Near Tring TV) Tirana, Albania
Cases:

Auto/Accidents; Civil Law; Contracts; Criminal Law; Damages; Family Law; Foreign Claims; Marriage/Divorce; Narcotics;

8 CENAMERI, Bledar (Mr.)

Address: Law Firm: Blvd. Bajram Curri P. Palma e Arte, 5th Floor Tirana, Albania CLO Legal Solutions

Contact: +355(0)44314122 (tel) +355(0)44314122 (fax) +355(0)694085520 www.cenameri.com

Cases:

Adoptions; Aeronautical/Maritime; Auto/Accidents; Banking/Financial; Child Custody; Child Protection; Civil Law; Collections; Commercial/Business Law; Contracts; Corporations; Criminal Law; Damages; Estates; Family Law; Foreign Claims; Foreign InvestmentsInsurance; Labor Relations; Marketing Agreements; Marriage/Divorce; Patents/Trademarks/Copyrights; Taxes; Transportation Law; Adoptions; Auto/Accidents; Civil Law; Commercial/Business Law; Contracts; Corporations; Criminal Law; Damages; Estates; Family Law; Insurance; Labor Relations; Marriage/Divorce; Narcotics; Patents/Trademarks/Copyrights;

Law Firm: Duraj Law Firm

Address: Blvd. Gjergj Fishta P. Gora 1, Kt. 2 Tirana, Albania

Contact: +35544532512 (tel) +35544532512 (fax) +355692737706 info@durajlaw.com www.durajlaw.com

Cases:

ELMAZAJ, SOKOL (MR.)

Law Firm: Boga & Associates

Address: Rr. Ibrahim Rugova

Contact: +355(0)42251050 (tel)

(P.O. Box 8264) +355(0)42251055 (fax)
Tirana, Albania +355(0)682007603
www.bogalaw.com

Cases:

Aeronautical/Maritime; Civil Law; Commercial/Business Law; Contracts; Corporations; Estates; Foreign Claims; Patents/Trademarks/Copyrights;

HAJDARI, ARTAN (MR.)

Address: Law Firm: Blvd. Deshmoret e Kombit Twin Towers, 2, Suite 9/1 & 2 Tirana, Albania Haxhia & Hajdari

Contact: +355(0)42280170 (tel) +355(0)42280171 (fax) venerajaupllari@lawfirmh-h.com.al www.lawfirmh-h.com.al

Cases:

Adoptions; Aeronautical/Maritime; Auto/Accidents; Banking/Financial; Child Custody; Child Protection; Civil Law; Collections; Commercial/Business Law; Contracts; Corporations; Criminal Law; Damages; Estates; Family Law; Foreign Claims; Foreign InvestmentsInsurance; Labor Relations; Marketing Agreements; Marriage/Divorce; Narcotics; Parental Child Abduction; Patents/Trademarks/Copyrights; Sports; Taxes; Transportation Law; Traffic Law.

HAKANI, ARBEN (MR.)

Law Firm: Hakani & Associates

Address: Rr. Vaso Pasha
P. 13/1, Katui i Zyrave, Apt. 4
Tirana, Albania

Contact: +355(0)42240200 (tel)
+355(0)42253422 (fax)
+355(0)682024555
www.hakani-attorneys.al

Cases:

Adoptions; Child Custody; Civil Law; Commercial/Business Law; Contracts; Damages; Estates; Family Law; Labor Relations; Marketing Agreements; Marriage/Divorce;

HAXHIA, MAKSIM R. (MR.)

Address: Law Firm: Blvd. Deshmoret e Kombit Twin Towers, 2, Suite 9/1 & 2 Tirana, Albania Haxhia & Hajdari

Contact: +355(0)42280170 (tel) +355(0)42280171 (fax) venerajaupllari@lawfirmh-h.com.al www.lawfirmh-h.com.al

Cases:

Adoptions; Aeronautical/Maritime; Auto/Accidents; Banking/Financial; Child Custody; Child Protection; Civil Law; Collections; Commercial/Business Law; Contracts; Corporations; Criminal Law; Damages; Estates; Family Law; Foreign Claims; Foreign InvestmentsInsurance; Labor Relations; Marketing Agreements; Marriage/Divorce; Narcotics; Parental Child Abduction; Patents/Trademarks/Copyrights; Sports; Taxes; Transportation Law; Traffic Law.

Address: Law Firm: Blvd. Deshmoret e Kombit Twin Towers, 2, Suite 9/1 & 2 Tirana

Contact: +355(0)42280170 (tel) +355(0)42280171 (fax) venerajaupllari@lawfirmh-h.com.al

Suite 9/1 & 2 Tirana, Albania Haxhia & Hajdari www.lawfirmh-h.com.al

Cases:

Adoptions; Aeronautical/Maritime; Auto/Accidents; Banking/Financial; Child Custody; Child Protection; Civil Law; Collections; Commercial/Business Law; Contracts; Corporations; Criminal Law; Damages; Estates; Family Law; Foreign Claims; Foreign InvestmentsInsurance; Labor Relations; Marketing Agreements; Marriage/Divorce; Narcotics; Parental Child Abduction; Patents/Trademarks/Copyrights; Sports; Taxes; Transportation Law; Traffic Law.

15 HOXHA, Eris (Ms.)

Address: Law Firm: Rr. Nikolla Tupe P.O. Box 48 Tirana, Albania Hoxha, Memi & Hoxha

Contact: +35542274558 (tel) +35542244047 (fax) info@hmh.al www.hmh.al

Cases:

Banking/Financial; Commercial/Business Law; Contracts; Corporations; Foreign Investments; Government Relations; Immigration; Insurance; Labor Relations; Marketing Agreements; Taxes;

16 HOXHA, Shpati (Mr.)

Address: Law Firm: Rr. Nikolla Tupe P.O. Box 48 Tirana, Albania Hoxha, Memi & Hoxha

Contact: +35542274558 (tel) +35542244047 (fax) +355692054943 info@hmh.al www.hmh.al

Cases:

Banking/Financial; Civil Law; Collections; Commercial/Business Law; Contracts; Corporations; Estates; Foreign Claims; Foreign Investments; Government Relations; Immigration; Insurance; Labor Relations; Marketing Agreements; Patents/Trademarks/Copyrights; Sports; Taxes;

17 HYSI, Eris (Ms.)

Address: Law Firm: Blvd. Deshmoret e Kombit Twin Towers, 2, Suite 9/1 & 2 Tirana, Albania Haxhia & Hajdari

Contact: +355(0)42280170 (tel) +355(0)42280171 (fax) venerajaupllari@lawfirmh-h.com.al www.lawfirmh-h.com.al

Cases:

Adoptions; Aeronautical/Maritime; Auto/Accidents; Banking/Financial; Child Custody; Child Protection; Civil Law; Collections; Commercial/Business Law; Contracts; Corporations; Criminal Law; Damages; Estates; Family Law; Foreign Claims; Foreign InvestmentsInsurance; Labor Relations; Marketing Agreements; Marriage/Divorce; Narcotics; Parental Child Abduction; Patents/Trademarks/Copyrights; Sports; Taxes; Transportation Law; Traffic Law.

Law Firm: Isufi International & Associates

Address: Rr. Ismail Qemali Kulla Fratari, Nr. 27 Tirana, Albania

Contact: +355(0)662100000 (tel) +355(0)4226935 (fax) +355(0)682045790 info@isufilaw.eu www.isufilaw.eu

Cases:

Adoptions; Aeronautical/Maritime; Auto/Accidents; Banking/Financial; Civil Law; Collections; Commercial/Business Law; Contracts; Corporations; Criminal Law; Damages; Estates; Family Law; Foreign Claims; Foreign Investments; Government Relations; ImmigratiInsurance; Labor

Relations; Marketing Agreements; Marriage/Divorce; Narcotics; Patents/Trademarks/Copyrights; Sports; Taxes; Transportation Law; Traffic Law.

19 KALO, Perparim (Mr.)

Law Firm: Kalo & Associates

Address: G-Kam Business Center Rr. Kavajes, 4th Floor Tirana, Albania

Contact: +355(0)42233532 (tel) +355(0)692090090 www.kalo-attorneys.com

Cases:

Adoptions; Banking/Financial; Civil Law; Collections; Commercial/Business Law; Contracts; Corporations; Damages; Family Law; Foreign Claims; Foreign Investments; Government Relations; Immigration; Insurance; Labor Relations; Marketing Agreements; Marriage/Divorce; Narcotics; Patents/Trademarks/Copyrights; Sports; Taxes; Transportation Law;

20 KUSHE, Muharrem (Mr.)

Law Firm: Kushe Law Firm

Address: Rr. Barrikadave P. 118, Kt. 3 Tirana, Albania

Contact: +355(0)42247561 (tel) info@kushe.al www.kushe.al

Cases:

Adoptions; Auto/Accidents; Banking/Financial; Child Custody; Child Protection; Civil Law; Commercial/Business Law; Contracts; Corporations; Criminal Law; Damages; Estates; Family Law; Foreign Investments; Government Relations; Immigration; Insurance; Labor Relations; Marketing Agreements; Marriage/Divorce; Narcotics; Parental Child Abduction; Patents/Trademarks/Copyrights; Taxes; Transportation Law;

21 LEKA, Renata (Ms.)

Address: Rr. Ibrahim Rugova (P.O. Box 8264) Tirana, Albania

Law Firm: Boga & Associates

Contact: +355(0)42251050 (tel) +355(0)42251055 (fax) +355(0)682007604 www.bogalaw.com

Cases:

Banking/Financial; Civil Law; Commercial/Business Law; Contracts; Corporations; Estates; Foreign Investments; Immigration; Insurance; Labor Relations; Marketing Agreements; Patents/Trademarks/Copyrights; Sports; Taxes; Transportation Law;

22 LENA, Erjon (Mr.)

Address: Rr. Gjin Bue Shpata Tirana, Albania

Law Firm: LLF Legal & Tax

Contact: +355(0)695337456 www.llf-al.com

Cases:

Adoptions; Auto/Accidents; Banking/Financial; Civil Law; Collections; Commercial/Business Law; Contracts; Corporations; Criminal Law; Family Law; Foreign Claims; Foreign Investments; Labor Relations; Marriage/Divorce; Patents/Trademarks/Copyrights; Sports; Taxes; Transportation Law; Traffic Law.

Law Firm: K & H Lawfirm

Address: Rr. Petro Nini Luarasi, Nr. 51 Tirana, Albania

Contact: +355(0)42237064 (tel) +355(0)4240893 (fax) +355(0)692361034; +355(0)694008039 info@kh-lawfirm.com www.kh-lawfirm.com

Cases:

Banking/Financial; Child Custody; Child Protection; Civil Law; Collections; Commercial/Business Law; Contracts; Corporations; Damages; Family Law; Foreign Claims; Foreign Investments; Government Relations; Insurance; Labor Relations; Marriage/Divorce; Patents/Trademarks/Copyrights; Taxes;

24 PENGILI, Enkeleda (Ms.)

Cases: Address: Law Firm:	Blvd. Bajram Curri, Nr. 10 Tirana, Albania Individual	Contact:	+355(0)699959663 e.pengili@gmail.com;

Adoptions; Auto/Accidents; Banking/Financial; Child Custody; Child Protection; Civil Law; Collections; Commercial/Business Law; Contracts; Corporations; Damages; Estates; Family Law; Foreign Investments; Immigration; Insurance; Labor Relations; Marketing Agreements; Marriage/Divorce; Parental Child Abduction; Patents/Trademarks/Copyrights;

25 PUTO, Erlir (Mr.)

Address: Law Firm:	Rr. Gjin Bue Shpata, Nr. 3/2 1006 Tirana, Albania Puto, Topi & Partners	Contact:	+355(0)44529797 (tel) +355(0)44529797 (fax) +355(0)682090608 www.putopartners.com
Cases:			

Adoptions; Auto/Accidents; Banking/Financial; Civil Law; Commercial/Business Law; Contracts; Corporations; Damages; Estates; Family Law; Foreign Claims; Foreign Investments; Government Relations; Immigration; Insurance; Labor Relations; Marketing Agreements; Marriage/Divorce; Patents/Trademarks/Copyrights; Taxes;

26	URUCI, Alketa (Ms.)			
	Address: Law Firm:	Rr. Ibrahim Rugova (P.O. Box 8264) Tirana, Albania Boga & Associates	Contact:	+355(0)42251050 (tel) +355(0)42251055 (fax) +355(0)682026554 www.bogalaw.com
	Cases:			

Banking/Financial; Civil Law; Commercial/Business Law; Contracts; Corporations; Foreign Investments; Government Relations; Immigration; Labor Relations; Taxes; Transportation Law;

27	VEIZI, Julian (Mr.)			
	Law Firm:	Individual		
	Address:	Rr. Irfan Tomini P. 32, Shk. 4, Apt. 45 Tirana, Albania	Contact:	+355(0)692144516 julianvezi@gmail.com;
	Cases:			

Adoptions; Aeronautical/Maritime; Auto/Accidents; Banking/Financial; Child Custody; Child Protection; Civil Law; Collections; Commercial/Business Law; Contracts; Corporations; Criminal Law; Damages; Estates; Family Law; Foreign Claims; Foreign InvestmentsInsurance; Labor Relations; Marketing Agreements; Marriage/Divorce; Narcotics; Parental Child Abduction; Patents/Trademarks/Copyrights; Taxes; Banking/Financial; Civil Law; Collections; Commercial/Business Law; Contracts; Corporations; Damages; Estates; Labor Relations; Patents/Trademarks/Copyrights; Sports; Taxes; Transportation Law;

Law Firm: Boga & Associates

Address:	Rr. Ibrahim Rugova (P.O. Box 8264) Tirana, Albania	Contact:	+355(0)42251050 (tel) +355(0)42251055 (fax) +355(0)682007605 www.bogalaw.com
Cases:			

VLORE

29	ZOTO, Ilir (Mr.)			
	Law Firm:	Zoto Law Office		
	Address:	Blvd. Ismail Qemali P. 538 Vlore, Albania	Contact:	+355(0)33227262 (tel) +355(0)33227262 (fax) +355(0)693820555 zotosoffice@gmail.com www.studiozoto.al
	Cases:			

Adoptions; Aeronautical/Maritime; Auto/Accidents; Banking/Financial; Child Custody; Child Protection; Civil Law; Commercial/Business Law; Contracts; Criminal Law; Damages; Family Law; Foreign Claims; Foreign Investments; Immigration; Insurance; Labor Relations; Marriage/Divorce; Narcotics; Parental Child Abduction; Taxes;

INTERNATIONAL PARTNERSHIPS RELATED TO LAND

Donor	Dates	Budget	Description
European Union PHARE		300 mill euro	FEOGA Agricultural support EDHIR democracy ECHO Humanitarian
European Union CARDS	2001-2004	187 mill euro	Justice and public order Public administration Trade and transport Environmental institutions Democracy
European Investment Bank			Basic infrastructure, energy, ports, water supply
International Monetary Fund		$60 mill	Enterprise privatization Poverty reduction facility
World Bank IDA		$719 mill	Poverty reduction support credit Fisheries Energy, transport

			NSSED sustainable development
World Bank IFC		$130 mill	Financial sector SME lending Industrial rehabilitation
UN Development Program	2006-2010		Millennium Development Goals Regional government capacity Environmental protection institutions
USAID			Agro-business capacity SME credit Local government administration capacity Rule of law
German government		320 mill euro	Water and sewer infrastructure Energy, hydropower
Greek government		50 mill euro	Agriculture and rural infrastructure
Italian government		353 mill euro	Electricity, water, sewer, roads
Japan		$52 mill	Agriculture sector adjustment
Switzerland			

Environment and Infrastructure

Project	Donor	End date	Budget	Description
National Water Strategy	PHARE AL9306	1997	400,000 ecu	Preparation of national Water Strategy
Feasibility Study for Sewage Treatment in Vlora	PHARE AL9306	1997	492,000 ecu	Reduce soil and water contamination by uncontrolled waste water disposal
Feasibility Study for Sewage Treatment in Pogradec	PHARE AL9306	1997	299,400 ecu	Reduce soil and water contamination by uncontrolled waste water disposal
Cleaning of Golem Beach	PHARE AL9306	1997	50,000 ecu	Demonstration coastal project

Master Plan for Dajti National Park	PHARE AL9306	1997	50,000 ecu	Protected land management planning
Karavasta Lagoon Wetland Management	PHARE AL9306	1997	346 200 ecu	Karavasta Ramsar biodiversity protected land/water management
Institutional Support for Environmental Protection	PHARE AL9306	1995	695,800 ecu	Organization, training and technical development of State Committee on Environmental Protection; national Environmental Action Plan
Strengthen Regional Environmental Agencies	PHARE AL9306	1997	92,200 ecu	Organization, training and technical development of regional staff
Additional equipment Regional Environmental Agencies	PHARE AL9306	1998	98,300 ecu	Equip the offices of the REAs
Benchmark survey of Patos-Marinze oilfield	PHARE AL9306	1997		Pollution control planning and feasibility
Comprehensive Impact Assessment of Uranium Exploration	PHARE	1999	125, 000 ecu	Develop Environmental Impact Assessment methodology
Equipment for Scientific Laboratories	Med-Pol UNEP		$40,000	Chemical laboratories for monitoring of Mediterranean coastal waters
Urban Waste Management	EU LIFE 96	1999	591,000 ecu	Landfills in six municipalities
Mediterranean Wetlands	EU LIFE MedWet	1998		Environmental, development and social study of Kune-Vaini lagoons
Biodiversity Protection	GEF W Bk	1999	$96,000	Prepare the Biodiversity Strategy and Action Plan
Lake Ohrid Conservation	GEF W Bk	2003	$184,000	Lake water monitoring and watershed management, institutional capacity and public participation
Durres Industrial Chemical Pollution	Italy		$7,600	Removal of toxic waste from port and creation of safe storage
Environmental Regulatory Framework	PHARE COP96	1999	200,000 ecu	Strengthening of Environmental Protection agencies -- enforcement
Environmental	PHARE	2001	300,000	National Environment Action Plan

Institutional Strengthening	COP97		ecu	implementation, policy formation for sustainable development
Conservation of Coastal Wetlands	GEF/PNU MedWet	2003	$1.7 million	Mediterranean Region -- six countries -- legal framework and methodologies; Narta Lagoon monitoring
Update national Environmental Action Plan	METAP W Bk	2001	$200,000	Develop a comprehensive national environmental policy
Environment Ministry Enforcement	DFID	2002	400,000 lb	Reorganization, training and management of the new Ministry of Environmental Protection
Institutional Strengthening of Environment Improvement	W Bk	2005	$250,000	Hot spot of Porto Romano, Durres, as model for handling of dangerous waste
Integrated Water Management and Ecosystem Management	W Bk	Start 2005	$4.87 mill	Wetlands in the Kune-Vain marsh area
Fier Arsenic Cleanup	EU	2005	1 million euro	Disposal of arsenic from nitrate fertilizer plant
Environmental Hot Spot Clean Up in Vlora	UNEP MAP	2005	$300,000	Develop remediation plan for clean up of Vlora PVC factory
Prespa lake Trans-boundary Ecosystems	UNDP GEF	2005	$928,000	Protected lands regulation and watershed management
Biosecurity National Framework	UNEP GEF	2006	$185,000/ $123,000	Prepare national Bio-Safety Framework with risk assessment, management and public participation
Institutional Strengthening of Environmental Ministry	DIFD	2005	£300,000	Strengthen the National Environmental inspectorate for monitoring and enforcement
Effective Institute of Environment	Netherld	2006	1 mill euro	Rehabilitation of Institute of Environment for monitoring
Strengthen Environmental Monitoring	EU CARDS	Planned 2005	2.5 mill euro	Monitoring system

Landfill for Hazardous Wastes	EU CARDS	2007	600,000 euro	Design of hazardous waste storage facility
Wastewater Treatment Plant Balsh Oil refinery	EU CARDS	2007	900,000 euro	Rehabilitation of the refinery facility
Construction of Landfill for Hazardous Waste	EU CARDS		3.5 million euro	Construction of hazardous waste facility
National Center and Network Environmental Monitoring	EU CARDS		2.5 million euro	National environmental monitoring network tied into European system
Environmental Laws Harmonization	EU CARDS	2007	2.5 million euro	Prepare environmental legislation and sub-acts to relate with European system
Technical Assistance to Ministry of Environment	Italy			Proposed 2 million euro under Cooperation Protocol Italy/Albania
Butrint National Park Biodiversity	W Bk	2005	$25,000	Feasibility and project design
Capacity development Biodiversity Strategy	GEF		$324,000	Review progress of Biodiversity Strategy and prepare second report
Karavasta Lagoon Management	W Bk	2005	$25,000	Preparation of project design
Ecosystem Management Lake Shkodra	W Bk	2006	$175 000	Trans-boundary pollution control and Biodiversity
Solid Waste Management Korce	SIDA	2006	15 million S krone	Solid waste management plan and institutional organization

Forest and Pasture

Private Forestry Development	USAID	1996		Communal and private forest transfer Communal Forest Users Associations
Forestry Project	W Bk Italy	1997-2003	$8 mill $8.5	Institutional capacity of Forest Directorate; communal forest transfer
Natural Resources Development	W Bk	Start 2005	$80 mill	Continue communal forest transfer Integrated management of watersheds

Korce TransBorder Wildlife	International Land Coalition

Agriculture

Project	Donor	End date	Budget	Description
Rural Development in Remote Mountains	DFID Oxfam			Small infrastructure projects
Mountain Area Development Program	DFIC IFAD		$23 mill	Poverty reduction and non-farm employment, irrigation rehabilitation
Northeastern District Rural development	IFAD		$18.2 mill	
Strengthening Business Capacity in Agriculture	USAID	2004 2005	$2.7 mill $2.0 mill	Assistance to dairy producers
Community Works Project	EU	2002		Albanian Development Fund managed small infrastructure projects
Hellenic Plan for the Balkans	Greece			Rural drinking water
Assistance to Trade Associations	USAID IFDC	1992-98		Creation of farm producers associations
Assistance to Trade Associations	USAID IFDC	1998-2002		
Assistance to Trade Associations	USAID IFDC	2002-2003		Agriculture producers associations and credit unions

Immovable Property Registration System

Project	Donor	End date	Budget	Description
Land Markets in Albania	USAID	1994-2001		Organization of IPRS First registration rural zones
Support for Immovable Property	PHARE	1994-		IPRS mapping capability

Registration System		2001		First registration of rural zones
Registry Organizational Improvement	USAID	2002-2004	$5 mill	First registration or urban and rural zones
Korce Region First Registration	EU	2004-2005		First registration

Urban Land Use

Project	Donor	End date	Budget	Description
Land Use Policy	PHARE			Institutional capacity and GIS
Integrated Development Tirana-Durres	EU CARDS	Planned 2005	1 mill euro	Sustainable integrated development master plan for the corridor
Assistance to the Port of Durres	EU CARDS	Planned 2005	2 mill euro	Update the Port Master Plan

Local Government

Project	Donor	End date	Budget	Description
Local Government Assistance	USAID	2005		Local budget and finance Property inventory
Civil registry and address system	EU CARDS	Planned 2005	2.5 mill euro	Address system
Local Community Development Program	EU CARDS	Planned 2005	7.5 mill euro	Infrastructure projects

USEFUL CONTACTS

H.E. Ambassador Pavli Qesku
Albanian Embassy
4th Floor
38 Gloucester Gardens
London SW1
England
Tel: +44 171 730 5709
Fax: +44 171 730 5747
Michelle Gillen
Albania Desk Officer
Department of Trade and Industry
Kingsgate House
Victoria Street
London SW1

England
Tel: +44 171 215 4849
Fax: +44 171 215 8598
British Charge d'Affaires Office
Rruga Vaso Pasha
Tirana
Albania
Tel/Fax: +355 42 34973
Adrian Cohen
Managing Director
ITS Travel Services
540 Royal Exchange
Old Bank Street
Manchester
England
Tel: +44 161 839 1111
Fax: +44 161 839 0000

GOVERNMENT CONTACTS

Office	Location	Tel No	Fax No
OFFICE OF THE PRESIDENT	Bulevardi Deshmoret e Kombit, Tirana	+355-42-28491	+355-42-33761
OFFICE OF THE PRIME MINISTER	Bulevardi Deshmoret e Kombit, Tirana	+355-42-34816	+355-42-34818
MINISTRY OF AGRICULTURE & FOOD	Ministria e Bujqesise, Tirana	+355-42-32796	+355-42-27924
MINISTRY OF CONSTRUCTION & TOURISM	Ministria e Ndertimit dhe Turizmit, Tirana	+355-42-32477	+355-42-27879
MINISTRY OF CULTURE, YOUTH AND WOMEN	Ministria e Kultures, Rinise dhe Sporteve, Tirana	+355-42-32488	+355-42-32488
MINISTRY OF DEFENSE	Ministria e Mbrojtjes, Tirana	+355-42-32675	+355-42-28481
MINISTRY OF EDUCATION	Ministria e Arsimit, Tirana	+355-42-34845	+355-42-32002
MINISTRY OF FINANCE	Ministria e Finances, Tirana	+355-42-28405	+355-42-28494
MINISTRY OF FOREIGN AFFAIRS	Ministria e Puneve te Jashtme, Tirana	+355-42-28311	+355-42-32971
MINISTRY OF INDUSTRY, TRANSPORT & TRADE	Ministria e Industrise, Transportit dhe Tregtise, Tirana	+355-42-32503	+355-42-27773
MINISTRY OF HEALTH AND ENVIRONMENTAL PROTECTION	Ministria e Shendetesise dhe Mbrojtjes se Ambjentit, Tirana	+355-42-32937	+355-42-32554
MINISTRY OF MINERAL AND ENERGY RESOURCES	Ministria e Burimeve Minerare dhe Energjitike, Tirana	+355-42-32833	+355-42-34052
MINISTRY OF JUSTICE	Ministria e Drejtesise, Tirana	+355-42-32704	+355-42-28359
MINISTRY OF LABOUR	Rruga e Kavaje, Tirana	+355-42-33429	+355-42-28340

MINISTRY OF INTERNAL AFFAIRS	Ministria e Brendshme, Tirana	+355-42-32794	+355-42-34983
MINISTRY OF HIGHER EDUCATION & SCIENCE	Mine Peza Street, No.4, Tirana	+355-42-32461	+355-42-27975
STATE CONTROL COMMISSION	Komisioni i Kontrollit, Tirana	+355-42-32491	+355-42-32491
GENERAL DIRECTORATE OF TELECOMMUNICATION	Myslym Shyri Str., No.42, Tirana	+355-42-32169	+355-42-33323
DEPARTMENT OF ECONOMIC DEVELOPMENT	Ministry of Finance	+335-42-28467	+335-42-28362

ALBANIAN EMBASSIES

AUSTRIA
Vienna
Tel. +43 1 364628
Fax. +43 1 3691229

BULGARIA
Sofia
Tel. +359 2 441110
Fax. +359 2 443349

CHINA
Beijing
Tel. +86 1 5321120
Fax. +86 1 5321116

CZECH REPUBLIC
Prague
Tel. +42 2 379329

EGYPT
Cairo
Tel. +20 2 3415651

FRANCE
Paris
Tel. +33 1 45535096
Fax. +33 1 45535132

GERMANY
Bonn
Tel. +49 228 351044

GREECE
Athens
Tel. +30 1 7234412
Fax. +30 1 7234457

HUNGARY
Budapest
Tel. +36 1 1227251

ITALY
Rome
Tel. +39 6 8380725
Tel. +39 6 8390201
Fax. +39 6 8313024

POLAND
Warsaw
Tel. +48 22 498516
Fax. +48 22 498516

ROMANIA
Bucarest
Tel. +40 90 793180

SWEDEN
Stockholm
Tel. +46 8 7310920
Fax. +46 8 7310930

SWITZERLAND
Geneva
Tel. +41 22 7311143

TURKEY
Ankara
Tel. +90 4 1466527
Fax. +90 4 1466516

Istanbul
Tel. +90 1 1615726
Fax. +90 1 1616109

UNITED STATES
Washington, DC
Tel. 1 202 223 4942

Permanent Mission to the U.N.
New York
Tel. 1 212 249 2059
Fax. 1 212 517 5204

HOTELS IN ALBANIA

TIRANA

Dajti
Bulevardi Dëshmoret e Kombit
84 rooms
Tel. 42 33326/27662
Fax 42 32012

Tirana International
Sheshi Skenderbe
163 rooms
Tel. 42 34295
Fax 42 34447

Europapark
Bulevardi Dëshmoret e Kombit
Tel. 42 35035
Fax 42 35050

Arbëria
Bulevardi Dëshmoret e Kombit
95 rooms
Tel. 42 42813
Fax. 42 42813

Diplomati
10 rooms
Tel. 42 35542
Fax 42 42457

Chataeu Linza Motel
Linza, mountain resort
6 km from Tirana
Tel. 42 35142
Fax 42 35143

BERAT
Tomorri
45 rooms
Tel. 624 62602

DURRËS
Adriatik
57 rooms
Tel. 52 23612
Fax. 52 23051

Durrësi
92 rooms
Tel. 52 23051
Fax 52 23612

Apollonia
96 rooms
Tel. 52 23051
Fax 52 23612

Hotel Restorant Pameba
14 rooms
Tel/Fax 52 24149

Blue Moon
Plazhi i Durrësit (Durrës Beach), Vila 14

ELBASAN
Skampa
99 rooms
Tel. 545 2651
Fax 545 2093

GJIROKASTRA
Çajupi
36 rooms
Tel. 726 3621
Fax 726 3626

KORÇA
Iliria
108 rooms
Tel. 824 2473
Fax 824 2855

KRUJA
Skenderbeu
38 rooms
Tel. 4210 (through Tirana operator)

KUKËS
Kukës
44 rooms
Tel. 4210 (through Tirana operator) ext. 699, 251, 269

LEZHA
Hunting Lodge
13 rooms
Tel. 4210 (through Tirana operator) ext.483

Llogara Tourist Village
22 rooms (chalets)
Tel. 63 2415

LUSHNJA
Ardenica Inn
10 rooms, located in an old monastery, Restaurant service
Tel. 4210 (through Tirana operator) ext. 2140

POGRADEC
Enkelana
60 rooms
Tel. 4210 (through Tirana operator) ext. 269, 259

SARANDA
Butrinti
75 rooms
Tel. 4210 (through Tirana operator) ext. 538, 417

SHKODRA
Rozafa
82 rooms
Tel. 224 2354
Fax 224 3590

VLORA
Adriatik
38 rooms
Tel. 63 2415

Grand Hotel Dhermi
Dhermi (Vlora)
50 rooms, underwater sports, boats, canoes and windsurf equipment for hire, restaurant,
disco
Tel. 39 366 3275. 4 (dial through Italy)

USEFUL BUSINESS CONTACTS IN EUROPE

Albania		
U.S. Commercial Officer Frederick Baron Econ/Commercial Officer U.S. Embassy Tirana Mailing Box A PSC 59 APO AE 09624 Street: Rruga Labinoti 103 Tirana Telephone: 355-42-33520 Fax: 355-42-32222	CEEBIC Employee Omer Dashi U. S. Embassy Tirana Riugahabinot 103, Tirana Telephone: 355-42-33-520 Fax: 355-42-32-222	Commercial Officer in the U.S. Mr. Arben Tashko First Secretary Embassy of Albania 1511 K Street, NW Suite 1010 Washington, DC 20005 Tel: (202) 223-4942 Fax: (202) 628-7342
Bosnia and Herzegovina		
U.S. Commercial Officer Patrick Hughes Mailing: (Bosnia) Vienna Department of State Washington, D.C. 20521-9900 Street: 43 Ul. Dure Dakovica Sarajevo, Bosnia and Herzegovina Tel: (387-71) 659-743 Fax: (387-71) 659-722	CEEBIC Employee Edin Fetahovic U.S. Embassy Sarajevo 43 Ul. Dure Dakovica Sarajevo, Bosnia and Herzegovina Tel: (387-71) 659-743 Fax: (387-71) 659-722	Commercial Officer in the U.S. Malik Skaljic Counselor/Deputy Chief of Mission Embassy of Bosnia and Herzegovina 1707 L Street, N.W., Suite 760 Washington, D.C. 20036 Tel: (202) 833-3612 Fax: (202) 833-2061
Bulgaria		

U.S. Commercial Officer Susan Weidner Senior Commercial Officer U.S. Embassy Sofia 1 A Stamboliski Blvd Sofia Telephone: 359-2-963-4062/2014 Fax: 359-2-980-6850 E-Mail:osofia@doc.gov	CEEBIC Employee Georgi Peev 1 A Stamboliski Blvd, Sofia Telephone: 359-2-88-48-01 Fax: 359-2-980-6850 E-Mail: osofia@doc.gov	Commercial Officer in the U.S. Mr. Panteley Penev Commercial Counselor Embassy of Bulgaria 1621 22nd Street, NW Washington, DC 20008 Tel: (202) 387-7969 Fax: (202) 234-7973
Czech Republic		
U.S. Commercial Officer Michael Murphy Senior Commercial Officer Kathy Kriger Commercial Officer Paula Potts Assistant Commercial Attache U.S. Embassy Prague Hybernska 7a 117 16 Prague 1 Telephone: (420-2) 2421-9844, 2421-9846 Fax: (420-2) 2421-9965	CEEBIC Contact U.S. Embassy Prague Hybernska 7a, 117 16 Prague 1 Telephone: (420-2) 2421-9844 Fax: (420-2) 2421-9965	Commercial Officer in the U.S. Mr. Miroslav Toman Head of Commercial and Economic Section Embassy of the Czech Republic 3900 Spring of Freedom Ave, NW Washington, DC 20008 Tel: (202) 274-9111 Fax: (202) 244-2147 Mrs. Zuzana Novakova First Secretary 1109-1111 Madison Ave. New York, NY 10028 Tel: (212) 717-5643 Fax: (212) 717-5064
Croatia		
U.S. Commercial Officer Patrick Hughes Commercial Officer U.S. Embassy Zagreb Mailing: APO AE 09213-5080 Street: Andrije Hebranga 2 Zagreb Telephone: 385-1-45-55-500 Fax: 385-1-45-53-126	CEEBIC Employee Damir Novinic, Commercial Assistant U.S. Embassy Zagreb Andrije Hebranga 2, Zagreb Telephone: 385-1-45-55-500 Fax: 385-1-45-53-126	Commercial Officer in the U.S. Mr. Aleksandar Heina Economic Counselor 2343 Massachusetts Ave, NW Washington, DC 20008 Tel: (202) 588-5899 Fax: (202) 588-8936
Estonia		
U.S. Commercial Officer David Katz Econ/Commercial Officer U.S. Embassy Tallinn Mailing: Box T APO AE 09723 Street: Kentmanni 20 Tallinn Telephone: 372-6-312021 Fax: 372-6-312025	CEEBIC Employee Reene Sepp U.S. Embassy Tallinn Kentmanni 20, Tallinn Telephone: 372-6-31-20-21 Fax: 372-6-31-20-25	Commercial Officer in the U.S. Mr. Jaan Salvlaid First Secretary, Economic Embassy of Estonia 2131 Massachussetts Ave., NW Washington, DC 20008 Tel: (202) 588-0101 Fax: (202) 588-0108
FYR Macedonia		
	CEEBIC Employee Arben Gega U.S. Embassy Skopje Ilindenska bb Skopje, F.Y.R. Macedonia Telephone: 389-91-116-180 Fax: 389-91-117-103	Commercial Officer in the U.S. Embassy of the Former Yugoslav Republic of Macedonia 3050 K St., NW Ste 210 Washington, DC 20007 Tel: (202) 337-3063 Fax:(202) 337-3093
Hungary		
U.S. Commercial Officer John Fogarasi Senior Commercial Officer U.S. Embassy Budapest	CEEBIC Employee Gabor Kaczmarczyk U.S. Embassy Budapest Bajza utca 31, 1062 Budapest	Commercial Officer in the U.S. Mr. Pal Kepisz Head of Commercial Representation Economic Affaris

Mailing: Department of State Washington, D.C. 20521-5270 Street: Bajza utca 31 H 1062 Budapest Telephone: 36-1-3228600/1217 Fax: 36-1-3422529 or 36-1-3328934	Telephone: 36-1-302-6100 Fax: 36-1-302-0089	Embassy of Hungary 2401 Calvert Street, NW Suite 1021 Washington, DC 20008 Tel: (202) 387-3191 Fax: (202) 387-3140 Mr. Tibor Zselinszky Commerical Counselor Embassy of Hungary 150 East 58th Street 33rd Floor New York, NY 10022 Tel: (212) 752-3060 Tel: (212) 486-2958 Mr. Gyorgy Szabo Commercial Attache Embassy of Hungary Hungarian Commercial Office 1130 Prudential Plaza 130 East Randolph Drive Chicago, IL 60601 Tel: (312) 856-0274 Fax: (312) 856-1080
Latvia		
U.S. Commercial Officer Mary Ruth Coleman Economic Officer U.S. Embassy Riga Mailing: Box R APO AE 09723 Street: Raina Blvd. 7 Riga Local Tel: 371-7-211-572 Telephone: 371-882-0046 (cellular) Fax: 371-782-0047 (cellular)	CEEBIC Employee Anna Zisser U.S. Embassy Riga Raina Blvd. 7, Riga Telephone: 371-7-211-572 Fax: 371-782-0047	Commercial Officer in the U.S. Mr. Normunds Popens Commercial Attache Embassy of Latvia 4325 17th Street Washington, DC 20051
Lithuania		
U.S. Commercial Officer John Stepanchuk Economic Officer U.S. Embassy Vilnius Mailing: Box V APO AE 09723 Street: Akmenu 6 Vilnius Telephone: 370-2-223-031 Fax: 370-670-6084	CEEBIC Employee Jonas Vasilevicius America Center Pranciskonu 3/6, 2005 Vilnius Telephone: 370-2-223-031 x149 Fax: 370-670-6084	Commercial Officer in the U.S. Ms. Dalia Grybauskaite Minister for Economic Affairs Embassy of Lithuania 2622 16th Street Washington, DC 20009 Tel: (202) 234-5860 Fax: (202) 328-0466
Poland		
U.S. Commercial Officer Maria Andrews Senior Commercial Officer David Ponsar Commercial Officer Alain Bobet Commercial Attache U.S. Embassy Warsaw al. Jerozolimskie 56/C 00-803 Warsaw Telephone: 48-22-625-4374 Fax: 48-22-621-6327	CEEBIC Employee Anna Janczewska (Warsaw) U.S. Embassy Warsaw al. Jerozolimskie 56/C 00-803 Warsaw Telephone: 48-22-625-4374 Fax: 48-22-621-6327 Barbara Blocka (Krakow) U.S. Consulate Krakow ul. Stolarska 9, 31-043 Krakow Tel/Fax:48-12-421-4909 Telex: 325350 KRUSA PL	Commercial Officer in the U.S. Mr. Andrzej Ilczuk Economic Counselor Embassy of the Republic of Poland 1503 21st Street, NW Washington, DC 20036 Tel: (202) 467-6690 Fax: (202) 833-8343 Mr. Andrzej Laganowski Commercial Counselor Embassy of the Republic of Poland 100 Park Avenue, 19th Floor

		New York, NY 10017 Tel: (212) 370-5300 Fax: (212) 818-9623
Romania		
U.S. Commercial Officer Bill Crawford Senior Commercial Officer U.S. Embassy Bucharest Mailing: APO AE 09213-5260 Street: Strada Tudor Arghezi 7-9 Bucharest Telephone: 40-1-2104042 Fax: 40-1-2100395 Telex: 11416		Commercial Officer in the U.S. Mr. Adrian Constantinescu Minister Counselor Mr. Marian Voicu Commercial Counselor Embassy of Romania 1607 23rd Street, NW Washington, DC 20008 Tel: (202) 332-4848 or 4852 Fax: (202) 332-4858
Slovak Republic		
U.S. Commercial Officer Gene Young Econ/Commercial Officer U.S. Embassy Bratislava Hviezdoslavovo Namesite 4 811 02 Bratislava Tel: 421-7-533-5990 Fax: 421-7-533-0096	CEEBIC Employee Pavol Matusek American Business Center Grosslingova 35, 811 09 Bratislava Telephone: 421-7-361-079 Fax: 421-7-361-085	Commercial Officer in the U.S. Ms. Ingrid Brockova Second Secretary, Economic Officer Embassy of the Slovak Republic 2201 Wisconsin Ave, NW Washington, DC 20007 Tel: (202) 965-5160 Fax: (202) 965-5166 Mr. Jaroslav Smiesny Trade Representative Economic and Commercial Section Embassy of the Slovak Republic 10 East 40th Street Suite 3601 New York, NY 10016 Tel: (212) 679-7044 Fax: (212) 679-7045
Slovenia		
U.S. Commercial Officer Paul Reid Political/Econ Officer U.S. Embassy Ljubljana Prazakova 4 Ljubljana Telephone: 386-61-301427 Fax: 386-61-301401	CEEBIC Employee Marko Mlakar U.S. Embassy Ljubljana Prazakova 4, Ljubljana Telephone: 386-61-301-427 Fax: 386-61-301-401	Commercial Officer in the U.S. Mr. Marjan Smonig, Counselor Republic of Slovenia 1525 New Hampshire Ave., NW Washington, DC 20036 Tel: (202) 667-5363 Fax: (202) 667-4563
Additional Contacts		
World Bank Janice Mazur Office of the U.S. Executive Director The World Bank Tel: (202)458-0118, 458-0120 Fax: (202)477-2967	EBRD Dean Peterson Senior Commercial Officer Office of the U.S. Director One Exchange Square London, EC2A 2 EH, UK Tel: (44-171) 338-6569 Fax: (44-171) 338-6487	

BASIC TITLES ON ALBANIA

IMPORTANT!
All publications are updated annually!
Please contact IBP, Inc. at ibpusa3@gmail.com for the latest ISBNs and additional information

TITLE
Albania A "Spy" Guide - Strategic Information and Developments
Albania A Spy" Guide"
Albania Air Force Handbook
Albania Air Force Handbook
Albania Army Weapon Systems Handbook
Albania Army Weapon Systems Handbook
Albania Army Weapon Systems Handbook
Albania Banking & Financial Market Handbook
Albania Banking & Financial Market Handbook
Albania Business and Investment Opportunities Yearbook
Albania Business and Investment Opportunities Yearbook
Albania Business and Investment Opportunities Yearbook Volume 1 Strategic Information and Opportunities
Albania Business and Investment Opportunities Yearbook Volume 2 Leading Export-Import, Business, Investment Opportunities and Projects
Albania Business Intelligence Report - Practical Information, Opportunities, Contacts
Albania Business Law Handbook - Strategic Information and Basic Laws
Albania Business Law Handbook Volume 2 Investment and Trade Laws Volume 2 Investment and Trade Laws
Albania Business Success Guide - Basic Practical Information and Contacts
Albania Company Laws and Regulations Handbook
Albania Company Laws and Regulations Handbook - Strategic Information and Basic Laws
Albania Constitution and Citizenship Laws Handbook - Strategic Information and Basic Laws
Albania Country Study Guide - Strategic Information and Developments
Albania Country Study Guide - Strategic Information and Developments
Albania Country Study Guide - Strategic Information and Developments Volume 1 Strategic Information and Developments
Albania Criminal Laws, Regulations and Procedures Handbook - Strategic Information, Regulations, Procedures
Albania Customs, Trade Regulations and Procedures Handbook
Albania Customs, Trade Regulations and Procedures Handbook
Albania Diplomatic Handbook - Strategic Information and Developments
Albania Diplomatic Handbook - Strategic Information and Developments
Albania Ecology & Nature Protection Handbook
Albania Ecology & Nature Protection Handbook
Albania Ecology & Nature Protection Laws and Regulation Handbook
Albania Electoral, Political Parties Laws and Regulations Handbook - Strategic Information, Regulations, Procedures
Albania Energy Policy, Laws and Regulation Handbook
Albania Energy Policy, Laws and Regulations Handbook
Albania Energy Policy, Laws and Regulations Handbook
Albania Export-Import Trade and Business Directory
Albania Export-Import Trade and Business Directory
Albania Fishing and Aquaculture Industry Handbook - Strategic Information, Regulations, Opportunities

TITLE
Albania Fishing Industry Business and Investment Opportunities Handbook
Albania Fishing Industry Business and Investment Opportunities Handbook
Albania Foreign Policy and Government Guide
Albania Foreign Policy and Government Guide
Albania Government and Business Contacts Handbook
Albania Government and Business Contacts Handbook
Albania Immigration Laws and Regulations Handbook - Strategic Information and Basic Laws
Albania Industrial and Business Directory
Albania Industrial and Business Directory
Albania Insolvency (Bankruptcy) Laws and Regulations Handbook - Strategic Information and Basic Laws
Albania Internet and E-Commerce Investment and Business Guide - Strategic and Practical Information: Regulations and Opportunities
Albania Internet and E-Commerce Investment and Business Guide - Strategic and Practical Information: Regulations and Opportunities
Albania Investment and Business Guide - Strategic and Practical Information
Albania Investment and Business Guide - Strategic and Practical Information
Albania Investment and Business Guide - Strategic and Practical Information
Albania Investment and Business Guide - Strategic and Practical Information
Albania Investment and Business Guide Volume 2 Business, Investment Opportunities and Incentives
Albania Investment and Business Profile - Basic Information and Contacts for Succesful investment and Business Activity
Albania Investment and Trade Laws and Regulations Handbook
Albania Investment, Trade Strategy and Agreements Handbook - Strategic Information and Basic Agreements
Albania Labor Laws and Regulations Handbook - Strategic Information and Basic Laws
Albania Land Ownership and Agriculture Laws Handbook
Albania Mineral & Mining Sector Investment and Business Guide - Strategic and Practical Information
Albania Mineral & Mining Sector Investment and Business Guide - Strategic and Practical Information
Albania Mining Laws and Regulations Handbook
Albania National Defense and Armed Forces Handbook
Albania National Defense and Armed Forces Handbook
Albania National Development Strategy Handbook: Important Programs and Developments
Albania Oil & Gas Sector Business & Investment Opportunities Yearbook
Albania Oil & Gas Sector Business & Investment Opportunities Yearbook
Albania President Handbook - Strategic Information and Developments
Albania Privatization Programs and Regulations Handbook
Albania Privatization Programs and Regulations Handbook
Albania Recent Economic and Political Developments Yearbook
Albania Recent Economic and Political Developments Yearbook
Albania Starting Business (Incorporating) in....Guide
Albania Tax Guide Volume 1 Strategic Information and Basic Regulations
Albania Taxation Laws and Regulations Handbook
Albania Telecom Laws and Regulations Handbook
Albania Telecommunication Industry Business Opportunities Handbook
Albania Telecommunication Industry Business Opportunities Handbook
Albania Transportation Policy and Regulations Handbook
Albania: How to Invest, Start and Run Profitable Business in Albania Guide - Practical Information, Opportunities, Contacts

TITLE
Cape Verde Business Intelligence Report-- Strategic, Practical Information, Contacts
Cayman Islands Business Intelligence Report-- Strategic, Practical Information, Contacts
Central African Republic Business Intelligence Report-- Strategic, Practical Information, Contacts
Chad Business Intelligence Report-- Strategic, Practical Information, Contacts
Chile Business Intelligence Report-- Strategic, Practical Information, Contacts
China Business Intelligence Report-- Strategic, Practical Information, Contacts
Colombia Business Intelligence Report-- Strategic, Practical Information, Contacts
Comoros Business Intelligence Report-- Strategic, Practical Information, Contacts
Congo Business Intelligence Report-- Strategic, Practical Information, Contacts
Congo, Democratic Republic Business Intelligence Report-- Strategic, Practical Information, Contacts
Cook Islands Business Intelligence Report-- Strategic, Practical Information, Contacts
Costa Rica Business Intelligence Report-- Strategic, Practical Information, Contacts
Cote d'Ivoire Business Intelligence Report-- Strategic, Practical Information, Contacts
Croatia Business Intelligence Report-- Strategic, Practical Information, Contacts
Cuba Business Intelligence Report-- Strategic, Practical Information, Contacts
Cyprus Business Intelligence Report-- Strategic, Practical Information, Contacts
Czech Republic Business Intelligence Report-- Strategic, Practical Information, Contacts
Denmark Business Intelligence Report-- Strategic, Practical Information, Contacts
Djibouti Business Intelligence Report-- Strategic, Practical Information, Contacts
Dominica Business Intelligence Report-- Strategic, Practical Information, Contacts
Dominican Republic Business Intelligence Report-- Strategic, Practical Information, Contacts
Ecuador Business Intelligence Report-- Strategic, Practical Information, Contacts
Egypt Business Intelligence Report-- Strategic, Practical Information, Contacts
El Salvador Business Intelligence Report-- Strategic, Practical Information, Contacts
Equatorial Guinea Business Intelligence Report-- Strategic, Practical Information, Contacts
Eritrea Business Intelligence Report-- Strategic, Practical Information, Contacts
Estonia Business Intelligence Report-- Strategic, Practical Information, Contacts
Ethiopia Business Intelligence Report-- Strategic, Practical Information, Contacts
Falkland Islands Business Intelligence Report-- Strategic, Practical Information, Contacts
Faroes Islands Business Intelligence Report-- Strategic, Practical Information, Contacts
Fiji Business Intelligence Report-- Strategic, Practical Information, Contacts
Finland Business Intelligence Report-- Strategic, Practical Information, Contacts
France Business Intelligence Report-- Strategic, Practical Information, Contacts
Gabon Business Intelligence Report-- Strategic, Practical Information, Contacts
Gambia Business Intelligence Report-- Strategic, Practical Information, Contacts
Georgia Business Intelligence Report-- Strategic, Practical Information, Contacts
Germany Business Intelligence Report-- Strategic, Practical Information, Contacts
Ghana Business Intelligence Report-- Strategic, Practical Information, Contacts
Gibraltar Business Intelligence Report-- Strategic, Practical Information, Contacts
Greece Business Intelligence Report-- Strategic, Practical Information, Contacts
Greenland Business Intelligence Report-- Strategic, Practical Information, Contacts
Grenada Business Intelligence Report-- Strategic, Practical Information, Contacts
Guam Business Intelligence Report-- Strategic, Practical Information, Contacts
Guatemala Business Intelligence Report-- Strategic, Practical Information, Contacts
Guernsey Business Intelligence Report-- Strategic, Practical Information, Contacts
Guinea Business Intelligence Report-- Strategic, Practical Information, Contacts

TITLE
Guinea-Bissau Business Intelligence Report-- Strategic, Practical Information, Contacts
Guyana Business Intelligence Report-- Strategic, Practical Information, Contacts
Haiti Business Intelligence Report-- Strategic, Practical Information, Contacts
Honduras Business Intelligence Report-- Strategic, Practical Information, Contacts
Hungary Business Intelligence Report-- Strategic, Practical Information, Contacts
Iceland Business Intelligence Report-- Strategic, Practical Information, Contacts
India Business Intelligence Report-- Strategic, Practical Information, Contacts
Indonesia Business Intelligence Report-- Strategic, Practical Information, Contacts
Iran Business Intelligence Report-- Strategic, Practical Information, Contacts
Iraq Business Intelligence Report-- Strategic, Practical Information, Contacts
Ireland Business Intelligence Report-- Strategic, Practical Information, Contacts
Israel Business Intelligence Report-- Strategic, Practical Information, Contacts
Italy Business Intelligence Report-- Strategic, Practical Information, Contacts
Jamaica Business Intelligence Report-- Strategic, Practical Information, Contacts
Japan Business Intelligence Report-- Strategic, Practical Information, Contacts
Jersey Business Intelligence Report-- Strategic, Practical Information, Contacts
Jordan Business Intelligence Report-- Strategic, Practical Information, Contacts
Kazakhstan Business Intelligence Report-- Strategic, Practical Information, Contacts
Kenya Business Intelligence Report-- Strategic, Practical Information, Contacts
Kiribati Business Intelligence Report-- Strategic, Practical Information, Contacts
Korea, North Business Intelligence Report-- Strategic, Practical Information, Contacts
Korea, South Business Intelligence Report-- Strategic, Practical Information, Contacts
Kosovo Business Intelligence Report-- Strategic, Practical Information, Contacts
Kurdistan Business Intelligence Report-- Strategic, Practical Information, Contacts
Kuwait Business Intelligence Report-- Strategic, Practical Information, Contacts
Kyrgyzstan Business Intelligence Report-- Strategic, Practical Information, Contacts
Laos Business Intelligence Report-- Strategic, Practical Information, Contacts
Latvia Business Intelligence Report-- Strategic, Practical Information, Contacts
Lebanon Business Intelligence Report-- Strategic, Practical Information, Contacts
Lesotho Business Intelligence Report-- Strategic, Practical Information, Contacts
Liberia Business Intelligence Report-- Strategic, Practical Information, Contacts
Libya Business Intelligence Report-- Strategic, Practical Information, Contacts
Liechtenstein Business Intelligence Report-- Strategic, Practical Information, Contacts
Lithuania Business Intelligence Report-- Strategic, Practical Information, Contacts
Luxembourg Business Intelligence Report-- Strategic, Practical Information, Contacts
Macao Business Intelligence Report-- Strategic, Practical Information, Contacts
Macedonia Business Intelligence Report-- Strategic, Practical Information, Contacts
Madagascar Business Intelligence Report-- Strategic, Practical Information, Contacts
Madeira Business Intelligence Report-- Strategic, Practical Information, Contacts
Malawi Business Intelligence Report-- Strategic, Practical Information, Contacts
Malaysia Business Intelligence Report-- Strategic, Practical Information, Contacts
Maldives Business Intelligence Report-- Strategic, Practical Information, Contacts
Mali Business Intelligence Report-- Strategic, Practical Information, Contacts
Malta Business Intelligence Report-- Strategic, Practical Information, Contacts
Man Business Intelligence Report-- Strategic, Practical Information, Contacts
Marshall Islands Business Intelligence Report-- Strategic, Practical Information, Contacts

TITLE
Mauritania Business Intelligence Report-- Strategic, Practical Information, Contacts
Mauritius Business Intelligence Report-- Strategic, Practical Information, Contacts
Mayotte Business Intelligence Report-- Strategic, Practical Information, Contacts
Mexico Business Intelligence Report-- Strategic, Practical Information, Contacts
Micronesia Business Intelligence Report-- Strategic, Practical Information, Contacts
Moldova Business Intelligence Report-- Strategic, Practical Information, Contacts
Monaco Business Intelligence Report-- Strategic, Practical Information, Contacts
Mongolia Business Intelligence Report-- Strategic, Practical Information, Contacts
Montserrat Business Intelligence Report-- Strategic, Practical Information, Contacts
Montenegro Business Intelligence Report-- Strategic, Practical Information, Contacts
Morocco Business Intelligence Report-- Strategic, Practical Information, Contacts
Mozambique Business Intelligence Report-- Strategic, Practical Information, Contacts
Myanmar Business Intelligence Report-- Strategic, Practical Information, Contacts
Nagorno-Karabakh Republic Business Intelligence Report-- Strategic, Practical Information, Contacts
Namibia Business Intelligence Report-- Strategic, Practical Information, Contacts
Nauru Business Intelligence Report-- Strategic, Practical Information, Contacts
Nepal Business Intelligence Report-- Strategic, Practical Information, Contacts
Netherlands Business Intelligence Report-- Strategic, Practical Information, Contacts
New Caledonia Business Intelligence Report-- Strategic, Practical Information, Contacts
New Zealand Business Intelligence Report-- Strategic, Practical Information, Contacts
Nicaragua Business Intelligence Report-- Strategic, Practical Information, Contacts
Niger Business Intelligence Report-- Strategic, Practical Information, Contacts
Nigeria Business Intelligence Report-- Strategic, Practical Information, Contacts
Niue Business Intelligence Report-- Strategic, Practical Information, Contacts
Northern Cyprus (Turkish Republic of Northern Cyprus) Business Intelligence Report-- Strategic, Practical Information, Contacts
Northern Mariana Islands Business Intelligence Report-- Strategic, Practical Information, Contacts
Norway Business Intelligence Report-- Strategic, Practical Information, Contacts
Oman Business Intelligence Report-- Strategic, Practical Information, Contacts
Pakistan Business Intelligence Report-- Strategic, Practical Information, Contacts
Palau Business Intelligence Report-- Strategic, Practical Information, Contacts
Palestine (West Bank & Gaza) Business Intelligence Report-- Strategic, Practical Information, Contacts
Panama Business Intelligence Report-- Strategic, Practical Information, Contacts
Papua New Guinea Business Intelligence Report-- Strategic, Practical Information, Contacts
Paraguay Business Intelligence Report-- Strategic, Practical Information, Contacts
Peru Business Intelligence Report-- Strategic, Practical Information, Contacts
Philippines Business Intelligence Report-- Strategic, Practical Information, Contacts
Pitcairn Islands Business Intelligence Report-- Strategic, Practical Information, Contacts
Poland Business Intelligence Report-- Strategic, Practical Information, Contacts
Polynesia French Business Intelligence Report-- Strategic, Practical Information, Contacts
Portugal Business Intelligence Report-- Strategic, Practical Information, Contacts
Qatar Business Intelligence Report-- Strategic, Practical Information, Contacts
Romania Business Intelligence Report-- Strategic, Practical Information, Contacts
Russia Business Intelligence Report-- Strategic, Practical Information, Contacts
Rwanda Business Intelligence Report-- Strategic, Practical Information, Contacts
Sahrawi Arab Democratic Republic Volume 1 Strategic Information and Developments

TITLE
Saint Kitts and Nevis Business Intelligence Report-- Strategic, Practical Information, Contacts
Saint Lucia Business Intelligence Report-- Strategic, Practical Information, Contacts
Saint Vincent and The Grenadines Business Intelligence Report-- Strategic, Practical Information, Contacts
Samoa (American) A Business Intelligence Report-- Strategic, Practical Information, Contacts
Samoa (Western) Business Intelligence Report-- Strategic, Practical Information, Contacts
San Marino Business Intelligence Report-- Strategic, Practical Information, Contacts
Sao Tome and Principe Business Intelligence Report-- Strategic, Practical Information, Contacts
Saudi Arabia Business Intelligence Report-- Strategic, Practical Information, Contacts
Scotland Business Intelligence Report-- Strategic, Practical Information, Contacts
Senegal Business Intelligence Report-- Strategic, Practical Information, Contacts
Serbia Business Intelligence Report-- Strategic, Practical Information, Contacts
Seychelles Business Intelligence Report-- Strategic, Practical Information, Contacts
Sierra Leone Business Intelligence Report-- Strategic, Practical Information, Contacts
Singapore Business Intelligence Report-- Strategic, Practical Information, Contacts
Slovakia Business Intelligence Report-- Strategic, Practical Information, Contacts
Slovenia Business Intelligence Report-- Strategic, Practical Information, Contacts
Solomon Islands Business Intelligence Report-- Strategic, Practical Information, Contacts
Somalia Business Intelligence Report-- Strategic, Practical Information, Contacts
South Africa Business Intelligence Report-- Strategic, Practical Information, Contacts
Spain Business Intelligence Report-- Strategic, Practical Information, Contacts
Sri Lanka Business Intelligence Report-- Strategic, Practical Information, Contacts
St. Helena Business Intelligence Report-- Strategic, Practical Information, Contacts
St. Pierre & Miquelon Business Intelligence Report-- Strategic, Practical Information, Contacts
Sudan (Republic of the Sudan) Business Intelligence Report-- Strategic, Practical Information, Contacts
Sudan South Business Intelligence Report-- Strategic, Practical Information, Contacts
Suriname Business Intelligence Report-- Strategic, Practical Information, Contacts
Swaziland Business Intelligence Report-- Strategic, Practical Information, Contacts
Sweden Business Intelligence Report-- Strategic, Practical Information, Contacts
Switzerland Business Intelligence Report-- Strategic, Practical Information, Contacts
Syria Business Intelligence Report-- Strategic, Practical Information, Contacts
Taiwan Business Intelligence Report-- Strategic, Practical Information, Contacts
Tajikistan Business Intelligence Report-- Strategic, Practical Information, Contacts
Tanzania Business Intelligence Report-- Strategic, Practical Information, Contacts
Thailand Business Intelligence Report-- Strategic, Practical Information, Contacts
Timor Leste (Democratic Republic of Timor-Leste) Business Intelligence Report-- Strategic, Practical Information, Contacts
Togo Business Intelligence Report-- Strategic, Practical Information, Contacts
Tonga Business Intelligence Report-- Strategic, Practical Information, Contacts
Trinidad and Tobago Business Intelligence Report-- Strategic, Practical Information, Contacts
Tunisia Business Intelligence Report-- Strategic, Practical Information, Contacts
Turkey Business Intelligence Report-- Strategic, Practical Information, Contacts
Turkmenistan Business Intelligence Report-- Strategic, Practical Information, Contacts
Turks & Caicos Business Intelligence Report-- Strategic, Practical Information, Contacts
Tuvalu Business Intelligence Report-- Strategic, Practical Information, Contacts
Uganda Business Intelligence Report-- Strategic, Practical Information, Contacts
Ukraine Business Intelligence Report-- Strategic, Practical Information, Contacts

TITLE
United Arab Emirates Business Intelligence Report-- Strategic, Practical Information, Contacts
United Kingdom Business Intelligence Report-- Strategic, Practical Information, Contacts
United States Business Intelligence Report-- Strategic, Practical Information, Contacts
Uruguay Business Intelligence Report-- Strategic, Practical Information, Contacts
Uzbekistan Business Intelligence Report-- Strategic, Practical Information, Contacts
Vanuatu Business Intelligence Report-- Strategic, Practical Information, Contacts
Vatican City (Holy See) Business Intelligence Report-- Strategic, Practical Information, Contacts
Venezuela Business Intelligence Report-- Strategic, Practical Information, Contacts
Vietnam Business Intelligence Report-- Strategic, Practical Information, Contacts
Virgin Islands, British Business Intelligence Report-- Strategic, Practical Information, Contacts
Wake Atoll Business Intelligence Report-- Strategic, Practical Information, Contacts
Wallis & Futuna Business Intelligence Report-- Strategic, Practical Information, Contacts
Western Sahara Business Intelligence Report-- Strategic, Practical Information, Contacts
Yemen Business Intelligence Report-- Strategic, Practical Information, Contacts
Zambia Business Intelligence Report-- Strategic, Practical Information, Contacts
Zimbabwe Business Intelligence Report-- Strategic, Practical Information, Contacts

www.ingramcontent.com/pod-product-compliance
Ingram Content Group UK Ltd.
Pitfield, Milton Keynes, MK11 3LW, UK
UKHW051457290926
15471UKWH00008B/1264

9 781433 000492